Humanistic Frontiers in American Education

Humanistic Frontiers
in American Education

ROY P. FAIRFIELD, Editor

Professor of Social Science, Antioch College
Coordinator of the Union Graduate School of the Union for
Experimenting Colleges and Universities

PRENTICE-HALL, INC., Englewood Cliffs, New Jersey

The royalties from this book are being shared with The Humanist.

13-447755-3

Library of Congress Catalog Card Number: 79–166138

Current Printing (last Digit):
10 9 8 7 6 5 4 3 2 1

PRENTICE-HALL INTERNATIONAL, INC., LONDON
PRENTICE-HALL OF AUSTRALIA, PTY. LTD., SYDNEY
PRENTICE-HALL OF CANADA, LTD., TORONTO
PRENTICE-HALL OF INDIA PRIVATE LIMITED, NEW DELHI
PRENTICE-HALL OF JAPAN INC., TOKYO

To Those *Humanists* Who Preach
What They Practice

It's well nigh impossible to express appreciation to all who are engaged in so complex a phenomenon as bringing together articles, permissions, and the variety of materials included here. Some of the efforts are indirect, in form of encouragement as from one's wife (thank *you*, Maryllyn); other is much more formidable and direct: from Paul Kurtz, leader of the editorial staff of *The Humanist*, who is attempting to make more humanist literature available to the American public; from my other colleagues on the editorial staff, David Cole Gordon and Khoren Arisian, Jr.; from each of the authors contributing articles; from Otto Krash whose Dewey-like querying throughout the project kept me on my toes; from J. W. F. Klein-von Baumhauer whose knowledge of humanism and language helped me sharpen the introductions; from the many publishers who generously granted permissions to use both short quotations and long articles (duly acknowledged); from Samuel Baskin and Antioch's Institutional Research Committee for modest funds to assist with routine costs; from student and faculty associates who must have tired hearing me discuss the project; and by no means last in my esteem, from secretarial and research assistants, Betty Jo Pool, Gerda Oldham, Nora Gunning, and Judy Scotnicki.

R. P. F.

Contents

Foreword

We are in the midst of a humanist revolution in education: the schools are being shaken to their foundations, as their most basic assumptions are being questioned.

The roots of the humanist revolution may be traced back to the revolutionary impact that John Deway had upon education. Today it has reached full force, not only because so many leading intellectuals and educators are committed to the movement for humanistic liberation, but also because, as witnessed by a recent poll, some two-thirds of American college students, when asked to identify their basic commitments, responded that they were "humanistic."

Thus there is much excitement and talk about the emergence of a new humanistic focus in education. There is, however, unfortunately, little clarity about precisely what humanism in education is or what its methods or goals should be.

Among the various ideals of humanism that one hears about—some of it familiar, some of it new—are the following: (1) the need for education to be relevant to the needs of students and to the problems of contemporary society; (2) the insistence that teachers should teach living students, not dead subject matter, and should emphasize creative learning, not abstract forms or rote memory or discipline for its own sake; (3) the commitment to experiment and innovation in educational curriculum and methods; (4) the view that students should be given the opportunity democratically to participate and share in wider phases of school life; (5) the effort to overcome the dehumanizing and alienating forces that large, impersonal educational institutions seem to generate; and (6) recognition that among the most important aims of education should be the development of critical intelligence and the fulfillment of the human potential.

The current upheaval in the schools has had many wide reverberations and dimensions: the movements for student power, student rights, and participatory democracy, independent study, international education, curriculum reform, the free university, black studies, the role of the schools in the community, their relationship to the federal government, and so on. Many significant reforms have already been made or are under way. This movement for genuine reform has in some instances, however, degenerated into disruption and confrontation, conflict and violence, rhetoric and romantic excesses for their own sake by those who either do not believe in reform or are unclear as to what it entails. And this has led to a bitter backlash which has lumped the humanist program together with the excesses of the militants and which thus threatens to overwhelm any real advances that already have been made in education.

It is important, therefore, that the humanistic frontiers of education carefully be defined and their worthwhile contribution be explored. This is what this book is about. It grew out of an invitation to Dr. Roy Fairfield, Associate Editor of *The Humanist*, to undertake a series on humanistic aspects of education. Some of the chapters in this volume have already appeared in *The Humanist* or elsewhere; most of them have not. Virtually all of them were written explicitly for this book. The authors present a wide range of opinion, and they include recognized leaders in their fields—liberals, radicals, conservatives, students, administrators, and faculty. Hopefully, out of this discussion will emerge a clear sense of the great ferment and vitality in education today and an understanding of the new directions that can be taken in forging new frontiers in education.

Paul Kurtz, Editor
The Humanist

Humanistic Frontiers in American Education

Introduction

The Humanist Frontier

**Humanism and
the Present Crisis in Education**

It takes no seer to recognize that the schools are in deep crisis. The student movement and the wide unrest on university and college campuses as well as in the high schools are symptomatic of the underlying sickness. Something is the matter with our educational system. And something drastic must be done. Does the humanist have anything significant to offer as a way out? This is what this book is about. There is a crisis and there is a frontier and we need to move beyond the errors of the past into the challenges of the future. The thesis of this book is that the frontier in education is *humanistic*.

It is almost impossible to read a newspaper, listen to the radio, watch television, or talk with one's neighbor today without encountering educational questions which threaten to overwhelm both sense and reason:

> Why doesn't our society value genuine competence more highly?
> If our schools are so bankrupt, as the critics claim, how did they manage to produce those very critics?
> How does one account for the youthful shift in mood from a psychology of being to one of becoming?
> Should a boy's refusal to cut his hair or shave his beard lead to suspension from school and possibly induction into the Army?

What would be the consequences of even wider closing of the Catholic parochial schools?

Does allocation of federal funds to parochial school children, done in the context of a "child benefit theory," strengthen or weaken the wall between church and state?

Is higher education a "national danger" as one critic claims?

Should the university do classified military research? Why? Why not?

Should blacks be encouraged to develop Black Studies, independent of the total curriculum?

What price *any* slowdown in integrating schools?

Is a man *free* if he has been educated to perceive world events within the framework of his own national heritage? Is it possible to develop a healthy minded world citizenship?

Do our schools foster pluralism? Do they impart the tools of critical thinking which enable citizens to detect shoddy reasoning as well as cogent argument?

What is relevant education? Who should develop it? On what time scale?

In a society as pragmatic as ours, what is the value of the utopian vision for a better society? a better school system or systems? for developing closer relations between school and society? for evolving work-study programs which push out the classroom walls?

Who should have the power to run our schools and colleges, or, for that matter, our total society?

Are the radicals in our midst interested in reform or revolution and what difference does it make? Are they aware of the potential consequences if they succeed in destroying both the school system and the society which has made it possible for them to dissent with both words and body?

Do our schools and teachers promote self-development of the individual or do they produce rubber stamps? (And what are the consequences of asking questions—and trying to answer them—in such an either-or framework?)

And what is the value of asking any question whatever?

How one approaches such questions as well as those asked by Ben Thompson in the Epilogue of this book depends, of course, upon his fundamental assumptions about life, learning, and liberty. The more open his philosophy or the more he searches for evidence to support or reject a viewpoint, the more confused he may become. For he soon learns that there are many sides to every question, not merely two. Hence the dilemma which any honest inquirer discovers: one appeals to authority or becomes dogmatic at enormous expense, for closure of any issue, whether logical, catechismic, passionate, or behavioral shuts one off from further evidence, logical classification, or imaginative insight.

In a very real sense the present century is the humanist century, the century in which man has become fully conscious of his *humanity*. And the discovery has profound implications for the serious questions we raise here.

The modern day humanist has a decided viewpoint. He might, on the one hand, agree with Lewis Carroll's observation in *Alice in Wonderland* that if you don't know where you're going, any road will take you there. Yet, as Paul Kurtz suggests in delineating the nature and spirit of contemporary humanism in the book, *Moral Problems in Contemporary Society: Essays in Humanistic Ethics,* although humanism is negative in that it rejects traditional supernaturalistic explanations of the universe, it is positive in that it insists that *human* values cannot be derived from transcendental sources. Rather, they grow naturally out of *human* experience.

Most humanists today also believe in the efficacy of objective intelligence and reason, and they are committed to the view that human beings are interdependent—hence there is a need for humanitarian service and fellowship if we are to fulfill our highest potentialities.[1] According to Professor J. P. van Praag, the noted Dutch humanist and leader in the international humanist and ethical movement, the humanist attitude is one which stresses the ideals of liberty, equality, and fraternity as well as the experiential and existential; and, it asserts that the world in itself is complete and without need of an independent creator.[2] This stated negatively: humanists eschew theistic "explanations," cosmically determined value systems, fanatic anti-intellectual, ideological, or social forces which seek to destroy men or dehumanize them. Stated positively, the proper concern of man is *man.*

Accordingly, the basic questions which humanists ask in any field of endeavor are these: What should human beings do to resolve their problems? What is the relationship between what they *say* and what they *do*?

The consequences of asking such questions are also fairly clear: humanism is *radical.* It will compromise with no alienating force, whether it be the educational system or something else which frustrates man. The humanist is radical because he wants to emancipate humans from bondage, any kind of bondage.

Educational issues today are so complex and so inextricably related to matters of political, economic, and social survival that easy solutions are virtually impossible. Thus, Robert Theobald and Noel McInnis in their essay later in this volume offer the following challenge to educators: "The possible is irrelevant, so it is only worth trying for the impossible. This is why education is crucial."[3] And one is reminded of the slogan which appeared on the walls of industrial plants during World War II, "The difficult we do immediately, the impossible takes a little longer."[4] One can only hope that this collection of essays will assist the reader in shortening the time it may require to do the impossible—so long as we remember that once we have resolved one impossibility, another or indeed ten others may grow in its place, much like the soldiers from the mythical dragon's teeth. The rate of growth seems exponential to the sensitive person. That's what it means to be human—to search constantly to assess the dilemma (both comic and tragic), then to strive for means to solve it with one's bare hands, or better yet, with his reason, and through exposure of his vital nerve centers to the vital nerve centers of others.

> No *deus ex machina* will suffice
> to slice
> a problem in twos or threes
> and force a *man* to his knees.

Perspectives

Some perspective may be gained on the current frontier in education by reminding ourselves that there have been several humanistic waves of educational endeavor since the pre-Socratic philosophers (about 660 to 300 B.C.) first rejected mythological or superstitious explanations and sought to account for nature in terms of natural causes and events. Fortunately, naturalistic Greek and humanistic Greek and Roman philosophers were not limited by sterile theistic doctrines which they had to incorporate into their educational theories. Education had a humanistic goal. If, as Protagoras suggests, "man is the measure of all things" and learning is placed in that context, man is free to evolve values, social systems, and philosophies of human destiny which fit *his* needs, not those of gods or oracles.

Renaissance educators such as Desiderius Erasmus and Thomas More were well aware of classical humanistic principles, for they abandoned medieval Christian theology and education and returned to the Greeks and Latins for the inspiration to derive a "new birth of freedom," to develop man's capacity for reason, which rejected the narrow confines of an ethic of sin, guilt, and dogma. Such a humanistic emphasis helped to secularize and liberalize the schools. Ever since the Renaissance which was essentially humanistic:

> One can distinguish at least three continually entwining lines of development; a more reflective line, a more social line, and a more scientific line. The reflective development goes particularly via German philosophy to, e.g., Jaspers. It has a strong moral and (in a general sense) religious woof; it is particularly occupied with education and counseling. The social line goes via Bentham, Comte, and Marx. . . . It strives

at formulating a humanist criterion of social action and is characterized by the triplet of inform, perform, and reform. The empirical development goes mainly via Bacon and the Anglo-Saxon empiricists to logical positivism, linguistic analysis and various kinds of scientists. In this latter field psychologists like Fromm and Rogers, and a biologist like Huxley, stress the specific responsibility of the human species on the basis of its specific nature. In a broader sense modern thinking contributes to all three lines of humanistic development. As well in the field of philosophy as in the field of science; that is, both social sciences like history, psychology, and sociology; and natural sciences like biology, physics, and astronomy. Together they constitute a really modern picture of life and the world.[5]

In a less technical sense Western education has continually acquired many humanistic characteristics. Insofar as it has stressed the value of the individual and developed means to enhance individual uniqueness, whether in the context of Lockean, Watsonian, or Rogerian psychology, the net result has probably been humane and humanistic. As van Praag suggests, insofar as scientific rationalism and even German idealism have given a rational bent to learning matrices, they have had a humanistic impact. And, at the interpersonal level, the vein of humanitarianism which runs from Erasmus through Ichabod Crane to Mr. Chips and the kindly and understanding teacher in today's classroom or free school, this is fundamentally humanistic. The same is true of the social consciousness evolving in our state universities and gaining momentum in the latest campus tutorial project or collection of funds for some catastrophe on the world stage.

What gives contemporary humanism its unique character is the heightened demand from students themselves for ways and means to be perceived as persons and not cogs in a mechanical system. At once they seek to cast off the alienating impact of technology, coercion into a system (*any* system), and the destructive paternalism of elders who have power, while they work to achieve a mind-releasing, freedom-enhancing condition which promotes further creativity. They seek to employ the insights of humanistic psychology, and to use the products of technology—such as the pill, LSD, psychedelic experiences, and electronic music—in order to derive an independence from authority-bound value systems imposed by an older generation. The result may be a "counter-culture."[6]

If one wishes to be on the humanistic frontier of education, then he must be willing to "hear it like it is" in the hearts and minds of the young for whom educational processes are in the final analysis intended. This does not mean that the traditional educational tools, such as reading and mathematics, are necessarily dehumanizing. It all depends upon the student's perceived need. *If* he asks for bibliographies, a particular specialized skill, or a body of knowledge which the teacher may have, one may say, fine. But the teacher would better serve his calling if he were to function as a midwife, developing perception, sharpening insight, feeling, hearing, and knowing, rather than behaving like a perambulating encyclopedia. Even to survive, the teacher must remain closer to the frontier of student awareness than ever before in history. (This is the insight of Kaare Bolgen's viewpoint, Chapter 22.) The teacher must be prepared to admit that it may be more humane to "let his student go" than to attempt to develop discipleship. It may even be more humane to encourage the student's use of television sets, hi-fi, movie cameras and projectors, McLuhan style, than to insist upon students' sitting in school six hours a day, five days a week, thirty-six weeks a year (cf. William Chase's essay, Chapter 17, as well as Ben Thompson's Epilogue, Question 5).

In other words, the humanistic frontier has no specific location in space-time; it is wherever young minds become aware of their own potential and devise means for developing that potential, without the deadening impact of preordained structures. This does not mean that some formal structures, of knowledge or skills, of buildings and campuses, of attitude and logic, of influential personalities (both old and young, living and dead), cannot be used constructively. In fact, such frameworks often serve as scaffolding on which to build philosophies of life and means for more humane living. Rather, it cannot be assumed that what was good for one person or generation is necessarily good for another. And "good" may be defined however one wishes! Once that insight is acted upon, almost everything that was once sacred (history, nationalistic indoctrination, architecture, sequential learning, polite language, etc.) may have to be modified or abandoned. And once old patterns of behavior may be questioned—whether teacher roles, student roles, school roles, required courses, or acceptable extracurricular activities—then *all* traditional standards and values are subject to restructuring (cf. Epilogue, Questions 1–25!). Moreover, if one accepts the view of participatory democracy so current today, that all human beings, including students and adults, should have a voice in those decisions and events which affect their lives, then conventional wisdoms about power, authority, and trusteeship in educational institutions are also subject to restructuring, *re*-restructuring, and other modifications.

One is reminded of Harold Kaplan's astute observations regarding "two wisely mature principles" which, he says, are "essential to any democracy on the deepest level of its self-awareness":

> One is that society will remain radically imperfect from any moral standard of judgment. The other is that the

medium of permanent criticism and dissent is necessary for the reform, control, and peaceful continuity of imperfect human societies.[7]

The humanistic frontiersmen represented in this volume "hear it like it is." They see nothing in any conventional wisdom as remaining especially sacred, not even the penetrating insights of John Dewey, one of the great humanists of the twentieth century (cf Otto Krash's views on Dewey, Chapter 11). Rather, the central issue of our day is whether human beings will develop values that will enhance human growth and hence contribute to social sanity. Growth and sanity relate to the way values are developed and knowledge is used and the subsequent results which are achieved for our ends, both personal and social. In short, knowing the multiplication table is not necessarily dehumanizing if such knowledge functions to enhance growth; but it might be a better strategy to develop skills at multiplying both in the mind and by computer— that is, *if* the having of such options is perceived in itself as freeing human beings for evolving further options. It is not a mistake to memorize a Shakespearean sonnet, Bach fugue, or chemical formula, *unless* the process of memorizing stunts further appreciation of Shakespeare or Bach, or discourages one's own artistic or scientific creativity. It is not necessarily detrimental to develop skills in mastering systems of analytic logic, *unless* such skills destroy one's capabilities to appreciate nonlinear processes or gestalts which are *also* part of human experience. The frontier lies beyond both the cerebrum and the aorta; it lies in the processes of self-realization and social reconstruction.

Bristling Discontent

The essays included in this volume raise a host of questions and suggest a great variety of alternative solutions. In fact, it would be surprising if anybody reading reflectively could go more than a paragraph or two at a time without stopping to annotate the margins of his book with questions, both substantive and methodological in nature. The lines bristle with discontent, discontent which the reader may not feel as intensely as any given writer. While a few of the authors may follow Samuel Johnson's admonition to "censure with respect and praise with alacrity," most diagnose sharply the educational problems of our time. The contributors to the student power symposium, for instance, do not mince words. I only regret that they couldn't have been brought together physically after the appearance of their articles in *The Humanist* in order to debate their alternative angles of vision. As it is, the reader will have to imagine (a process more creative, perhaps, in the long run) what one might have said to another.

The common theme of the essays in this book might be summarized as follows: American education is in crisis. It faces disaster at all levels. Something must be done quickly if we are to rescue humans from continuing damage. The authors in this book do not say this quite as dramatically as the titles of two recent books, *Death at an Early Age,* and *Our Children are Dying,*[8] but they say it clearly enough. Humanists believe that something still may be done—*if* there is the will to do it. Educational means, they insist, must be humane; they must not be the acts of scholarly or administrative despots, however benevolent. They know that educational reform requires the radical restructuring of our schools. It is not easy, however, to tinker with the system if those in power are determined to maintain their controls. Even where educators are willing to ease up on the controls, some method must be found to keep them from feeling—as they did at Columbia University—that they are "up against the wall," or, if they can face such feelings, to channel such facing creatively. We're well aware of the psychological extension of Newton's law of physics that every action brings about equal and opposing reactions. So how to effect meaningful dialogue may be a matter of encouraging listening lessons, constructing feeling lessons, in short, squeezing the human disposition to change into encounter or sensitivity group molds of many shapes and sizes which, one may hope, leaves the potential changer open to new winds of logical argument, new evidence for evolving creative generalizations. Too, old logicians and administrators, comfortable with their own particular brand of linear analysis (which has worked for them up to this time) may need to develop respect for other linear models as well as the gestalt approach to a given problem. We may wish to borrow from Eastern civilization as well as from other cultural and subcultural experience.

In short, no humanist can view the school landscape in America without serious concern about "up-tight" teachers who force their own hang-ups on their children, authoritarian professors who insist upon using last year's notes for their students while developing new experiments in industrial and government research, running-scared administrators (often afraid of their own shadows when *one* parent phones to register *one* complaint about such items as sex education or the use of a controversial novel) who seem to spend their days and nights devising Procrustean curriculums, class schedules, and codes of dress in order to have smooth-running schools. The humanist is also concerned about frightened students, often too cowed to devise their own learning strategies, too brainwashed to respond to the question, "What do you want to learn?" or too angry to search for the consequences of rebelling without a cause. So another common theme of these essays is really a methodological one. The authors focus their microscopes on those societal viruses which threaten to infect today's students with a disease beyond all hope of therapy. Their generalizations are often large, but their data are concrete. Their assumptions are varied, but their arguments are clear. At every point their vision is one of a better society where the good of the individual is not subordinated to the forces of social continuity. They wince when they observe a phenomenon threatening to destroy the individual's capacity to respond or the opportunity for realizing his potentiality. They are aware of the ever-latent conflict between individual liberty and societal stability. In fact, several authors express fear that the more militant radicals may wish to blow up the system simply to watch the pieces fly. And yet, they call for action—to improve the governance of public school and private university, to develop relevant learning matrices and curriculums, to evolve more sensitive human beings who will not let themselves get boxed in by any system, to realize "a new birth of freedom." All would probably agree that a major purpose of education is to evolve the courage to develop the examined life, not for mere formal credentialism, but more importantly for the release of creative energies at every moment of consciousness, *in* school and out. Authors like Edgar Friedenberg, Judson Jerome, and Abraham Maslow stress poignantly the critical importance of establishing individual authenticity. Kaare Bolgen demonstrates keenly some of the agonies and insights required to feed such authenticity. Learning situations which do not accomplish that may not be worthy of the name "school" though we are all too aware that it's difficult to establish one's unique identity if thrust into any kind of ticky-tacky box, whether it be called Grade Eleven American History or High Rise Dorm No. 70!

Educational specialists are prone to divide education into preschool, elementary, secondary, undergraduate, graduate, and professional subareas. Indeed, one might easily collect a group of essays concerning the humanistic frontiers in each of these categories. After all, the Head Start program is a kind of frontier at the preschool level insofar as it searches for means to boost children out of cultural deprivation, though it may dehumanize if it raises expectations which cannot be fulfilled. At the elementary level, many exciting developments are occurring, including the nongraded classroom, multimedia approaches to learning, and the devising of materials which stress the gestalt approach to human development. At the secondary level the discovery and problem-solving approaches, plus more independent study and the use of multi-media, begin to realize some of the objectives mapped out in George Leonard's provocatively humanistic book, *Education and Ecstasy*. Evolution and revolution among undergraduates suggest that students are being encouraged to "do their own thing" in classroom and residence; they are also being encouraged to develop decision-making processes which affect the quality of campus life; some of these trends have dehumanizing implications, too, especially insofar as drugs accentuate alienation. The pressures for humanistic reforms are less evident in the graduate and professional schools, though here, too, there are some exciting experimental innovations; for instance, the Tufts University Medical School is substantially altering its curriculum by gearing it more closely to social need and student motivation; teacher education is making greater use of internships and independent study; the Union for Experimenting Colleges and Universities, a consortium consisting of some twenty institutions, is pioneering in restructuring the Ph.D. by minimizing formal requirements and maximizing independent study, project formulation and solution. In short, where there is vision and courage, there is also action.

This collection of essays makes no pretense to represent all of the divisions of education or include all the new frontiers. Rather it brings together men intensely concerned about persons and American education. Hence some alternative patterns of protest, prescriptions for action, dilemmas for deliberation are found here in a variety of expressions which will enable the keen methodologist to identify contradictions, decipher dichotomies, assess assumptions. And it seems fairly safe to suggest that few will finish this collection of thoughts and proposals with the notion that ideology has come to an end, as Daniel Bell concluded in his work, *The End of Ideology.* The serious reader may find it challenging to summarize the ideology succinctly and make a sketch of the society which might result if the proposals were translated into action.

Most humanists today are critically aware that to utter words or abstractions without also taking into account their effect upon practice would lay them open to the formalistic hypocrisy which they abhor and which young people today wish to eschew. Such are the poignant paradoxes and ironies we face. And however much the paradoxical, ironical, or even humorous situation may constitute the human dilemma, the radical humanist would hope to make an analysis of those situations a fundamental part of relevant learning and acting. Then, to be a participant in paradox, irony and humor could prove to be constructive and not lead to paralyzing cynicism and a wishful earthling cry, "Stop the world, I want to get off."

I

General
Diagnoses

Introduction

We may joyfully or sardonically cry, "Give us this day our daily illusion!" But it is the better part of sanity to develop a fine distinction between illusion and reality. Without such distinction, it may be difficult to locate oneself in a desert landscape, or in a ghetto or a school john filled with graffiti. Theodore Brameld, long a catalyst in urging Americans to do something about the crises of our times, addresses himself critically to such illusions and realities, urging us to rid ourselves of cant and rhetoric.

How can we "turn the society around," for instance, if the task of the school is merely to transmit the cultural heritage? Must everybody internalize nationalism or learn technologies which have the future of the dodo bird? Can we expect major breakthroughs in individual creativity or self-direction in learning if teachers merely perpetuate their own values? And how long shall the teacher remain a eunuch? And implicit in Professor Brameld's questions is the question: if queries about explosive issues force powerful men to overreact, why value questioning? In other words, do questions kill? This may well be the central theme of this book, a problem deserving wide discussion across the American landscape. For it is quite commonly accepted that a person who isn't part of the solution (answer?) may be part of the problem (question?). And we know, too, that an unsolved question (a person?) may require restructuring (personal change?). Hence to open with Brameld's viewpoint suggests that we may need to ask rather bluntly, "How competent am I in detecting the difference between illusion and reality?" or "What glasses must I don to sharpen my perception?" or, "What logical tools must I develop to distinguish between shoddy and keen analyses?"

Closely related to such questioning about questioning is that pertaining to relevance. Who among us wants to think or feel that his life is an exercise in futility? Hence it's important early in this book to face the problem of relevance. True, the word has been overused, but has the concept? Aren't we all concerned about *that-which-relates-to-us,* that which is relevant?

Mario Fantini helps us see the need for major surgery through the students' eyes, just as students later (cf. "Voices Through the Mortar," Chapter 16) tell us what they want to relate to. And we may ask, Why the shift in youth's mood? Why do more students have more courage to speak their minds more than their fathers and grandfathers did? Or do they? How does the teacher, the parent, the principal facilitate student involvement to turn the curriculum around to achieve relevance while not destroying the knowledge base which we need to build a bridge, destroy a slum, or scan a poem? And what models are available for constructing a more responsible governance process to run schools and colleges? Is the corporate model adequate? neighborhood controls? bureaucratic procedures? or do we need a model which no imagination has yet conceived? If so, how and whom do we encourage to dream *toward* it? And after thinking about Fantini's proposal for "altering at least three basic pillars which support our conventional schools," one may wish to ask: "alter or smash?" And what price either alternative?

Edgar Friedenberg has, of course, given us all many new angles of vision about youth in America. Nor does he disappoint us here. Once Professor Friedenberg points it out, how can one deny that a diploma or degree is a "political document," an "access to status and role"? But once we admit that, what can anybody *do* about it, personally, socially, or even politically? Do any of us *want* to? What would we gain (or lose), for instance, if we faced up to psychological reality and awarded a Bachelor of Servility or Bachelor of Courage or even Joy (depending upon the circumstances) rather than a Bachelor of Arts? or a Doctor of Servility rather than a Doctor of Philosophy? Likewise, at the political level, would a Doctor of Affluence & Access (DAA) be more appropriate than Doctor of Education? We have lived so long in this country with the medieval bachelor's and doctor's captions that it's not easy, even in experimental circles, to direct much thought toward a suggestion that I once made that we need to face up to the realities of learning processes and award a Doctor of Learning.[1]

But more importantly, when Professor Friedenberg reminds us of the behavioral consequences of school socialization, namely, "the hazing of potential poets and critics into submission," then humanists among us may feel the urge to burn down the schools to get rid of the rats. Although I have little confidence in curriculum reconstruction as a panacea, for it's too often perceived as *thing* or is too gimmicky to cut into real problems, I'm inclined to urge the inventing of course titles and processes which will describe humanizing ways. Better Imagination 101–102, Dreaming 203–204, and Goofing-off 307–308 than the illusion that the taking of 12, 16 or 20 years of neatly dovetailed courses is *necessarily* encouraging people to become human. Which brings us back to facing the reality of potential illusion: "Give us this day our daily illusion!"

Can we?

1

THEODORE BRAMELD

Illusions and Disillusions in American Education

I

The volatile state of education today is illustrated by articles recently featured on the covers of two mass-circulation magazines: "Angry Teachers—Why They Will Strike 300 Times This School Year" and "Students Against the World."

These feature stories are unprecedented. Neither could have been imagined a few years ago. Each symbolizes the phenomenal unrest that is permeating educational events. They signalize a movement that is shattering the whole facade of beliefs, processes, and structures so resistant to inadequacies in the vast institution of modern education.

I use the term "facade" deliberately because education in America as well as in other parts of the world is demonstrably an artificial if not an obsolete enterprise—artificial and obsolete in the sense that it distorts, conceals, and avoids many of the most fundamental perplexities and compulsions of our age. Hence, here is a series of great "illusions" and "disillusions" of contemporary education. By the former I mean the fallacies and shibboleths that remain only too apparent. By the latter I imply more than a negative connotation: Disillusionment is often the forerunner of reawakening and renewal. It is largely in this sense that I speak of "disillusion."

This paper was originally published in Phi Delta Kappa, **50**, *No. 3 (December 1968), 202–7. Reprinted by permission.*

Since one cannot list all that might be included in such a series, I am compelled to oversimplify. Nevertheless, my examples should serve to establish the contention that education is being forged as a double-edged sword. With one edge, it proves a novel capability to cut through the facade; in this sense it plays the indispensable role of exposing its own obsolescences. With the other edge, it enables us to consider how this capability may be channeled toward more impelling alternatives—toward reconstructed beliefs, processes, structures, and most crucially toward new and urgent goals that are the fruits of its own disillusions.

II

Here, then are ten of our illusions:

1.   Education's primary task has always been and must always be to perpetuate the customs, attitudes, practices, and institutions that prevail from generation to generation. This still-dominant characteristic, although not always explicitly rationalized, is maintained not only by many educators but by remarkably large numbers of psychologists, sociologists, and anthropologists. Terms familiar in this context may include "adjustment," "socialization," "enculturation," and "transmission."

2.   It follows from No. 1 that the primary task of teaching is to assure such perpetuation, thereby qualifying each successive generation for induction into and approval by adult society. This task is exemplified by the heavy emphasis placed upon preparatory curricula of the secondary school, and thus upon the kinds of training that enable the young to climb the social and economic ladder by admission to higher institutions of education, preferably those of such prestigious standing as virtually to assure acceptance by the more affluent sections of that society.

3.   Conversely, the primary task of learning is to respond to the task of teaching noted in No. 2. Today, this capacity is being refined and accelerated by the new technology—particularly by the multimillion-dollar "educational hardware" industry. With its proliferation of automatized gadgetry, the learner can be increasingly "prepared" in highly systematized conveyor-belt teaching factories, hitherto known as schools.

4.   Largely because of the assumptions embodied in Nos. 1, 2, and 3, educational institutions have been effectively organized and controlled chiefly by means of hierarchical structures of authority centering in school boards and boards of trustees as well as their appointed representatives: college presidents, deans, superintendents of schools,

confront degrees of novelty if only because the evolutionary process is itself always novel—a generalization demonstrated sometimes dramatically but oftener modestly in their struggles to combat and control their inanimate and animate environments. Anyone, for example, who has watched the Australian aborigines is struck by the fantastic ingenuity with which they search out and discover food, invent their own tools, and demonstrate other abilities and skills suitable to their arduous needs. How more truly, then, do complex and sophisticated cultures prove their own genius for originality, discovery, and inventiveness.

The point I wish to make penetrates still more deeply into the whole psychology of learning and teaching than is commonly assumed. It takes issue with the behaviorist assumptions recently obsessing so many psychological practitioners under the influence of B. F. Skinner and his followers. It equally undergirds a major quality of the nature of human power. Surely, however, to belabor further the creative capabilities latent if not always overt in human experience is itself redundant. One may only recall the amazing achievements that abound in the arts—in painting, the dance, sculpture, music, architecture, and others—through millennia of history and across all continents.

A great deal more could be said about our first illusion, but even these sparse remarks would be wholly superfluous were we not so often befuddled by the metacultural assumption of education regarded so predominantly as a "reinforcing" or "socializing" process.

2.   The view to be repudiated here is that education, especially for the increasing middle classes of America, France, Japan, and other countries, must be designed to assure both the young and their parents that they should go to college and that in order to do so they must meet admissions standards established *by* the colleges.

Lively criticism is generated against this complacent view. Not only are we questioning why the typical high school curriculum should so often be tailor-made for the conventional college-bound student, but more seriously we may question whether the curriculum is defensible even for him. To a shocking extent both the high school and college curricula are structurally the same as they were 30 or 40 years ago—an "eggcrate" of courses with little if any significant relation either to each other or to the central streams of life around them. Most are still bound by the all-too-familiar rubrics of English, mathematics, science, social studies, and foreign language, plus a smattering of peripheral subjects.

3.   Until our second illusion is dissipated, the illusion that worthwhile learning can be successfully automated is unlikely to be challenged either. To put the point differently, as long as ambitious, competitive grade-seeking motivations remain paramount, school and

college hierarchies will respond eagerly to the already high-pressure promotion campaigns of General Electric, Westinghouse, and other huge corporations in open collaboration with the "software industry" of book publishing. But the focal question is whether the kind of efficient, stimulus-response learning induced by this technology can actually produce "educated" people. Disillusionment lies in the greater likelihood, given a free rein, that it will produce excellently conditioned human beings but neither autonomous nor creative ones. *Walden Two, 1984,* and *Brave New World* are only too ominous alternatives.

4. The plausibility of radical challenge to automatization and computerization in education remains remote, in turn, as long as our fourth illusion carries its own heavy burden of influence—namely, that the best organization of education is to be found in models of business, with directors and managers properly in command, and with the rest of the personnel of education largely subject to their orders. The line-staff structure of education thus becomes the most prevailing one. It is also a major source of current student and faculty revolt. Behind this revolt is an awakening if still semiconscious realization that the analogy with business models is blatantly false—rather, that education should be conceived as an institution designed not to reinforce efficiency or comparable virtues of the prevailing power structure but rather to encourage critical-mindedness, distinctiveness, "dissentual knowledge," and participation by both students and faculties in every segment of educational life.

5. I have mentioned faculties here, and thus we return to the illusion of conventional teacher and professorial subservience to educational control. It would be difficult to find better samples of exposure to this illusion than a widely quoted statement by Mrs. Ruth Trigg, former president of the Department of Classroom Teachers of the National Education Association:

> I maintain that a teacher who finds himself in a situation where conditions are such that good education is an impossibility, having exhausted every other means of improving those conditions with no success, should walk out. I further maintain that this teacher shows more dedication to his profession than does the teacher who stays on the job, perpetuating mediocrity. Perhaps the child's education will be interrupted for a week or a month, but what is one week or one month when measured against years of education, all less than adequate? If the teacher's militancy leads to improved conditions of learning, the child's opportunities are enhanced for a lifetime.[1]

Here surely is a remarkable repudiation of encrusted mores of the teaching profession. Yet it is only a more general statement of a more pointed one by David Selden, an official spokesman for the labor-affiliated American Federation of Teachers:

> I think the best thing that can happen to the country is a nation-wide teachers' strike to bring about the vast improvement in schools that we need.[2]

If one recalls events in several cities in the light of what Mrs. Trigg and Mr. Selden have said, he will agree that illusion No. 5 may be on the verge of collapse. And if he underscores such a likelihood with the record of teachers' organizations in several other countries, he must perceive this phenomenon even more clearly. In Japan, for example, Nikkyoso, the national Teachers' Union, is not only the largest union in the entire country but one of the most militant, most politically minded opponents of the economic, social, and educational establishment.

6.   Closely related to the intensifying militancy of teacher power is, of course, student power. This fallacy is pinpointed by Professor Alaine Touraine of the University of Paris:

> The student revolt is not merely a crisis of the adaptation of the universities to the modern society, nor is it only a revolt of youth against tradition. Rather, it signals the birth of new conflicts, the first act in the drama of putting the new, computerized industrial state on trial. But it is within the universities that its future lies, because it is there that learning takes place. The student movement is no longer the *avant-garde* of a peasant or worker movement, but the *avant-garde* of itself.[3]

Increasing minorities of students all the way from Rome, Madrid, and Paris to Rio de Janeiro, Mexico City, and Tokyo are defying the creaky apparatus both of learning-teaching and of time-exhausted curricula.

Such student upheavals suggest profound, if also subtle and intricate, connections between student unrest and black unrest. Both kinds overlap, as witnessed at Columbia University, San Francisco State, and in the courageous lunch-counter sit-ins. But whether the alignment is tenuous or not, its roots spread deep into the malaise hinted at by Professor Touraine—a malaise typified by such widely recognized symptoms as alienation with all their accompaniments of guilt, frustration, hatred, and (in the existentialist sense) meaninglessness.

This is surely not to say that the student and the black share *identical* travails. But they do often share *common* ones. The average black is the victim of white racism, as the Commission on Civil Disorders and other commissions so impressively demonstrate. The average student is the victim of outmoded policies and programs which ubiquitously and covertly generate negativism and skepticism toward education and its supporting triple structure of the industrial, political, and military. Both students' and teachers' uprisings, now chronic, herald a deep-seated want of self and social fulfillment quite as urgent as do the blacks' uprisings herald theirs.

The comparison may be carried further. Just as militant organizations such as the Students for a Democratic Society reject the classic sociopolitical theories of radical change, and along with them the dominance of the entrenched generation, so the black power movement rejects most of the older liberal doctrines characterized by integration and equality of opportunity.

On a personal note: twenty years ago I, too, was much persuaded by these doctrines. As a staff member of both the Bureau for Intercultural Education and the Center for Human Relations Studies at New York University, I tried to contribute to well-meaning integrative ventures. Today I am convinced that they have largely failed. Instead, I empathize with Negro leaders I have come to know in the Roxbury ghetto of Boston—all of whom, from militant to moderate, regard black power as the clarion call of their programs. Moreover, after having read one of the most deeply moving and enlightening books I have ever encountered—*The Autobiography of Malcolm X*—I am somewhat better prepared to identify with the mood of both blacks and students.

At the same time, let me seriously question whether the frequently defiant and disillusioning posture of student activism is any more mature than black nationalism is as a decisive answer. Both movements are manifestations of anguish, of strength, of courage, of self-respect and group identity. But both need to be superseded by a more clearly affirmative and powerful set of democratic strategies and goals. To recall an old concept from Hegel, student power and black power are both in a stage of "antithesis" against the older "thesis" of traditional patterns. But both should strive to reach much further than this, just as Malcolm X had himself begun to strive further toward "synthesis" during the last months of his young and tragic life.

7 and 8. These two illusions may be combined, because both confront the need for what I may call "the disillusioned curriculum"—the overemphasis of the technological and the underemphasis of the esthetic, moral, social, and humanistic. In both cases, the fallacy centers in what is anticipated in previous comments upon the revolt of the younger generation, white and black alike. Its correction lies in thorough rebuilding of curricula of the public schools and colleges—a rebuilding already inherent in sweeping demands for relevance for maximum satisfaction of human needs and aspirations.

Here again difficult questions confront us, for on paper there are almost as many curricula as there are curriculum planners. Yet the crucial question remains clear: *whether learning and teaching both as process and in substantive quality can cope directly, constantly, penetratingly, with the central character of human life itself.* Plenty of evidence points to the answer; indeed, some schools all the way from Summerhill in England to Tamagawa Gakuen in Japan are already proving that this kind of energizing and transformative adventure is both practicable and vastly exciting.

Of course, the curriculum envisaged here does not minimize necessary transmissive skills such as reading. What it does demonstrate, as John Dewey so brilliantly wrote in one of his more neglected and least remembered books, is that "interest and effort" in education are reciprocal, not antagonistic, propensities of human learning. To promote this kind of reciprocity is never easy—certainly not when high school students have often become so miseducated and unmotivated both by the eggcrate curriculum and by ordained learning requirements.[4]

The disillusioned and therefore innovated curriculum is, by contrast, geared at every stage to the very real experience of learners, no matter their age. Consequently, half of their school program occurs, not in the formal classroom at all, but in the local, regional, national, and ultimately international community. It means that teachers are effectively trained anthropologically and sociologically as well as psychologically; hence, both they and students engage in continuous and expertly directed involvement, in nearby ghetto life as well as distant foreign cultures. It means that the surrounding natural and social environment is constantly utilized as a boundless resource of learning. Finally, it means a freshly designed model of the "community school"—not the caricature we often hear about but one providing wide, busy, two-way avenues equally travelled in both directions by adult learners and by nursery school children.

9.   This illusion, you recall, is the hoary one of the alleged evils of economic support and federal control of education. Notwithstanding the expanding political iniquities of the Vietnam War, we have pretty well exploded the myth of local and state financial adequacy for education. But we have hardly begun to think through a political philosophy sufficiently updated to realize not only that enormously strengthened federal support is necessary but also that carefully formulated practices of federal authority are necessary.

Thus, the relevant issue is not in the least whether we can or should artificially dichotomize federal support and control. Rather, the issue is whether such control is or could be democratically and authentically expressive of the largest possible majority of people. Here, of course, power becomes central once more. Behind it is the question of whether we can still construct a nation with the locus of power genuinely centered in that majority. I doubt if we can, unless the military-industrial network is superseded by patterns of modern democratic socialization mandated by and geared to the maximum needs of the citizenry as a whole. Simultaneously, "decentralization" counterbalanced with federal control becomes a concomitant principle—not for the sake of new forms of authority that could be just as disillusioning as the old, but for the sake of cooperatively developed community plans and tasks through which parents, students, and teachers engage in unrestricted dialogue to arrive at tenable, functioning, and self-correcting guides of operation.

But these samples of controversial contention themselves precisely illustrate the meaning of a modernized and revitalized curriculum—a curriculum focusing on the pressing, concrete problems of mankind and subjected to the most searching, unmitigated questions and criticisms that can be raised in the adventure of teaching and learning.

10.   The illusion of nationalism, as exemplified by the truncated programs of UNESCO, is another example of much the same sort of archaism mentioned just above.

Thus far in this agenda we have paid far less attention to power as ends than to power as means. Even so, it is hoped that power as ends is at least implicit in what has been said about means—in, for example, the as yet only partially, crudely articulated goals of student power and black power.

Nevertheless, a desperate demand arises in education for much more *explicit* attention to these goals—above all, to the goal of a realizable international order. Here is a theme demanding more patient, more probing diagnosis and prognosis than does any other single problem endemic to our time.

The pity is that, to an alarming extent, the means and ends of a viable community of nations remain neglected by most education. One hears occasional lip service to the United Nations. But what in actuality is required is vastly more than this: the problems and expectations of all mankind should become nothing less than the pervading theme of *every* curriculum, beginning in its own terms of maturation at the kindergarten level and extending to the college and adult levels. Here surely is a captivating theme—one compelling us to utilize and discover all that we can know about the earth's resources and ecology, about population control, about the dangers and promises of technology, about the deep-seated conflicts that pervade political-economic struggles, and certainly about the similar as well as dissimilar value patterns of cross-cultural ethnic and racial clusterings. It is a theme that can galvanize and provide direction as no patchwork remedies of the curriculum can possibly provide; that can replace the emptiness and sterility of much of the present program; that can arouse the younger generation (in partnership with the older) to seek and express its own significance and purpose; and finally that can strive for the establishment of a UNESCO with authority to construct a planetary, democratically directed program of education.

Like the preceding nine illusions, the disillusion of nationalism is not to be interpreted in a merely negative sense. The corollary of this disillusion can be the positive and universal affirmation of an earth-wide humanity—of life-vitalizing goals that could and should transcend our long overworked illusions.

W. Warren Wagar, in *The City of Man,* has a magnificent epitomization of what a curriculum could mean to all our children and to all our citizens:

> Whoever enlists in the cause of man in this age will find no time for nostalgia. We are the link between the traditional civilizations of a well-remembered past and the emergent world civilization. We stand between. If we break under the strain, there will be no future. All posterity is in our keeping. Such a task against such towering odds joins man to man and weaves meaning into the vast fabric of confusion. It can be the difference between the life and death of the soul.[5]

2

MARIO D. FANTINI

Relevance = Humanistic Education

The world exists for the education of each man . . . He should see
that he can live all history in his own person . . . All history be-
comes subjective; in other words, there is properly no History;
only Biography . . . Every soul must know the whole lesson for
itself—must go over the whole ground. What it does not see, what
it does not live, it will not know.

Ralph Waldo Emerson, *History*

In a staggering number of ways, man has become subservient to the civilization which he has created: his job is threatened by automation, his lungs are impaired by the pollution of technology, and "the alienation of modern man" is as hackneyed as "once upon a time." No less hackneyed is the "inadequacy of American education." It is patently accepted that the schools are failing to educate on their own terms; ghetto children often read below grade level, and the institution of assimilation has produced a generation of cultural exiles. This generation is not merely concerned with the school's inability to accomplish the conventional objectives, but is questioning the validity of those objectives themselves. They are demanding a new kind of educational system in which the individual human being is the ultimate concern—a humanistically oriented institution. Let us examine two statements reflecting student interests, one black, the other white. Both are from high school aged youth. First the black students of the Freedom School, Eastern High School Freedom Annex, Washington, D.C.:

> What we understand by education is the obtainment and application of all one's knowledge for the benefit of the group which in turn will benefit each individual within the collective. To this end what must constitute the basic part of one's education is the understanding of people more than things. We realize that once people understand themselves, their knowledge of things is facilitated, that the exclusive knowledge of things does not guarantee knowledge of people, and

in fact contributes to the erosion, disintegration, and destruction of the creativity of man.

Therefore our Freedom School must: (1) make Black People aware of who they are, (2) make Black People aware of who they must identify with, (3) enlighten Black People to the creative and scientific tools that are needed in order to obtain whatever we want to mean as freedom.[1]

Second, issued by the Montgomery County Student Alliance, entitled "Wanted: A Humane Education":

Some of the county school system's announced goals are being met. County students on the whole are equipped with certain skills and facts, and test scores and grades show that the school system has by and large prepared them for college.

The most significant effect of this emphasis on measurable, "acceptable" performance has been to subordinate greatly other basic goals of a desirable educational climate—goals which are less tangible but which, we feel and the county school system says (rhetorically) it agrees, are of far greater and more lasting importance. It is these latter goals that have, practically speaking, been almost totally ignored by the county school system and the way it operates. Feedback to see whether these much more vital aims are being fulfilled has just not been sought by school officials; to our knowledge the county schools have shown little willingness to confront these questions and bring about the fundamental changes in attitude and organization that are necessary. . . .[2]

The existing American school, like schools everywhere, is a social, political, and cultural instrument of the total society. The values and behavioral patterns of the community at large are nurtured and perpetuated via the educational institution. In fact, the school is a microcosm of its surrounding environment; and, therefore, it is a vulnerable and obvious target in any movement toward societal reform. If the society is victim to hypocrisy, so the school will demonstrate fraudulence. The student movement is attempting to legitimize societal objectives by changing the traditional goals of education.

The students' fight for power in their own schools is not aimed at a benign, benevolent dictatorship. They view their public schools and universities as having deprived them of the *me* in the learning process. The ubiquitous cry for "relevance", among even the most disparate factions of the student movement, is affecting the theoretical complexion of educational planning. University catalogues now describe courses which lean more toward encounter groups than massive lectures. Freshmen reading lists are omitting *Jane Eyre* in favor of *The Autobiography of Malcolm X,* and courses which include community participation are becoming more popular than the prestigious scholar's lecture series.

For years, the United States has been comfortable with a social system of norms—that which is done is, by necessity, good, and you will adjust or you will suffer the consequences. American institutions have reflected that same value scale. The school's primary concentration is in the area of smoothness, or efficiency, and anyone who disrupts the peace of the institution is reprimanded. Consider the demands which are made of our youngsters:

> Students don't ask that orders make sense. They give up expecting things to make sense long before they leave elementary school. Things are true because the teacher says they're true. At a very early age we all learn to accept "two truths," as did certain medieval churchmen. Outside of class, things are true to your tongue, your fingers, your stomach, your heart. Inside class, things are true by reason of authority. And that's just fine because you don't care anyway. Miss Wiedemeyer tells you a noun is a person, place or thing. So let it be. The important thing is to please her. Back in kindergarten, you found out that teachers only love children who stand in nice straight lines. And that's where it's been at ever since. Nothing changes except to get worse.[3]

The blind faith of the fifties ("apathy," as it was once called) has given way to a catapulting outrage in this decade. The old credentials are toppling despite the enormity of their past success. Because a man is a teacher neither makes him virtuous nor omniscient; similarly, a man is not automatically honorable because he is chairman of the board of a corporation or, for that matter, President of the United States. Young people judge their peers and elders in human rather than power terms. Does he listen? Does he understand? Does he care? These are the questions which determine the worth of an individual man in a humanistic society.

Moreover, students are asking that schools deal with social realities, social injustices, in direct ways. It is not enough to *know* that there are slums, starving human beings, and discrimination. To know about them is one thing, to do something about them is quite another. The conventional educational process develops an adjustment orientation, i.e. it teaches us to *adjust* to slums, discrimination, etc., rather than to *reconstruct* these negative environments.

One is reminded of the scene in the film, "The Graduate," in which Benjamin Braddock returns to his California home, the superficially accomplished product of a "fine American education." There is a great cocktail party to celebrate his remarkable achievements, and he alternates between nodding politely to his parents' friends and rushing to his own room for escape. The guests (presumably the upper-middle class, revered segment of the American population) congratulates him between drinks, and linger long enough to deliver a kiss, a proud tear, and then turn away to continue the business of having a party. Benjamin, in a stupor of self-doubt and disbelief at what's going on around him in the name of his graduation, is looking for anything with a hint of honest affection or concern. A man rushes up to him in earnest, and says he must talk to him. The ever-hopeful Benjamin jumps at the chance, and they walk outside for the conversation. "Benjamin, I have one word to say to you." "Yes, Sir?" "Benjamin," (long pause, expression of intensity), "plastics!" The scene is already famous, and, in a very amusing fashion, takes the myth of the respectable, the elite in our society, and portrays pathetic buffoonery instead.

The myth of materialism has been under attack for some time now, but the travesty of academia is a new target for the young population. Just as a successful industrialist is not necessarily admirable in affairs other than business, so a distinguished scholar may not be a decent teacher. At several college campuses, students now publish catalogues which evaluate the professors and their respective courses. This method serves to inform prospective course participants of the day-to-day value of a teacher and his course work. Whereas the university still selects faculty members on the basis of published works and scholarly reputations, today's students are using different criteria. It isn't enough to be competent in a discipline; a good teacher must be able to translate that information in a meaningful, tendentious manner to his students. To glance at these student catalogues is a lesson in irony; one would be amazed at the number of prominent academicians who fail because they read directly from their own publications or rely on graduate assistants for grading papers and student conferences!

The classical approach to education places ultimate value on the disciplines, and these areas of cognition govern the activities of individual students. If one is a student of history, for example, one must be familiar and fluent with a plethora of details and philosophical viewpoints in order to pass a regents, college final, and the eventual doctoral examination. The commitment here, on the part of the institution, is to something called history; the student's role in the historical process is of no interest to a group of five who judge a doctoral candidate during oral examinations. And yet, a candidate who succeeds is called a doctor of history, though his command of the subject is in the realm of abstraction. There is no professional judgment regarding a student's participation in historical realities—after all, that's the student's own business. The classical criterion is absorption of subject matter, not activity.

It is paradoxical that many theories of knowing require doing, yet our institutional methods have repeatedly contradicted this most basic assumption. Henri Bergson described the highest form of knowledge as duration, the only process which provides the possibilities of real insight, profound understanding—a process which is not simply cognitive, but involves the total personality. He illustrates his concept of knowledge with the example of photographs of a street in Paris. If one were shown fifty snapshots of a street in the city of Paris—all angles of the building, the sidewalk, the people—they could not replace the total sensation of walking down that street on a sunny, noisy day. It is essentially the difference between description and definition—the surrounding qualities of an experience versus the experience itself.

Our educational system has dwelled on descriptions of ideas, paintings, skills, etc. It is definition, however, which *affects* the life of a human being, and this definition is achieved through a variety of educational experiences. Education does not end with the blackboard; it is an ongoing process which is determined by the makeup of each individual child. Cognition, after all, is valuable insofar as it serves emotion, yet the existing school has reversed that procedure. Emotions are used as devices to motivate children in a classroom, and are the means rather than the ends of contemporary education. For example, teachers will discuss a high student interest topic such as the hippie movement not as a strategy for connecting with the learners' *intrinsic* concern for identity, but as a tactic for connecting the learners to *extrinsic* content, e.g., the Western Explorers (hippies have something in common with Columbus—they are self-searching, exploring). All roads seem to lead to cognition. Laughter and tears are prohibited in the classroom; they are considered an obstruction to the learning process. The youngster who displays his emotions—even if he's excited about what he is learning—is subject to censure.

To criticize American schools for failing to achieve success using existing educational methods is to minimize and ultimately ignore the fundamental dilemma of education in the United States. Even from the most selfish point of view, the economic structure (a service-oriented economy) is making an unprecedented demand for sensitive, aware people. Madison Avenue does not sell products on the basis of cognition; the old commercials with the authoritative man in white offering laboratory tested statistics are relics on television. Advertisements appeal to the audience's sense of humor, its sexuality, its wildest fantasies. Business has changed since the days of *The Man in the Gray Flannel Suit;* corporations want a different brand of executive model. The ability to deal with people, to have them trust you, is a personnel criterion from the Garment Center to Wall Street. The rudiments of human relations are no longer superfluous to American business, yet the schools have treated them as an extracurricular luxury.

All facets of contemporary American society are veering away from pure intellect; abstract art, the theatre of confrontation, from *Portnoy's Complaint* to the nod of the intellectuals toward rock music. We are in the post-Freudian era, where repression is the only obscenity, and sensual pleasure is applauded. Consider the vocabulary of the young: "uptight," "hang loose," "dig," "being 'into' something"—all emotional adjectives. It is no longer freakish to be in analysis; group therapy sessions attract audiences as large as those for off-Broadway plays. The success of *Hair* on Broadway would have been inconceivable ten years ago, and the well-made play of yesterday is laughed off the stage. Pomposity is no longer tolerated among the young, and there is an openness concerning neurosis (even pride) which is unprecedented. The days of hiding a crazy relative in the attic are long gone.

The school has so far avoided the growing mood of the young: the shift from a *normal* to *individual* psychology, from *a psychology of being* to a *psychology of becoming*. Not only is it boring to adjust, it is also harmful and restrictive to individual growth. A Scandinavian social scientist has said that we are born originals and are turned into copies. We are immersed in an age of rebellion which lauds originality, and disdains conformity. The era of the young also seeks knowledge for intrinsic purposes, unlike previous ages. In a sense, this is a very moral view of learning; that it be an end in itself. In other words, only that which is a particular concern should be taught in the schools.

Relevance, after all, is not based on the needs of the academic disciplines, but on the needs of society and the people who comprise that society. No existing institution is prepared to deal with the search for identity, anonymity in urbania, or the increase of violence in the United States. In order to change the content of American education—from subject matter to people—we must create an entirely new kind of school. From what the students are expressing, we can piece together at least four different sets of educational objectives:

1. Social reality and the school's curriculum have to be intrinsically connected.
   a. The school must acknowledge the realities by setting up a structure in which students are engaged in the examination of these realities.
   b. Students will learn the skills and behaviors needed to influence social realities.
   c. The skills and behaviors for social change will be applied by the students to the social realities.
2. Power, identity and connectedness have to become a legitimized basis for curriculum development with the aim of expanding the repertoire of responses students have in dealing with these concerns.
3. Diversity, both cultural and individual, and its potential for cross-fertilization has to be encouraged and expanded through educational objectives and organization that allow and legitimize such an aim.
4. The school and the community it serves have to exist less as

separate entities and instead develop responsibilities and lives of authority that are more integrated and shared.[4]

The humanistically oriented school must allow the students into the institution—to have a voice in social and academic policies, and to be involved in the workings, rather than the sounds of democracy. This first step will at least, bring the student into appropriate perspective within the educational structure. He is no longer the subject in the kingdom of the professional, and he has some sense of potency in the learning environment. Not only does student participation benefit the youngsters, but it also eases the burden of the educator; too often the school administrator makes judgments in an experiential vacuum, and relies on research and evaluation when he delineates educational policy. With student participation, he is offered a whole new set of factors for his professional life.

More germane than the appearance of the school as a total society is the functioning of the classroom in a humanistic institution. The present public school classroom in the United States revolves around the teacher —the teacher's need for quiet, for neatness, for order. The children, as early as the first grade, have to adjust to the teacher's idiosyncrasies or suffer the consequences. Voices must be quiet if the teacher has a headache, is in a bad temper, etc. A recent conversation with a twelve-year-old youngster in a prominent Manhattan private school revealed the inordinate imbalance between students and faculty. This particular student was taken to the principal's office for having been rude to his teacher. During the administrator's harangue, the child asked why it was all right for the teacher to be rude to him? He was immediately suspended.

This conventional atmosphere of one versus many is undoubtedly the most efficient; grappling with one personality among thirty obliterates the multiple situation. It also denies the nature of thirty human beings (who happen to be the "clients"), and acknowledges the existence of one (the public "servant"). Think of the teachers who adopt a pedagogical strategy by their third year, and remain loyal to it until retirement. Unfortunately, this strategy is usually one of didactic bombardment, rather than subtle direction, and all students are treated as a cumulative blank slate. It is a tribute to our children that they have learned *despite* these conditions.

Establishing a relevant educational institution will therefore involve altering at least three basic pillars which support our conventional schools:

1. Governance.   There must be a shift from professional dominance to a meaningful parental and community role in the education process. Meaningful participation stands arm's length between professionally circumscribed participation on one hand and total control by students, parents, and community residents on the other. It calls for student, parent, and community roles in the matters of budgeting, personnel, and curriculum. The vehicle of participation may be structures at the individual school level or elected bodies on a neighborhood basis. In either case, one of the chief criteria is proximity of educational decision-makers to the affected schools. The chief political criterion is accountability of the professional and the school system to the students and community.

2. Substance.   There must be an evolution to a humanistically oriented curriculum and a modification of the skill-performance standard by which educational quality is primarily measured. The heavy emphasis on cognitive subject matter must be at least tempered with materials that bear some relevance to the students' lives and with newer kinds of content and procedures that help ghetto students answer deep personal concerns and often rediscover their own integrity. Curriculum that represents an alien, boring, and false culture must be abandoned (ghetto children *can* be well-educated without being robbed of their own sub-culture). Evaluative criteria, in particular, must be expanded to include ways of judging student abilities other than by the verbal means notoriously weighted to the middle-class.

3. Personnel.   The educational system must be opened to a far broader base of talent than the conventionally prepared career educator. The staffs of schools must vary along a wide horizontal spectrum from the professional to the layman, the latter including parents, community residents and students themselves. They must vary vertically as well, to include not only professional educators but also specialists from other disciplines and professions. Moreover, the training of teachers must be vis-à-vis and *in* the reality of community needs and expressions.

The movement toward educational reform is leading us into a neo-progressive era. The unrelenting cry for individual recognition has reached an unavoidable volume. It is not enough to please the teacher—as a matter of fact, the teacher's satisfaction is the least important aspect of a humanistic classroom. If a child "fails," it is the responsibility of the institution and its staff; if he is bored, unprepared to cope with class material, punishing him merely shirks responsibility and ultimately prevents the school from change.

The growth and development of every child is the paramount concern of education. This growth cannot be partial—merely academic—but must encompass all aspects of man's behavior. Intellectual aptitude is farcical unless accompanied by emotional maturity, and the latter is absent in today's classroom; we have demanded emotional acquiescence. The school which we are working toward will acknowledge not only the existence of emotions but the value of them. Each child will be considered and educated first as an individual, then in relationship to his peer group, and, finally, as a present and future member of society.

The student movement and its pleas for relevance, the significance of the individual, and the need for change will form the foundation of the new school. The curriculum will revolve around the student's particular and projected concerns. Consider the implications of our past efforts at glossing over the reality of history, our existing social system:

> Juvenile delinquency may be the healthy revolt of pupils against the injustice of a social system (of which the educational system is merely the preparation, the apprenticeship). The Peasants' Revolt in the fourteenth century, the Pupils' Revolt in the twentieth—are they not fundamentally the same? Is this not just the human spirit kicked about and longing to be treated with justice and dignity? I remember reading a Vicki Baum novel which described the forces in a native who ran amok and I realized for the first time that this phenomenon was a sign of pathology not in an individual but in the society which drove him into blind despair.[5]

It is true that American society is the larger version of our existing schools; a society which praises peace and chooses war, extolls justice and practices inequity, and calls itself a democracy despite Mayor Daley, Governor Strom Thurmond, and Justice Abe Fortas. The discrepancies in the United States are overwhelming, and the public school system includes those paradoxes. In this sense, the schools are performing their function—they are a condensation of the community-at-large.

We are fortunate to be participating in an age which refuses to accept the delusion of American society. Young people everywhere challenge the necessity of fraudulence and are fighting for something better, something different. The schools have already been changed by the mere presence of that awareness. We have the opportunity to transform that awareness into a working institution, to "escape from the classroom," and to begin the business of education in its finest sense. Such a transformation will be a significant step toward a healthy, human America. Isn't that, after all, what we want?

3

EDGAR Z. FRIEDENBERG

Status and Role in Education

The central function of education in a complex society is the allocation of the various credentials that define the status of the bearer and the range of social roles that he may be permitted to fill. The role that an individual comes to occupy in society on the basis of his credentials from school virtually determines his social identity, both in his own eyes and those of society. By "credential," of course, I mean far more than a transcript or a diploma; these certainly, but, properly speaking, the credential includes the entire dossier collected, preserved, and transmitted by the school or used by it as a basis for recommendations to those authorities on whom the student's life-chances depend.

Much of the emphasis placed on the credential in modern society is an expression of its commitment to universalistic values. Formal education is expected to further universalism by promoting achievement —doing rather than being—and appraising it impersonally regardless of the needs of or other claims to consideration by the candidate.

And to the degree that the society is egalitarian as well as universalistic in its values the school will also be expected to admit candidates for credentials to its programs solely on the basis of potential or actual competence in the skills the program demands. Such a society conceives itself as engaged in a continuous talent search, which it is obligated to conduct competitively and impartially for the purpose of maintaining

This article was originally published in The Humanist, **28,** *No. 5 (1968), 13–17, 32. Reprinted by permission.*

a graded talent pool adequate to its enterprises and, generally speaking, without much concern for what the process does to those who are placed in the pool's shark-infested waters. And it regards the schools as its instrument for this purpose and hardly any other.

The schools' devotion to the task of keeping the talent pool stocked with properly labeled and fairly priced items wins it the public support it depends on, but also involves it in fundamental conflicts both internally and with its community. It affronts those students who dislike being processed and labeled as a product. It creates cynicism and despair among students and educators who perceive that, in any case, the credential is awarded in recognition of qualities quite different from the competences it is supposed to certify. And, because of its universalism, the school's talent searching involves it in continuous, covert conflict with its local community, of which maneuvering over school integration provides the best examples.

School systems in the United States are locally controlled, and local control of education is rooted in local political and status systems. It must therefore often conflict with commitments to universalism in an increasingly cosmopolitan society. The intensity, and hence the capacity for damage, in such conflicts tends, however, to be limited by the steady attrition of real local power in an increasingly centralized society. As the scope of local control is reduced by the application of state-aid formulas, the control of textbook production and instructional services by the mass media, and the push toward uniformity exerted by a geographically mobile population that demands interchangeable schools, the local response tends to become more ritualized as it becomes impotent. This does not make it less acrimonious, but merely more passive, so that conflict serves neither to clear the air nor to exert a clear influence on policy.[1]

But local control remains an important influence on the process of status allocation in the schools because it retains considerable veto power and manages thereby to impose local norms on enterprises of great pith and moment. The character of these norms, and their relationship to more cosmopolitan norms, profoundly affect the outcome of this process. Local assessment of students, on the basis of values that may be unrelated or even negatively related to the abilities that will actually be required of them in the roles for which they are becoming qualified, may largely determine their life-chances. As an extreme example of this process, one may conceive of a beard or long hair ultimately costing a youth his life by occasioning his suspension from school, barring him from college admission, and leading to his induction into the armed services. At the level of higher education, it seems to me fair to observe that the Regents and administration of the University of California, by invoking narrowly authoritarian norms of personal conduct when confronted by the hippy cosmopolitanism of student activists and causing their leaders to be jailed, have managed to make a criminal record an essential part of the credential by which those students of the university who were most deeply concerned about education may be recognized; the Ph.D., surely, is a less reliable index.

Ultimately, what any credential comes to certify will be determined by the play of political forces among the groups who participate in the certification, whether they represent local customs, scholarly interests, or the burden of investment. The school, functioning as a certifying agency, serves partly as the vessel within which these contending forces are contained and reach equilibrium, and partly as one of the forces that contribute to the outcome. School personnel themselves judge students according to norms derived from their position in life that express their values and anxieties as well as—and doubtless far more than—academic standards. A school or university credential is in many ways a political document that expresses the vector sum of a set of social forces that determine what kinds of people will be accredited and on what terms; and hence what kinds of people may legitimately influence policy in a given situation. This aspect of the credential's function may or may not involve the way the competences it is supposed to certify are defined, but this does not usually matter crucially. Our society does not value competence very highly. It depends more on the rationalization of production and maintenance than on craftsmanship for quality control, and learns to content itself with lowered standards in those areas—of which teaching is a prime example—where rationalization does not work.

At the level of general education, I need look no further than the last graduation exercise I attended for an example of unconcern with the relevance of the credential to competence even during the very ceremony at which it is being awarded. At this institution, it is customary for the president of the senior class to make a short speech presenting the senior class gift to the university. The young man who did so stated that, instead of giving the school some costly object, the senior class had decided to spend its money on repairs for a dilapidated old fountain, which, he justly observed, "hadn't ran for several years." He further noted that this was "the most expensive gift any senior class had ever given the university." Nobody even winced.

It is possible, perhaps, to define liberal education in such a way that proficiency in its arts need not exclude either graceless and ungrammatical use of language or an unimaginatively materialistic sense of values, but I do not believe that many of my colleagues at that graduation would accept such a definition. Their conceptions of a college education were pretty conventional. They had simply ceased to expect the degree to mean anything at all in terms of the conventions they still accepted. In less striking ways we have all been living with our disillusionment for years, gradually adjusting to it by ceasing to expect high-school graduates to show any real mastery of the "fundamentals" required for college entrance, expecting employers in turn to retrain our graduates on the job instead of relying on the competences for which we had certified them. Except for the advanced physical scientists, who don't really graduate anyway since they are hired by their own major professor or his colleagues to work in another part of the military-academic complex, employers usually have to retrain graduates, since, if they are hired to work with machines, the equipment they learned on at school is usually obsolete by industrial standards; and if they are hired to work with people—as for example, teachers or lawyers—the ideology they were taught in school is usually so naive as to impede their function and must be unlearned on the job.

School credentials, though they determine access to status and role then, I would maintain, are not thought of as certificates of competence. But they certainly mean something, and something society regards as important. And society is right; the process of allocating this access is indeed vital, at least in the sense that the chorus in *The Mikado* use the word:

> Behold the Lord High Executioner:
> A personage of noble rank and title.
> A dignified and potent officer
> Whose function is particularly vital.

Ko-ko himself, it will be recalled, proved incompetent to perform the duties of his post, but satisfied his sovereign with an affidavit that he had done so and an explanation that the affidavit should not be interpreted literally. His very professional deficiencies proved essential to the preservation of the Royal House, while his symbolic discharge of his function tended to preserve freedom and order in the community. In his case, the personnel-selection system of Titipu worked; it put the right man in the job, thereby ensuring that the job never really got done. And this was exactly what was required.

In the more complex society of the United States, the function of the credential is often analogous, though not strictly so. What we require of a credential is that it reliably designate its holder as a person who will get part of his job done, will provide a symbolic substitute for those aspects of it that cannot be publicly denied without creating intolerable social strain but cannot really be performed without creating even more intolerable social strain, and who will unfailingly and discreetly discharge those of his functions that cannot be included in the job-definition or even admitted to be a part of it, but which the actual power distribution of his community requires. This is really more than was demanded of Ko-ko; for a public executioner's role provides little opportunity for partial fulfillment and hence little complexity. But it is no more than is demanded of a school superintendent as he struggles to reconcile what his community really wants to do about its Negro youth with what is officially required; or of a lawyer, or a business executive—indeed, of the practitioner of any profession old enough to have defined its obligations and its ethics under conditions very different from those under which it must now be practiced.

Therefore, when we award a social role and the status that goes with it to a candidate, we want to be sure that he has some skills that cannot tactfully be attributed to practitioners of the role he is seeking; and these will strongly affect his appraisal, though in disguised or covert terms. Communities want to be sure that teachers will control children whether or not this impedes learning; that policemen will enforce their mores regardless of what may have been formally taught about civil rights, before they hire them for the job. Few communities, however, would rest content merely with the reassurance that new recruits to positions of social responsibility understood the requirements of their position well enough to be willing and able to betray its traditions when these became socially dysfunctional. We demand that the credential also tell us something positive about the incompetence that we require as a part of a candidate's qualifications—about what Veblen calls his trained incapacity, or a horse-trader calls being well-broken. We expect it to assure us that the bearer will respect the conventional limits of the roles it makes available to him. To permit the members of a profession to make the fullest use of their technical powers would spoil the existing fit among society's various roles, impede the operation of its status system, and generate such hostility and mistrust as to jeopardize the place of the profession in the society. What tact and diplomacy do for individuals, trained incapacity does for role-definitions and role-expectations; and the credential must certify to that incapacity. A social worker must not only understand the dynamics of social stratification and of group work; he must be incapable of turning the poor on and using his skills to organize them into an effective political action group if he is to earn a good credential.

This is ironical, but not unusual, and is probably as true of most societies as of our own. What is new is that, in the United States, the accrediting function of the school has expanded so far that it issues not just licenses to enter particular trades or professions, or to continue more specialized education, but what amount to licenses to live. The schools have simply accepted the responsibility of recording and transmitting the kind of judgment of the candidate's personal qualities that a society less guilty about social stratification and less concerned to provide equality of opportunity would have left to private judgment, either of individuals or of cliques. Such judgments still affect recruitment and advancement crucially, even in our society; but they are acceptable as much more legitimate if supported by the credential of an official agency. The school grades students on citizenship and emotional adjustment, but this is less important than the fact that value judgments about the student's acceptability within the social structure permeate course grades as well, and at this level they cannot effectively be challenged as reflecting cultural bias. Similar judgments, as Aaron Cicourel and John Kitzuse have observed in *The Educational Decision-Makers,* also strongly affect high-school counselors' judgments as to whether students should be admitted to a college-preparatory program and hence whether they will ever obtain a college degree at all.[2]

I am not certain whether it would be fairer to say that in this way the school introduces into the student's credential a personal judgment masked as a bureaucratic assessment, or that it depersonalizes its students by in fact reducing what is most human about them to a rationalistic appraisal. Both, perhaps; and either would be bad enough in my judgment. Yet, even granting that these processes occur, it would still be logically possible for the school to alter its assessment according to the role the student was preparing to fill, to leave him with a dossier indicating that he might make a very good scientist but a poor office worker, an excellent revolutionary but a rather unpromising naval officer, and so on. And of course the school does this insofar as it takes account of different aptitudes and levels of performance in various subject-matter fields and records variations in personality among students as it perceives them. I am very skeptical, however, that these ways of accounting for variability and suiting the student to the available opportunities are effective over a very wide range of behavior or personality. Despite their terrifying array of testing and psychological services against which even the Constitution provides little defense, schools usually seem bent on turning out and labeling an all-purpose grind that will keep nobody awake.

This uniformity of viewpoint expresses a school mystique that pervades to a considerable degree every school I have observed, despite differences in location, curriculum, or social class served, even nationality. The mystique seems to be international. Of course there are tremendous differences as well; there are no up and down staircases, or any other kind, in glassy new suburban schools. But sooner or later, if one stays around, the characteristic flavor breaks through. I recall, for example, a five-day visit I made within the past year as a consultant to a high school widely—and justly—esteemed as one of the best in the United States for its academic standards and level of instruction. It had also just opened a magnificent new plant and was run with unusual urbanity. My hosts, or clients, had generously arranged for me to meet with student groups as well as staff under as little supervision as the routines of the place permitted. They could not, however, transcend the routines. There just was no way to permit a group of students to meet with me longer than a period unless we planned it that way—and then they had to. There was no place the students and I could sit together and smoke, even tobacco, while we talked. Nevertheless, after several days I had about concluded that this school was enough like a college in its atmosphere and its intellectual level to make the experience of attending it qualitatively different. Then, on the last day there was a fire drill during the morning, and the facade collapsed. Classes were interrupted, of course. Those like myself who happened to be in the library at the time were turned out hurriedly. The teachers and vice principals who had seemed bright and reasonably flexible during the discussions we had been having during the past four days turned into a horde of up-tight little men, blowing whistles and screaming at the youngsters, who were forbidden to talk as they marched out of the new glass and ferroconcrete structure into the snow. Several of the teachers looked a good deal more turned on, too, than they had during our seminars, now that they were really doing their thing.

Even in this nearly completely college-preparatory high school, its college-bound youngsters were still being assessed and recorded by a staff committed to a pattern of values that disparages qualities our colleges and our society could use a great deal more of. What kind of credential does the student get who refuses to interrupt intellectually exacting work in order to act out an imposed collective civic fantasy? Can he still get into a good college? Or are we going to make do with the talents of those who don't take themselves quite that seriously, or possess quite that much autonomy? What kind of credential does the student get who responds as I did to the principal's insistence that fire drills are required by law with the observation that extreme zeal in obeying the law is itself a *ressentient* way of behaving, and that a school that turns compliance with regulations into a devotional pageant is indoctrinating its students in servility as surely as it would be if it decked its halls with "Support your local police!" banners? This is, after all, a useful insight for a student of the social sciences to have, and one that comes rather easily at least to hippier high-school students; and there is a good chance that those who develop it earlier will make more honest artists and even more effective executives.

And if the school is justified in insisting, for the sake of its own internal order and commitment to the official values of the community, that fire drills take precedence over and must be used to disrupt its regular instructional activities, then where does a youngster turn to get away from this constraint and learn more freely, doing his own thing, unconcerned with fires, neither setting nor fleeing them? What kind of credential does he get? The answer is clear enough; he gets a term in

juvenile hall as a truant and a credential that says he is either a delinquent or mentally ill. And, of course, he has even less chance to learn
on his own than he has of sneaking through the meshes of school routines.

We must still explain, however, why society has become so rigidly
insistent on subjecting all its youth to protracted formal socialization,
and why, in any case, it has made the public-school system the single
instrument of that process—except for the use of the Selective-Service
System, which, in effect, extends the compulsory school-attendance age
to 21 or so for middle-class male youth and provides an alternative form
of compulsory socialization for school dropouts who are usually of lower
status. As Paul Goodman has so often pointed out, our society permitted
many alternative ways of growing up until a decade or so ago. Moreover,
standardized testing has developed so massively in the United States,
both in quality and in the scale of its enterprise, that it would be both
simple and economical to furlough young people from schools as long
as they reported to the testing center for a day or two each year and
demonstrated that they were making normal progress toward the prescribed goals of the curriculum. That no such social arrangement is
provided suggests very strongly that the achievement of these goals,
which must be defined in terms of openly demonstrable competence,
constitutes little more than a pretext for compelling the student to submit to schooling and submerge himself in its routines. The content of
the curriculum is of little significance except insofar as what is done with
it conveys to the student the values, threats, and anxieties whose impact
he is required to sustain. In schooling more than any other kind of
communication the medium is surely the message.

And the school mystique provides the medium. Those who accept
it well enough to emerge after 16 years with a favorable credential can
usually be trusted to have sufficiently conventional goals, motives, and
anxieties to find the larger social system into which they are released
rewarding. To those who have learned to endure and even have fun in
a small trap, the big trap built to a similar plan but on a much more
lavish scale and with much richer bait looks like freedom. It offers,
in any case, all they are likely to have learned to desire or even imagine.
"TV dinner by the pool! Aren't you glad you finished school?" the Mothers
of Invention chant, succinctly and sardonically, in "The M.O.I. American
Pageant." Most youngsters probably are.[3]

But saturation of the young with the school mystique has, I believe,
more fundamental functions than creating a respect for our common cultural heritage as exemplified by a desire for gracious suburban living. To
survive the school and earn its commendation and support in gaining
access to desirable roles and status, the student must come to accept
as virtually inevitable certain value-positions that determine his most
intimate responses to other people and to his own experience. These

responses get built into his very nervous system in the form of an anxiety gradient, and they set the limits of his life space by limiting how far he can swing and how confidently he can resist the inroads of social sanctions on his self-esteem. This, after all, is what socialization means.

Wide acceptance of the value-positions conveyed by the school mystique keeps our social institutions going and reduces conflict; it stabilizes our society. But this is just another way of saying that the schools support the status quo, and, particularly, that the restriction of opportunity to those who come to terms with it virtually ensures that our society, in all its echelons, will be led by people who either cannot conceive of better social arrangements or despair of ever getting them adopted, and with good reason. This seems to me the final irony—the school, by controlling access to status on terms that perpetuate the characteristics of mass society, while serving simultaneously as the registrar and guarantor of competence, holds competence in escrow. And it does not release it until competence has demonstrated, over a period of years and under a variety of provocations, that its bearer has other qualities that make him unlikely or even unable to direct his competence toward major social change. By placing the school in control of the only legitimate channel to status and power, we virtually ensure that those who gain status and power will use them to perpetuate our difficulties rather than to create new and radical solutions.

The problem is not that the schools are conservative—official social institutions are inevitably conservative. The problem is in the nature of what is to be conserved, of the specific social values of which the school is custodian, and to which it demands adherence as the price of accreditation. What are these values? They constitute a complex and seamless pattern, but the following emphases are revealing: There is first an anxious and sometimes brutal intolerance of deep feeling between persons, of emotional commitment to others. This permeates school routines; love and loyalty are violations of its code and are severely punished. In some ways this is evident—the school forbids any kind of physical expression of affection at the same time that it maintains and supports a teasing attitude toward sexual attraction; its erotic ethos is basically that of a key club with unpaid bunnies. Love between members of the same sex, though a real and valid aspect of adolescent growth, is of course even more brutally punished, and hippiness, which refuses to limit itself by considerations of gender at all, is perhaps most condemned. Calm, gentle, long-haired boys arouse genuinely pathological hatred in physical education teachers.

But it is not only physical love and honest, personally expressive sexuality that get the school up tight. Affectionate regard and care among peers is contrary to standard operating procedure, which prescribes instead jolly, antagonistic co-operation and competition. The school breaks up what it calls peer groups bound together by strong personal ties as cliques, which it sees as anti-democratic and potential sources of resistance and subversion. In class, co-operation between friends is cheating. It is evident that this pattern of values is, or has been, functional in breaking youth to the demands of middle-class life in a mobile society dominated by impersonal bureaucratic structure. But the middle class itself has begun a strong revolt against the emptiness and lack of feeling this way of life imposes; not only is hippy youth primarily middle class, but industrial executives as well as isolated professionals have begun seeking a restoration of feeling and authenticity in group therapy sessions, T-groups, and other prostheses intended to replace the functions that friendship and respect for one's neighbor perform in cultures that do not stifle them.

For lower-status, or otherwise "culturally deprived" youth, the schools' insistence on impersonality is anathema. Murray and Rosalie Wax, in a continuing series of published studies of the effect of imposing formal education on the Oglala Sioux, have made it clear that this issue is the focus of a complete educational stalemate. Sioux children will not adopt American competitive folkways and refuse to respond to the teacher at all; adolescents sit in third grade year after year in derisive silence rather than meet the teacher's terms. Similar difficulties, as the Waxes point out, arise in encounters between lower-status urban youth and the schools; and one wonders why so common and serious a source of educational frustration has not resulted in a more flexible response to the children. But in the allocation of status and role the frustration is functional; it ensures that youngsters, whether Indian, Negro, or just unusually autonomous, who refuse to be depersonalized will get bad credentials that will stigmatize them as lazy or slow learners, keeping them down without involving the school in a disagreeable overt conflict about values.

A related, and perhaps even more fundamental, aspect of the school mystique is its support of vulgarity, especially shabby-genteel vulgarity. If there is one single social function of the school on which, more than any other, a mass society depends for stability, it is this: the hazing of potential poets and critics into submission, depriving them of the self-confidence that might have turned them into prophets rather than technologists.

This is accomplished by investing authority in personnel who themselves obviously either do not understand the material they are dealing with or are either intolerant of contradiction or defend themselves by treating the whole issue as a "fun thing"; and by grouping together in class students of such different backgrounds that no meaningful discussion is possible. It is all in *Up the Down Staircase;* but though life in Calvin Coolidge High and its counterparts is sometimes farcical, its social function is deadly serious, and it works. By defining the role of the teacher and school officials as fairly low in status, society ensures that, though there will be many competent teachers, all students will nevertheless be exposed for significant periods of time to the cognitive style and emotional attitudes that pervade life at the "common man" level. The fact that higher-status students are unlikely to accept this view as their own, and that students of whatever social status who feel a need for freedom and personal expression will loathe it as constrictive is all to the good. The school does not perform its integrative function by convincing its students that the way of life of the common man is beautiful and his view of reality profound. Rather, it demonstrates to them, over and over, that the common man is going to win and they are going to lose, no matter who is right, so that if they are wise they will learn to avoid challenging him. The lesson is not that the system is admirable but that you can't beat it.

Most of us learn this lesson; later, if we become professors at a state university we simply assume that we mustn't buck the legislature. Our administrators depend on our having this insight to assist them in their funding. Most of the good credentials go to those who learn it early and well. And in this way a shifting sea of unhappy and resentful people who live by wheeling and dealing keep their society going and avoid breaking one another up in direct confrontation. But the poets become frightened and sound the alarm; they, at least, are faithful to their function:

> Take a day
> And walk around
> Watch the Nazis
> Run your town
> Then go home
> And check yourself—
> You think we're singing
> 'Bout someone else!
> But you're plastic people!
> I know that love
> Will never be
> A product of
> Plasticity![4]

the Mothers sing. And the schools bear some of the responsibility for the truth of their vision of the Great Society.

II

Some
Specific
Problems

Introduction

The educational landscape is so cluttered with problems that it's a major undertaking to delineate specific problems sharply enough to do something about them. The temptation is to dodge the issue by resorting to metaphors: it's a can of worms—too many variables—a disaster—a case of pure bankruptcy. It may be any or all of these, or even some combination of them. But neither laymen nor educators can afford to look away in the hope that the problems will vanish; in fact, we may have tended too much to do that anyway, forgetting that priceless adage relating eternal vigilance and the price of liberty.

This is not to suggest that the problems included in this section even begin to be representative. Many of the missing ones, including black studies and black power, student power, and educational ecology are located elsewhere in this book. But the issues which Messrs. Rapport, Kampf, Shaw, Blanshard, and others discuss do elicit great concern among educators everywhere.

Surely there has been no issue as burning during the past decade as the Vietnam War and its implications for teaching/learning matrices on the campus. Many a university has expanded at an explosive rate as a consequence of developing government contracts, including military research. Professor Anatol Rapoport's viewpoint regarding the university as a "community of scholars" raises many questions: What *is* a "community of scholars"? Has one ever existed on land or sea, or is it a cloud vision? And why is there a "defense community"? What values, if any, hold it together? And when the value question arises, of course, one must ask about the value of having an ideal such as "complete dedication to the truth and the whole truth." Does such an ideal conflict with the pragmatic methodology of science? Then, too, what is "pure science" or "pure research"?

In reading the Kampf essay immediately after that on military research, one is afforded an excellent opportunity to compare assumptions. If, as the brilliant M.I.T. professor concludes, "American society is a disaster" and "higher education is a national danger," then, because the two things are inextricably linked, those in positions of power who do nothing about their problems are delinquent. Whether or not the radical- izing or politicizing of faculties will produce a new era of morality, one in which professors refuse to do classified research, may remain a ques- tion. But it is no academic question, even for academics, if individual teachers, searching their consciences, must take a stand and act accord- ingly to avoid charges of hypocrisy which students rightly hurl at so many teachers (though they may not avoid hypocrisy themselves!). With revolution, variously defined and perceived, in the air, the issue must be joined. Students of power who see the allocation of power as the central issue of our day may wish to quiz Kampf further, however, about his call for "a meaningful reform of power." And one doesn't need a Ph.D. to ask: How high is the probability that the radical faculty will radicalize their colleagues? Will the "critical intellectual" have enough balls to act as Kampf, his colleague Noam Chomsky, and the whole stable of editors at the *New York Review of Books* wish them to act?

To those involved in teacher education (training?) the question of *the best way to do it* seems like an eternal perennial, or a perennial eternal. As much evidence may be mounted on one side of an argument as on another. Pick your criteria, mount the evidence, and draw a con- clusion! Repeat! Repeat! Having devoted the proverbial twenty-five hour day and eight-day week to the problem during much of the past decade, I am profoundly concerned about the many questions raised in my chapter of this section. I have been so involved in discussing them with students and colleagues, then trying on solutions for size, I've often lost my perspective. In fact, it was not until I wrote this essay that the common factor of *immersion* emerged. And this immersion viewpoint may be one which many will wish to attack.

But I hope it can be attacked with joy rather than bitterness or the vindictiveness with which so many individuals and groups have attacked sex education throughout the country. As a veteran of many such battles during her tenure with SEICUS, Esther Schulz is eminently qualified to suggest the best routes through such turf-torn battlefields. Her questions, too, should evoke much thought and discussion. Why is it that sex is so vital to life yet so often kept under a blanket? And what constitutes socio-economic class differences in attitude? Shall we live to see the problems related to sex education in any kind of perspective (depending upon criteria) as long as sex is perceived as object rather than as part of larger gestalts? Too, what can the women's liberation movement do to open up such perspectives? Will men be liberated humanistically as long as women are made objects or sex slaves, as long as commercial advertising is so flagrantly dehumanizing? Can any parent or teacher in this country, or throughout the world for that matter, avoid the critical issues related to the vast variety of citizen views of sex?

The Shaw and Blanshard pieces dealing with parochial school education approach a whole congeries of problems from different angles. Paul Blanshard, long a critic of Catholic power and its democratic implications, always cuts directly to the core of a problem. And though the details of the Supreme Court decisions during the next decade may differ from those of the past ten years, we're still talking about the hand-writing on the wall between church and state. That is, assuming there is much of the wall standing, it raises some more questions: Are you convinced that the spirit of the Founding Fathers, as embodied in Jefferson's Act for Establishing Religious Freedom (passed by the Virginia Assembly in 1786) or in the First Amendment has been maintained by the Supreme Court in the two cases which Blanshard discusses? What is your opinion of the "child-benefit theory" of school funding? Is the principle humanistic? Dare you predict whether Blanshard's Jeffersonian objective will prevail?

But if more federal money is *not* poured into Catholic education, what alternative is there to the further decline in the numbers of Catholic students and schools as already outlined by Russell Shaw, a most informed Catholic publicist? And how do Shaw's views relate to Mario Fantini's observations about the decentralization of school controls? Logically, shouldn't every effort be made to effect local, lay control? Or is this a contradiction of terms in an organization with so many hierarchical characteristics? Why do so many people fear Catholic power and values, especially in a society which ostensibly prizes pluralistic forms of power, prestige, and program? After all, is the public school so value free? Or, as Jack Nelson suggests in Chapter 14, has nationalism become the American religion? Yet, for that matter, is *any* learning process value free? If not, need we worry about "Catholic mathematics," "Catholic Spanish," and "Catholic social science" when any and every curricular process could be biased? A vital question remains: Who is capable of conducting Bias Therapy to help any person detect his biases and discover what difference those biases make in his life?

The question of values is also central to Professor Darcy's insights about turning economic education around so that attention is given to human consequences as well as efficiency. Or more accurately, perhaps, our efficiency has provided the technological platform making it possible to perceive the human potentiality which can be actualized when a society moves beyond subsistence to affluence. It's the insight so basic to the futuristic possibilities which Robert Theobald and Noel McInnis perceive in their essay (Chapter 19). But many questions obtain: Which Americans are sufficiently sophisticated in citizenship to see the connection between their individual acts (whether smoking a cigarette, flushing a toilet, or driving a car) and the total environment? How many members of the Depression generations, men and women 45 to 80, would agree with Darcy that scarcity is, indeed, a bogey? And what difference does it make when they take their attitudes to the polls or put their money where their mouths are in party or pressure politics or both? And how does such a concept as "opportunity cost" help relate such seemingly unrelated events as building a new airport to accommodate B-747s and erecting several hundred low-cost houses for the same amount of money? Will the groundswell of concern over the contamination of our skies, rivers, and landscapes become such a tidal wave as to wash away our Neanderthal attitudes about "doing our own thing" with land, water, and air?

As I read Darcy's comments about the necessity for him and his colleagues to become specialists in "the science of value," I am reminded of the Cambridge (Massachusetts) scientists of the post-World War II period. How poignant it was to watch them agonize over their newly-developing human and social concerns following their development of the atomic bomb! Perhaps we should rush with compassion to welcome economists on this new frontier; awareness may be painful, but it may be a necessary precondition of change if we are to survive.

4

ANATOL RAPOPORT

Classified Military Research and the University

The university should be a community of scholars dedicated to the pursuit of truth—a hackneyed phrase, perhaps, but a deeply meaningful one to those so dedicated.

Not every socially useful institution can or need be a community. A department store, for example, may be an eminently useful institution, a triumph of marketing techniques, an indispensable adjunct to urban society. But a department store is not, and need not be, designed as a community. The only connection between its various services, from selling furniture to duplicating keys, is geographic proximity for the convenience of the shoppers. Neither the shoppers nor the sales people at different counters need to have anything to do with each other in order for the department store to fulfill its function properly.

I reject the department-store model of the university, the so-called "multiversity," because it is incompatible with the community model; and, I repeat, this does not in any way reflect any judgment on my part as to which of the institutions is the more important to a society. I do have an opinion, but it is not relevant to my argument. It follows that I reject the notion that the university must serve "society" in whatever way society wants to be served as long as such service does not jeopardize other activities essential to the university's mission. The implication of this notion is that such other activities are not jeopardized by

This article was originally published in The Humanist, *29, No. 1 (1969): 4–10. Reprinted by permission.*

the services rendered by the university, as long as the two functions are kept apart. I argue, however, that if different activities in a university have no effect upon one another, then this is prima facie evidence that the university is not a community and therefore its primary function has already been jeopardized.

My objection to conducting classified research in a university is that such activities jeopardize the community a university ought to be and to which members of the university, faculty and students alike, ought to aspire. The community is jeopardized not so much by the distinction between two classes of faculty, those "in" and those "out." After all, every specialist is privy to knowledge inaccessible to those outside his specialty. The university community is jeopardized by secret military research by virtue of the fact that for the most part those who participate in such research owe allegiance to another community, a loyalty that is, in my opinion, incompatible with the loyalty to the community a university ought to be. Moreover, the defense community (or the "strategic community," as it is sometimes called by some of its prominent members) is now a reality, while the community of scholars is still only an ideal. There are many hindrances to the realization of this ideal, but the overlap between the academy and the defense community is, I believe, one of the most important of these factors.

The intellectual defense community arose in the United States in the course of the infiltration of military research into the universities since World War II. The circumstances and some of the effects of that infiltration are well known. It must be kept in mind that actual figures tell little of what has happened. Its most important effects have been not quantitative but qualitative; and they must be considered not only with regard to what is happening to universities but also with regard to what is happening to the war business. Specifically, not only has a large sector of the academy become militarized but the war business has become intellectualized; and because of this it has become highly attractive to many people who work with their brains.

It must be borne in mind that dedication to truth as a way of life is a primary motivating factor to relatively few people. Most of us have absorbed the cultural values around us as a matter of course. Among these is an appetite for prestige in terms of the culturally dominant criteria: being near to the foci of power, being valued for one's expertise by those who possess great social prestige, being asked by the wielders of power to advise on matters of policy, etc. These satisfactions, so long denied to the American scientist and scholar, coupled with considerable intellectual challenge in the design of military technology and of global diplo-military strategy, were, I am sure, an important factor in the creation of the scientific-technical defense community. It is a large community. The director of the Willow Run Laboratories made this point when he refuted the notion that the results of classified research were available to very few.

"This is...not so," wrote MICHIGAN Dr. Evaldson. "Witness, for example, the Project MICHIGAN annual Radar Symposium, ... attended by 400 to 700 people." Dr. Evaldson is quite right. The scientific-technical defense community is large. And it is a genuine community, another point made by Dr. Evaldson when he wrote: "Indeed, in some classified areas of activity, the dissemination of results may be more timely and more complete in its coverage of the people engaged in the subject fields than is true in some unclassified areas." In other words, what Dr. Evaldson seems to be saying (and I agree) is that the defense community is more of a community than the academic-intellectual community.[1]

But the defense community, it seems to me, is held together by values quite different and essentially incompatible with the values that ought to hold together the academic-intellectual community. I say "ought" because I keep in mind that the latter is still only an ideal, while the former actually exists. Moreover, it seems to me, the intellectual community is hindered from maturing by its infusion of academe with the spirit and aims of the defense community.

The primary value of the would-be intellectual community is the unfettered search for the truth and its free dissemination. Closely allied but, at times, only a derivative value is the use of knowledge in the service of humanity. The primary aim of the defense community, on the other hand, is to put power at the disposal of specific groups of men. Since scientific knowledge is a source of power, the defense community seeks such knowledge; and since this knowledge is genuine only if one is aware of truth, the defense community adheres to standards of scientific truth in matters relevant to its pursuits. But in this scheme the awareness of truth is a derivative, not a primary value. In matters not relevant to its pursuits, the defense community is often indifferent to truth. It either takes for granted the world picture of the power wielders or eschews altogether the task of trying to understand the world in which we live.

Please note that I am not here distinguishing between the degrees of dedication to truth of various individuals. It would be presumptuous to make such judgments. I am merely pointing out that complete dedication to the truth and the whole truth is an integral component in the ethics of the ideal intellectual community, but not of the defense community (defined in terms of its mission), except to the extent that truth must be established in the pursuit of specific knowledge.

It seems to me that this must be so; otherwise I cannot explain the totally uncritical acceptance by the defense community of all the clichés of conventional wisdom whenever it feels called upon to justify or to rationalize its activities. In the language of the defense community, war research is assumed, as a matter of course, to be a "service to society." Preparations for war are blithely assumed to increase the nation's "security." War itself is justified as a regrettable but necessary means in the pursuit of "national interests." Journalistic inanities are freely incorporated by the defense community into the lexicon of political discourse, whenever its members engage in such discourse.

If the members of the defense community were also true members of the intellectual community, then they would, of course, be completely entitled to defend their world picture. The intellectual community is inherently antidogmatic; and the views of an Edward Teller or a Herman Kahn would be entitled to be heard and discussed side by side with those of a Linus Pauling, a Kenneth Boulding, or an Erich Fromm. But the defense community is not part of the intellectual community. The loyalties of its members are elsewhere, primarily to power, and to truth only in so far as knowing truth helps in the pursuit of power. The work of the defense community does not, in my opinion, help mankind. It is, on the contrary, a threat to mankind. Now this opinion is, naturally, challengeable; but it is also a challenge. The defense community is not obliged to respond to this challenge. Under the present arrangements it is able simply to hide behind the cloak of secrecy.

Dr. Evaldson, in his defense of classified research, warns against the tyranny of peers. I should think this term is more appropriate in the context of juvenile groups than in the context of an intellectual community. Secrecy protects the war researcher not from the tyranny of his peers but from the scrutiny of his peers. Clearly the intellectual community could not function if the intellectual products of its members were not at all times subjected to scrupulous, at times merciless, scrutiny of all the members of the community. Certainly the intellectual is responsible to his peers, and not only in matters of careful methodology, scrupulous regard for facts, rigor of reasoning, etc. These are scientific standards. But the intellectual community is not just a scientific community. It is a community dedicated to the growth and the preservation of the spiritual human heritage, of which science is only one component. In a genuine intellectual community, not only the scientific validity but also the significance of findings ought to be subjected to scrutiny, analysis, and prognosis; significance, that is, not only in the sense of relevance to other areas of science, but also of relevance to man's life and, above all, to man's outlook.

Let us, then, consider a biologist who is doing "basic" research instigated by a felt need in the defense community for more knowledge about pathogenic micro-organisms, knowledge that will facilitate the creation of strains more resistant to antibiotics. The work itself may be of fundamental importance to biology and may be pregnant with "spin-offs." However, the identity of the contracting agency and the secrecy attending the research bespeaks the intended use of this knowledge. Now the "academic freedom" of the scientist to seek such knowledge is not at issue. What is at issue is the fact that, if he does his work in secret, he is not obligated to justify it, if challenged on moral grounds. It is irrelevant whether the example chosen is realistic or not, or what particular parts of war research happen to be done in what specific universities at this time. As long as research is done in secret, we do not know what research is done where, and why. I think a member of a university faculty has a right to know what research is being done under the auspices of his institution; not only the titles of contracts and their sources and budgets but also the content of the research, its applications and implications. I think that the fraud perpetrated by the Central Intelligence Agency on Michigan State University is a blot on that university's name, and I know personally that many faculty members of that university felt a deep shame when the unsavory role of their institution was publicly revealed.

In a teach-in held recently, a university vice president pointed out that participation in classified research often broadens the contact of a scientist with the advancing of a science. This is meant, I take it, as a justification for classified research on the ground that such participation fulfills the professional needs of a scientist. In my opinion, this is the only valid point in the defense of classified research. But if the faculty members of a university are to be a community (and I always start from this premise), then the professional needs of some faculty members should be weighed against the moral needs of others. Many faculty members feel strongly that the utilization of man's intellectual faculties and of scientific insights for the purpose of increasing the military might of a war-waging state is degrading and immoral. Again, at the risk of redundancy, I must emphasize that the freedom of some scientists to engage in an activity regarded as immoral by others is not being questioned here. What is being challenged is their right to do so without their colleagues' knowledge about what these scientists are doing and why.

Recall the controversy concerning subversion on campus of a decade and a half ago. There were those who were genuinely devoted to academic freedom and who staunchly defended the Communist's right to his view as a member of a university faculty. They were most concerned, however, with the alleged secrecy of the Communist's activities and commitments. They felt they had a right to know who their colleagues were, not in order to persecute them but in order to be in a position to dissociate themselves from them if their consciences demanded it. An intellectual should have the opportunity to dissociate himself from colleagues who, by serving a war-waging state, violate his moral sense. He should also have the right to dissociate himself from an institution that has become an adjunct of a war-waging state. He cannot do so if research is cloaked in secrecy.

To summarize, the following arguments have been used in defense of classified research on campuses:

1. Academic freedom has been invoked. The appeal to academic freedom is, in my opinion, irrelevant. If such freedom means anything, it must include the freedom to disseminate knowledge to everyone, not just to privileged groups. The scientist ought to be free to undertake any research that interests him, but he should be in a position to defend his choice to his colleagues. Secrecy cancels this responsibility and is therefore antithetical to academic freedom.

2. Service rendered to the military establishment has been equated with service rendered to society. I think it is time to turn a jaundiced eye on the proposition that what is good for the Pentagon is good for the country, or, for that matter, that what is good for this country is necessarily good for man. A university community ought to be an integral part of a world intellectual community and ought to dissociate itself from the power struggles waged by states, blocs of states, and superstates. In this respect, the goals of the intellectual community ought to resemble the goals of a genuinely dedicated religious community, not, of course, in the sense of shared dogmas but in the sense of shared values.

3. Unclassified "spin-off" from classified research has been cited in the defense of such research. This is no reason for keeping classified research on campus. Spin-offs would presumably occur wherever such research is done. All in all, it is not likely that science would be impoverished if all military research would suddenly stop, let alone if it were excluded from universities.

4. I will simply dismiss the defense of classified research on the grounds that it brings in money or helps maintain the interest of the military contracting agencies in the research potential of a university. I reject the idea that a university is an enterprise "in the business" of doing research. I have not heard this conception of the university explicitly defended on all campuses, but I must say in all frankness that it is implicit in many of the arguments that I have heard in defense of classified research.

This orientation has also a broader connotation. In the popular mind, the image of a university as a "research business" and an "education business" has become prevalent. Ironically, it is this image that has "legitimatized" the activity of the intellectual in our culture in which the business enterprise is the universal model of all organized activity, all the way from the theater to war. In the business world, growth, solvency, and success in competition are the imperatives of existence. They have been traditionally the dominant values of our society. It has come about, however, that these values are now not only being questioned but actively rejected by a growing sector of our youth; and I am convinced that the ferment on campuses is an expression of a deep resentment on the part of this sector that expects to find other viable values in what ought to be an intellectual community, but instead finds the predominant values of an outlook it has rejected. The *gleichschaltung* of universities to the needs of the business and miltary world is the most salient symptom of the university's failure to provide a new source of values. Exclusion of classified military research will not, of course, remake the university into a semblance of an intellectual community, but it is an indispensable step in that direction.

5.   Participation in classified research has been cited as a factor in nurturing the scientific interest and the creative interest of the participants. I concede this argument, but at the same time plead for weighing the benefits so derived against the demoralization of other faculty members. The well-known free market principle embodied in the admonition "If you don't like it here, you can go elsewhere" ought to apply more properly to the members of the scientific-technical defense community than to those who view themselves as members of an incipient world intellectual community. The former already have institutions with aims coinciding with their own—the military research institutes specifically created to serve the needs of the military establishment. The latter should also have the right to build their own communities dedicated exclusively to the pursuit of truth, to the dissemination of truth, unencumbered by the needs of the military establishment for secrecy, and to service rendered to all of humanity rather than to groups engaged in a struggle for power.

5

LOUIS KAMPF

The Radical Faculty:
What Are Its Goals?

Whether the radical faculty can be spoken of as a corporate body is not clear. However, many of us who call ourselves radicals and who also teach at a university, feel that we have a common purpose, and that we share some basic assumptions about the world.

We assume that the American social system is a disaster. How odd! After all, in terms of abstract models, our economy is a success: the rate of growth is steady; most of the major financial problems have apparently been taken care of; and there is no large-scale unemployment. Capitalism has been an apparent success and no major revolution is likely to occur in the foreseeable future. Yet, American society is a disaster. And it is so precisely because abstract economic success has given America an inordinate amount of power. This power is dangerous both to the citizens of America, and to the millions in other countries whose well-being depends on our rulers' determination of the national interest.

In much of its research, in the training it provides, and in the ideologies it helps to formulate, higher education is an instrument of this power. The stated educational objectives of the academy—the mask of liberal education—serve as a ritual, as one more nostalgic memory. The academy's primary function is institutional, not educational; we all have our degrees, but our real task is the administration of power. Higher

This article was originally published in The Humanist, **29**, *No. 6 (1969): 9–10, 25. Reprinted by permission.*

education is a national danger. Certainly, it presents a grave threat to our intellectual culture.

Radical academics are not likely to overwhelm their colleagues with the inevitability of their logic. But this hardly matters. Were we to convince a few deans, for example, that the goals of the radical faculty are desirable, or good, or even correct, there is little they could do to implement their new convictions. For, it is unlikely that many of them have the institutional power to effect radical change on the campus.

So no amount of discussion—or even agreement—amongst radicals and their administrators will make the tensions between us and the academy disappear. The myth of a liberal consensus helped to depoliticize most American intellectuals and students after World War II. But it has become increasingly difficult to hide our country's real divisions and struggles behind the screen of an impotent dialogue. Vietnam, the black revolution, student strikes, and the general disaffection of the young have seen to that. No, our problems are not to be located in a failure of communication.

The radical faculty does not simply want to be communicated with, or heard, or given representation on committees where it will be dutifully listened to and then ignored. What it wants, instead, is a meaningful form of power. But for radicals the possession of such power does not imply—as it does for members of university corporations—manipulation, the wielding of force, or the attempt to control the lives of students.

What then are the radical faculty's goals? Stated abstractly, they should not be very different from those of any academic humanist, honest enough to face the social implications of his beliefs. The humanist ideal is best summed up in Matthew Arnold's formulation: "Getting to know, on all the matters which most concern us, the best which has been thought and said in the world; and through this knowledge, turning a stream of fresh and free thought upon our stock notions and habits." Arnold assumed that knowledge, both scientific and humanistic, should lead to the criticism of life—that its proper end is to make us better human beings, to make us more humane. In a university which pretends to be doing "value-free" research, these are radical goals indeed.

Some corollaries to Arnold's propositions come to mind: that proposals for research be honest; that grants be awarded only to projects intended for the betterment of humanity and the improvement of general knowledge; that there be a boycott of industrial and war research; that no research be initiated for the sake of professional advancement; and that professors not use the university as a base for making private fortunes or world reputations.

Some more distant implications are implicit in the humanistic ideal. The college president who treats his faculty as a debating society is not a humanist. Surely an elementary component of any humanistic education is that the administration of learning be open and honest. There should be no closed meetings of the faculty or the corporation. Indeed, the division between students, faculty, staff, and administration has no place in any institution that claims to be primarily concerned with learning. To exclude students—and faculty, for that matter—from the decisions made by the corporation is to treat them with condescension.

We must all become full participants in the entire university enterprise. Too many academics treat their pieces of turf as sacred and untouchable ground, and therefore react in terror to student demands for power. Students (Does one really need to say it?) are not an invading horde. They are not children to be threatened with punishment when they get out of line. They ought, in fact, to be the center of any university community, but that would clearly threaten entirely too many vested interests.

Another lesson to be drawn from Arnold's admonition that scholarship be turned to humane ends is that we must learn to understand—indeed sympathize with—the moral outrage that, given our students' institutional impotence, inevitably expresses itself in militant activism. A profound dedication to humane values is the force that generates the current student rebellions. Students at Berkeley, Columbia, and elsewhere have had the gall to use the academy's humanistic rhetoric as a guide to action. They have yet to learn that rhetoric is intended to be hollow.

Perhaps the imperatives of the humanistic ideal for higher education can best be put negatively. The university, any humanist should know, ought not to be a service station or cafeteria. Its chief activity ought not to be research. It should certainly not be an instrument of the "national interest." Conversely, it must not be allowed the comfortable pretense of being an ivory tower.

Perhaps the morals I have drawn from Arnold's formula, though reasonable or even edifying, represent little more than a childish reversion to utopian wish-fulfillment; no doubt they are products of a mind not accustomed to the sobering realities of power. Humane scholarship, honesty, democratic procedure, compassion—such notions, given the nature of our universities and of the society they so accurately reflect—are wildly utopian.

So let us forget about the university as a humanistic abstraction. For, is it not obvious that the goals of the radical faculty cannot be stated solely in terms of the university? That its goals must necessarily involve society as a whole? The matter is no different for student radicals. If they really want institutional power, that power will have to be wrested from those who hold it. I cannot envision anything of the sort occurring without a shift in the society's allocation of power—a shift which will not occur through the good graces of benevolent rulers. There is a struggle being waged in the universities, and radicals must not ape their adversaries in making power its own end. It is worth attaining only if it is to be used toward attaining meaningful educational—that is social, and personal—goals. If institutional power is to serve students in determining and fulfilling their lives, they will need as guide not only a new model of the university, but a new model of man and society.

What then are the radical faculty's goals for society? They are no different from those of any other radical. I think they have been stated clearly by André Gorz in his important book, *Strategy for Labor:*

> Economically, it [Socialism] can mean nothing but collective ownership of the means of production, that is to say the end of exploitation. But socialism is also more than that: it is also a new type of relationship among men, a new order of priorities, a new model of life and culture. If it is not all this also, it loses its meaning. This meaning, to define it in one sentence, is: the subordination of production to needs, as much for *what* is produced as for *how* it is produced. It is understood that in a developed society, needs are not only quantitative: the need for consumer goods; but also qualitative: the need for a free and many-sided development of human faculties; the need for information, for communication, for fellowship; the need to be free not only from exploitation but from oppression and alienation in work and in leisure.[1]

Gorz's words can serve us as a basic text. We radicals know that, since men must not be mere means of production, our first task is to eliminate the inhumanities and contradictions inherent in property relationships. For only their elimination will give us the freedom to envision a new man and a new culture.

Such social objectives have some clear implications for colleges and universities. Rather than detail a complete program—a task which, in any case, ought to be a basic component of any education—I shall make the following related suggestions:

1.   Admission policies should not be geared toward getting the "best" students for any given institution, but toward finding the institution which will be best for the student. It should be recognized that the "best" students are almost invariably the economically privileged.

2.   We radicals want a university which does not stress professionalization (hideous word!) at the expense of the student's human faculties and natural talents. He must be given the opportunity of developing these at his own pace and by his own methods.

3.   The university should become a place where students and faculty can pursue their cultural and social needs as ends in themselves.

Ordinarily, the fulfillment of these needs is constrained by the university's master, the social system. We should begin our search with an inquiry into that system, an inquiry which must be allowed to challenge the system—and the university—itself.

4.   Our goal is a university that transcends the obsessive inwardness of the quest for personal fulfillment: that is, a university which makes students and faculty aware of their social roles. The notion of absolute individual freedom is one more ideological trap set by the system. For, it allows us an escape into a private universe dissociated from our social role.

Capitalism, of course, typically transforms collective needs into individual ones. The academy encourages this transformation—with notorious success—by its brutal stress on individual accomplishment (read competitiveness). Students and faculty who are well attuned to the academy's schedule of rewards learn to plan carefully and rationalize their work with a view toward squeezing the most out of the system, or even beating it. There is a pathos in the attempt, for it is doomed to failure; the very failure to understand the social function of one's own competitiveness leads to inevitable defeat at the hands of the system.

Only when students and faculty begin to understand their roles as producers will they be capable of developing their individual roles in terms of commonly—not privately—attained freedoms. Rather than learning to beat the system, we must learn to direct our work toward those individual satisfactions that will benefit the whole. But, the powers that be know that if we stopped cutting each other's throats, we might, figuratively, cut theirs.

So once more, what is the meaning of these goals if we consider the actualities of power? Does the radical faculty have any power at all? It does, to a degree. However, whatever strength we have does not so much derive from our own organizing efforts as from the contradictions of American higher education. I shall merely allude to a few.

Deans, presidents, members of corporations never seem to tire of humanistic rhetoric; yet, higher education is used for the wider reproduction of labor. They pay lip-service to the traditional notion of the critical intellectual; yet, the system rewards professionalism and bourgeois accommodation. They encourage the tacit assumption that education is the province—even the property—of students and teachers; yet, both the latter know that they are alienated from the products of their labor. Most insidiously, they have encouraged their faculties to think of higher education as an instrument of social mobility and amelioration when, in fact, it generates new class hatreds to replace the old, and leads students to view their teachers as agents of social oppression.

The contradictions are also apparent in broader social terms. Industrial capitalism has created a set of needs which it cannot meet, because they do not relate to the concept of economic man, and the latter's goal of individual consumption. Industrialism has destroyed the natural environment, thus giving rise to real—indeed desperate—collective needs. Those needs cannot be met by our present social and political structures, because they contradict the criterion of profitability.

The needs should be familiar: air we can breathe without risking lung cancer; housing and city planning that address themselves to building a humane environment that is not reserved for the economically privileged; services such as nursery schools, clinics, and transportation; and, perhaps most importantly, the development of communities having enough cohesion to address themselves—freely and in their own terms— to matters of culture and group leisure. All these needs are fundamentally biological and natural; yet, they can be dealt with only by cultural and institutional means, by the imaginative collective use of our resources. I feel safe in saying that none of these needs will be met. They will not be met because they contradict the economic imperatives of our system.

In our society's failure to resolve the contradictions fathered by these needs the university has played an important role. Most obviously, departments of planning, architecture, and economics rarely encourage— except in their rhetoric—students and faculty to explore what the real needs of the community are. Academic security and prestige, not to speak of comfortable grants, come to those who meet the demands of their profession. The dangers of the professionalism that academic life encourages—especially to social scientists and planners—should be obvious. Academics tend to reduce any complex human activity to the construction of abstract models. Build a more elegant model, and academic success will be your need.

Left to itself and separated from the rest of the world, such activity would be harmless enough, though extravagantly wasteful. But any profession sees itself as an elite, as a guild of experts whose models should be humbly admired by the ignorant and fervently institutionalized by those in power. The models may involve monstrosities like counterinsurgency, or urban renewal, or planned unemployment, or atomic warfare, but who can show concern for such human trivia or community needs when the rationality of one's model—one's very expertise—guarantees the correctness of the enterprise?

Any professional elite will almost invariably sell its expertise to those with economic and institutional power; further, it will shape the very nature of its field to the demands of established institutions. The contradictions of industrial capitalism are thus reinforced by the dynamic of professionalism. Are there departments of social science which encourage their students and faculty to work as equals with those constituencies and communities that most desperately need them?

But something curious has been happening with the young. Some of them, to everyone's surprise, have taken the humanistic rhetoric of the academy seriously. Consequently, they have become nearly incapable of living with the contradictions of capitalism and the hypocrisies of the professions available to them. Many students are engaged in an almost frantic search for alternate careers and for alternate models of consumption—for a way of life in which production is subordinated to human needs, and activity is not simply geared to production.

This search should, of course, be an integral part of higher education. Scholarship, instead of bending students toward exclusively professional concerns, should be the servant of self-discovery. If so, it must begin with an inquiry into its own nature and into the institutions which are engaged in its administration. But for scholarship to perform such a function, scholars will have to reclaim the traditional role of the critical intellectual; further, they will have to establish that role's centrality for academic culture. Will anything less than a cultural revolution on our campuses make such an occurrence possible? Yet, this revolution is necessary for the academy's survival; if it is to be suppressed, I have little doubt that most institutions will blow apart or at least crumble.

The primary academic goal, then, of the radical faculty is the development of an alternate culture. As industrial capitalism generates more elaborate bureaucratic structures, the need for autonomous bodies making decisions democratically becomes increasingly urgent. We radicals want universities and colleges to be such bodies.

This means making the university a much freer place than it has been; it means student, faculty, and community participation in the administration of learning and research; it means real freedom in the pursuit of scholarship. At the least, the radical faculty wants programs which will afford concerned students the opportunity to use the academy not for the production of professional competence and learned monographs but for the production of democratic relationships between people. Our most serious students demand alternatives to bourgeois relationships; they should be given the freedom to develop a significant minority culture.

I have few illusions, if any, that the radical faculty will be joined by most of its colleagues in pursuing these goals. Academics, as I mentioned earlier, have their vested interests. They constitute a privileged caste whose leisure is derived from the surplus value of the masses. The official academic ideology has it that such exploitation is necessary if knowledge and culture are to advance. This strikes me as self-protective myth-making. In any case, the leisure of a chosen few is not necessary for propagation of culture; if it is, there is something wrong with that culture. That professorships which guarantee the idleness of their incumbents have become a mark of distinction is disgusting; it is a sure sign of cultural decadence.

To countermand this merchant mentality, we radicals must create a different style of life for academics, one not based on individual consumption. We must also develop a more significant set of loyalties: not to alma mater; not to a profession; certainly not to the national interest, but to a vision of a decent and humane life for all. We do not know precisely what form this new academic culture or the relationships within it will take—nor do we want to know. For it is in shaping the future that students and faculty must be free to communally determine their own fate.

Some of these goals we shall attain—not as a generous gift from our administrators. Gifts we do not want. Gifts are handed out by kind daddies, and we find paternalism degrading. No, we shall attain some of our goals because America's major institutions need the liberal university. The universities are the training grounds for the professionals that industrial society demands; they are the center for research which guarantees economic growth. Therefore, America's financial and industrial centers of power cannot afford a university which alienates masses of its students; nor can they afford a university which is an armed camp.

So some of our demands will be met in the hope of absorbing us into the liberal academic consensus. We understand this and the risks it involves. But the risks are also those of the academic establishment. For, whether we become absorbed or grow into a real force depends on our own clarity of vision. It depends on our determination to settle, ultimately, for nothing less than a free university in a free society.

6

ESTHER SCHULZ

Education for Human Sexuality

Historically most schools in this country have carried on the day-to-day business of educating the young as though sex did not exist. With few exceptions, the formal educational approach to sex, if indeed there was any approach, was confined to a rainy-day film in an all-girl or all-boy physical education class or a hasty, embarrassed lecture on the dangers of venereal disease.

Within the last few years, however, schools seem to have discovered sex. From New York to California and Alaska sex education programs have appeared. Teachers, administrators and parents inevitably have the subject on the agenda at meetings, and newspapers, national magazines and television have joined in enthusiastically with features on "The Birds, the Bees and the 3 R's."

While some schools and some individual teachers have for years been giving their students some information about sex, the extent and the intensity of interest is new. And while those of us who have been working in this field for years are pleased that a long-neglected area has finally come to the surface of public attention, we see some danger signs.

For one thing, there is a desperate, panicky note about many of the inquiries we receive at the Sex Information and Education Council of the United States (SIECUS). Written by parents, teachers, administra-

©1968 by Harcourt Brace Jovanovich, Inc. Reprinted from Family Life and Sex Education: Curriculum and Instruction by Ester D. Schultz and Sally R. Williams, by permission of the publisher.

tors, ministers, doctors, the letters have a common plea: "What do we do when we *have* to do something about sex education in our schools?"

Also, the "bandwagon" approach to sex education that is building up in many communities is similar to the atmosphere that marked the launching of Operation Headstart—the early childhood enrichment program that was hailed as the educational salvation of the disadvantaged child. Oversold and underplanned in many communities, the program left behind it a residue of disillusionment that did much to discredit an excellent program. In the rush to begin sex education programs without proper preparation or teacher training, some schools and communities seem bent on repeating the Headstart experience.

To avoid this pitfall and to lay a firm basis for a sex education program, schools and communities must first work out their own mutually satisfactory answers to the three basic questions of sex education: Why teach about sex? What is to be taught? and Who is to do the teaching?

The first question is the most important one in many respects because the answer to it will provide the philosophy, set the tone and direction of the course. In a discussion guide prepared for SIECUS, Dr. Lester A. Kirkendall says, "The purpose of sex education is not primarily to control and suppress sex expression, as in the past but to indicate the immense possibilities for human fulfillment that human sexuality offers." Unfortunately, this positive approach is far from characteristic. The real impetus behind much of the clamor for sex education programs is the desire on the part of parents and educators to reduce the number of out-of-wedlock pregnancies, to curb venereal disease and to counter what many adults see as a frightening revolution in the sexual mores of teenagers (whether there is actually a significant change in behavior as opposed to *talk* about behavior is a moot question). While these aims are often unspoken, countless contacts with schools and parent groups throughout the country indicate that these are the real goals that they want to accomplish with a sex education program. It is not surprising, therefore, that many of these programs contain an "hidden agenda" designed to get students to conform to what parents and teachers see as the moral status quo, an idealized image of adult morality that often has very little to do with reality. Kirkendall says that "most parents, could they but be assured that their children would lead conventional lives and would 'stay out of trouble' without being 'given' sex education, would doubtless heave a sigh of great relief."

Courses that begin with this "stay out of trouble" mentality and go on to establish specific and limited guidelines for student thinking defeat the very purpose of sex education. In the first place, they do not work, since anyone who has had any experience with young people knows that they simply drop a mental curtain when the moralizing and the sermonizing begin. Secondly, this approach hardly prepares young people to deal with a complex and uncertain world where standards of all kinds are in a state of upheaval. And finally, whose code is to be taught in the schools of this pluralistic society?

The minute a school tries to establish a code about masturbation, for example, or premarital sex, petting and necking, dating and other such subjects it is putting itself in a precarious position. If the school system says one thing and youngsters go home to parents with another set of standards, the children are confused and the system is likely to be discredited.

In contrast to this "tell them what. is right" approach the ideal sex education program gives students a chance to assess a wide span of behavior, to see how it applies to the society in which they live and to determine whether they are ready to abide by the sanctions society offers. It prepares students to decide on a set of values that they choose for themselves, values on which they base their behavior and make their judgments. If what they choose is contrary to what is acceptable, then they must be ready to face the censure of society.

The other side of the coin of the moralistic approach is the attempt to avoid entirely the sensitive area of values and judgments and to simply "give them the facts" to center the program on biology, anatomy and the mechanics of reproduction to the exclusion of all else.

Because of this tendency to limit sex education strictly to reproduction, Dr. Mary Calderone, founder and Executive Director of SIECUS, evolved a new phrase—education for human sexuality—that connotes a broad approach including the behavioral sciences, psychology and sociology, as well as the purely biological aspects of sexuality. SIECUS emphasizes that the primary aims for sex education are to help each individual understand himself as a sexual being in the total sense and to use that knowledge in a responsible manner.

Given this framework, with its positive orientation and broad scope, the answer to the next question about sex education—What is to be taught?—follows naturally. The approach to planning a sex education curriculum should be no different than the approach to English or math. Young people are not expected to learn English in one course or in sporadic presentation. Neither should sex education be handled this way. The curriculum should be a sequentially planned learning experience at levels which can be assimilated by the students in various age groups. As in other courses, the presentation and the material will change as the child's understanding grows and develops. There is fairly general agreement that children should have a sound understanding of the biology of reproduction and the physical changes of puberty by the time they reach junior high school so that as adolescents they can focus on the values and attitudes and relationships that are so crucial during these years.

In addition to being sequentially planned, sex education, if it is to be an academically respectable part of the curriculum, must make use of the insights into the entire learning process that we have gained over the last few years. In all other areas we have moved away from the old concepts of rote learning, drill and memorization of facts. We now start in the earliest grades with a research approach to learning. In math we want students not merely to memorize the multiplication tables but to understand numerical concepts. In history, instead of asking for a textbook list of five causes of the Civil War, we give students documents and newspapers from the period and urge them to reach their own conclusions. Only when we come to sex education do we lose faith in this approach and revert to telling students what to think. If sex education is to take its rightful place in the curriculum, it must be as soundly planned as the math courses and as free from cant and indoctrination.

It would be a mistake to leave the impression here that planning a good course and then putting it into practice is an easy matter. Even schools that start out with the best of intentions can bog down in the execution. A recent evaluation of one program of several years duration showed that although the objectives had a heavy behavioral science emphasis, little of this had filtered down to the classroom. The students were receiving mostly information on reproduction and the negative aspects of the sex act. Parents seemed delighted with the program, but student reaction was decidedly less enthusiastic. The students wanted more opportunity to discuss their real concerns such as responsibility for sexual interaction, the double standard and other ethical-moral problems.

But who in the school system is competent to lead such a discussion, to deal with such sensitive issues and help students as they search for answers? This is, in the minds of many many school people and parents, the crucial question—Who is to do the teaching? There is almost universal agreement that the teacher is the key element in a good program. No matter how carefully planned the course, how sound the philosophy, how strong the community backing, the ill-prepared or fearful or embarrassed teacher can destroy the entire effort.

This concern was expressed in an editorial in the December 18, 1965, issue of the *Saturday Review*. Education editor Paul Woodring pointed out the difficulties of teaching a code of behavior in a society where there is no such thing as a standard code and he concluded that a separate course on sex is not desirable primarily because "when they venture into the moral issues we doubt that teachers are better qualified than parents." Unfortunately this concern has not been disproven in the minds of many people.

It is true that teaching such a course properly demands not only thorough knowledge of a variety of subjects—biology, psychology, sociology—but, and most important, it demands an attitude of openness and understanding, a self-knowledge and awareness of hidden prejudices and a willingness to be honest with students. While these qualities are certainly not present in every teacher, there are people in every system who have the basic attitudes and who can be trained in subject matter and methodology. In many of the successful programs such as the one in Anaheim, California, teachers of various subjects, even a librarian, were chosen on the basis of their interest and willingness to participate and then given extensive training.

The training of teachers is at present one of the major problems in the development of good sex education programs. With communities pressuring school administrators to do something *now*, much of the teacher training amounts to stop-gap measures. Workshops varying in length from one to two days to six weeks are cropping up across the nation. In some cases young people are brought in to engage in group discussions with teachers that are designed to "sensitize" them to student reactions and to their own attitudes.

Secondary level students can state their major interests as a basis for planning course content. However, use of adolescents in short-term sensitivity groups where they have stated their basic problems and beliefs with no follow-up for those who have "bared" their souls needs a second look. Another teacher training format now in use is complete concentration on methods and materials which reverts to earlier patterns of normal school type preparation. In any case the area of teacher training is still in the experimental stages and, perhaps more than any other, needs further study to find the best methods to prepare teachers for a crucial task.

The three main components of sex education programs—philosophy, curriculum, and teacher training—are all caught up in the explosion of interest that has transformed a subject once spoken of in schools only in whispers into a subject as popular and respectable as the new math.

We can only hope that when the flurry of activity and atmosphere of panic in which many schools and communities are approaching sex education has leveled off, there will be an opportunity for some sane and sober thinking. When this period comes, there will be time to look with depth at what we are trying to do in preparing our youth to meet the challenge of life as *individuals*. If the school is to prepare students for a productive and satisfying life in today's stressful and challenging world, a curriculum must be established which will contribute to a healthy positive attitude toward the sexual aspects of man's nature. When this is accomplished, hopefully, the individual's sexual nature will contribute to his self-development and happiness and at the same time conserve and advance the welfare of society. The major hope then is that we will not have tried to turn out a group of conformists into a society that demands individual choice. Ignorance, misinformation, fear and negative attitudes about being a male or female member of society can and must be dealt with in sex education. Helping young people to find well thought out and comfortable patterns for expressing their sexuality is the ultimate goal of sex education. If we succeed we will see the results not only in individual lives but in a healthier and sounder society.

7

ROY P. FAIRFIELD

Teacher Education:
A New Immersion!

Internship . . . Microlecture . . . Module Scheduling . . . Nondirection
Free Structure . . . Process . . . Humanistic Psychology . . . Microlab . . .
Experiential . . . Revolution of Awareness . . . Sensitivity Training . . .
Videotaping . . . Communication Arts . . . Innovation. . . .

Such is the verbal arsenal of humanistic teacher education of the past several years, and there is little doubt that words we've never thought of, processes we've never dreamed of, will be added to the arsenal during the next decade.

The imperative is clear: traditional ways of training teachers will not do! It is painfully obvious that mere imitation of "master" teachers is hardly enough for those injected with the revolution of relevance or identifying with the counterculture. It is painfully obvious that neophyte teachers become strong by flexing their own muscles rather than by riding on the strengths of a cooperating teacher. It is painfully obvious that the lecture system at any level of education has limited utility—fine perhaps when a teacher is able to synthesize a large body of material in a brief moment, but virtually worthless for dispensing routine information: a teaching machine is probably more reliable. It is also painfully evident what does *not* happen when freshmen go into one end of the teacher training hopper in some of our larger university factories and come out like sausage-seniors. If and when teachers' techniques, their values, their mind-sets, their life styles are "laid on" students, whether second-graders or high school juniors, the results are often killingly ticky-tacky; the processes kill creativity and kill joy. Too, when those teachers encounter genuine dissenters, those students convinced that the revolution is *now*, the result is disastrous—for the teacher; such encounters often drive teachers from the profession.

OK. So the usual techniques don't work. So the lock step of course preparation, observation, student teaching, and certification is no longer adequate. What next? How does one prepare for the kind of attitude, needs, and learning climates discussed elsewhere in this book? How does a fellow, 18 to 22 years old, planning a high school teaching career, prepare to teach students half of whom are not even born! Or a girl the same age prepare to teach first grade, *ninety percent* of whom are not born! How do we develop a strategy for teaching in a world which seems to be in constant flux? We are now closer to 1984 than the year 2000, but what is the implication of that fact for those who will live beyond that millenial milestone?

There are other critical questions, too: if Marshall McLuhan is truly prescient, if those who extrapolate technology are accurate, if way-out school designers forge substance from their fantasies—if, if, IF,—then our entire environment may well be perceived as a learning environment. If, for instance, the Philadelphia Parkway School becomes a national or worldwide norm, shall we need teachers in any traditional sense or mode? If the several versions of the University Without Walls, currently being evolved in various parts of the country, become norms, what will the undergraduate teacher look like, do, or become? If the process concepts built into the Union Graduate School, wherein Ph.D. candidates take a self-determined route to that charmed degree, are extended in some major proportion, will there be a function for the graduate professor? Threatening as it may be to potential teachers in every discipline at every level, teaching as usually conceived is probably on the way out. It is quite clear that there is little place for the teacher-as-authority *if* the major responsibility for learning is placed on the student, *if* the major task of the teacher is to put himself out of business! And the same might be said about the parent-as-teacher if his major task is to shove his charges out of the ticky-tacky boxes which his culture, his language, and his values have made for him.

Just as the promise of abundance without sweat has brought the work ethic under question, so has the vision of a humane world in which all men and women are dignified equally brought the education-as-preparation-for-work under serious scrutiny. This does not mean that learning will not be important in years to come. Rather, it means that we shall learn for a greater variety of reasons and in a greater constellation of situations. "Legitimate" learning will not be confined to schooling. No doubt we shall continue to learn mathematics, accounting, engineering and anatomy in order to sustain some of the technological gains we've made since the dawn of the scientific revolution. But new learning is necessary to close the gap between technology, which speeds ahead seemingly out of control, and cultural developments (family, politics, habits, values, etc.), which plod along at a medieval pace. Tomorrow's teachers may have to be as expert in convincing a student that writing poetry or letters to friends, making movies or inventing an American tea ceremony are as "legitimate" as learning mathematics. Said another way, things have always gotten *done* in America by people who felt fulfilled by the doing; but to balance that phenomenon, things need to get felt, thought, smelled, touched, and tasted by those who feel fulfilled simply by living.

Approach to the What?

One thing seems eminently clear from the new departures in teacher education: most efforts have stressed the importance of *human immersion*. Even the more analytical and potentially gimmicky techniques, such as the use of videotaping techniques to get potential teachers to study the disparate phases of teaching (lecturing, listening, nonverbal presentation, discussion, etc.) in order to develop such skills, even these skills provide the teacher a better means for immersion into processes of communication which induce learning. The extension of student or practice teaching processes into the internship, wherein students assume full responsibility for a classroom or for a group of students under the general direction of a college instructor, this is immersion par excellance—or with a vengeance! One thing is sure: it's a survival situation which distinguishes the fittest and the dread! Or take the matter of encouraging neophyte teachers to find new structures which are nonstructures and are less threatening to *their* student-learners, again the object is to remove arbitrary authority from the processes so that student-teacher relationships become ones in which all parties are immersed in a learning process rather than a gaming with one another. Likewise, by introducing sensitivity training of some sort into teacher education, if a would-be teacher discovers better ways of perceiving self as self, as well as self as related to the power of groups, he or she may be less reluctant to plunge into new learning situations, face changing realities, and welcome risk-taking. In fact, that teacher may wake up in the morning with the joy and anticipation of facing countercultural chaos rather than dreading it.

Naturally, immersion assumes that the teacher has some sense of where he is in the learning process; he needs to be sensitive, courageous, and intelligent. He must have a better sense of the conflict or integration of facts and theories, the cognitive and affective, the static and dynamic. He will not despair that the only thing constant is change if he is immersed in the changing—and if he feels that he is part of the changing for human fulfillment rather than human destruction. That he will need to struggle with subjectivity-objectivity problems, that he will be torn between conflicting political forces, that he will have to decide upon the balance of knowing and feeling, almost goes without saying. It is important perhaps for teachers of teachers to make clear that there are some parameters for the potential teacher to emulate, that the good teacher is one more open than closed in his human relations, more cosmopolitan than parochial, more knowledgeable than ignorant, more process-oriented than thing-oriented, more sensitive than callous to human feeling (his own and other's), more immersed than withdrawn, more widely experienced than narrow, more of a listener than a talker. And the new teacher may need courage lessons more than math or English if he or she comes to realize the greater *need* for listening lessons, world-awareness lessons, and even swimming-in-experience lessons! And he needs to sit at the feet of student innovators as well as teacher innovators.

Approach to the Who?

It is not my intention to take each word, each concept of process, suggested at the outset of this essay and trace its evolution, its development, and its outcome. Those interested can find such discussion in the educational journals. Rather, this is to suggest that humanistic teacher education is *in process*. And, I hasten to say that the old apprenticeship system, self-consciously used since the days of Solomon, Socrates, and Confucius, is not in itself bad! In fact, millions of persons have lived fulfilling lives in understudy roles. Yet we face a major problem today. We know that "master teachers" are not necessarily humanistic since the hurricanes of change are destroying all fixed relationships between people—a devastating threat. Such teachers are all too likely to expect emulation rather than immersion. They usually see the need for the prospective teacher to be like them rather than like whatever the neophyte perceives himself as wanting. Too, the master or critic or cooperating teaching situation often doesn't permit the flexibility which is imperative in a changing world. Nor is it, often, more than a factory system when large numbers are involved.

The internship method, evolving rather rapidly in the Sixties, is no doubt a better one when authorities and would-be authorities *let the intern be*, in the best sense. With early philanthropic foundation support of major universities and later federal support of teacher education facilities along a broader baseline, the internship is now widely used. No doubt several social forces, other than desire to experiment, led to such an outcome: teacher shortages, especially for special students and inner city children; the seeming failure of anything to work in ghetto schools; the revolution of rising minority group expectations and the pressure which that put on school officials; and, the rising sense of outrage over the ways many students were being "killed" when closeted in traditional classrooms and curriculums. The increasing use of the internship and other techniques discussed throughout this volume have made some dent on the educational landscape although the interface between hard-core, establishmentarian school officials and would-be humanistic teachers-in-training has sometimes led to some very unhumanistic behaviors in all quadrants of the educational community, to wit, firings, threatenings, co-optings.

My own experience is probably not untypical of those working in this particular phase of teacher education, hence a few words about a specific program. Since 1964 the Antioch-Putney Graduate School of Education, a legal branch of Antioch College, has worked with several hundred teachers-in-training. It's difficult to talk about *the* Antioch-Putney program, for it really consists of many individual programs rather self-consciously derived as processes by individuals. For this reason and another, the fact that both individuals and the institution are changing rapidly, makes it downright impossible to take word pictures of "it". One needs a movie camera, tape recorder, videotape, a lively imagination, pencil and paper, as well as an airplane, automobile, and extrasensory transit mechanisms, to grasp the full sweep of the processes. But despite such a disclaimer, here are a few impressions.

Students (prospective teachers) are literally spread around the country, sometimes in one of our several centers, sometimes doing independent study (under a contract or covenant with a faculty person) at home or abroad. They work in a variety of teaching situations (both student teaching and internship types), in free schools and Head Start, in elementary and secondary private and public schools, in tutorials and community colleges, in rural, urban and suburban areas, in community-controlled school districts (Antioch-Putney efforts were vital in developing the renowned Adams-Morgan Program in Washington, D.C.) and in dictatorial districts. They evolve their own programs with the assistance of faculty persons who serve both as facilitators of learning and as conventional teachers. And when I say that they evolve their own programs, I mean that even within the parameters established by teacher certification strait-jackets, they determine the curriculum in a unique way. Any given group at any of the centers decides what it needs most in any given academic period of time; then they opt for that. Sometimes discussions of what to do, whom to involve, and how to do it is as important an aspect of the learning process as the actual doing. They also participate in the process of evolving their own transcript, for we post-register rather than preregister their courses; in many respects the chore of writing a formal transcript is a task of creative writing. Although an individual may opt for a traditional designation of course title, for example, "Political Science: ," what follows the colon depends upon what he has done rather than what he *might have* done had he done it with a prearranged description.

In short, the focus is on human interaction between faculty and student, among students as teachers-in-preparation and their students, between prospective teachers and school systems. There is a greater effort to integrate theory and experience concurrently than in most other teacher training programs. An Antioch-Putney student is also encouraged to *know*, to know that which he needs to know to teach a class, to discover the realities of the politics of schools, to rediscover himself, to develop the tactics of community action, to understand the alternative learning processes, and so forth. Furthermore, Antioch-Putney students are so immersed in their internships that they sometimes fail to see the forest for the trees; this is at once the beauty and the horror of it all—something like life! Too, they *are immersed* in evolving their own governing structures, at their respective centers as well as for the total program. Antioch-Putney administrators and faculty must be rare birds, serving more as facilitators for governance and learning than directors in the normal sense. One learns to assume many roles or he does not survive. The term "coordinator" sums up function better than do the usual titles.

The Antioch-Putney program will never be fully developed in the normal sense; it's not in the design. Rather, unless it develops some form of educational arteriosclerosis, it will continue to grow organically in facing the difficulty of shoestring financing, in resolving the complex conflicts between humanistically oriented students and beleagered school officials, in expanding from a small elitist group of prospective teachers to a larger and more heterogenous group capable of developing genuine cultural pluralism, in confronting the problem of burning out dedicated faculty people at an alarming rate. But our graduates are *in the field*. Some of them have developed free schools; others, working in a more conventional system, find delight in "teaching as a subversive activity." Some have used the Antioch-Putney facilities and processes as the means of discovering that teaching is *not* for them; others have even invented new professional strategies through which they've become captains of their own being, serving as consultants in facilitating the development of communes as learning communities. In an era of fantastic and potentially debilitating change, we hope that our graduates, accustomed to living in several locations, fresh from the adventure of the discovery of self, and familiar with the processes of linking humanistic theory and action, will continue to be capable of giving birth to freedom in their classrooms or wherever else they may venture. Never has there been so great a need for more relevant effort.

This is not to suggest that Antioch-Putney is always humanistic, or that it is the only humanistic teacher-training venture in existence. Nor has it necessarily been emulated self-consciously. Other events are occurring. The internship is now so widely accepted that universities are "placing" studnts in active teaching roles, north to south, east to west. When one learns, for instance, that a California university has located a master's candidate in a Detroit seventh grade, one sees some of the parochialism of college-as-place shattered. Increasingly universities and colleges are making community involvement a vital part of the learning process, extending the work-study concept initiated at Antioch in the twenties into a mind-blowing number of configurations. Prospective teachers are being encouraged to dip deep into community experience at every level. Too, there is an increased awareness that tomorrow's teachers need not be enrolled in today's courses called "Education 101A" or "My Major 303" to be preparing for teaching. In fact, if changing phenomena become the norm, then that teacher has the greatest prospect for survival if he adopts such views as "the world is my oyster" or "nothing human is foreign to me" or "I am a citizen of the world."

More specifically, institutions are changing. The School of Education at the University of Massachusetts recently declared a moratorium on all courses, reconstructed their curriculum to provide for a wider range of options in training for teaching, including the option of spending more time away from the campus than on it. Medical schools such as Tufts, Oklahoma, and Cincinnati are employing community-action and sensitivity processes for training doctors; the wider adoption of such processes may eventually produce more human doctor-teachers. With national medical exams to protect the public, there seems to be no reason why we cannot have medical schools without walls; after all, not all the clinical facilities in the world are located within the medical school cloisters. There is some evidence, too, that the law schools are encouraging more community immersion through legal aide involvement; a return to the apprentice system may also have long-range implications for the law teacher. One music educator, Guy Duckworth, is touring the country pointing out that musical instruction must be brought into the twentieth century. He observes that "A lot of educators approach piano instruction...like they were teaching shepherds and shepherdesses." What he says about student dissenters "telling us something"; namely, that "they are looking for teaching that is more relevant," has application for every field of teaching, whether formal or informal, whether kindergarten or graduate school.[1] If teachers refuse to change, they may get driven out by student dissenters and militants—not only at Columbia and San Francisco State but also at Timbuktu Tech and North Gumshoe Community College. Although teachers have been less pressured than administrators since the Berkeley incidents of October, 1964, students are increasingly aware that the Emperor's colleagues are *also* naked. Some teachers in America may find refuge behind the ramparts of tenure, credentialism, professionalism, narrow role definitions, and other such crenelated structures, but these structures are crumbling, becoming dysfunctional in a society which sets function as an ultimate criterion of workability.

New (?) Questions . . .

Those immersed in humanistic education of teachers may have to design a whole host of "unthinkable" questions: If schools become obsolete, where will the teachers go? Is there a humane way to put a traditional teacher out to pasture if his or her twenty years of teaching is really only one year repeated twenty times? Is it humanly possible for any person, perceiving himself as *person*, to change rapidly enough to keep up with a changing world and its changing demands? What should teachers do to induce humanistic change as compared with dehumanizing change? Where shall teachers stand during such revolutionary times? If the revolution is actually here, as some say it is, how does this change the teacher's self-perception as professional? Is it possible for teachers to become co-learners with their students, become immersed in their problems and lives to achieve new forms of self-respect, dignity, and self-hood? What are the consequences of a teacher's search for status at any cost or of maintaining the teaching-learning gap between self and student? Should teachers maintain loyalty to discipline, to school, to student, to professional organization, to all, or to none of these?

There are many *how* questions, too: How can teachers of teachers develop in their charges enough personal security to enable them to take risks? *How* can we identify and train teachers who can live with the ambiguities and contradictions of a changing world; who can evolve and appreciate the paradoxical qualities of being human in a world where the comic and the tragic often intersect sharply at a single moment of one's life; who can live in a world where a teacher is most likely to destroy a student if he struggles too hard to create him, where he may lose the student if he holds on too tightly, where he may become impotent if his will to power is too strong, where learning may lead to leaving if the teacher pushes too hard without clarity about his own purposes, his own impact, his own being? How can we develop teachers who will not be threatened by a word, a gesture, or a glare of rebellion in a student's or colleague's eye?

How questions are usually answered in our culture by technology or gimmickry, by a blueprint or a ground plan. But these are not enough today. True, microteaching, microlabs, teaching machines, computer processing, all may help facilitate learning. But even as we are enmeshed in such technology and in a sense are being programmed toward 1984, there are many humanistic forces abroad in the world: youth determination to develop a counterculture; new energies working on way-out architectural designs, community building and free-form institutions; wide concern about genocide. Teachers of the world can and must be part of the re-evaluation which is the revolution. And such re-evaluation, at every time, space, and institutional integrity, can be a creating process—*if* teachers and teachers of teachers learn to say "No" to those people and processes which would destroy them as people. After all, "Learning is beautiful!"

8

RUSSELL SHAW

The Changing Catholic School

As any reader of the newspapers knows, the American Catholic
school system is in the midst of radical change. Catholic schools are experiencing multiple changes simultaneously and at every level, extending
from an upsurge of interest in early childhood education through programs of sweeping reorganization in seminary education. It is impossible
to describe, much less analyze, all of the changes at every level of education in a chapter of this length. Rather, I shall concentrate on what is
happening to Catholic elementary and secondary schools, both because
they make up far and away the largest part of the formal Catholic educational effort in this country and because, in certain respects at least,
they are the most significant part of this effort.

The most obvious thing about Catholic elementary and secondary
schools at the moment is that there are fewer of them now than there
used to be, and they enroll fewer students than they used to enroll.[1] In
the 1968–69 school year there were 2,248 Catholic secondary schools and
10,338 Catholic elementary schools in the United States, enrolling a shade
under five million students (4,982,927). While this represents a very substantial educational system indeed, it also marks a substantial decline
from the peak year of 1964–65, when there were 5,600,519 students enrolled in 13,249 schools. Present indicators point to more school closings
and continued enrollment declines in the years immediately ahead, although there is general agreement that, barring outright financial collapse, a leveling-off point will eventually be reached.

As important as statistics on school closings and enrollment declines for the total picture of what is happening in Catholic education are figures which illustrate the dramatic change in the composition of the Catholic school teaching force during the 1960s. Although Catholic education is generally thought of as an overwhelmingly clerical enterprise, with priests and nuns making up the vast majority of teachers, this has never been true in this century in American Catholic colleges and universities and is now no longer true on the elementary and secondary levels either. Thus, whereas in 1960–61 there were 108,169 full-time teachers in Catholic elementary and secondary schools—79,119 priests, brothers, and nuns and 29,050 lay people—in 1968–69 there were 119,850 teachers, of whom 66,224 were religious (priests, brothers, or nuns) and 53,626 were lay. On the secondary level, in 1960–61 there were 43,733 full-time teachers (32,910 religious and 10,823 lay), while in 1968–69 there were 57,108 full-time teachers (34,214 religious and 22,894 lay).

This change in the makeup of the Catholic school teaching force is in turn directly related to two of the most urgent problems now confronting Catholic education: soaring costs and the declining number of religious teachers. The costs of education generally have risen sharply in recent years, but the financial pressures have been exacerbated for Catholic schools by the need to hire a growing number of relatively more expensive lay teachers. Over the years, the contributed services of priests, brothers, and nuns teaching in Catholic schools have played a major role in keeping the schools afloat financially. ("Contributed services" are the dollar difference between the generally minimal salaries and other benefits received by the religious teachers and the salaries they would receive for comparable work in the public school system.) No accurate national figure is available on the current value of these contributed services, but it is generally agreed that it is several thousand dollars—perhaps in the $3,000 to $4,000 range—per year per teacher.[2]

While the number of religious teachers has grown slowly throughout most of the past decade, the growth has been nowhere near fast enough to keep pace with the demand for teachers. Thus the Catholic schools have been obliged to turn more and more to lay people as staff. And while the salaries paid lay teachers in Catholic schools are generally lower than those in public schools, an increasing number of dioceses and individual schools have been setting lay teacher salaries at from 90 percent to 95 percent of the local public school salary scale. The result, of course, has been an enormous increase in the salary item in Catholic schools' budgets.

Furthermore, in the last few years, the problem has not been simply that the number of religious teachers was not increasing fast enough to keep up with the demand, but, more serious, that the number of available religious teachers has been declining absolutely. New vocations to the priesthood and religious life have dropped off substantially (in some cases, alarmingly), and the number of ordained clergy and older religious leaving religious life has been rising. A growing number of Catholic schools in the last few years have been notified by the religious communities which have staffed them that several or perhaps all of their teaching religious were being withdrawn because the communities' manpower (or womanpower) shortage made it necessary for them to cut back on their institutional commitments. Such schools have thus been faced with the choice of either finding other religious teachers to take their places—frequently an impossible thing to do—or hiring lay teachers to replace them —and thus adding drastically to operating costs; or closing down entirely.

If the picture looks grim, however, it is not entirely so. For one thing, many Catholic school "closings" to date have in reality been consolidations in which two or more parochial institutions merge to form a single school. Consolidation has been defended and indeed urged by some Catholic educators on grounds of more efficient administration, greater economy, and, most important of all, better education. In many cases, it seems to have delivered on all of these promises.[3]

Many Catholic education officials also contend that the enrollment decline of recent years is less the result of school closings than of the action of diocesan school systems in adopting and strictly enforcing limitations on elementary school class size in order to improve the student-teacher ratio. While educators continue to argue about optimum class size (and there is evidence that the skill of the teacher is a more important factor than the number of students in the classroom) it is nevertheless accepted that the jammed Catholic school classrooms of years gone by (50, 60, or more pupils per teacher in some places) presented an inordinate challenge to even the most competent teacher. In recent years, however, class size has been steadily reduced and the pupil-teacher ratio has improved markedly. Whereas in 1960–61 the pupil-teacher ratio in Catholic elementary schools nationwide was 40:1, in the 1968–69 school year it was about 33:1. (On the secondary level, the ratio was about 20:1 in 1960–61 and about 19:1 in 1968–69.)

While these significant changes in the number of schools, number of students, composition of the teaching force, and the rest have been occurring, even more important shifts have been taking place in the attitude of American Catholics toward their schools. It would be going too far to suggest that Catholics no longer want Catholic schools. The available evidence—both research-based and that obtained more informally by word of mouth—indicates that the American Catholic community remains attached to its schools and wants to see them continue and prosper.[4] But this attachment is a quite different, and probably more healthy, thing than the almost automatic allegiance to the schools manifested by American Catholics throughout most of this century. While it is difficult to generalize about such matters, it would probably not be too wide of the mark to describe the current attitude of Catholics toward Catholic schools as "friendly but selective." That is to say, other things equal, most Catholic parents will still choose to send their children to a Catholic school. But where other things are not equal—where, for example, the Catholic school is judged to be inconveniently far away, or excessively expensive, or academically inferior to the local public school, or simply not the "right" school for a particular child—many Catholic parents today have no hesitation about choosing a public or private school for their children in preference to a Catholic school.

Several stages can be marked out in the shift in attitudes of the Catholic public toward Catholic schools. The first stirrings of change came in the mid-1950s and focused for the most part on the academic performance of the schools. A number of Catholic intellectuals, notably the historian John Tracy Ellis, pointed to evidence that American Catholics had up to that time not had an impact on American academic and intellectual life in proportion to the numbers. The question of the hour was: "Where are the Catholic Salks and Einsteins?" Since the obvious answer was nowhere, the finger of blame came to be pointed at Catholic schools, which were said to be providing their students with an inferior education. (It is perhaps worth recalling that the wave of discontent with the performance of Catholic schools roughly coincided with the post-Sputnik national dismay over the performance of American schools generally. Catholics often exhibit a tendency to see their problems in isolation, even though the evidence would suggest that the problems are in many cases by no means uniquely theirs.)

While criticisms of the academic performance of Catholic schools were often justified, at the same time the criticism appears in retrospect to have arisen in part from an exaggerated notion of what schools can accomplish and a misapprehension as to the relationship of a school to its sponsoring community. Put simply, it can be argued that a school—any school—to a great extent reflects the aspirations and values of the community which has created and sustains it. Thus, assuming the truth of the charge that Catholic schools in the past assigned a relatively low priority of importance to creative work in the arts and sciences, it is probably true that this is less a criticism of the schools than of the intellectual aspirations of the American Catholic community (aspirations which, it might be noted in passing, are understandable in view of the largely immigrant and peasant origins of American Catholicism in the late nineteenth and early twentieth centuries). In any case, as the socioeconomic status of American Catholics has moved dramatically upward in the last quarter of a century or so, there has been a change in its intellectual aspirations and, so far as one can judge, a corresponding new emphasis on intellectual achievement in Catholic schools. Recent studies indicate, for example, that Catholic high school graduates are now somewhat more likely to enroll in graduate school following the completion of college and that Catholics who attended Catholic high schools are equally as likely as Catholics who attended other high schools to elect college courses in chemistry, physics, mathematics, the social sciences and English.[5]

While the criticism directed at the academic performance of Catholic schools in the 1950s may in some cases have been exaggerated, it did have the salutary effect of stimulating a good deal of soul-searching and action on the part of Catholic school officials. In recent years the idea of "quality" education has reached near-shibboleth status in Catholic educational circles. We have already noted the effects of the concerted effort to reduce class size and the pupil-teacher ratio, particularly on the elementary level. In addition, agencies like the National Catholic Educational Association in Washington, D.C., have been extremely active in efforts to upgrade the quality of Catholic schools, and the national Sister Formation Conference, an organization sponsored by communities of religious women, has conducted many programs to improve the professional preparation of nuns going into Catholic school teaching. It is thus fair to say that Catholic schools are today doing at least as good a job in academic terms as public schools.[6] There are exceptions, of course, since there are some exceptionally good Catholic schools and also some exceptionally poor ones (just as there are exceptionally good and exceptionally poor public and private schools). On balance, however, Catholic schools have no reason to offer apologies so far as the quality of the education they provide is concerned.

More recently, however, Catholic critics of Catholic schools, at least the more sophisticated among them, have focused their objections not on the academic performance of these institutions but, more fundamentally, on the question of whether it is necessary or even desirable that they exist. There are many aspects, theoretical and practical, to this sometimes heated controversy, but in general the argument of Catholics who challenge the value of the American Catholic school effort runs more or less along the following lines:

The Catholic schools, it is said, were a nineteenth-century response to a crisis situation. As waves of Catholic immigrants from Europe arrived in America, the Catholic leadership was confronted with the grave problem of retaining their loyalty—and, more particularly, that of their children—to the old-country faith. American public schools of the time were not merely inadequate for achieving this purpose but positively inimical because of their strongly Protestant orientation. Thus the movement to create a separate Catholic school system quite logically gathered steam in the middle years of the century and culminated with the decrees of the Third Plenary Council of Baltimore (1884), mandating the establishment of a Catholic school in every Catholic parish and obliging Catholic parents to send their children to such schools unless there were grave reasons for them to do otherwise. (It should, however, be noted that this particular mandate, while it certainly gave a tremendous impetus to the growth of the Catholic school system, was in fact never fully carried out and probably could not have been, given the limited financial resources of American Catholicism.)

Today, however, so the argument continues, the situation has altered radically and the conditions which called the massive Catholic school system into existence simply do not exist any longer. By no stretch of the imagination can American public schools be regarded now as covert "Protestant" institutions, and thus the danger that they might subvert the faith of Catholic children has vanished. Viewed in this light, the American Catholic school system appears as an anachronism and, more than that, a positive obstacle to the achievement of other goals by the Catholic community. Among other things, the schools tie down vast Church resources—money, facilities and manpower—which should now be devoted to other activities, such as alleviating the misery of the inner-city poor. The religious education of Catholic children can be handled as well by the home and by out-of-school religious education programs, and the Catholic schools (most of them anyway) should be phased out and the money and personnel now assigned to them reallocated to other, more pressing needs.

Thus runs the Catholic argument against Catholic schools. It has by no means become the majority opinion of American Catholics, but at the same time it has had a real impact, though one which is difficult to measure, on the attitudes of the Catholic public. It has played a considerable role in the unrest now apparent among members of religious communities, especially the younger ones who are seeking more "relevant" and "meaningful" forms of service than those they judge to be available to them in Catholic school classrooms. Quite possibly, too, it has contributed to some extent to the current wave of defections from religious life.

The response of Catholics who see a continued vital role for Catholic schools proceeds on several fronts. It is, it should be noted, by no means a simple defense of the status quo. Supporters of Catholic schools are virtually unanimous in agreeing that many changes must be made if the schools are to remain viable and are to continue to perform a useful service to the Church and society in the years ahead. Provided the changes are made, however, such people (I am one of them) contend not only that Catholic schools are still useful but that they are as much needed today as they have ever been.

For example, that the public school can be accepted—from the Catholic's point of view—as an adequate replacement for the Catholic school is at the very least a highly dubious proposition. It is true that American public schools are no longer "Protestant" institutions, but that does not mean that their educational program is therefore value-free. Many people would agree that there is no such thing as value-free education since values of one kind or another are inevitably conveyed by the very process of education. Thus, it is argued, by omitting certain areas of human experience from their program, the public schools "teach," implicitly at least, that these are matters of no great importance and can reasonably and safely be passed over by the student. For the Catholic, the most notable instance of such omission in the public school program is the religious dimension of human experience; and, since omission of the religious dimension is tantamount to the ideology of secular humanism, the Catholic would argue that the public school is committed de facto to the inculcation of secular humanist values.[7]

A specific example may serve to illustrate the point. Public schools are generally committed to "teach" the value of brotherhood. Catholic school supporters have no objection to this—in fact, they welcome it—but at the same time they are obliged to object to the assumptions which underlie the public schools' approach to this particular value. In a Christian view of the matter, the ultimate rationale for brotherhood is the fatherhood of God: that is to say, since all men are creatures of God, all stand in essentially the same relationship to one another. Quite obviously, however, the public school, by court decree and constitutional interpretation, is in no position to say anything about the fatherhood of God. Rather, it is obliged to teach, explicitly or more likely implicitly, either that brotherhood has no explanation beyond itself (it is a value because it is a value because it is a value) or that brotherhood is important because its observance makes it possible for men to live together harmoniously in social relationships (which is true, to be sure, but in a Christian view only part of the truth and a radically inadequate explanation of why brotherhood is a value).

Nor is it accurate to say that Catholics or, for that matter, other religious believers can compensate for what they regard as the deficiencies of the public schools by giving religous education in the home or in out-of-school programs. The practical difficulties alone are substantial (fatigued and bored children, harassed parents or instructors or both). Even more disturbing are the psychological problems: for if the child is being indoctrinated in a secular humanist value system in school, the task of substituting a different value system in an out-of-school program is, educationally speaking, rather staggering.

This, it should be said, is not to be read as an attack on public schools. Catholic school supporters wish them well and are increasingly anxious to be of whatever assistance to them they can. The old-time denunciations of "godless" public schools have generally disappeared from the rhetoric of Catholic educational literature. Catholic educators also recognize that a good deal more must be done to strengthen and upgrade the

Church's out-of-school religious education efforts. Elementary self-interest alone would dictate such a course of action, since Catholic schools are already able to accommodate only a shrinking minority of Catholic students, and the rest are clients of public education and out-of-school religious education.

From the Catholic point of view, nevertheless, the peculiar advantage of the Catholic school is that it is able to integrate religious values and beliefs into the total school program. In this way the student is introduced, in the school setting and not in some peripheral, non-school program, to this dimension of human life. This integration of religious values and beliefs into the Catholic school program is, however, by no means the same thing as religious permeation of the school curriculum—the latter being a factually and theoretically dubious concept at best. There is, after all, no such thing as "Catholic" mathematics or "Catholic" French, and it is difficult to imagine how religion either can or should permeate the teaching of these subjects in a Catholic school. The point of integration, rather, is that religious education stands on an equal footing with other subject areas in the school curriculum; that the religious dimension of human experience can, when appropriate, be examined without embarrassment or ellipsis in classes like history or the social sciences; that, in short, religious values and beliefs can be treated in the Catholic school as normal and full components of the student's total education and life, rather than being passed over in silence or shunted off to after-school hours (there to compete for the student's interest with piano lessons, ice-skating classes, and similar fringe educational experiences).[8]

It is difficult to say how convincing this rationale for the Catholic school sounds to people who have not had the experience of attending a Catholic school themselves. To state the matter impressionistically, however, one might say that people who have attended Catholic schools generally find that a particular way of looking at the world is bred into their bones as a result. As James T. Farrell, not the most likely source of encomia of Catholic schools, once said of his experience of Catholic schooling:

> I got a sense that there was something before me and something after me, that there was depth of experience, and that I was living in a continuity where there was an idea of greatness and grandeur and also mystery and reality. Where you face tragedy, you face yourself. You ask yourself if you sin or not. That can have the effect of making you see rather realistically.[9]

Even the most enthusiastic Catholic schoolman would hesitate to claim a great deal more than that for the "religious" effects of Catholic schooling in most cases.

A good deal of criticism has nevertheless been expressed by Catholics in recent years about the religious outcomes of Catholic schooling. As in the controversy over the academic-vocational effects of Catholic schooling, the criticism seems to arise at least in part from a confusion over the relationship of the school to the sponsoring community. The research done by Andrew Greeley and Peter Rossi at the National Opinion Research Center shows rather conclusively that Catholic schools of the recent past were quite successful (even surprisingly so) in developing in their students a commitment to such things as regular attendance at Mass, regular participation in the sacramental life of the Church, acceptance of the teaching authority of the Church, adult involvement in church-sponsored groups and activities, and so on.[10] One might surmise that the school was successful in this way largely because these were the elements of religious behavior most highly esteemed by the Catholic community at large; the school, in short, was reinforcing—with marked success—values already impressed on the child by the home and the church.

The objection now being heard is that these values are too limited, representing a minimal concept of religious commitment. In many respects, this is true. It seems apparent, for instance, that Catholic school graduates have not been any more active than the American public generally in such causes as racial justice, world peace, and the eradication of poverty. The question is: Is this something for which the Catholic schools are to blame? It seems rather that the schools have simply reflected the value system of American Catholicism, with its emphasis on individual piety and religious practice and its relative lack of emphasis on social justice and social charity. If this is the case, supporters of Catholic schools would contend that it does not represent an argument for closing down Catholic schools but rather for consciously giving relatively higher priority to the values of social justice and social charity in the Catholic school program (as in fact now seems to be happening in many places) in a planned effort to instill greater commitment to these values in Catholic school students.

Another matter of sometimes heated controversy in Catholic educational circles is the question of Catholic school "priorities." With some oversimplification, it comes down to whether Catholic schools should concentrate on educating white, middle-class, Catholic students or black, poor, largely non-Catholic students. As a matter of fact, Catholic schools are presently doing both, for despite the flight of the "white" churches to the suburbs in recent years, large numbers of Catholic schools remain behind in the core areas of many large American cities and continue to operate there, drawing students from the surrounding community without much concern for their religious affiliation.

Among those who have urged a larger role in the inner city on Catholic schools is the former U.S. Commissioner of Education, Harold Howe

II, who in 1968 said Catholic schools could make a significant contribution to the solution of urban educational problems because their relative freedom from political pressure and bureaucratic red tape enables them to inaugurate innovative teaching programs and adopt desegregation policies in a manner frequently denied to public schools.[11] Many Catholic educators agree but question whether massive reorientation of the Catholic school effort toward the inner city is either feasible or desirable. On the dollars and cents level, it seems apparent that Catholic education, cut off from its base of financial support in affluent urban and suburban parishes, would scarcely have the wherewithal to accomplish much in the way of significant educational innovation in the inner city. If, furthermore, one accepts the diagnosis of the Kerner Commission that "white racism" is the underlying cause of the American racial crisis, it would seem to make excellent sense for Catholic schools to seek to Christianize the racial attitudes of their white clientele rather than abandon whites for the most part and rush pell-mell into the inner city. While the outcome of this particular argument remains somewhat murky at the moment, it seems fairly safe to predict that there will be no dramatic increase in the number of Catholic inner-city schools, but rather that serious attempts will be made to upgrade the efforts—especially the innovative élan—of Catholic schools which are already there, while at the same time Catholic schools in "white" areas strive to eliminate de facto segregation and do more to instill a commitment to racial justice in their students.

Despite their current problems—of finances, personnel, and rationale—Catholic schools are scarcely at the point of vanishing en masse from the American scene. Quite a few, however, have disappeared in the last few years, and quite a few more will probably do so in the years immediately ahead. Prophecy is difficult, but it appears that the American Catholic school system is now in a period of fairly drastic contraction; stabilization is likely to come sooner or later, but at precisely what point it is now almost impossible to say. This process is painful for many American Catholics, whose attachment to the Catholic schools is deep and strong, but its results are not likely to be altogether bad. If nothing else, the Catholic school system of the future will in all probability be more compact, more efficient, and more committed to "quality" (in both academic and religious outcomes) than ever before. Despite their current embarrassments, Catholic school people feel an underlying optimism about the future: the optimism of a man who has a worthwhile product to sell and feels it is only a question of time until its value is universally recognized.

9

PAUL BLANSHARD

Public Money and Church Schools: Two Supreme Court Decisions

After 20 years of avoidance and delay, the Supreme Court has at last handed down two decisions that will serve to reopen and ultimately to answer this question: Under what circumstances can public money be constitutionally used for direct or indirect aid to sectarian schools? Strange as it may seem, the Court has never given an across-the-board answer to that question in the past, and its partial answers have been rather confusingly exploited by defenders and opponents of the separation of church and state for their own benefit.

The two new decisions, among the most important in the history of American law, were handed down on the same day, June 10, 1968. Both cases came to the Court from New York. The decision in one of them, *Flast v. Cohen,* was a great victory for believers in the separation of church and state.[1] The other, the case of *Board of Education v. Allen,* was bad news for those same believers.[2] If I had to appraise the two decisions in one package, speaking as an ardent Jeffersonian, I would have to say that the news was 55 percent bad and 45 percent good. The Court has given new rights to taxpayers to challenge unconstitutional grants to religious institutions, but at the same time it has seriously weakened the legal grounds for such a challenge. That same Court, which went all-out against prayer and Bible-reading in the public schools in 1962 and 1963, has now turned slightly to the right on the financial

This article was originally published in The Humanist, **28,** *No. 6 (1968): 11–13, 31. Reprinted by permission.*

issue. Only time can tell whether the slight right turn is merely a jog in the road or the beginning of a new era of concessions to sectarian pressure.

Let the good news come first. The Flast victory is not simple, but its results can be quickly summarized. Florence Flast, former president of the United Parents Association of New York, and six other taxpayers challenged in a Federal court the use of tax funds under the Elementary and Secondary Education Act of 1965 for such things as teaching arithmetic and reading in parochial schools. A special three-judge Federal court ruled by a vote of 2 to 1 that the plaintiffs had no right to sue, basing that judgment on an old Supreme Court ruling of 1923 (*Frothingham v. Mellon*), which held that taxpayers who have only a general financial interest in a practice that allegedly violates the Constitution cannot use the courts to challenge that practice. The theory behind the old decisions was that courts must not be swamped with obstructive suits unless the litigants have a substantial and direct financial interest at stake. This theory had been used for 45 years to block many very important suits challenging serious violations of the establishment clause of the First Amendment: "Congress shall make no law respecting an establishment of religion, or prohibiting the free exercise thereof."

Led by Leo Pfeffer of the American Jewish Congress, and backed by the New York Civil Liberties Union and various teachers and parents groups, with amicus briefs from the National Council of Churches and Protestants and Other Americans United for the Separation of Church and State, the plaintiffs challenged this obstructive theory before the Supreme Court and argued that illegal appropriations to religion have a specific and important unconstitutionality under the First Amendment that the courts have an obligation to heed and forbid. In a long and thorough ruling read by Chief Justice Warren, the Court held by a vote of 8 to 1 that the seven New York taxpayers have the right to sue to block the challenged expenditures for religious schools, chiefly on the ground that in voting the educational expenditures Congress had allegedly breached a very specific limitation on its taxing powers. Although the decision did not consider the constitutional merits of the attack on such expenditures, some of Warren's general words were very encouraging:

> The concern of Madison and his supporters was quite clearly that religious liberty ultimately could be the victim if government could employ its taxing and spending powers to aid one religion over another or to aid religion in general. The Establishment Clause was designed as a specific bulwark against such potential abuses of governmental power, and that clause of the First Amendment operates as a specific constitutional limitation upon the exercise by Congress of the taxing and spending power conferred by Article I.

Now, at last, all the fuzzy and, I think, unconstitutional devices for giving money to church schools under such labels as "poverty" and "welfare" can be sifted and analyzed. I suppose it will take at least two years for a comprehensive and definitive decision, and the outcome is in doubt, but the issues can now be squarely faced.

A Step Backward

The victory in the Flast case was only procedural. The defeat in the second (Allen) textbook case was substantive on its merits, and that is why it hurts. It hurts also because Warren came out on the concessionist side, rather surprisingly, and Thurgood Marshall also voted with the sectarian school champions. In the present circumstances Warren's defection may be less important than Marshall's alignment, since Marshall will presumably sit on the Supreme Court for a long time.

The issue in the textbooks case was this: The New York State education law, as enacted and amended in 1965 and 1966 required local boards of education to buy textbooks and lend them free of charge to students in parochial schools. Two local boards challenged this requirement and argued that it was forcing them unconstitutionally to aid religion by aiding religious schools. They won the first round in their court battle when a New York State Supreme Court judge held that the law violated both Federal and state constitutions. But the highest New York court, the Court of Appeals, held 4 to 3 that the law did not violate anybody's constitutional rights because it was "meant to bestow a public benefit upon all children, regardless of their school affiliations."

This was, in substance, the famous child-benefit theory, which had been rather fuzzily defined by the Supreme Court in the New Jersey bus decision of 1947 (*Everson v. Board of Education*), in which the Court had declared by a vote of 5 to 4 that tax money might be used to finance bus rides for children going to sectarian schools without violating the Federal Constitution. When the two New York local school boards appealed to the Supreme Court on the textbook issue, they were really asking the Court to reanalyze its own thinking on the child-benefit theory and decide whether textbooks could be squeezed into the limits of that theory. (The Supreme Court had once allowed public funds to be used for textbooks in sectarian schools, but this was before such use had been challenged under the religion clause of the First Amendment.)

I have always felt that the four justices who dissented in the Everson bus case were correct in resisting the application of the child-benefit concept to school buses; their reasoning had at least some faint justification. Buses do not enter classrooms or partake of the educational process itself. There is nothing ideological about them. In the 1947 bus decision the five-man majority ruled that bus transportation could be considered a safety measure for the public streets, similar to police protection, provided for children as children and not for the parochial schools themselves—although the Court admitted that bus service could help sectarian schools to maintain themselves and increase their enrollment.

This time the Court went beyond its bus concession and voted 6 to 3 to sanction as constitutional the New York textbook arrangement on the ground that it is a benefit merely "to parents and children, not to schools." Justices Black, Douglas, and Fortas dissented. Justice White spoke for the Court.

The prevailing decision, although it limits the child-benefit theory to textbooks alone, contains enough broad concessionary phrases to permit indefinite expansion of tax aid to the "secular" aspects of church schools. The Catholic press hailed it with glee, describing it as a Magna Carta for parochial schools. One New York monsignor said: "Hopefully now, those who cling to the outdated dogma that parochial-school students have no claim to public assistance of any kind will now join the rest of us in working for children's benefits and quality education regardless of school attendance."

Some of Justice White's phrases were broad enough to justify the monsignor's optimism. They virtually transferred the financial argument about sectarian schools from the field of the separation of church and state to the field of social utility. White said:

> ...private education has played and is playing a significant and valuable role in resisting national levels of knowledge, competence, and experience.... Considering this attitude, the continuous willingness to rely on private school systems, including parochial systems, strongly suggests that a wide segment of informed opinion, legislative and otherwise, has found that those schools do an acceptable job of providing secular education to their students. This judgment is further evidence that parochial schools are performing, in addition to their sectarian functions, that task of secular education.... We cannot agree with appellants either that all teaching in a sectarian school is religious or that the processes of secular and religious training are so intertwined that secular textbooks furnished to students by the public are in fact instrumental in the teaching of religion.

This reasoning omits the two most basic conflicting truths about the nature and control of Roman Catholic schools, that (1) they are financially an organic part of the Church they serve, and (2) their official policy is to see that every subject taught is "permeated" so far as possible with the Catholic outlook. (Justice Douglas in his dissent covered part of this ground.)

Justice Black who, oddly enough, wrote the Everson decision on which the present Court majority chiefly relied, struck back sharply at that majority. "I believe," he said, "that the New York law held valid is a flat, flagrant, open violation of the First and Fourteenth Amendments, which together forbid Congress or state legislatures to enact any law 'respecting an establishment of religion.'" He was particularly caustic in rejecting the analogy between buses and textbooks. "Books," he said, "are the most essential tools of education, since they contain the resources of knowledge which the educational process is designed to exploit. In this sense it is not difficult to distinguish books, which are the heart of any school, from bus fares, which provide a convenient and helpful general public transportation service."

Then Justice Black launched into gloomy prophecy:

> It requires no prophet to foresee that on the argument used to support this law others could be upheld providing for state or Federal government funds to buy property on which to erect religious-school buildings or to erect the buildings themselves, to pay the salaries of the religious-school teachers, and finally to have the sectarian religious groups cease to rely on voluntary contributions of members of their sects while waiting for the Government to pick up all the bills for the religious schools.

Fortunately, the prevailing textbook opinion did not specifically justify all these forebodings. By inference the Court still held to its previous judgments that no money may be appropriated directly to sectarian schools for the major aspects of their maintenance. White insisted that under the New York law "No funds or books are furnished to parochial schools and the financial benefit is to parents and children, not to schools." He pointed out that no religious textbooks as such were involved, only secular ones, and that each textbook loaned had to be approved by a local public-school authority. The pupils in the sectarian schools had to apply individually for the books. He held that the lending of textbooks under such circumstances had "a primary effect that neither advances nor inhibits religion."

Unfortunately, since the appeal in this case came up without a detailed record, the complete truth about the sectarian techniques employed in the selection and use of textbooks for parochial schools was not available. In practice under the New York law, the "individual" role of pupils and parents in the selection and use of textbooks in parochial schools is purely nominal. The priests and sisters select the books that are most acceptable to the sectarian outlook, send in the names of pupils in bundles, and distribute the largesse. The local public board "approves" the selections as a matter of routine.

Justice Fortas in his sharp dissent denounced the "transparent camouflage that the books are furnished to students; the reality is that they are selected and their use is prescribed by the sectarian authorities." Then he added:

> The child must use the prescribed book. He cannot use the different book prescribed for use in the public schools. The state cannot choose the book to be used. It is true that the public-school board must "approve" the book selected by the sectarian authorities; but this has no real significance... this program is not one in which all children are treated alike, regardless of where they go to school. The program, in its unconstitutional features, is hand-tailored to satisfy the specific needs of sectarian schools. Children attending such schools are given *special* books—books selected by the sectarian authorities.

Justice Douglas in his rambling but very eloquent dissent struck at the assumption that the textbooks given to sectarian-school children would be nonreligious simply because they would not bear a specific religious label. He cited several nominally nonreligious books that, although they would be eligible for selection in religious schools as "secular" books, actually opposed evolution or taught embryology incorrectly because of a religious bias.
Douglas said:

> ...the statutory system provides that the parochial school will ask for the books that it wants. Can there be the slightest doubt that the head of the parochial school will select the book or books that best promote its sectarian creed?...If the (public) board resists, then the battle line between church and state will be drawn and the contest will be on to keep the school board independent or to put it under church domination and control. ...
>
> How can we possibly approve such state aid to religion? A parochial-school textbook may contain many, many more seeds of creed and dogma than a prayer. Yet we struck down ...an official New York prayer for its public schools, even though it was not plainly denominational.

The Future

The first results of the Flast decision will be a clearance of many church-state lawsuits that have been waiting at the doors of Federal and state courts. The American Jewish Congress estimates that there are 36 such suits now pending in 24 state and 12 Federal courts, and more than half of them are concerned with the use of public money for sectarian schools. In handling the appeals in some of these cases, the Supreme Court will now be compelled to analyze the complex educational laws of the Johnson Administration and decide which features, if any, violate the principle of the separation of church and state. Hundreds of millions of tax dollars are at stake, but money is not the most important issue. The primary issue is whether our educational system will revert to the European pattern under which the governments compel men to support religious institutions with their tax contributions. To that extent the issue is one of religious and nonreligious freedom.

Even if the outcome in the Supreme Court is in doubt—and there must be some doubts after the broad and permissive language of the textbook decision—there are mitigating factors to be considered. Many of our states have prohibitions on their statute books banning aid to religious schools in much more specific language than the language of the Federal Constitution, and a new laxity in Supreme Court interpretations of the Federal Constitution will not necessarily weaken the state statutes. We can assume that the battle against tax funds for religion will continue unabated in the states, and in that battle the law is heavily weighted against public appropriations for church schools.

Moreover, the Supreme Court has not yet specifically renounced the best part of the Everson bus decision of 1947, the famous paragraph that may be considered the guiding star for all defenders of the separation of church and state:

> The establishment of religion clause of the First Amendment means at least this: Neither a state nor the Federal Government can set up a church. Neither can pass laws which aid one religion, aid all religions, or prefer one religion over another. Neither can force nor influence a person to go to or remain away from church against his will or force him to profess a belief or disbelief in any religion. No person can be punished for entertaining or professing religious beliefs or disbeliefs, for church attendance or nonattendance. No tax in any amount, large or small, can be levied to support any religious activities or institutions, whatever they may be called, or whatever form they may adopt to teach or practice religion. Neither a state nor the Federal Government can, openly or secretly, participate in the affairs of any religious organizations or groups and vice versa. In the words of Jefferson, the clause against establishment of religion by law was intended to erect "a wall of separation between Church and State."

The most dangerous possible loophole in this paragraph is the phrase "to teach or practice religion." What is the teaching and practice of religion as distinct from the other activities of a religious school? The champions of public taxation for sectarian schools argue that only a few of the activities of their schools can be described as the teaching or practicing of religion. The rest, they claim, are primarily secular, and are thus eligible for public financial support. If the Court should accept this theory, perhaps 90 percent of the costs of sectarian schools could come out of public treasuries without violating the First Amendment. The drift of Justice White's language in the Allen textbook decision was in this direction, and the alarm of Justice Black concerning that drift seemed quite justified.

But the first part of that famous paragraph in the Everson bus decision still stands, and its strong general prohibition against any aid to religion has not been specifically revoked. Any realistic analysis of the procedure and emphasis of American parochial schools must result in the finding that aid to such schools is in truth aid to religion. The promotion of religion is the primary purpose of these schools. Such considerations lead to the hope that the Supreme Court is now engaged in only a slight and temporary retreat from its great record in the church-state field, and that in the end the justices will return to their original Jeffersonian moorings.

10

ROBERT L. DARCY

Economic Education, Human Values, and the Quality of Life

Among economists and noneconomists alike, the discipline of economics is widely perceived to be little more than the science of efficiency. Mainstream economists for more than a century have occupied themselves primarily with the discovery, elucidation, and application of the principles of optimal choice and decision making under conditions of scarce resources, with given values or preference functions. Since land, labor, and capital are scarce (i.e., not available in unlimited quantities) so the argument runs, it is necessary to *economize* by making wise decisions concerning the allocation of existing resources to achieve the highest possible levels of economic welfare.

The criterion of efficiency (i.e., obtaining the greatest output and satisfaction from a given quantity of resource inputs) has not only dominated, but virtually preempted, the value system of the conventional economist; and courses in economics, especially in the universities, have fully reflected this orientation. But since efficiency is a *value* concept (i.e., a criterion of choice concerning goodness and badness), it follows that economists and economic educators have shown concern for value, albeit primarily for values that can be expressed monetarily. Indeed, as recently as a generation ago, it was customary to designate economics "the science of value," and offer courses in "value theory." Books and articles were published by economists under such titles as *Value and Capital, The Theory of Value, Value and Distribution,* and so on. Thus, economic science sought to explain the process whereby market values, or prices, were determined and how these criteria of choice (i.e., prices) in turn directed the allocation of resources to those uses assuring the highest levels of efficiency and human satisfaction.

More recently, the term "value" has fallen into disuse among mainstream economists (few university courses in conventional microeconomic analysis today are labeled "Theory of Value"); but preoccupation with the efficiency value concept has nevertheless persisted. Benefit-cost analysis and the Planning Programming Budgeting System, for example, have recently emerged as popular techniques for securing optimal resource allocation in the *public* sector of the economy, making use of imputed benefits and costs where values are perceived but not directly measurable in money terms.[1] Such techniques represent an extension of traditional marginal cost—marginal revenue calculus for profit maximization in the business sector. Efficiency analysis is thus carried beyond rational *individual* choices (i.e., those aimed at maximizing profits, consumer satisfaction, or factor income) expressed in the private sector of the economy through observable and quantifiable market prices. Let it be emphasized, however, that the applications of benefit-cost analysis to actual project proposals are not always carried out in a manner designed to clarify all relevant benefits and costs—or even to include all of them.

Beyond Efficiency

The values that people hold do not emerge from a vacuum, nor are they totally independent (despite their stubborn resistance to change) of the socio-technological environment of the time. Preoccupation with the *value* of efficiency in economics presumably was a response to the *fact* of scarcity in our technologically backward economic world a century ago when the method and scope of economics became crystalized. What is significant and unfortunate is the failure of economics to adjust its orientation and basic premises sufficiently to keep pace with the changing times; or as Thorstein Veblen put it, to be "an evolutionary science."[2] Not that economics is a fossilized discipline: significant changes have indeed been occurring "at the margin." The difficulty is that economics still suffers an identity problem, both externally and internally. While a growing number of economists now perceive their discipline to be *the study of how society organizes to develop and use its resources under conditions of technological change and institutional lag,* nevertheless the popular notion persists that economics is really nothing more than a study of profit maximization for business firms, utility maximization for consumers, efficient resource allocation and income distribution by the market forces of supply and demand, plus the macroeconomic process whereby aggregate demand creates its own supply. Since that is what economics *was*, that is the way academics write their texts; so that is what economic educators teach, and what economics students too often learn. If one is not really interested in profit or utility maximization, and "efficient" resource allocation under assumed conditions of scarcity, or in full production and "growth," but inquires instead about such phenomena as poverty, pollution, and social imbalance, then economics seems to have very little indeed to offer its students.

Clearly, however, the United States in the last third of the twentieth century is not characterized by an economy of scarcity. We are an affluent economy, notwithstanding the persistence of poverty for some 10 to 15 percent of the people. The salient features of today's environment are the twin facts of *affluence*—per capita personal income by 1969 exceeded $3,500, or $14,000 for a four-person family—and *interdependence*. The latter is amply demonstrated by environmental pollution, nationwide labor disputes, civil disturbances, electric power blackouts, and periodic cycles of unemployment and inflation. Values that are relevant to these contemporary economic conditions and problems in contrast to the obsolete premises and value implications of scarcity and individualism are needed today as modern criteria of choice if individuals and the community as a whole are to make wise socio-economic decisions affecting the quality of their lives. *The processes and fruits of economic growth have carried the American people beyond scarcity; now we must grapple with the difficult task of carrying our values beyond efficiency.*

"We" refers to the entire community, of course; but certainly it includes economists and economic educators. For the theorists and teachers of "values theory" have more in their bag than the tools of marginal analysis and optimality.[3] Unfortunately, they have been hiding much of their light under a basket. Seen in new perspective and liberated from the artificial constraints of monetary quantification, the concepts and principles of economic science can point the way toward, and help legitimize, a much broader range of socially relevant values than efficiency alone.

What are the other values? And what is it in our world of diverse and conflicting values, that economists can say about performance criteria other than efficiency? And once they have said it, what difference will it make?

Such values as economic justice, freedom of choice, equality of opportunity, resource development and conservation, economic progress, income security, international harmony, social balance, and improvement in the quality of life not infrequently are found in company with efficiency and economic growth.

Consider, for instance, the policy declaration of the Economic Opportunity Act of 1964: "to eliminate the paradox of poverty in the midst of plenty in this Nation."[4] It seems plausible that the values of justice, security, equality of opportunity, and the quality of life are all relevant criteria of choice that might lead the American people to declare a war against poverty. On the other hand, the values of efficiency and stable growth may seem threatened by an antipoverty program; and in the absence of a rational-empirical case for the former values, the traditional "tough-minded" efficiency values might prevail. Thus, "you can't eliminate poverty by simply giving money to poor people because then nobody would work and everybody would wind up poor." But suppose national poverty is perceived as a bogey, that the value of our annual output (Gross National Product) is seen to be a *trillion* dollars and GNP *per person* is $5,000 per year—not $5,000 per family or per worker, but $5,000 of goods and services for every man, woman, and child in the country. Suppose the American people become aware of the fact that it is possible to close completely the poverty-income gap, perhaps by means of a negative income tax, at a cost of only *one percent* of the GNP![5]

What do these statistics signify? Simply that the U.S. economy in the aggregate is phenomenally affluent: we produce roughly *four times* the quantity of goods and services necessary to provide all 60 million American households with an annual income above the official poverty thresholds set by the Social Security Administration. Now, if there is some linkage between knowing what *is*, knowing what *can be*, and knowing what *should be*, it would seem highly relevant to decision makers to know the facts of American affluence in order to make enlightened value judgments about programs concerning the elimination of American poverty.[6]

Market Demand and Human Needs

A familiar principle of equity in law and taxation prescribes equal treatment for equals, and unequal treatment for unequals, with the proviso that differentiation be based on reasonable criteria such as age or income, rather than hair color! Traditional teaching about the efficiency-oriented market appears to have assumed everyone to be equal, if not in income (i.e., consumer voting power) itself then in income-earning capacity, or "productive intelligence" as one economist sardonically labels it.[7] But as we all know, families are not equally endowed with income: the top 10 million families have *eight times* as much income as the 10 million families at the low end of the scale. Nor with "productive intelligence." Indeed, many families have no property resources with which to command income in the market, and some have little or no valuable *human* resources to offer for sale in the labor market. As a result, families with little or no income are ignored by the market mechanism; for as we should recognize, the market operates to meet effective monetary *demand*, not to satisfy human *wants*. Increasingly, therefore, we circumvent market processes that fail to generate enough earned income to sustain life. Rather, we opt for such alternative values as security (freedom from want), justice (to meet minimum human needs), equality of opportunity (to enable children of the poor to develop their physical, intellectual, and other capabilities), and for the quality of life—with perhaps a nod to the underconsumption school of macroeconomic theory, for legitimation.[8] Why? In part, as George Bernard Shaw observed so eloquently almost half a century ago, because "poverty...infects with its degradation the whole neighborhood in which they live. And whatever can degrade a neighborhood can degrade a country and a continent and finally the whole civilized world...for though the rich end of the town can avoid living with the poor end, it cannot avoid dying with it when the plague comes. People will be able to keep themselves to themselves as much as they please when they have made an end of poverty; but until then they will not be able to shut out the sights and sounds and smells of poverty from their daily walks, nor feel sure from day to day that its most violent and fatal evils will not reach them through their strongest police guards."[9]

Interdependence and Externalities

Shaw was saying that poverty is not an individualistic phenomenon, where the principle of exclusion operates (i.e., all the benefits and costs accrue exclusively to the individual) as in the case of the consumption of a hamburger (without onions). It entails *externalities,* or spillover effects for third parties or the entire community. Poverty entails *social costs* in the form of dependency, hostility, crime, mental and physical illness, and other types of pathology that pollute the social environment. As middle-income urban residents put it: "As our cities decay, we all become poor." Poverty and urban blight are not the only condition which impose social costs, of course. The beginning of the seventies brought a frenzied awareness of environmental pollution—of the air we breathe, the water we drink, the food we eat, the land we see, the noise we hear, the society in which we live—traceable directly to *the way we produce and consume goods and services.* The concept of externality (i.e., social costs and social benefits) helps us appreciate that programs to eliminate poverty and rebuild the cities are highly rational behavior after all, traditional monetary efficiency criteria notwithstanding. This emphasis on externalities is one of the distinctive and most valuable features of benefit-cost analysis. It demonstrates the economists' awareness of the need to move beyond the simplistic monetary quantification of market prices and costs. It equips the economic educator with additional means of helping students and the general public recognize the value implications of national affluence and social interdependence. And it can help turn the American mind set away from the bogey of scarcity, the anachronism of individualistic advantage, and the *quid-pro-quo* orientation toward valuing.

The other side of the externality coin takes the form of *social benefits,* or spillovers that enhance the wellbeing of the community at large, as opposed to private benefits that accrue solely to the individual purchaser or consumer of a good. Social benefits occur in many forms, but take education as an example. Recent developments in the economic analysis of human resources include the significant finding by Edward Denison that about *one-fourth* of U. S. growth in real national income during the period 1929–57 resulted from increased educational attainment, or "investment in human capital." By contrast, only about *one-seventh* of our growth came from investment in conventional capital such as plant and equipment.[10] Increased schooling resulted, of course, in the private benefits of higher earnings for individual workers. But a more remarkable consequence of this qualitative improvement of human resources in the contribution made to growth of the economy as a whole, and the likely if undocumented benefits accruing to the community at large in the form of such expanded stocks of "human capital" as literacy, political awareness, social competency, mobility, and esthetic sensitivity.

The implication of these findings is that society may benefit much more from investing in human development than simply accumulating more machines, and the value implication is that informed and rational people may judge it good to provide more social funding for education.

Value Implications of "Opportunity Cost"

Another economic concept which can help clarify and legitimize behavior that might be shunned if only static-efficiency values were considered is *opportunity cost.* This concept refers to the goods or services that must be *foregone* in order to allocate resources to the production of *other* goods and services. Thus, the opportunity cost of a ton of napalm is the amount of food, fuel, or medicine that could have been produced if the manpower, capital, and natural resources that were used to produce the napalm had instead been employed to the production of alternative goods. The opportunity cost of another Caesar's Palace in Las Vegas might be 500 low-cost family dwellings for Negroes in suburban Detroit, or half a dozen new vocational schools for children in rural Appalachia. The concept of opportunity cost helps one see more clearly the kinds of choices and tradeoffs we can make as members of the economic community; it may also help us think more clearly about the real costs of a major effort in the seventies to reduce environmental pollution before man's ecological niche is hopelessly damaged.

Theory of Economic Progress

Another major area of economic analysis that provides insights for the teacher and student of values is economic development, especially in the context of the underdeveloped nations, which has attracted an enormous amount of professional attention since the end of World War II. The familiar static efficiency models of resource allocation have given way, in recent development theory, to truly dynamic socio-economic models that accommodate such variables as the quality of human resources, technological change, and the change-resisting nature of ceremonial social values and obsolete institutions. As economists and other scientists have sought to apply their findings from abroad to our own situation at home, there has emerged a heightened awareness of opportunities and need for human development and institutional adjustment in the United States. There is a growing concern over the performance gap that sees our technology and productive capacity expanding rapidly while the quality of life seems simultaneously threatened by social upheavals and environmental pollution. One may wonder if the trends are simply coincidental, or whether they are functionally related in an ironic pattern of accelerating "progress" toward destruction.

Pertinent to this concern is a provocative discussion included in the U.S. Department of Labor's 1968 Manpower Report suggesting the need for a "more qualitative orientation" to employment that focuses attention not only on "how well the economic system absorbs individuals into employment and meets their financial needs, but also [on] the adequacy with which it satisfies quite different kinds of needs—physical, psychological, and social."[11] In other words, contrary to traditional economic analysis, man is seen now to be more than a consumer and more than a means of production. He is a human being with individual needs for integrating work into his total scheme of life and for human fulfillment. A similar, and more comprehensive discussion of qualitative factors on socio-economic life—concerned with indicators of progress rather than merely growth—is given in the document, *Toward A Social Report,* issued by the U. S. Department of Health, Education, and Welfare on the eve of the Johnson administration's departure from office.[12]

One implication of the knowledge beginning to emerge about the process of socio-economic development is that qualitative, hard-to-measure, nonpecuniary elements may not be dismissed from the analysis without serious loss of relevance for the whole exercise. In the past, economists have been inclined to avoid the study of complex social problems preferring the pure elegance and determinancy of traditional efficiency analysis to the messy models demanded if we are to understand and deal with the real world. But, the point is, economists now are beginning to modify their orientation and priorities; and this greatly enhances their ability to help solve the crucial value problems of our day.

The Rational-Empirical Approach to Value

In addition to the economic concepts discussed above (namely, affluence, interdependence, externalities, opportunity cost, nonefficiency performance criteria, investment in human development, and the quality of employment) there is a systematic five-step method of analysis that can be used by economic educators when examining questions of value and policy. This rational-empirical-comprehensive method involves: *first*, a careful definition of the problem (utilizing historical, statistical, and theoretical techniques); *second,* an explicit identification of objectives (validity of which can be tested by facts and reason); *third,* consideration of the full range of alternative measures that might be adopted to achieve the objectives (avoiding the fallacy of the excluded middle, whereby a technicolor world is simplistically perceived as black and white); *fourth,* analysis of the probable consequences of the various alternative measures (estimating the tangible and intangible benefits, costs, and "other effects"); and *fifth,* selecting the best course of action in light of the chosen objectives and values.[13]

How "Relevant" Is Economics?

So these are some of the economic concepts that might shed light on the analysis of value. At this point, I would emphasize that the burden of proof is squarely on economists and economic educators to demonstrate the *relevance of their discipline* to help solve problems relating to issues beyond efficiency. If anyone doubts this, consider the statement by a prominent environmental planner: "We have to look at economics if only to dismiss it."[14] And cringe at the words of the literary editor of a major journal of opinion, a self-styled "Humanities man," who decries proposals made by behaviorial and social scientists to develop "a system of social indicators" and to offer suggestions on "ways for men to organize their relationships more satisfactorily." "Well, gosh, all hemlock," the editor writes: Save us from the "invading jello" of the social experimenters.[15]

As already indicated, it is not entirely without reason that critics of economics and other social sciences assume an anti-intellectual position.

On the one hand, it is a fate similarly imposed on Christianity (and on statistics) by intuitive literary-esthetic types whose exposure to the field has been both superficial and personally frustrating. And on the other hand, it is a largely-deserved rebuke to the clan of efficiency, individualistic advantage, and pecuniary values. In any case, to persuade skeptics that economics may indeed offer helpful analytical insights in defining and applying human values will require a purging of old prejudices as well as the teaching of new perceptions. And this is precisely where the teachers of economics come in.

The task of the economic educator as a specialist in "the science of value" is to identify and explain concepts, facts, and principles that shed light on a broad range of consequences, private and social, that result from economic decisions and behavior. Teachers can also identify areas where concepts and data are presently lacking to meet the demands of intellectually curious students, and responsive economists can direct a portion of their energies to filling some of these demands. The resulting enhanced perception of socio-economic processes can produce both deeper understanding and greater consensus on economic values, goals, and policies, and thereby help us to resolve socio-economic problems.

In a democratic society, however, where decision making is broadly based, the mere existence of knowledge will be of limited significance. Social action requires that awareness and knowledge be widely distributed. The socio-economic educator must begin to teach economics to large numbers of children and adults, not merely as the science of efficiency and income maximization, but as a social science whose subject matter—for example, the facts of affluence, interdependence, externalities, technological progress; the concepts of opportunity costs and social imbalance; the principles of human resource development and institutional adjustment—are relevant to a whole range of value issues.[16]

Of course, this discussion rests on a "faith" in the validity of five interrelated propositions: namely, that more knowledge is better than less; knowing what *is* (and how and why it is) can help one to know what *ought to be;* widespread dissemination of knowledge increases the probability of its social application; people will express preference for the good (with respect to values, goals, and policies) if they can but identify it; and finally, social judgments based on evidence and reason, whether they are qualitatively superior to intuitive judgments or not, have a decided advantage in generating the social consensus that is requisite to social action.

Without confidence in a rational-empirical method of valuing perhaps discussion is useless. If confidence in such reasoning is lacking and the whole approach is judged to be misdirected, pernicious, or naïve, then we must look elsewhere for insight into the problem of value. And we must surely do so with an urgency and diligence not previously witnessed in the American intellectual community. For if we fail to solve the crucial problem of value methodology—if we fail to develop *a way of knowing the good* (in operational terms, and always tentatively, of course) and of *establishing social consensus* on values, without resort to force or chicanery—then we face a frightening drift into a future where accidental currents of technology and social power will largely shape the quality of our lives. Small wonder, to paraphrase author Norman Cousins, that such a prospect gives opportunity the face of disaster.[17]

III

Look Back
to the Future

Introduction

It is difficult to envision any humanistic frontier without John Dewey. One of the intellectual and moral giants of the twentieth century, he ranks with Bertrand Russell and Alfred North Whitehead, with Sigmund Freud and Winston Churchill, as an Everest among the Himalayas. Even those who disagree with him must admit that he made a difference in their lives.

Father of progressive education in America, he was a founder of such liberal and liberating societies as the American Civil Liberties Union, the National Association for the Advancement of Colored People, and the American Humanist Association, among dozens of others with which he was actively involved. He was both activist and thinker. Nor did he avoid politics even when he was abused for his efforts. In 1946, he joined labor leaders to lay groundwork for a People's Party. Avowedly antifascist and anticommunist, he spent a lifetime thinking and writing about the need for developing an "ideal" balance between individual freedom and institutional forms. His great humanness was felt in Tokyo and Peiping as well as in Moscow and Mexico City, for his frontier was the whole planet. And despite his very active involvement in worldly affairs, his published works are estimated to number more than 1000!

One looks back to the future in thinking of Dewey because so much of what he thought and did was so remarkably contemporary and relevant. Far from having failed, as critics of progressive education are so wont to claim, Dewey's philosophy has never been tried on any substantial scale. An editorial marking his eightieth birthday sums up his impact:

> There are countless school children today and yesterday whose lives have been influenced in a constructive way by this one man who never shouted, and whose formally stated philosophy often is a stiff dose for more subtle minds. . . . One thinks of him as refining into gold the rough ore of our tumultuous pioneer experience. . . . He is yankeeism at its best—shrewd, wise, humane.[1]

Both Dewey's thought and the commentary on Dewey's thought constitute the "stiff dose" to which the editor referred, and Otto Krash's essay is no exception. Just as Dewey was unlikely to let us get away with inquiry without inquiry *about* inquiry, neither is Professor Krash. And his questions about the assumptions which underlay this book are symbolic of both Dewey's mental toughness and that of both admirers and critics. The questions which Krash asks, of both humanists and Dewey, are pivotal in the construction of a foundation for human action. What is the genesis of human thought? What are the consequences of deriving many humanisms? Is *anything* human humanistic? Which social forms should humanists advocate? And which humanistic impulse constitutes a challenge to Dewey?

Lest Otto Krash be judged solely upon his logical analysis, however, I quote a letter responding to my question: How did Dewey affect *your* life?

> The man lived so compassionate a life. His modest size and eager soaking up of life's experiences. His willingness to be "out on a limb" in his own personal as well as technical principles. It is difficult to approach his intellectual honesty and accounts of his life without a response of love and compassion on one's own part and in return. My listening to him speak to premedical students in a jammed auditorium at Columbia University, and the reverence paid him and the record of his thought at his ninetieth birthday party and the added aura of worth surrounding him as Nehru stopped his round of diplomatic chores to pay homage, recounting his opportunities to read Dewey while he was in jail and detailing the effects of Dewey on his own thought. The greatest power Dewey had over me as I read his work, being moved always to extend my own thoughts, develop my own imagination, asking always, "What does this mean to me in my work with teachers?" These are the dominating characteristics: the measure of the man? How does one take the measure of a man? As long as controversy swirls about the work of John Dewey, I will be pleased. For he provides a matrix of thought where each of us can freely inquire, and extend our minding . . . as he might say it.[2]

So let us gladly inquire.

11

OTTO KRASH

Several Humanisms
and John Dewey

What is humanism? One *Humanist* editor indicates that

> Humanists have been debating for years the proper
> definition of humanism. It is clear that humanism is not a
> dogma or creed, and that there are many varieties and mean-
> ings for humanism.

He goes on to suggest that a characteristic emphasis of contemporary
humanism is a "concern with the good life and a commitment to democracy."[1] But doesn't that leave us in a dilemma that is so characteristic of
much current humanist literature; namely, is the good life inclusive of
democracy among other ways of life? Or is the good life identical with
democracy? Is humanism a generic description of human association or a
selection from among many ways of living and a specific program for
achieving the good life?

Many find humanism a generic characterization of human experience,
but then disagree about what those generic traits are and how we go
about discovering them. For instance, Paul Kurtz asks:

> Is it possible to find a common ground between various
> forms of humanism? It should be clear that there is no essence
> to which the term 'humanism' corresponds. Rather, any
> definition of humanism can only be roughly drawn by
> reference to certain generic tendencies that humanists have
> manifested.[2]

He finds:

> ...an important difference in contemporary humanism be-
> tween those, such as Marxian humanists, who believe that the
> problem of man is essentially *social,* and those, such as liberal
> democratic humanists, who emphasize the need to enhance
> the qualities of individuality.[3]

He concludes by observing,

> Perhaps what we can use today is a new humanist manifesto,
> written by both Western and Eastern humanists, which spells
> out the rights of the individual and criticizes all those forces
> in the modern world that seek to constrain him.[4]

A few issues of the magazine later, Mihailo Marković of Yugoslavia de-
scribes characteristics he takes to be basic in Marxist Humanism:

> Marxist philosophical anthropology is a strong expression
> of revolt against the human condition in capitalist society.
> Capitalism and some initial forms of socialism have shown
> that privatization of individual, class, national, and racial
> egoism, one-sided obsession with technology, material posses-
> sions, and political powers degrade man, develop destructive
> instincts, and eventually make human existence empty and
> meaningless. Marxist humanism is a radical negation of a
> society in which man is so depraved and in which possibilities
> of a fully developed life are so reduced
>   This negation has a democratic character. The humanist
> ideal implicit in this negation expresses certain deeply rooted
> basically assumed preferences. This could be empirically
> established by investigating which among rival norms of be-
> havior masses of people would follow, all other conditions
> being equal.[5]

Our dilemmas increase. Are the generic traits of humanism individualistic
or social? Professor Kurtz compounds our difficulties when he refers to
"generic tendencies that humanists have manifested." Generic to the
manifestations of humanists, but not characterizations of human experience? And shall we look, not to generic descriptions, but rather to
manifestos or the norms followed by large masses of people for developing a program to achieve humanism?

Is humanism a *preference,* as both Kurtz and Marković indicate? Or,
is humanism some "golden mean" between universal and relative values?
Herbert Feigl states:

> In my view we may reject extreme relativism. The relativist,
> especially the anthropologist, has confused mores and folk-
> ways with morality. If we dig deeper into human nature,

we find that in some social contexts certain moral ideals essentially work themselves out. So I think that a unified set of supreme moral values can be empirically discerned as inherent in the conscience of man, even if it is not always displayed in his behavior.

...I assume a sort of synthesis between a 'nothing but' and a 'something more' view of morality; namely, morality on the one hand is relative to human interests, and moral values do not come down from on high nor are they dictated by the deity. There is a golden mean that combines the valid element of monism, i.e. that ethical principles are universally applicable, with the empiricism of relativism, which teaches that human values are related to human nature. If you want a label for this, call it *scientific humanism*.[6]

This scientific humanism with universally applicable values that are also relative to human nature complicates our several and conflicting conceptions of current humanism.

In rethinking humanism in reference to the work of John Dewey, I believe that he too is a source of confusion as well as inspiration. As we have seen, humanists are confusing! Is humanism a description of human relationships that reveals basic characteristics of man? Is humanism a preference and a program for achieving the best that the human creature can become? Is humanism identical with life, or is humanism one among many ways of life? Are we to look for generic traits in human experience that we may characterize as humanistic or must we select particular human experiences and reject others in the name of humanism?

Support for this confusion can be located in Dewey's writing, and it accounts in some measure for the difficulties theoreticians have had with Dewey's analyses of the processes of thought as well as his description of social institutions. Two specific sources that lend themselves to a dualistic interpretation of humanism are located in Dewey's definition of philosophy in the *Encyclopedia of the Social Sciences* and in his generic account of significant thinking processes in the volume *How We Think*. In the former he states,

> Definitions of philosophy are usually made from the standpoint of some system of philosophy and reflect its special point of view. For the purpose of this account the difficulty may be avoided by defining philosophy from the point of view of its historical role within human culture...[7]

Confusion arises here when we accept the initial premise that definitions of philosophy reflect a special point of view and Dewey's attempt to circumvent this difficulty by examining "the historical role of philosophy in culture." Is Dewey avoiding the problem or creating an additional problem? What is this cultural theory of philosophy? And isn't this

Dewey's special point of view? What is this *new* conception of philosophy being proposed by Dewey? More to the point of this investigation—in what way does Dewey leap from description to prescription? What are the intermediary analyses by which Dewey develops this new conception of philosophy from a descriptive account of its historical role in culture?

Can we arrive at a substantive and structural account of philosophy and its functions by merely describing Grecian cultural characteristics? If this is being proposed, then we are confused when particular Greek cultural characteristics and interests are singled out and others neglected. If one of the hazards in historical research is the necessity for selecting among the welter of cultural characteristics, what ground is Dewey employing in making his selections? And, what value criteria are being used as a basis for such a selective process? Dewey clearly states the values he employs and the values he selects, but he leaves us with our initial confusion: does a descriptive account of philosophy's function in culture provide us with a new standpoint in philosophy?

Another source of the confusion between generic accounts of human experience and the selection of some human values with which to evaluate other values is his account of significant thought processes in *How we Think*. His descriptions are classic and often repeated in philosophical and educational literature. For Dewey, thought begins in a situation that is taken as disturbing. His homely illustrations refer to circumventing a stream blocking one's forward progress, analyzing reasons for the presence of poles both aft and astern a ferry boat, and accounting for a "messed-up" room. In each instance, thought is initiated by a disturbance that becomes a prime impetus for resolution by developing hypotheses, gathering data relevant to the hypotheses, and acting on that data. These "steps" of thought are not necessarily sequential. Here again a descriptive account of how we think is projected as the structure and form of thought. In what manner has Dewey converted a generic description of thought into *the* way we think or how we *should* think? Why is this description a model or procedure for how we ought to think? Surely thought processes occur in many forms.

Early in my teaching career, I enjoyed presenting Dewey's classic illustrations to undergraduates in philosophy of education. Save in one instance, students volunteered many suggestions for resolving "the disturbance." We converted these suggestions into hypotheses and attempted to prescribe possible tests in action. This met Dewey's conditions for significant thought.

On one occasion, however, I was stopped short by a student who, when confronting the example of a messed-up room proposed that we "straighten it up!" On previous occasions, students had proposed that we work with the ideas of burglars, a childrens' party, or a temper tantrum.

Such suggestions fit Dewey's analysis neatly, but "cleaning up the room" seemed to be a "resolution" of a sort beyond the parameters of Dewey's account! As Dewey says,

> The first result of evocation of inquiry is that the situation is taken, adjudged, to be problematic. To see that a situation requires inquiry is the initial step in inquiry.[8]

And if the situation is not taken to be problematic in the sense of developing hypotheses, what then? No significant thought occurs? Is it possible that thought as hypotheses-formation is one mode of thought that could be ignored in preference for others? And, is it common for housekeeping to ignore the consideration of other purposes? "Setting things aright" can preclude the development of hypotheses for problem solving of another sort. What is the mode of thought that habitually imposes form or a solution upon situations, in contrast to the mode of thought that attempts to account for the sources of disturbance?

Here again, Dewey provides us with a generic account of thought which he seemingly converts into *the* form and structure of thinking. This theoretical formulation does not provide sufficient analyses with which to bridge the gap between the genesis of thought and thought that is taken as significant; namely, how we *do*, and how we *should*, think. It is insufficient analysis that converts *How We Think* into how we should think or converts mere description into a design for significant thought. Dewey's discussion of philosophy and thought in these two sources reinforces the type of humanist who finds humanism in a generic description of life.

Some of this confusion is occasioned by Dewey's naturalism.. In response to an essay on his philosophy, Dewey remarked,

> Before taking up the issue raised by Mr. Parodi, I want to thank him for his grasp of the main purpose of my philosophical writings: "To reintegrate human knowledge and activity in the general framework of reality and natural processes". For I doubt if another brief sentence can be found to express as well the problem which has most preoccupied me.[9]

Knowledge and thought are natural processes, existents in reality. The genesis of thought is experiential; natural, in nature. But difficulties arose when Dewey seemed to argue that the adequacy and validity of thought depended upon its genesis. As Ernest Nagel observes,

> Dewey has sometimes argued, or at least given the appearance of arguing, that the validity of previous logical systems may be determined on the basis of the character of the historical period during which they originated. . . . In general the validity of a belief is not determined by its origin. But a

belief, taken as the conclusion of controlled inquiry, involves
a prior reconstruction of experience, and if a belief, to be
rightly understood, requires an understanding of the methods
of the testing and criticizing it, then its meaning as well as
its validity can not be rendered without reference to the
procedures of which it is a product."[10]

Some of the difficulty is lessened when we accept the natural genesis of
thought without *necessarily* referring directly to its genesis in accounting
for its accuracy or validity. In Nagel's terms, the validity of thought is not
determined by reference to its origin or genesis. Yet belief as a conclusion of thought can not be clearly understood apart from the procedures
by which we arrive at that belief.

In contrast to this emphasis upon natural processes and the genesis
of thought underscored by Dewey in his response to Parodi in 1939, his
emphasis seems to have shifted to the problems of inquiry in a work
written with Bentley and published ten years later:

Whatever relative novelty may be found in my position consists in regarding the *problem* as belonging in the context
of the conduct of inquiry and not in either the traditional
ontological or the traditional epistemological context."[11]

It is precisely this relation of the adequacy of thought and its origin, the
relation of inquiry to nature and experience, of logic to the ontological,
that leaves us with a fundamental confusion among alternate conceptions
of humanism. Whether humanism is a generic description of experience
or a set of preferences among various kinds of human experience.

Surely we cannot believe that whatever we *take* as human nature has
only one natural process of development: that the gamut of human behavior (including both infamy and honor) is *all* humanistic. If this were
the case, then there would be no need for further analysis—all is humanism. And we could not distinguish the valuable from the nonvaluable in
human experience. Evaluation would be impossible.

Dewey clarified the issue to me when he recommended that we take
problems *in the context of inquiry,* for it is within this context that Dewey
has provided us with the conditions for evaluating experience.[12] Humanism could then be a set of preferences accompanied by rational justification within the context of inquiry.

In an exchange with Ernest Nagel, Dewey makes the following distinctions:

I should not dream of denying either that valid objects of
thought are *conditioned* by prior existence or that they are
indirectly applicable to them by means of operations, themselves existential, which are integral elements in the *complete*
object of thought.[13]

If I am accurate in my interpretation, then problems (such as defining the characteristics of humanism) are taken as problems in inquiry where logic has to do with the relations among propositions. These logical relations have an *indirect* not a direct relation to experience. And, as Nagel indicates, the meaning and validity of these relations cannot be rightly understood apart from the procedures of which they are the product. Some of these procedures have reference to prior reconstructions of experience. So Dewey cannot be accused of establishing a direct relation between significant thought and the genesis of thought as developed earlier in this essay. He cannot be held responsible for converting a description of experience into a prescription for thought or of reducing logic to its experiential or biological origins.

Humanism to Dewey can be taken as his vision of the potentialities of experience and his preference for a critical evaluation of human experience. Dewey's primary concern seems to be with "the complete object of thought."[14] To discuss the logical relations between propositions detached from the constructions and reconstructions of experience that precede and that might follow the development of logical principles (the laws of logic) is to nurture false dichotomy between thought and experience—a dichotomy that Dewey resolves or attempts to resolve in his analysis of the complete act of thought. Without resolving this dichotomy, men would be unable to evaluate experience and would be involved in logical games governed by arbitrary rules that had no relevance to experience. This view of an unbridgeable gap between logic and practice governs much of past and current philosophy.

Dewey had faith in the potentialities of human experience. He had great faith in the extension of intelligence. That he seems to find his vision one with experience as well as in an evaluation of experience is a reflection of that great faith.

Either type of humanism will be better for understanding the ideas provided in the life work and living example of John Dewey. In addition, perhaps the distinction between descriptive and normative proposals often seemingly unclear in Dewey's writing poses the problems for contemporary humanists. Can humanists rest their case on descriptions of experience and culture? Or must humanists specify those characteristics of experience they find desirable or humanistic? Should humanists find primary value in social or individual experience? Which social forms should humanists support? What social programs do humanists offer to man?

Dewey's humanism offers a faith in the potentialities of experience and a theory of inquiry that provides standards for evaluating that experience. What do contemporary humanists offer?

IV

Relevance
Like It Is:
Curriculum and/or
Process?

Introduction

Despite the insights of John Dewey, Sigmund Freud, Alfred, North Whitehead, Jean Paul Sartre, and other distinguished philosophers and psychologists of the twentieth century, both students and educators still tend to think of a curriculum as *a thing* rather than a process. This is manifest in many of the statements in this book. It is implicit in the following two essays, which might better be called Blacks Studying rather than Black Studies. This is no mere semantic exercise; all too often, even in free structured programs such as the Antioch-Putney and Union Graduate schools, some students approach learning as if it were something "out there" rather than a process in which their minds, books, films, and various experiences were part and parcel of a gestalt. Perhaps the very effort to reduce events to words or symbols of happenings escalates the tendency to consider the curriculum as an objective reality?

Comparison of Professor Lerner's logic and style with those of Alston Brower's highlights at least two approaches to black studies. The reader, black or white, may decide for himself which of the two authors, the teacher or the student, comes closest to hearing it like it is. Also, when one considers the nature of the symbols in the content of black studies, whether nonverbal or verbal, in standard English or the vernacular, he may derive some insights about curriculum as either thing or process.

Both Abba Lerner and Alston Brower raise other questions, too. I wonder, for instance, if teachers and administrators can continue to talk about "lowering standards," "corrupting the academic community," or "high risk students" without exploding the dynamite planted in the statements some of the high school students make in writing for the underground press. Would it not be more humane, or even more politic, to admit that open admission processes imply the acceptance of *different* standards? By assuming the former attitude, doesn't one transform the self-fulfilling prophesy into the self-defeating one? This is not to suggest that we should "lower" expectations. Instead, don't we need to focus on the *locus* of expectation, relating the curricular processes to the perceptions and needs of the individual, regardless of race, creed, or clan, rather than some abstract body of knowledge per se? If one takes that approach rather than the one suggested by Abba Lerner, what implications does it have for blacks learning? or for blacks evolving what Alston Brower calls "the correct questions concerning the survival and development" of his people?

Nor can the problems of educating a subcultural group be divorced from those in the so-called mainstream. Should either black or white feel proud to recite the American Creed, to salute the flag, or to stand to sing "The Star Spangled Banner," especially such lines as "land of the free and home of the brave?" Can blacks identify with people and governments (local, state, and national) which have consistently oppressed them? Such are the questions implicit in the writing of Professors Jack Nelson and Christian Bay. And they rightly inquire, too, how much brainwashing occurs as students read chauvinistic history books or succumb to social pressures to conform. When is the argument for national security mere rhetoric? When is physical threat a reality? And who decides the "when"? Is love of country more important than love of reason to examine that country? Then, too, how does one approach curriculum construction (whether thing or process) to build a healthy respect for nation without promoting chauvinism? Or a healthy balance between national citizenship and world citizenship? Or is such balance impossible in view of the schools' using every subtle device to keep us natiocentric?

Both Nelson and Bay analyze the American failure to develop citizens who are free men capable of developing free-standing selves. And this failure, despite the millions of students who have taken every variety of civics courses! Must we not admit that our concept of citizenship has been too narrow and our processes too restricted to classroom activity (contrary to the spirit of John Dewey, who would make school and society one process)? Nelson and Bay also imply that it is possible to teach values, either by example (Bay) or through curricular devices (Nelson). If so, what is holding us back? If not, why try? Why not let the student grow up with the values he gets from his parents and peers? Where do you stand on the issue, and what are you willing to do to implement your views?

"Voices Through the Mortar," a collage of expressions from underground school newspapers, raises other kinds of questions: If schools were to espouse the morality implicit in these students' pleas, would we need to debate the issues of defense research? If teachers really listened to their students, listened with third and fourth ears, would junior and senior high school learning be as barren as students say it is? or as I know that it can be after having visited hundreds of public classrooms during the past decade? So why do teachers continue to play authority figure? What is intrinsically wrong about the set-up? If we were to change the environment, as William Chase suggests in his essay (Chapter 17), would that make a significant difference?

Whenever I read underground newspapers or watch TV accounts of campus disturbances, I am reminded of experiences on two successive days a few years ago. Visiting a distinguished southern university, I participated in an informal but agonizing debate over the sterility of a required freshman course in western civilization in which the 800 students could hardly see or hear their instructor as he droned through exquisite irrelevancies. Asking a former colleague whether or not anybody in power was doing anything about it, he responded crisply, "No." The next day I visited a very modern junior high school with free-form architecture, wall-to-wall carpeting, no halls, lots of open space, moduled scheduling, team teaching, and so forth. Both teachers and students seemed joyful as they moved about freely, quietly. Suddenly the archaic image of the 800 students in a single room hit me, and I blurted to my wife and hosts: "Hey! this school is a dissent factory! How could any of these students possibly go to Distinguished U and not feel like blasting the walls down?"

12

ABBA P. LERNER

Black Studies:
The Universities in Moral Crisis

Demands for black and "third world" studies and for black and third world control of black or third world departments or colleges in American universities have been supported by arguments ranging from the compelling to the ridiculous, pressed for by means ranging from the ineffective to the intolerable, and inspired by motives ranging from the most noble to the most despicable. The responses by faculties and administrations have covered almost as wide a spectrum, from inexcusable inaction on the most justifiable requests to unprincipled surrender to bullying bigotry.

For rational action in this situation the first requirement is the identification and the separation of the objectives behind the demands. The main objectives as they appear to me are here presented roughly in the order of their justifiability and their urgency. They are:

1. To remove any still existing discriminations against members of minority groups, thereby increasing the percentage of minority students and faculty in the universities.

2. To develop more appropriate and more impartial criteria for the admission of minority students and for the appointment of minority

This article was originally published in The Humanist, **29,** *No. 3 (1969), 9–10, 23. Reprinted by permission.*

teachers and administrators by supplanting or correcting such criteria as may be culturally biased against them.

3. To provide help and encouragement to disadvantaged and discouraged students and potential students (whose difficulties are in large measure the result of past racial discrimination).

4. To develop and expand the study of topics of concern to black and other minorities where these have been neglected—possibly because of conscious or unconscious prejudice.

5. By these and other means to cure black and other minority students of unwarranted feelings of inferiority that are the residues of discrimination against them in the past.

6. To bring about "reverse discrimination" in favor of members of the minorities in admissions, scholarships, appointments, promotions, etc., as partial compensation for the shameful discrimination against the minorities in the past.

7. To bring the proportions of minority students, faculty members, and administrators on the campuses into equality with the proportions of the minorities in the general population.

8. To overcome self-deprecation of black and other minority people—the result of past suppression—and to raise their pride in their color, race, or culture, by playing down, suppressing, or denouncing as "racist" any studies, researches, or criticisms that might tend to weaken such pride.

9. To limit the teaching of black and third world subjects and the manning of black and third world departments to black or third world people.

10. To establish departments, colleges, dormitories, etc., that, officially or unofficially, will be basically segregated in their student body and that will instill the habit of seeing all problems in terms of race and foster feelings of racial superiority over other groups.

11. To combine pride in "blackness" or in "third-worldness" with hatred of all "whites" (or nonblacks or nonchicanos, etc.) as intrinsically and incurably racist.

12. To achieve and escalate confrontations with university authorities by ever increasing "revolutionary demands" (i.e., demands that by their nature cannot be granted) for the purpose of disrupting and destroying the universities as the easiest first step towards destroying the society served by universities.

II

In pressing for some of these and related objectives, militant leaders have tried to shut down universities by so-called "strikes." In this they have universally failed; only small minorities having been peacefully and democratically persuaded to stay away. The militants have thereupon moved from the democratic way of persuasion to the antidemocratic way of intimidation, and have resorted to the disruptive tactics of confrontations and harassment developed by the group calling itself Students for a Democratic Society. Together with the S.D.S. they have engaged in violence and sabotage "to bring the universities to a grinding halt"—in the now-classic cliché.

In this they have in many cases been able to mobilize all kinds of unrelated discontents and to exploit all kinds of sentimental hangups. They have been able to involve many students and some teachers in staging and in escalating confrontations. They have provided bored students with the excitement of circuses, "rags," and small "social revolutions." They have exploited anger and shame at past discriminations and sympathy with the present sufferers from the past discriminations as well as the concern of all students for more individual attention and their inevitable impatience with the inevitable delays that stem from the ways of even the best-intentioned administration (in this context usually called bureaucracy). They have taken advantage of the awakening of apathetic students into wholly admirable eagerness for concern for and participation in the conduct of the university. But most of all have they been helped in the escalation of confrontation and violence by an ability to transform an appreciation of campus harmony and mutual understanding that would make police unnecessary, and an abhorrence of interference by totalitarian governments with freedom of speech, into an unthinking hostility to "police on campus" even when their only purpose there is to *protect* freedom of speech, and the general operation of the university, from physical violence.

Surprised by the disruptions and confused by the mixture of worthy and unworthy objectives, the faculties and administrators find themselves caught between unthinking, possibly malicious, conservative politicians on one front and unscrupulous revolutionary demagogues on the other; the two extremes in effect aiding each other. Thus trapped they are sorely tempted to lean over backwards to achieve peace even if it means bending some of their principles or even some of their prejudices.

Some prejudices will have to give, but the bending of principles constitutes just that kind of appeasement of the worst of the objectives that encourages the further escalation of the worst of the terroristic instruments of confrontation. Yet tension tends to cloud our vision, so that what in steadier times was clearly seen as incompatible with the proper functioning of a self-respecting university in a free country tends to be overlooked in the presence of greater threats, and our sensitivity to the fundamentals is warped.

This was brought home to me in looking over a statement of the basic principles as they appeared to me (and to some colleagues) before we were subjected to these pressures (and before the "black" demands had been fused with those of other minorities in "third world" demands). I was shocked to discover that I had not fully escaped the brainwashing by the campus tension or by the howling of the mobs outside as I tried to work in my study. Over 20 years ago I joined Roosevelt College in Chicago (now Roosevelt University) in part because it had revolted against the imposition by its trustees of a quota to limit the percentage of Negro students and had refused to register the color of students. And now I caught myself toying with the thought of buying some peace by deferring to color in selecting a student for admission or a teacher for an appointment.

III

It is in this contrite spirit that I present for consideration and possible guidance in our present crisis this statement of principles, set down in a more peaceful time when they seemed so obvious and so well-established as to be hardly worth spelling out. But in times of stress it is often the most obvious that needs the most emphasis.

1. We deplore any discrimination in opportunities for study or for teaching or for employment on account of color, race, creed, national origin, language or surname, or any other consideration irrelevant to academic potential or achievement.

2. We recognize that Negroes and others have been discriminated against, and are still being discriminated against, and that decency and efficiency call for doing all we can to end this discrimination.

3. Past discrimination is responsible for continuing disadvantages to prospectively successful students, in poverty, in lack of confidence, and in lack of home encouragement and support. It would therefore seem very likely that investment in special encouragement of and financial support to such disadvantaged potential students would be socially profitable as well as morally satisfying.

4. Such special help should be directed to *all* potential students who are in need of it. Because of the existing conditions of poverty and discouragement a very large proportion of such help would automatically go to Negroes, even if no attention is paid to the color of the students to be helped.

5. Paying special attention to color could be perfectly appropriate as a prima facie *indication* of probable need for help. It would not be justified as a *criterion* for help.

6. Teachers are often tempted to grade handicapped students more leniently, and to use criteria of color, nationality, race, etc., in a "reverse discrimination" favoring members of minority groups. Such temptations should be resisted as strenuously as possible for two reasons. One is that it affects the efficiency of the educational institution by lowering standards and inducing resentments both in those who fail to get the preferred treatment and in those who believe that they have not been favored as much as others or as much as they should have been (as a kind of vicarious compensation for damage done by others to others in previous decades or centuries). The more important reason is that the grades and degrees earned by the "favored" groups become suspect and tend to be discounted and even overdiscounted, so that discrimination against them instead of being diminished is perpetuated.

7. In the case of the hiring of teachers, "reverse discrimination" is even less defensible. In some case the instructor's special experience or knowledge of the habits, life, and language of certain groups of students may be a genuinely valuable quality, and this may go with his color. But in such cases the special qualification should be judged on its own merits and carefully scrutinized against its being merely an excuse for discrimination because of color, possibly in response to outside pressure—whether this is pressure by governments, regents, alumni, or students.

8. Such "reverse discrimination" would also have the effect of damaging the status of the "favored" groups. Experience in teaching at an institution would tend to be taken not as evidence of their having been examined by the institutions and found worthy but as evidence of the institution having given in to pressure, and the experience would tend to be discounted or dismissed as of no conclusive significance.

9. A policy of subjecting purely academic considerations to the objective of increasing (or decreasing) the proportion of the faculty that is of a particular color, creed, nationality, language or surname, or any other nonacademic consideration, would corrupt the academic community, damage the academic standards of the educational institution it infects, and constitute an attack on academic freedom as severely to be condemned as the imposition of restrictive quotas on the proportion of Negroes or of Jews to be admitted to educational opportunity.

10. All this is not to deny that great efforts should be made to seek out and encourage available Negro and other minority teachers who have been discouraged or to help such potential teachers to acquire the necessary training and experience.

11. Minority teachers are more likely than others to be lacking in formal certification even when they are really quite qualified to do the work required. It would therefore be even more useful in their case than in general to have sufficient flexibility to be able to appoint competent people lacking the formal requirements. In many cases this could be achieved by provisional appointments where there seems to be a good enough chance that the appointee could prove himself.

12. Both of these measures would be severely hampered by "reverse discrimination" such as in pressures to increase the *proportion* of Negro (etc.) teachers so as to correspond to, say, their proportion in the population. Such pressures, if yielded to, would strengthen the fear, often quite justified, that the termination of an experimental appointment, while attracting no attention in the case of a white appointee, would be denounced as racist discrimination in the case of a Negro (etc.). This is likely to make those in authority especially reluctant to make provisional or experimental minority appointments. Feeling that such an experimental appointment of a Negro or other minority instructor would be practically equivalent to granting tenure, they would actually be forced against their own consciences to engage in racial discrimination *against* the minorities.

13. There have been those who would compromise the principles here stated and undertake to double the proportion of Negroes on the faculty, even at some supposedly minimized sacrifice in the quality of the university, for the sake of relieving the pressure for "proportional quotas." Such compromising would increase rather than decrease the pressure. It would show that the pressure works, and it would strengthen the demands.

14. Negro (etc.) faculty appointed under especially lowered standards would also find themselves in a difficult and defensive situation. In danger of being charged with having "sold out to the white establishment" they will experience strong pressures to prove they are no "Uncle Toms" by showing themselves visibly in the forefront of all extremist claims. This is an additional reason why a compromising of standards for the sake of meeting a target would increase rather than decrease the pressures for further compromising.

15. There is also the danger of chairmen of departments under pressure or imagined pressure from administrators or from black student organizations (direct or through the administration) finding that they can meet quotas only by lowering standards. They would then be tempted to avoid resistance by evading normal faculty procedures in the name of pressure of time or what not.

16. The issues are clearer still in the matter of pressure for "black" studies. There are courses, and there could be more, that could be considered part of a "black curriculum." The filling of lacunae, if genuine, cannot be objected to, and complete freedom for experimenting in new courses, whether sponsored by students or anyone else, is only for the good. But arguments like that which declares "white" literature to be "irrelevant" to black students of literature, or vice versa, are completely unacceptable. All courses must be open to all students on a nondiscriminatory basis, and should fit into fields where their significance and relevance can plausibly be established.

17. The university should be especially alert against proposals intended as instruments of black power, and of antiwhite (segregationist, racist) policies within the university. Such proposals seem usually to demand black studies, taught by black faculty, for black students only (or similarly restricted to other minority groups). These proposals strike directly at the heart of the basic principle of free academic inquiry, and must be resisted. The notion, for example, that there should, on these terms, be freshman courses in literature and composition, or in science, taught by black faculty for black students is thoroughly pernicious, to say nothing of extending this principle to more advanced study. We must be scrupulously on guard against any acceptance of black racism as in any way any better than white or yellow racism. It is more easily explained but not one whit more justified.

13

ALSTON BROWER

Black Studies
and Changing Times

How do you see it? Everything moves, changes up fast. Fat Chubby Checker rolling out of Columbus doing the twist and marrying dat *European*. Fall back nigguhs! Then there was the Newark Riots. Who rioted? A Plot by the Insurance Industry or what? Martha and the Vandellas got on radio and asked (I said) asked the *Peeepulll* (All power) to get in off the streets. For the music that weekend was staccato rhythm of gunfire, dancing, ricocheting thru the paper-thin walls and ript some ex-slave's temple completely out leaving her rocking senseless and that young boy what's his name on the front of *Life* magazine in a pool of technicolor red blood and there was another one who got shot some forty or more times. That excellent example of how cowboy shows and the military industrial complex gives rise to sadism gave rise to a leap. Watching the Nevada testing grounds. That is those people, *The Man*, are *Sadist*, ruthless, purposeful maniacal sadist pumping out lead automatically like spitting watermelon seeds. And then saying "Get out of the streets!" forgetting the money they made inciting nigguhs to riot.

They said it. The sex, the excitement of personal appearance at the Apollo, the money all of it went out of their voices, they said, "Don't come out tonight—curfew." They said we *was* gonna be jammin' at the such and such club but we gonna cancel tonite. They said it and I wonder how many casualties they saved. How many nigguhs woulda got shot going to the bowling alley but then again how many said, "Ah, shut up bitch," and got down anyway.

Anyway, the human agents of state force and violence got down for real. And over in New York, the nationalists were in the streets telling nigguhs in Harlem, *Harlem,* New York, "Yall aint togethah. Yall aint nothin. Nigguhs over in Newark say yall aint nothin! Naw, Babee, yall aint shit. Why don't yall get it onnn. Yall sposed to be so *Badd.* Nigguhs over Newark is gettin down. You hear *Nigguhs*?! They gettin down. They ain't drinkin wine, they ain't gettin high, they gettin down. Boy, I hope they come over here fuck yall up after dey clean out Newark. Yeh, Nigguhs. That's right, clean yall out. Don't you realize nigguhs *he* din't got but sooo much military might! He got Vietnam, Jim, he got the whole world; you understand? He is what they say overcommitted! You dig. So if New York and Newark was to both get down: We could *rip* his ass and all but ah, yall din't nothin but yall be carefull. . . ."

And so goes the agitation to smash, to get down on this dog *white man.* But the nigguhs don't do nothin. But then again they did it in '65. Maybe it was a test, Martha and Vandellas, maybe they wanted to see if the brothers would respond. Anyway, while Newark smoldered, John Coltrane died and the hip nigguhs got occupied with that and on and on. . . .

And this is just in a week's time. Riots became events you checked on like baseball scores. You wake up—the count has jumped from 25 to 29 cities simultaneously in rebellion—and go to bed and wake to hear the count up or down. Assassination became a national holiday. You are handed a test and asked to identify if this is rococo or what. And we came into those testing offices under different influences. Some were about Trane or Fanon or about clothes or money or really some of everything. Different strokes for different folks. But then again we were all Black. And that man was declaring war on us everywhere and everyone reacted the same to that question about Beethoven or just about everybody. We all considered that question jive and irrelevant. On whatever level, from run and jump and hoop the pill to premed, we all thought or came to the conclusion that it was basically jive. And we would say how come they don't put some *Miles Davis* or some *Etta James* on that test; or go to a class and come back and say, "Man, forget *that*; or else get by, get over the best you can." Events, Events, Events.

And this Thing we were into getting more and more outside each day. What to take seriously? Astrology? Money? Degree? Islam? Needle? Blank Mind? Drop out?. . .and then they also are pumping questions, raising alternatives. The more you listen the weirder it gets. Drop In? Higher mathematics? How about graduate school? Or else they are laying Kissinger and Schlesinger on you and modernization theory and lecturing about *the world view.* And what is our world view? Dancing in the streets? Another generation of new Negros? Revolutionary violence? The urgency is to choose? We are reading Fanon, ignoring the chapter

"The Pitfalls of National Consciousness" and concentrating of the necessity of violence. Violent determinism became a world view. Fatalism. At last this hell on earth will be ended. We gonna die with our tikis and gators on. We gonna X this nonsense and Malcolm was Xed. Who pulled the trigger? What difference do it make? And what can we do about it? Makes no difference. *Get it on!* It was madness like inflationary spiral. The cost of livin was going, goes up every day and we have less and less capital to put in the game. Many brothers and sisters went to the mountaintop during this period. The cost of living was mighty high. And it didn't stop. We just got used to it. And now that you have been selected as one of two "high risks" to come to *college* from St. Louis out of total group of twenty candidates; or two of seventeen from East Harlem; or some number of some number from the "infinite" number doing their own thang or somebody's own thing to Simon Legree's funky beat. There are basic questions you have to answer no matter what your subjective state is while going to college. Why are they letting me in here? What should I do since I am here? Then what should we do since we are here? If we gonna do this thang and They still be about Beethoven, how we gonna be able to *do our thang?* Black Studies is conditioned, is determined by these factors: One—the social-material conditions and mix of such conditions comprising the lived histories of the students involved; two—the range of subjective approaches the students bring to the *College;* three—the manner in which the *college* responds to these questions. Why are they letting me in here? This question is presented as an accusation as to why. The why is liberal white guilt; pacification program; devil trickery; black brain drain or whatever. The why is today an accusation. We are calling you out, Charlie (or Dr. Philips, be it as it may)! Buildings are seized. And the response is the first lesson in how the system works, how the man does His Thang. Sometimes they scare; sometimes they crack down hard; sometimes carry you to court; sometimes talk you into confusion or to co-opt development with a few crumbs from the table. In this process, people start to research, to Think on the man's action. And this is black studies.

The second question is the double clutch fake, knockout punch. Because however the *college* responds to question one, the second question follows naturally, dialectically, and will deliver results. This is where everything accelerates, events get clearer and clearer, even though sometimes there is confusion. Inflation is your life. Those are the stakes. It is clear for one that wolf tickets and accusations are the furthest things away from change. So you must *do something* and even deciding where to start is a serious problem. With racism? With economy? With Swahili? With German? With His money? Without it? This is Black Education: The presence of alternatives and the necessity of developing a criterion in order to act.

We look back at freshmen pictures and see the difference. *It is* happening to us. History is going down. And we theorize we must seize the time. The question is, are we fast enough? Yah well ah bloods run away with Olympics every year. Somebody comments that in year 2000 the "citizen" is going to be on platinum nickles on the reverse side of a chitterling.

That is black education. You *have* to choose and you *have* to get down. Fanon was clear on that, saying in effect that every generation has a role in history and they either accept it or reject it. You either take care of business or space out. We now consider consciously, systematically, what will it take to do this thang. We are clear that we are not playing marbles. We are preparing ourselves to intervene on history. We analyse, we theorize, we do our homework. We decide, this is what we should do. How? We lay it out abstractly.

But we are not in control of ourselves as products of our pasts or others, nor in control of any material resources. So doing it is another matter. And since even with victory there will be change, we have to, with fair regularity, answer the question: Since we are clear on what we should do, how best to move? And we constantly reexamine the question of what to do and what we are? Was forty acres and a mule a hip program, and what about forty acres and a Cadillac? This week everybody doing the cat-walk. They doing it everywhere, even Jackson, Mississippi. Plus it is a strong possibility that public educational facilities will cease to operate for three to four months this year. Then again, upwards to five million workers in heavy industry and transportation are likely to strike this year. They are just getting around to changing those Beethoven questions. John Coltrane was a mean dude. So was Eric Dolphy, an Booker Little, so was Fred Hampton. Like any war, some make it; some are casualties; some are lost in action; some are permanently confused; and some space out.

Keep on pushin. We're a winner. The cost of living is high. Whatever the forms, the essence is having to make choices. The choices are inextricably bound up with the political-social-economic history of black people and their survival. There is more than enough to study. More than enough to investigate. More than enough to do. The point is that we must do it *by any means necessary,* and no matter what the costs. Wherever the term Black Studies came from, it is just a phrase, it's not what's happening. People use it as a tool to further their interests in what's happening. Some would say Black Studies is another form of Bantu-stand education. Some say it's this or that. Really, it is the sum total of experience that occurs as a result of the choices that the black student makes as an individual and as part of various groups. Given a common historical background, this is the essence of the experience emerging from the bubbling over of the melting pot. What will we do with this "black education"? What you did. What everybody does. Some of everything. It boils down to a struggle. Some will; some won't. What else can you say? The proof will be in the pudding.

Another day and more events. My Lai. New York Panther 21. Nixon throws a party for all those who support his HEW veto. And on and on. You see we have to communicate like this. Dig where this thing is really coming from. We have to be careful these days. The cost of living is escalating hand and glove with the war.

We can discuss what to do only after you are objectively ready to do it no matter what it costs. We are not shooting marbles. We are not engineering logically consistent social science fiction models. And we must decide (for example) what are the theoretical and practical implications of Nixon decisions. What preparation, strategy, and line of action shall we move on to deal with the social consequences of those decisions as identifying a definite trend in society. How shall we employ our expertise and experience in the best interests of our community, given a relatively clear understanding subject to revision based on analysis of the significance of that trend as well as other trends. School is never out. It's just that people get tired or fade away or get ript off or whatever. But *school* is never out.

The secret to making school an asset to black people is asking and attempting to answer through practice the correct questions concerning the survival and development of people on more substantial material and cultural levels. And finally, we learn the world is bigger than black even though the abyss we know best is black. With all of this in our heads and hearts finally we must go and meet the man.

And always the thought in the back of our minds: How will it be for us when we are fifty-one or -two and our chances for making history are slipping away. Then we will know for real if we asked the correct questions and made the right choices. All power to the people.

14

JACK L. NELSON

Nationalistic Education
and the Free Man

The societal dilemma of national security and individual liberties occurs in any open, democratic nation. Conflicts between the preservation of the nation and the preservation of free men emerge as the limits of freedom for individuals are tested. The Oppenheimer case, the (Joseph) McCarthy hearings, loyalty oath and disclaimer cases, draft card burnings, the House Committee on Un-American Activities and other security investigations, evolution of the John Birch Society, the Minutemen and other similar organizations, all attest to the strength and passion of this conflict. They also attest to the variability of perceptions of what constitutes national preservation and free society.

In dicatorships, the conflict is easily resolved by the imposition of the rulers' perceptions of national interest without special regard for individual liberties. In nations which profess democracy but practice totalitarian rule the conflict is merely an embarrassment, e.g., the Greek junta, the Diem regime in South Vietnam, and the Hungarian and Czechoslovakian invasion by Russia. In other nations the conflict reflects a deep moral issue of what is the greater good, national security despite potential loss of individual freedom or freedom despite potential loss of national security.

It is this division which often occurs in the United States and other nations—sometimes arising in countries considered totalitarian as in Russia when an intellectual or scientific group publicly opposes national dogma—that creates the social conditions for wide pendulum swings between right and left wing perceptions of the national interest. The winning rhetoric maintains sway for a period, then a countermovement develops and gains power. Thus, isolationism, internationalism, McCarthyism, pacifism, neoisolationism, superpatriotism and others are viable options at varying periods.

The basic dispute over what constitutes patriotic behavior and attitudes accounts for many current social disturbances. The draft card burner perceives his actions as patriotic in an attempt to correct a national immorality, while the policeman who arrests him sees the action as illegal and unpatriotic. Civil rights disorders are viewed by some as highly appropriate and patriotic activities to arouse the national conscience, but others search for anti-American conspiracies to account for the same behaviors. An increase in government spending for defense will be seen by some as encroaching socialism and presumably against the national ideal. Others may view the increase as improving national security, thus patriotic in its form, and a third group will perceive it as escalation and contrary to national goals. The behaviors are essentially the same, perceptions of the motivations and consequences of them are widely disparate.

Under these conditions, it becomes imperative to indicate the premises for discussing the schools as nationalistic instruments for developing patriotic citizens. When the concept of citizenship education is enunciated in school materials, it normally refers to course work in national history and government and to patriotic exercises. In many instances it also includes special course work or programs in whatever are considered to be contra-national ideas. Courses about communism exemplify the latter approach. The premise for requiring course work in American history and government in American schools is that the "good" citizen needs to develop a love of country and this is accomplished through knowledge of its history. This presumes an illustrious, or at least positive, history. The premise for teaching about communism is that one should know the national enemy in order to fight it properly.

My premise, however, is that patriotism and "good" citizenship rest upon some essential components of a political philosophy: (1) a free and open society; (2) individual human dignity; (3) a system of rights for all citizens. Consistent with these points is the notion of social change predicated on democratic justice. This framework provides patriotic education different from the traditional. It presumes a free man as basic and the open exchange of ideas as an operative necessity. It is contrary to the premises noted earlier for requiring American history and courses about communism in that no presumption of heroic history or enemy identification is necessary. Rather, *any* ideas, interpretations, and concepts are open to inquiry in a rational and forthright manner. This would not exclude education about heroic events and individuals nor agreement on the nature, intents and identification of national enemies. It does not, however, mandate or imply that decisions in these areas are made for and taught to students. Instead, students would be considered free, with dignity and rights, capable of contributing to and dealing with social change. The role of schools in this form of nationalistic education would be to provide students with analytic and synthesizing tools with which data, attitudes, and other types of evidence can be weighed. The tools of critical thinking can be applied to national history, government, international affairs, human rights, and myriad other topics without nationalistic censorship. The fact is, however, that education as a social institution has not been a model of open inquiry.

A society that places high values on national interest—chauvinsim—will expect its social institutions to reflect that concern. This is especially true of those institutions that are designed to convey the public morality.

The relation of education to a conflict between nationalistic interest and free inquiry is obvious. There is a presumption that education has a lasting impact on students in both cognitive and affective areas. Not only mathematics but also concepts of morality are taught in schools. Additionally, the movement toward mass education and democratic government lead to increased concern over the nature of that education. In the tradition of Washington, Adams, Jefferson and others, the schools are seen as means for enlightening the masses for self-government.

Schools have long been seen as major agents of socialization. Societies continue to rely on institutional means for imparting knowledge, beliefs, attitudes and behaviors. Churches, mass media and schools dominate sizable portions of the waking hours of children and youth and are considered to be significant elements in the development of social, political, economic, religious, and personal values. Of the various socialization agents, the schools are often singled out to play specific roles in conveying social values. Churches tend to be independent from broad public control, have limited and voluntary memberships, and consume relatively small proportions of a child's life. Mass media retain considerable autonomy although they are governmentally controlled through federal commissions, have voluntary and uncountable audiences, and are basically information and entertainment devices with limited intentions, despite their results, for value implantation. The family and peer groups are other strong socializations elements, but they are so diverse and distinct that particular social values are not easily fed into them.

It is because the schools occupy a unique position among social institutions that they are subject to pressures and requirements regarding national values. Compulsory education to age 16 or 18 for all children; state and local control over curriculum, teacher selection, and text usage; intentions to influence student behavior and attitudes; and a highly structured environment which tends to supplant the family as an inducer of morality in the young, all contribute to the rationale for using the schools to impart national, social, economic, and other values. The key issue is the determination of which values are to be expressed in the schools. The traditional approach taken in schools is to emphasize specific information, rituals, behaviors, and ideas which are highly nationalistic in nature and to portray negatively any reference to information, rituals, behaviors or ideas which are considered to be contra-national at a particular point in time.

Studies of textbooks, curricula and written requirements for instruction in patriotism and in anticommunism demonstrate the vitality of pressures to instill nationalistic views through the schools.[1] The studies indicate a variety of means for both dimensions of nationalistic education—positive instruction *for* patriotism, and negative instruction *about* areas considered contra-national. This is clear in studies of textbooks in American history which treat the activities of the rebels in the American Revolution as heroic, and the activities of the British and Tories as less than humane, courageous, or intelligent.[2] Billington summarizes this condition found in American junior high school texts:

> The impression that nearly all convey, even more persuasively than can be shown by quotations from their pages, is that the colonists were completely right and the British, although not consciously tyrannical, completely wrong. By repeatedly asserting American virtues, and by consistently labelling British measures as 'stupid' and products of the 'shortsighted, stubborn men who ruled the British Empire,' they have reduced an unbelievably complex series of events into a simple contest between 'good' and 'bad,' between 'hero' and 'villain.' This is not only untrue, but poor history.[3]

It is only fair to note that Billington's study, as have others, found nationalistic bias in texts in countries other than America.

Another area in which nationalistic education demonstrates the bipolar characteristic of good and evil is in regulations enacted to govern schools. A recent analysis of state laws and written statements regarding the teaching *of* patriotism and the teaching *about* communism shows this condition.[4]

A 1961 Florida law includes the following:

> 2. The public high schools shall each teach a complete course of not less than thirty hours, to all students enrolled in said public high schools entitled 'Americanism versus Communism.'
> 3. The course shall provide adequate instruction in the history, doctrines, objectives, and techniques of communism and shall be for the primary purpose of instilling in the minds of the students a greater appreciation of democratic process,

freedom under law, and the will to preserve that freedom.

4. The course shall be one of orientation in comparative governments and shall emphasize the free-enterprise-competitive economy of the United States as the one which produces higher wages, high standards of living, greater personal freedom and liberty than any other system of economics on earth.

5. The course shall lay particular emphasis upon the dangers of communism, the ways to fight communism, the evils of communism, the fallacies of communism, and the false doctrines of communism.

6. The state textbook committee and the state board of education shall take such action as may be necessary and appropriate to prescribe suitable textbook and instructional material as provided by state law, using as one of its guides the official reports of the House Committee on Un-American activities and the Senate Internal Security Subcommittee of the United States Congress.

7. No teacher or textual material assigned to this course shall present communism as preferable to the system of constitutional government and the free-enterprise-competitive economy indigenous to the United States.[5]

A California State Board of Education statement in 1962 contains these:

2. The State Board of Education, in adopting the Social Studies Framework, has recommended that there be study about communism in secondary schools.

3. Local school district governing boards are responsible for establishing courses of study, and should direct attention to studying about communism.

4. The principal emphasis in teaching about communism should be consistent with the ideal of developing well-informed American citizens; and while such study should be objective and scholarly in its approach, it should develop clearly the threat of communism to the free world.[6]

And a 1952 statement in New Hampshire notes:

The schools do not *teach* controversial issues, but rather provide opportunities for their *study*. The schools *teach* the American heritage (our established truths and accepted values) and, in doing this, provide opportunities for pupils to *study* controversial issues under competent guidance. For example, the schools provide opportunities for pupils to *study* other forms of government, such as communism and facism, in order to *teach* pupils the values of American democracy.[7]

These are only representative statements from the seventeen states which reported written regulations on the teaching of patriotism or communism or both.[8] Many states provide teaching materials and guides for such courses.

Another group of studies deals with the impact of pressure groups on nationalistic education in America.[9] These groups generally present a position on patriotism which incorporates a belief in unchanging values and symbols and a relatively clear perception of what is good citizenship and what is not. Patriotic organizations have a long tradition in America and have been remarkably effective in influencing what is taught in American schools about national and contra-national ideas. The influence occurs in local communities through direct or indirect action on school boards and PTA groups, presentations of monuments and patriotic artifacts to schools, assembly programs, letters to editors of local papers, and other means. At the state level, these organizations maintain close contact with legislatures and state school officials to insure "proper" patriotic education. They also conduct essay and other contests on patriotic themes which are often operated through school auspices. At the national level, the activity includes sponsorship of legislation, organizational resolutions on patriotic education, review of textbooks and other materials used in schools, and some coordination of local programs.

This utilization of the schools for nationalistic purposes is neither new nor unique to America. V. O. Key noted that all national education systems indoctrinate youth with national values.[10] Studies of Chinese, Russian, English, German, and other educational systems bear out his statement.[11]

In America, nationalistic education followed easily from prerevolution notions of the schools as a means for imparting "rightness" in religious and social conduct. The earliest laws regarding the establishment of schools in the colonial period expressed the conviction that morality could and must be taught. The Massachusetts School Laws of 1642 and 1647 provided that children be taught "to read, understand the principles of religion and the capital laws of the country," as a means of keeping "that auld deluder Sathan" from completing his "project to keep men from ye knowledge of ye Scriptures."[12]

The Revolutionary War and resulting nationalism led to a variety of prominent statements and laws designed to implement the concept of self-government by enlightened citizens.[13] The school became an important device to assure the proper instruction of citizens. Massachusetts, in 1789, had a law which required that "instructors of youth...take diligent care, and to exert their best endeavors to impress on the minds of children and youth...the principles of piety, justice, and a sacred regard for truth, love to their country, humanity and universal benevolence, sobriety, industry and frugality, chastity, moderation and temperance, and those other virtues which are the ornament of human society, and the basis upon which the Republic Constitution is structured."[14]

From these and similar charges to schools to educate for civic responsibility and proper moral character, emerged a continuing series of activities to insure proper nationalistic training. Laws, such as those cited earlier in this paper, require or prohibit instruction in certain areas of national concern. During the period from 1917 to 1920, several states prohibited instruction in German.[15] Books emphasizing patriotic speeches, songs, and rituals have become required in schools. Statements of schools goals show strong nationalism that is conveyed through the curriculum. Hiring and retention practices of districts demand nationalistic commitments from teachers.

Teachers have been subject to extensive regulation in regard to nationalistic education for a long time. Not only have they been admonished to teach the common morality, they have had to operate under restrictive statutes designed to prevent ideas considered to be un-American from being promulgated in the schools. It is interesting that nationalistic requirements for teachers were not standard until after the Civil War. The first laws prohibiting state certification of teachers who were not American citizens occurred in North Dakota and Idaho in the 1890s.[16] Kentucky began the network of laws requiring loyalty oaths from teachers in 1862.[17] The disclaimer affidavit, which became especially popular in attempts to eliminate teachers with communist backgrounds from the schools during the past quarter century, had noble ancestry in a Nevada law of 1907 which required teacher and professor signatures affirming loyalty and adding:

> And I do further solemnly swear (or affirm) that I have
> not fought a duel, nor sent or accepted a challenge to fight
> a duel, nor been a second to either party, nor in any manner
> aided or assisted in such a duel, nor been knowingly the
> bearer of such challenge or acceptance, since the adoption
> of the Constitution of the State of Nevada, and that I will
> not be so engaged or concerned directly or indirectly in or
> about any such duel, during my continuance in office.[18]

There is a wealth of literature on loyalty oaths and disclaimers required of teachers that indicates the social distrust of free and open education. The national paranoia reflected in demands that educators be more moral, more American, and more conforming than ordinary citizens is evidenced in the kinds of regulations cited earlier and still governing schools. These policies restricting free education are only exemplified in this paper. The history of nationalistic censorship, textbook and curricular requirements, surveillance of teachers, and periodic reversions to witch-hunt tactics to "ferret out un-American ideas" is long and complex.

The result of a tradition of nationalistic education which emphasizes controlled textbooks, curricula, and teachers is a cult of nationalism without inquiry—indoctrination to pronationalism and against anything viewed by powerful pressure groups as contra-national. David Spitz indicates this aspect in relation to humanism:

> It follows, therefore, from this idea about the exalted value of patriotism—a view which, for purposes of contrast, I deliberately put here in extreme form—that the teacher's duty is to inculcate the primary obligations of citizenship loyalty to, nay reverence of, the state and obedience to the law. He may, to be sure, have his pupils recite the words, 'In Democracy that state is for man, not man for the state,' for this rhetoric is still esteemed, but he must make certain that they understand (as the citizens of Orwell's 1984 came to understand) that words are not always what they seem.
>
> There is, however, an alternative judgment about the value of patriotism. In this conception the state, the nation, the country are but instrumental to the requirements of man— man as self and man as humanity. The individual is the supreme end; the country but the means to the fulfillment of that end. To argue otherwise, to reverse this order of value, is held to be a perversion of purpose. Consequently, nationalism is regarded from this standpoint as little more than a form of incest, even of insanity. It degrades rather than elevates man. It debases democratic and religious ideas of the value, the significance, of man.
>
> For the teacher who holds this alternative view, the primary obligation of the school is not to the nation but to humanity. And patriotism, which is the cult of nationalism, is necessarily to be scorned. At the very most, it may be defended as a temporary and necessary expedient; but under no circumstances is it to be revered as an intrinsic good. This, however, I need hardly add, is not the value that most of our teachers and the overwhelming bulk of the community attach to patriotism. Hence, the pressures of conformity move rather to sustain the first conception, that which puts love of country above love of man. . . .[19]

There is a wide variety of ways in which nationalistic education remains in schools. They appear to ebb and flow with social conditions, increasing in intensity when significant threats to national interests are perceived, and decreasing in more tranquil periods. The present situation regarding student unrest has already developed a nationalistic reaction which may have considerable impact on the schools and patriotic teaching. The "new patriotism" described by Sisson,[20] which would incorporate notions of continuing revolution from Jefferson, the Adamses and others, may be an ideal for an open society of free men, but appears to be unlikely in the prescriptive framework of the old patriotism. And it is the old patriotism which controls the schools.

A new definition for nationalistic education which would make it in the national interest to develop free men through open inquiry and the presumption of change would drastically change the present conditions in schools. It would permit challenges to prevalent national values, symbols, and rituals, and it would not demand unquestioning acceptance. This alteration would not, however, resolve the dilemma of national security and individual liberty, for many would view this restructuring of schools as a form of anarchy which would destroy the nation rather than improve it.

But if the schools fail to provide an arena for open discussion of national values, what social institution will? To the extent that nationalistic education is continued as blind faith in American superiority, there are serious questions raised about the development of free men. In a sense, the freedom to contemplate national ideals now occurs outside of schools rather than as a part of formal education. This may be one explanation for student perceptions of educational hypocrisy. Despite the pronouncements of free inquiry in schools and the verbal support for studying "controversial" issues, there are large segments of school time in which inquiry and controversy are not permitted or are conducted in a closed arena, that of positive national caricature.

15

CHRISTIAN BAY

Education for Citizenship

In my judgment all modern industrial nation-states, East and West, are fast becoming similar in their ways of coping with citizens, especially in their treatment and prevention of dissent. For one thing, all men of power, both in public and private organizations, have a vested interest in making our society appear as complex as possible so that they may seem indispensable.

To say that vested interests exist doesn't deny that some men of influence are capable of rising above them, to let their lives serve as models of justice, brotherhood, and sensitivity. But I do assert that unless there is an overpowering commitment to ideals or a will to be humane, powerful men are likely to exploit the less fortunate. And it is obvious that they will get away with more abuse of power, the more convincingly they dress themselves and the established system in the garb of righteousness, justice, democracy, and other eighteenth-century symbols of enlightenment which we've espoused for so long.

Like death and taxes, maldistribution of power is a fact of social life not readily eliminated. Only complete regimentation or a new kind of man could conceivably abolish the daily struggles between the strong and the weak, in which advantages and victories almost always go to the strong. Jean Jacques Rousseau had this in mind when he observed that democracy might work for a community of gods but hardly among men;[1] so-called civilized society had clearly substituted economic and political for physical strength as the roads to privilege. Only a radically more effective education for citizenship, Rousseau believed, could make democratic government realizable. In a society based on economic competition and greed, so-called democratic voting would be merely a contest between selfish interests at the public's expense. Only with the kind of political education that could produce the General Will—what people would want for their country if ignoring their own private or group interests—would a civilized, just, and democratic society become feasible.

It is a characteristic of man, Aristotle remarked, "that he alone has any sense of good and evil, of just and unjust, and the like;"[2] yet I would add that it is also a characteristic of almost all social organizations to counteract the individual's sense of justice. Man is potentially a humane animal, but is capable of becoming a hater or a cool psychopath if sufficiently tortured, especially during his defenseless days of infancy and early childhood. Social organizations do not plan the care and feeding of psychopaths and haters; rather, it occurs because of a deep malaise in our way of life, a way failing to meet our human needs. A paradox remains as an existential fact of life: the person has in his heart a sense of justice, but virtually every organization he joins or touches seeks to blunt it in him. To be socialized, to be educated, conventionally means learning appropriate behaviors—appropriate not in terms of the person's feelings about right and wrong but in terms of the establishment's interest in preserving the social system that perpetuates it.

Born Free but Chains Everywhere

Psychologically, the trouble begins with Mother, who teaches us to speak politely rather than frankly. Then there's Teacher, who demands neatness and predictability, pressing her young charges to internalize all the "correct" answers, and normally impatient with individual dissenting views about right and wrong. Then there's the Peer Group, whose very price of admission is conformity, in speech, conduct, and even haircuts and clothes. Then, of course, there's the rest of society, in which it becomes all to clear, all too soon, that a person usually gets ahead by avoiding convictions of social justice; above all, a person must avoid action in defense of justice, except in rare cases where his elders and allegedly betters, or their superiors on the job, might be supporting a particular crusade. The United Appeals Crusades are OK, in fact commendable, but no other crusades are if you know what's good for you. A sense of civic responsibility is fine, indeed a good advertisement for your firm or the Junior Chamber of Commerce; but don't get hung up on a sense of political responsibility, *please*, unless it's good, safe, clean, and conservative. Don't be a citizen in any real sense; don't get the idea that your own sense of justice should outweigh your elders' and betters' stake in the convenience of keeping business as usual. Above all, don't waver in your loyalty to the ideals of democracy *as we practice them*, by way of our gerontocratic oligarchy, or rule by small minorities of elderly men.

Schools and colleges have a particularly vital bearing on the development or retardation of citizenship orientation. I would assume that most of us agree in principle that schools and colleges are desirable institutions, and that education is "a good thing." On the other hand, I suspect that we may disagree on what a good school or a good college is; in other words, what its purposes are. Before spelling out my own position on this crucial issue, I want to clarify my conception of freedom; for I believe that beneath controversies on the nature of education lurk unexamined disagreements concerning the nature and value of freedom and education's role in expanding our liberties.

Freedom's Foundations

Briefly, I identify "freedom" with "expression of the self"; and by "the self" I understand the combination of intellect, emotions, and a sense of identity that make an individual unique. Each healthy self is in a process of continual development, and by "freedom" I mean expression of actual as well as potential qualities of the self. Now, self-expression, or freedom, has three requirements: the individual must have the *capacity*, the *opportunity*, and the *incentive* to express himself, and thereby develop his self further.

Correspondingly, there are three crucial aspects of freedom: "phychological freedom" refers to man's capacity to express himself; "social freedom" refers to his opportunity; and, thirdly, "autonomy" refers to his openness to new ideas and to his incentive to experiment with new kinds of self-expression, and thus continue developing his self.[3]

1. Psychological freedom is roughly the same as absence of severe neurosis or psychosis, or crippling anxieties or guilt. The basis for psychological freedom usually lies in a secure and loving human environment in infancy and early childhood. Emotional security in our early lives enables us to develop our selves; if this development is impaired, it may take psychiatric help to regain spontaneity. Does education produce this capacity to be free? Indirectly, perhaps, in that Dr. Benjamin Spock and others have been able to educate many parents and teachers about what children need. But without a minimum of psychological freedom, education may be impossible, since all the individual's energies are confined within his intricate neurotic system of self-defense.

2. *Social freedom* is roughly the same as absence of coercion; pressures blocking the individual's inclination to act or refrain from acting. Physical violence, up to and including murder, represents the extreme of denial of social freedom; but under "coercion" must be subsumed not only jails and threats of "or else" coupled with demands or requests. There is coercion, even violence, in poverty and other traditional kinds of deprivation, too, unless one continues to take them for granted. The coercer may be a dictator, a thug, a superior, or a policeman; but traditional *circumstances* may also be coercive. While psychological freedom has to do with security in infancy and childhood and psychiatric repair work, social freedom has to do with politics and economics. In my view, the only legitimate purpose of any government is to maximize the social freedom of all, with priority given to the least free. In short, government is doing its legitimate job only to the extent that it is reducing violence and coerciveness at home and abroad, the first priority of giving redress going to those suffering the worst deprivations. Governmental violence can be justified, if at all, only to the extent that it forestalls or diminishes worse violence.

3. *"Autonomy"* refers to the individual's spiritual independence, his ability to be and remain his own man, rather than the instrument of others' interests or designs. A person is autonomous to the extent that he is able to choose whether to conform or not to conform to the rules which he confronts. He may be lacking in autonomy and yet *feel* free if he simply takes for granted that there is only one way to live, one way to believe, one way to behave.

As neurosis is the negation of psychological freedom, and coercion is the negation of social freedom, so the negation of autonomy connotes manipulation, indoctrination, propaganda, or brainwashing.

There is one tricky aspect of autonomy when compared with the other two concepts: while a champion of freedom will likely approve of the highest levels of psychological and social freedom, he will probably not favor *maximal* autonomy. Naturally, most reasonable men would agree that neurosis should be reduced to the fullest extent; also, the less social coercion, the better. But manipulation and indoctrination fall into a different category, for no society or community can survive without some manipulation. In fact, mutual manipulation is at the core of close human relationships, between spouses, lovers, friends. We are continually busy trying to indoctrinate others with the view that we are pretty good guys ourselves, even lovable perhaps, and we want to induce others to see things our way.

Among the intricacies of autonomy important here: (1) There cannot be a goal of "maximal autonomy" because only a Robinson Crusoe, *without* his man Friday to manipulate him, could approximate this condition.

(2) Yet autonomy can and should, however, be maximized in given contexts, especially in the context of citizenship. We must encourage citizens to question the legitimacy of many laws, even to imagine breaking them...though obviously not including autonomy to murder. I am not opposed to citizens being manipulated into abiding by the laws against common crimes. On the other hand, I favor sufficient autonomy to *question* the legitimacy of turning intrinsically innocent and harmless behaviors, like pot-smoking or cardplaying on Sundays, into misdemeanors or felonies. (3) Autonomy requires education, though not necessarily school-type education. To be able to choose between available styles of life it is necessary to know what choices are available, and indeed to know vicariously how other kinds of people tick. Fiction as well as the theater are giant reservoirs of human models that one can accept or reject, but above all learn to *understand.*

This is what education is *for*: to achieve insight into one's own potentialities by learning to empathize with a wide range of people and problems, people real or fictitious, dead or live. Such learning builds persons and not robots, men who become autonomous as they grow in awareness of a wide range of their inner needs and requirements as human beings. This not only means exploring the individual's inner world, but also the world around us, including the whole range of political realities and ideologies past, present, and possible future.

Do Educators Educate?

We can now propose a general definition of "education"; so we may consider whether or to what extent our schools and colleges do educate. By "education" I mean the liberation of the intellect; i.e., the ability to think for oneself. Negatively conceived, what education liberates *from*, apart from blank ignorance, is the whole range of childlike beliefs and traditions from the home, church, and peer group; not that one must part with such beliefs, but that he becomes able to choose freely which he'll retain and which reject. Having developed the skills for making that decision, he is no longer confined within a prison of indoctrination, with walls impenetrable to facts, evidence, and moral challenge.

Positively conceived, what education liberates *to* is responsible human and social relationships, including citizenship. A person learns not to condemn automatically or withhold empathy from people whose behavior violates his own values. He learns that good citizenship is not a matter of doing as he is told, by teachers, parents, or political authorities, but doing what is just and fair to other human beings on the basis of insight, foresight, and sympathy, which add up to empathy.

Do our schools and colleges in fact educate young people in the sense of liberating their intellects? Not if they can help it. With few exceptions, schools and colleges are mainly interested in turning out "products" that are in demand by business, industry, government agencies, and—schools and colleges! Few employers want autonomous persons, for they are notoriously difficult people, difficult to push around, difficult to coerce into demeaning or immoral work. Almost universally, employers want highly trained, well-polished, "intelligent" young people with few commitments beyond settling into comfortable jobs permitting them to raise their own children in some nice suburb. Typifying the spirit of the times is the frequency with which teenage boys are suspended or expelled from school for refusing to cut their hair—as if the outside of their heads were more important than the inside! In such instances principals are often quoted as saying their schools must insist on good appearances, otherwise employers won't hire their graduates.

The word "education" is often bandied about loosely. Possibly this helps achieve consensus in favor of education? For many, the word simply denotes going to school to acquire a diploma leading to higher social status and income. Now, this process may be valuable enough, even a good investment, for the individual; but it is disastrous to our long-term public interest. The end product is bad citizenship and bad politics.

Every organization, and certainly every state, is top-heavy. Their leaders have a vested interest in expanding their own power and privilege at the expense of the population, to explain away and rationalize the flourishing injustices that surround us. Schools and colleges are also social organizations, ultimately run by those same people, the aging oligarchs who in the name of liberal democracy are the firmly entrenched rulers. Allowing for individual exceptions, those in power in any country tend to think it's a pretty good country such as it is; therefore it ought to change as little as possible. Quite naturally, then, those running our school systems and colleges take a dim view of education, as I use that term, especially citizenship education. Despite all their rhetoric they are fearful of "real citizens," opposed to "pseudocitizens," who are induced by their conscience to become political activists in pursuit of justice or just causes.

A few years ago I met a most impressive man, Edward Gottlieb, a high school principal from New York City, who must have been unique in that kind of a position. In a brief discussion of his own work he said something like this: "If a year goes by without a single political confrontation between our students and school authorities, then I feel our school hasn't been doing its job."[4] He is one of those rare school administrators who is also a committed educator believing in political education to citizenship. It might be easy to claim that this man can't be a good administrator; by conventional standards good administration means smooth operation, without eruptions of any kind, especially hostile confrontations between students and staff. I'd reply that a conventional administrator does not help educate for a free and just society; instead he administers training for the Smooth Society.

Expanding the conventional perspective further, a "good" teacher presumably promotes a tidy and orderly classroom; she makes her pupils behave in accordance with her standards. The more she makes her children scared of being different, wary of giving unexpected answers or asking unexpected questions, the better she "suceeds." Her "products" tend to become timid, repressed little conformists, or soldiers, rather than young individuals with their birth-gift of natural curiosity intact, let alone stimulated in directions fruitful for future growth.

Paul Goodman observes that colleges exist to undo some of the harm high school does to children, just as high school ought to undo damage suffered at home and in the lower grades. A fundamental and long overdue reform is to reverse the pay scales for our teachers; higher salaries, qualifications, and status should go with teaching the lower grades. Ultimately, preschools teachers should be paid the most, college teachers the least, since elementary teachers can do more good or more harm toward developing freedom, autonomy, and responsible citizenship than college professors. As it is now, most students enter college with their intellects completely ossified by nonuse and nonchallenge. They have learned a wide range of facts plus know-how in the arts of "getting by." They have a few skills and possess "good" nationalist attitudes. They are proud and smug about our so-called democracy's superiority over other systems. But most have little or no intellectual equipment for becoming *real* citizens, concerned with improving their society, or with making it more just.

Mind you, the situation is not entirely bleak. We live in an affluent society with many students in school until their midtwenties. Many are not as easily intimidated as in former years about the dire necessity of preparing themselves for the struggle for survival in our competitive society. Somehow they know they're not going to starve. As increasingly evident since the first Berkeley Revolt in 1964, the so-called Spock generation, raised in child-centered homes, have developed an ability to defend themselves by way of saying no—despite the school system. They are symbolized by those students opposing the Vietnam War who wear buttons with the motto, "I'm a Spock baby. I won't go!"

But there is certainly a lack of constructive adult models of citizenship in our schools. Traditionally, our teachers have been among the most intimidated, even henpecked professions, too scared to assert themselves even against obnoxious directives from higher up in the school hierarchies. And, what is more shameful, because collegiate academic freedom has been much wider for along time, most professors have been poor citizens, reluctant to join students even in confrontations where they felt student demands were just. Their own research or careers have too often been judged more important than meeting the moral challenge of doing the right thing as responsible citizens. Yet in our role of educating for citizenship, the kind of men and women we *are* is far more important than anything we say or do in the classroom. The means conjoining students' battles for human freedom and justice both on and off the campus. This implies involving them in course planning, not merely involving them as window dressing or in a safety valve context; rather, it means helping them gain competence to develop learning strategies consistent with their emerging selves, encouraging them to evolve and to solve real problems, not pseudo problems designed by professors. This means that teachers must be more open than closed, more vulnerable than defensive, more accessible than programmed. It also means that a teacher must learn to see the student as the student sees himself rather than as a basket to be filled with knowledge or an object to be manipulated for the teacher's ego satisfaction.

I suspect the only hope for this world is that we somehow manage to free the next generation from the conformity demands that every establishment of elders since the beginning of time has tried to impose on the young. Or rather, it is *their* task, the task of the young themselves, to bring about this discontinuity with our dismal history of man's cruelty to his fellow men.

This, as I see it, is what student power is all about.

16

Voices Through the Mortar:

THE HIGH SCHOOL UNDERGROUND SPEAKS

The tidal wave of student dissent rising at Berkeley in 1964 has washed through the public classrooms of America, picking up momentum through the years. This is evident in the mass media. Also, an increasing number of underground school newspapers has appeared in various forms to give vent to student voices, their reactions to Vietnam, perceptions of racial issues, views of selves as human beings, attitudes toward schools, and so on.

This collage is constructed from some of those newspapers. The voices are black and white, of junior and senior high students, of ghetto, suburbia, and small town, of students all across America. It seems best to publish them anonymously, although I can attest that each expression is genuine, was written primarily for local reading. Appearing here essentially as originally published, the pieces are edited only to protect individuals and specific schools. I regret not including more, to provide a better measurement of the many dimensions of frustration, joy, insight, pathos, tragedy, and beauty which wide reading of these publications affords. They are representative, however; and they suggest that students have something to say about their conditions of existence and are saying it loudly across the land.

The following symbols, used after each statement, identify the nature of the source: *L*, from a Student Log; *LE*, Signed Letter to Editor; *A*, Article for a paper; *E*, Editorial; *P*, Poem.

Views of Self

Know why I am writing in my log? There is no one else to talk to. I just wish my Mother and Father would sit down with me and let me talk to them. They don't even give me a chance to plead my case!

I dread getting up in front of the class. I'd rather do anything but give a presentation. I wonder what people will think of me afterwards.   [L]

I didn't go to school today. I had the flu and was sick all weekend. I could have gone today, but I just couldn't face it. It was good to stay at home and do nothing. Sometimes in school I get so nervous and think I am going to crack up. At school I'm told what to do, how to do it, and when to do it. I just don't like the pressure. I wonder if teachers realize this?????   [L]

In history class today I read some letters written to a family who had lost a son in the WAR. These letters make you appreciate that your family is together. It makes me realize my true feelings for my brothers and parents. Sometimes people don't realize how much they love someone until it is too late.   [L]

Almost everyone I know has a mask to shield himself and hide behind. No one knows me, I mean really knows me. Not even my own Mother. I can't talk to her. I know why I must have to hide my true personality. Last night my Mother and I got into it over a letter from a friend. She wanted to read it and I didn't think she should. There was nothing in it though. She asked me why I didn't leave home. What would you do if your own Mother said for you to get out? I felt like leaving right there, but since I am a senior I want to finish school. . . ? The next time she tells me to get out, I am going. Only one problem: where??   [L]

My first year in Jr. High School was a mess. I was always walking the halls, trying to be known as D.J. I had so much fun doing nothing. Then, when report cards came, I realized that I had to quit playing. But it was too late. I had failed and had to go to summer school. I felt bad going to school while everyone else was working and playing, so I quit going. I was wrong to quit school, but I made up for it when I went back.   [A]

I like Martha Thompson because I think she have a nice voice. Mabe because she is cute. Mabe because I like the way she move. And the way she keep her cool. She say she is a cool girl. From a cool world. I am the one to cool her down.   [A]

The Classroom and Studying

School is getting me down. Everybody piles things up on you. They're all cramming to get stuff in before semester. If I could change the school system, I would add more years in high school. This way students could take more courses and not be so loaded down. As it is, some students have a full schedule every year in order to have all the subjects they need or want. I guess my idea wouldn't go over well with some students.   [L]

Everybody is talking to someone but me. I think I must be invisible. I wish that school was out.

I look around this study hall at the people who are studying and I say to myself, "Learning—HA!" [L]

This is my schedule for school: I sleep first period. I type second period. I dream third period. I skip or sleep fourth period. I dream again fifth period. And I talk sixth period. So being awake one out of six periods is a bore—I think I'll quit school! [L]

I couldn't get anything done in class today...too many "Payton Places" to listen to! [L]

This class is boring!!! But, I can't say that I haven't learned anything. Everybody in this school is boring. This whole d——— school is boring! [L]

I sure hope that I can learn to sew well in Home Ec. We've just started and I don't know the first thing about it. So far everything has gone okay. I admire people who can sew and cook well. I think its important to know how to sew and cook well for your married life. You know, I worry about whether or not I'll be a good wife and Mother. I want to please my husband and I hope I'll raise my children right. [L]

The Classroom

What is it I see?
What are these machines
Sitting before a larger one?
It looks as if the bigger
One is talking to the others.
But as I look closer, I
Realize what I see...
Are not machines, but rather
Humans.
Why do they hide in their
Cases acting like machines?
Why don't they show what they feel?
Could it be the situation
They are placed in?
Could it be just because
There are so many and
The big one can't talk to
Them all. [P]

My Thoughts During English Class

Wandering minds
Staring eyes,
My doesn't that
Sunny window
Look inviting?
Talking teachers,
Open mouths,

Up-stretched hands,
"Who knows the
Answer?"

Yawns and concentration
Don't mix with
Confusion.

Anger too!
"Do we have to
Do that?"
Aren't there any
Pillows?

Corner-taking.
Whispers.
Are they bored too?
Why are they laughing?
I didn't hear the joke.
Listen better, more.
Concentrate on teacher now.
Time goes on.
"Again, who knows / The answer?"
Writing and words.
French? No, English.
Still only first period?
Time goes on.
Why is the window
So beautiful? Signifies freedom.
Yes, that's it. Freedom.

Who cares what the
Answer is.

Word structure
Gives splinters.
Stay away.
Why do the policemen
Stand at the door?
Wood inside,
Brick outside.
Ancient, yet standing.
Chains on the door.
Strait-jackets in the rooms.
Locks and bolts.
Flags in each room.
Restrictions on everything.
Smelly food.
Leaky roofs.
Beer drinking wardens
In each room.
    Jail?
No, guess again.   [P]

I think that a person learns more from doing reports and independent reading than by taking notes from a lecture and memorizing them. My sophmore year I had a lecturer for history. She just stood up and talked. She asked for a discussion period but no one ever talked. If you disagreed with her, she threw you a cut or embarrassed you. She also did this if you answered your question with wrong answer. I think that she must have been a robot!!!   [L]

I have some homework to do. I hate to do work at home. It doesn't seem right spending the whole day in school studying and then having to come home and spend the whole evening the same way. The thing that gets me is that everything is done for the future. My whole life is almost full of preparing for the future.   [L]

Two Views

The second period Social Problems Class is way out of hand. Mr. F. and Mr. S. need to be more strict. Order is needed.

There is no rebellion in the other Social Problems classes because the students know that the other teachers mean business. Here, obedience is a meaningless word.

All that is done is laughing, giggling and cutting up others. This is disturbing and unnecessary behavior for Seniors.

I don't think that Mr. F. and Mr. S. are very lenient. I think you run the class just right.

I don't think that a Civics class should be conducted out of books, but out of our government as it is being run, today. Quite naturally the class will get out of hand discussing things, this I think is what the problem is—noise

Students planning to go on to college need to learn subjects like Civics and History. But I am afraid that we are going to be lost, because there is not enough control for those of us who want to learn.   [A]

This can be handled in various ways, but I agree with you. We are too old to be watched over like babies, with you being some kind of police.

As far as other classes are concerned they are no better. Tests in other classes were hard mainly because the teachers do not tell you anything. They would give you grades and always make some stupid jokes.   [A]

I decided to observe the class to find the studious and creative ones. I started with John; he is never idle, is always seeking something new. He tries to do his very best.

The next conspicuous person was Peter. The only time you hear from him is if he's disturbed by his grade. And why shouldn't he be?

Janet keeps things uptight, namely her man. She is a very hardworking young lady. At least this is the impression she gives.

We have a few palmists in our third period class. Terry is one. Whether she makes them up or George, I don't know. At any rate, they're always good.

Donna is constantly trying to turn out something good. If she would come to class more often, she would be a good asset.

The observer of all observers is Ron. His eyes are always in the middle of things.

All in all, I think the third period class is a marvelous one. It takes all types of people to make the world.   [A]

On School Activities

We had a mock election and assembly today. All the speakers were very good. Some of the kids were very rude during the speeches, but for the most part it was interesting and fun. The kids that acted as campaigners for each candidate provided good entertainment after their candidate's speech. The only thing that messed it up was one teacher who went around telling everybody to shut up. We went for a mock assembly and wanted to have it like the ones we saw on television. But if we had been quiet and not participated like she wanted, it would have really been a boring experience. I guess that's the way some teachers like it! ! ! There's not as much for them to do that way!   [A]

Today we had a Youth Forum. I wish that I could have some of the knowledge those people have. I feel like a spanish peanut among a bunch of walnuts.   [L]

I think the Assembly we had was the best we ever had. It was a nice program. Every one at the assembly was very nice. The ballet dancers danced very nicely. The best part was how they do their dances. The men were brave they can lift the women if they were very light.   [E]

The Assembly talk by Mr. F. was to talk to the Girls and Boys about not playing Dice and taking other people thing And to hang your coat up in your locker and take them off in the building if He catch you he is going to call you and call you home and sent you home and give you a vacation.   [A]

Student Council is working with the YMCA to get the teen center ready for this Saturday's game, when we hope to open it after the game. That's one thing for our town that we really need—someplace for teenagers to go just to get out of the house, see your friends, and have some fun. I think having Student Council organize it should get it off on the right foot, with the right kinds of kids showing up. Not that everyone isn't welcome—it's just we don't want it to turn into a hood hangout and spoil it for the rest of us.   [L]

Our football team is a disgrace. The boys can't open their mouths unless something filthy comes out. The lobby is plagued with them and at times—especially lunch—no girl can walk through the lobby without hearing something filthy. Should this go on? The school puts these boys on a pedestal and all they do is stay drunk on weekends. The whole idea of honor is sickening to me. We are so warped!   [L]

Student Council adopted the "Dean's List" system to honor scholastic students of scholarship standing. During the meeting, one student asked to abolish the honor roll. If this is to be, then why not abolish the athletic awards? After all, scholarship is more important than athletics. Some people have changed high school and college into a sports training camp and are forgetting the supremacy and importance of being scholastically inclined.   [L]

I think it is very intresting and very educationed for kids in school to have sex education. For one thing, they are baring the facts and are learing them the right way, which I think is a lot better than the trash they pick up in the street.

I have heard parents complain but they should be glad because this way they learn the facts the correct way. I am sure there are many people who feel the same as I do about this all important subject of today.   [LE]

The trouble with boys is that they just can't keep their hands off of girls. Boys have to feel them and they just have to touch them on their legs and ass and breast. When the boys are talking to a girl he has to use foul language. When a boy is going with a girl then get what he wants then him and his friends will start talking about you like a dog. Boys hit on girls like they are some pushover or something. If the girl is too fat or too skinny they talk about that. Boys can most of the time persuade parents to buy them what they want or let them stay out all hours of the night. [A]

The trouble with girls is that they run around all day playing and picking and pulling on the boys, they also argue over little things and yelling all up and down the halls.

The other problem is that they're running outside every 5 minutes and uses profanaty every time something comes out of their mouths. [A]

> School is a place we go to learn
> To get the grade in which we have
> earned.
> School is a place to get along with
> others
> Not to talk about their mothers.
> School is a place in which you shouldn't
> fight.
> It teaches you about your bill of rights.
> School is a place in which it teaches
> you respect.
> Not a place in which you neck. (If you
> know what I mean)
> School is a place in which everyone
> should go
> Not a place to seek your foe. [P]

I learned a lot about life by talking to one of my teachers today. He said that he felt so immature. Well, he couldn't have gotten this far in life if he really were. He tries to make everything perfect. Maturity isn't perfection. [L]

Views of Teachers

Did you ever have a teacher who picked on you? One teacher lives to yell at me. She'll ask me a question and when I answer it, she says she couldn't hear me. And then she makes me answer again. It wouldn't be so bad if it was true, but I've asked some of the other kids in the back of the room if they can hear me and they say yes. I wish she would turn up her hearing aid! If anything, I am too loud in class! L

I found out today that teachers are human. Before this year, I didn't realize that. It seemed that all teachers were really stuffed shirts. I feel that I have reached one step toward maturity by realizing that teachers are people. [L]

I know a teacher that can't teach for nothing. Every time I come to he or her room I get a headache. The [one] I'm talking about lets the children take the advantage of him. What we learn in the class isn't worth coming to school for.

Can you guess who is the teacher? [LE]

This is one man the world could hate and his name is Mr. A. I guess he can't be nice around here or can he. Well any way he always pick on people, like this boy I know name Don. Don don't take P.E. and Mr. A. tell Don that he is scare to take P.E. and Mr. A. calls Don names. He isn't all that bad and he isn't all good either. I guess you could say he is in between. I think he should be tort to be kinder to us and Don. [A]

I think that teachers don't care if you miss school. They don't want any extra work for themselves by giving a make-up test so you have to take it the day you come back. Maybe I look like a kid who would cheat, but I don't care anymore. I feel like giving up, but what good would that do? [L]

The subject in which has come very strong in my mind is the fact that teachers are underpaid.

I am a student attending Madison and for all the wear and tear a teacher receives here all day, they could never be overpaid. They have spent so much time training and in turn, have given so much knowledge to others.

If it wasn't for our teachers the kids wouldn't have any knowledge. Sure he can learn something at home, but why let him settle for second best? He can get the best from a trained teacher.

So I say, "Raise the pay for the teachers of today!!" [A]

General Attitudes Toward School

Ask not what your school can do for you, but what you can do for your school. [L]

Adams High is a boring school. Some kids don't get enough sleep at home. It's hot here and the floors are dirty, the shades are broken. The drinking fountains are not cold enough. They're too far down. The boy's bathroom has writing all over the walls and all the book shelves in the boy's room are broken off. The boys should not bring their cars to school. It makes too much noise. The windows should be tinted. The chairs should be padded and the classrooms should be cooler. How can *we* make this a better school? [A]

I love school and I think most of the teachers at Adams are great. Teachers try so hard to teach, but the students are not interested. Look, we come to school to learn and I think our teachers do a good job. If you think our teachers are punks and no good, go home and have your parents teach you. It is hard to teach 30 students and try to be a friend when there is talking, screaming, throwing spit balls, and answering back. I wish teachers had the right to slap the heck out of some of these fresh mouths. When students learn how to behave and most of all, respect a teacher, then they can ask for improvement in teaching and teachers. [A]

Yesterday we had the pleasure of having two visitors at Jefferson High. One was an exchange student named Eva from Brazil. The other was from Maryville and her name was Linda.

We asked them what they thought about Jefferson.. Linda said it was a big school, old, well kept, and respected. We asked them about student relations. She said it was fabulous. She was relieved to know that there was no racial prejudice shown. Eva agreed.

Linda says that Maryville didn't have much school spirit, nor the facilities that Jefferson has. They don't have good relations with teachers. They do not cooperate with Student Council.

The girls talked about their Civics class. They have 45 minute lectures and seminars. We asked them: did they think that if Martin Luther King Jr. had been shot when it was warmer would there have been more violence than there was in our city? and both said yes.

Did they think that we are through with riots completely? The girls agreed 100 percent NO.

Did they think that pregnant girls should be allowed to finish school? With only the slightest reservations, the girls agreed that they should continue. [A]

Washington is a very nice school but the people don't know that. The big boys pull false alarm and try set the school on fire and teacher don't do nothing about it they should get the police up at the school and find the people who doing all these things. I believe the teachers are scare of the big boy by nixe year the school will be torn down if the teacher don't do nothing about. The only clean place in school is in the gym. [A]

Race and Education

I was asked to give my opinion on education. Being a Black man, I connect myself to his state of education. To me, education means life itself. It's a ray of hope for the poor. But I think the School is not teaching us enough Black History. About Black people, such as: Fredrick Douglas, a man took a giant step toward freeing the enslaved man. Thurgood Marshall, the first Negro ever to be on the Supreme Court. Another man which every man should take their hat off to, Dr. Rev. Martin Luther King for a man who has a dream of racial equality. Why don't the Black man have recognition? Why? [A]

The discussion in Sr. Soc. St. 421 led to questions concerning administration of our school. A committee was appointed to select areas of student interest and to use them while interviewing Mr. Jones.

Mr. Jones stated "the color of a teacher doesn't make any difference as long as he is qualified." He feels that Jefferson should be intergrated because all can learn from each other. White and black should intermingle.

He commented, "Jefferson is a fine school and the students' pride is greater this year. We are looking for improvement in the offices, new windows, painting in class rooms and halls, a new heating system and the cafeteria will be renovated." When asked his opinion of students smoking pot, he replied, "I hope they do not. It is getting into an area of possible addiction." He discussed the difference between the positions of Principal and Asst. Principals. He feels that the relationship between the community and Jefferson could be improved. The parents are what we need to take part in the school, especially the men.   [A]

Doris

> Doris is a Negro girl,
> Who has but one worry in the world.
> She goes to a school of white,
> And doesn't show any of her fright.
> She hasn't time to spare,
> But the students just stop and stare.
> She goes in the class room with all of her nerve,
> Of course I know she feels disturbed.
> She dares not say a single word,
> She sits like a frighten little bird.
> Hi! Doris turned as if she were old,
> Saw a girl that looked very bold.
> She didn't think that it could be,
> For she was a friend you see.   [P]

I was glad to see the ten Johnson High students visit our Social Studies 4th period class. These students were juniors, but they expressed themselves like seniors. Our seniors take over. Our seniors were afraid to say much. I guess they felt inferior or out of it.   [A]

I think they felt this way because it is not often we have a predominantly white school sit in our class and express their opinion of their family life to us. I, as well as a few other students were surprised because the students' parents seemed to want to keep them under them. Their parents were sort of strict and they felt this was wrong. I got the impression from several that they would be very glad to graduate and get out on their own.   [A]

The reason I think we didn't say too much was that most of what the students from Johnson said we were already thinking. . . . And believe me, we were looking with amazing and startling eyes!

As our discussion went on, there was talk on the way our parents were trying to make us see everything as they did when they were growing up. . . .

In some ways students are teaching parents nowadays. Children are learning more and more about life and many things parents never heard of. They should try and understand us and not always tell us what's wrong all the time. We have to live for ourselves.   [A]

Wednesday, Mrs. Smith and Mr. Standish took 21 students to Maryville High School. We arrived at about 9:15. My guide was a senior, Linda Ladd. She took me to her Drama class which I thought was interesting because we do not have one at Jefferson.

In spite of all the talk of racial problems, I feel that I couldn't have enjoyed myself more with a group of students of my own race, because they really were friendly.

They also took us out to an elementary school, a round building with no walls to divide the rooms and no windows. I feel that this school could be very educational for a student that really tries hard, but could be a problem for some that aren't very educationed.

On the whole, my visit was a good experience, because I think it is very good for students of different races to get together sometimes.   [A]

The Students of Davis, as you know, want to change the name of their school to Martin Luther King High School. Davis students said that when a school student body changes from white to black, then the school should be changed in order for black students to be proud of their race. I, also, believe that this is true.

Mr. Ross, a teacher, raised this question: "How many white schools are named after Negroes?" Naturally, we said none. He asked what would happen if the Board members tried to name Carnegie or James after a famous Negro person. Naturally, we said that the students of either school wouldn't approve having their schools renamed after a Negro because a majority of the students are white. The same situation is at Davis—the majority is Negro. Why must these Black students stick with a White school name?

I feel this is important and must not be overlooked at the next Board meeting.   [A]

Fashion

Do you like the current trend in men's clothing? The pinks, yellows, oranges, purples, limes, and other gaudy silk suits? with shoes to match? I can't hold my peace any longer. Besides costing a fortune, when will they realize that they take away from their masculinity?   **A**

Well I think that mini skirts are "smashing." And mini skirts would look alright on some people but not on a person with no legs hardly or no shape then that would look just terrible. But otherwise a girl would look just fine. And even if a girl looked okay with a mini on she wouldn't look very good in the cold like that I mean, in the snow! Now check that out!   [A]

Dropouts

Lincoln has set down rules for its teachers and students to follow. These rules should be followed.

Boys drop out of school because they meet the wrong people—the ones that shoot dice, drink syrup and sniff glue. After they do all of this they think that they are men and too big to be students again.

The reason for the girls dropping out is pregnancy. I think that when a school sets up rules it should stick to them. But nowadays if a girl knows the right teacher she can get back into school even after having a baby in the middle of the year. I think that this is wrong.

When a girl gets pregnant in the middle of the year and the school puts her out then she should not return. And she certainly should not be allowed to come back to school just in time to graduate.   [A]

Some students say to themselves I don't care if I don't pass. But I tell you this, every student is concerned about passing.

But if they do stay back I can tell you its a hurting feeling. Some time this stops a person. When they feel they got nine or ten years of schooling behind them and in their mind is ambition. But they are not going to pass and so, they *drop out*. So some teachers should realize how they can hurt a person ambition and career. And a student should say to themselves if I want my future to come out right do right.   [A]

School as Preparation

In June, over three hundred Seniors will be graduating. How has education prepared us?

Life isn't just a job! It isn't just money. And it isn't even being a success in the job that you choose. What about life's everyday problems? What about common sense that isn't in books? What about the conflicts that a person feels within himself? The ability to accept the "bitter with the sweet"?

I talked to my classmates, trying to find out how much they thought school had to do with the subject.

They were asked: How has school really prepared you for life—such as getting along with friends, relatives, boy friends and girl friends?

Martha Smith: School in several ways has prepared me, such as getting to school on time, and less absences which are to me most vital in succeeding with a job.

Linda Johnson: I think that High School has not prepared us for everyday life. Some of the teachers have, but the majority have not. But, it has helped as far as getting along with people. Because there are so many different kinds of people in a High School, you get the experience

of knowing them, understanding, and liking the different qualities of people.

Karen Ramsey: School has prepared me for present and future. It has
gotten me ready for finding a job, and for knowing the real meaning of
'getting an education'.

John Green: I came to school to meet people. My life at school and
at home are two different cups of tea.

Deborah Connors: It's a place to come to.   [A]

I think that teachers should not give grades. A person might be smart
in one class and not interested in the others. A person going into the
world as an artist has no need for English, history, and math. He should
be able to choose his classes. Then he would be interested in what he did.
But you know as well as I that this kind of thing will never happen.   A

Knowing about life is knowing how to deal with certain people and
problems, knowing how to socialize, and how to talk your way in and out
of certain situations. But education is much more important than this so-
called knowing-about-life, especially when trying to get a good-paying
job. Take some of the people that think they know about life: they don't
have a good-paying job. Knowing about life won't help pass a test, but
education will. Those people who think it can be done, I'd like to see
it.   [A]

Ideal Schools

Schools of today should be ten stories high with carpeting,
escalators and a place to eat whatever you wanted to eat at lunch. They
should have air conditioners and computers instead of teachers. Buildings
should be circular and very beautiful on the outside and inside. They
should have one side of the building for classrooms, the other for whatever the children want to do with their free periods. Computers should
answer and ask questions. During free periods, students should have
this great big room for playing records, ping pong, bowling, watching
TV, swimming, or doing whatever they want to do. Then, at the end of
the year, after exams, the computer should tell the students if they passed
or didn't pass their courses.   [A]

V

Technology
and
Education

Introduction

Those who doubt that we live in a technologized society haven't awakened from their Rip van Winkle slumbers! Those who doubt that each of our lives is touched by this revolution, perhaps the most pervasive in the history of the planet, must be suffering from an advanced case of leprosy! But there is room for doubt whether technology is a mixed or unmixed blessing. Readers over thirty-five will recall their elementary school geography lessons and the glory which was America for having outstripped the world in every technological statistic imaginable: greatest number of cars, largest production of coal and steel, the hugest this and the tallest that. But we are now in the Age of Ecology. One is not necessarily un-American if he questions the implications of these superlatives for the quality of life in the United States. Now there may even be room for a mature discussion of Friedrich Georg Juenger's *The Failure of Technology*, whose subtitle is "Perfection Without Purpose."[1]

But we are not about to set back the clock, that major instrument of the industrial revolution.[2] The challenge is to develop technology to perfection *with* purpose. The challenge is to evaluate and to apply technology for what it is. There is an inextricable relationship between the rate of social and the rate of technological change; it's *rate* of change that's the new phenomenon in the world. And, though human invention and creativity have long been recognized as amoral phenomena, this old idea meets a new challenge when we attempt to apply moral and social controls, when we attempt to build a technological society which does not stultify but leaves man free for further creativity and invention—pre-1984 style. More vividly, we may ask, how can we develop strontium 90 for the future of man rather than his demise? Or, in pedestrian terms, can we construct an automobile civilization without suffocating ourselves in our own fumes?

William Chase reminds us that we have hardly begun to utilize technology to further the learning matrices in which children have their daily being. Chase, along with Thompson (see below, Epilogue), would challenge us to "put up or shut up" in using technological innovations creatively. And one must also wonder if Americans are psychologically capable of developing the same attitude about public school buildings that they have about private property, namely, a readiness to knock it down when it's no longer functional. If we continue to use obsolete buildings and learning processes, what are the consequences? Do American parents have the guts to apply the demolition ball to schoolhouse walls in order that schools without walls may utilize a total community as a learning gestalt? Can parents tolerate their children's return home, to use learning centers built into their own houses, as Dr. Chase suggests that they may? Or is the thrust to use the school as a baby-sitter so strong that such a return home ironically enough seems like a nightmare? Are we ready and willing to accept on a wide scale other social inventions, such as child care centers, mobile teaching units, perambulating teachers, and other arrangements perhaps beyond our wildest imagination, to take into account the fact that we're closer to 2001 than we are to the medieval setting in which most learning ostensibly occurs today? Are we willing to pay for such social inventions in order to accommodate ourselves to the rate of technological change?

A few years ago I heard a university president become ecstatic about a federal educational program which he had helped design since it featured a five-to-one ratio between the staff and the disadvantaged children it benefited. Paradoxically, the student-teacher ratio on his own campus was climbing rapidly! After his speech I queried, "If the ratio of students and faculty were five-to-one from kindergarten through the Ph.D., do you think we'd need a federal program such as the one you have outlined?" He was obviously miffed, but the point is simple: Americans are *not* committed to education, technologized or nontechnologized, as deeply as human need demands. And as the numbers of students have increased, every effort has been made to find "easy," "inexpensive," "efficient" (pick your word) ways out of a dilemma—often to seem as if something were happening although the means chosen have all the qualities of a gimmicky panacea. And that, too, is a challenge of technology: with pressures of "soft hardware" salesmen almost irresistible, those calling the tune often seem more content with a brass band than a quartet. Since it's easier to see a teaching machine, wall-to-wall carpeting in a classroom, or some other *thing* than it is to understand more subtle learning processes, technology may seem to offer more results than it can deliver. Those concerned with human outcomes cannot stand by quietly if they see a dehumanizing use of human beings.

17

WILLIAM W. CHASE

Technology, Ecology, and the Learning Environment

Something very new and very important is happening. The entire focus on the purpose of school is being revised; forms of initiative and learning rates are being changed to encourage students to discover their own answers. And as the boundaries of man's world expand into outer space, it is only natural to anticipate changes in thought, attitudes, modes of living and occupation, and education. Hence, facilities now on the drawing boards must serve dual purposes; not only must they provide learning environments for today, but they must also be imaginative enough to serve in the year 2000. After all, for the high school teacher starting out next September and teaching until the 21st century, half of the students he will face during that period are not yet born!

Planning educational facilities today for practices not even dreamed of is at best an impossible task. Recent technological developments are being adapted to school needs; there's no denying that. As Basil Castaldi suggests,[1] school planners must prepare themselves for the tasks ahead by asking such critical questions as: Do current trends indicate greater or lesser attention to the individual learner? Do they offer greater emphasis to program enrichment? to self-instruction? to supervised study? to reorganization of learning experiences? to creative use of automated instructional aids? to increased student participation in determining their own learning experiences? Answers to these questions may set some of the patterns for the future.

Education can no longer be regarded as a process with a beginning, middle, and an end. Rather, it is a never-ending pursuit. By 2000 A.D., learning will not be a *part* of life; it will be an essential condition of living. Already traditional institutional autonomy is being replaced by emergency patterns emphasizing interdependence in the expansion and improvement of learning as school officials at every level find ways to coordinate their efforts more effectively. They are learning to relate to federal agencies dealing with health, welfare, housing, and community planning, with business and labor and with such educational resources as museums, libraries, performing arts and educational television agencies formerly on the periphery of the formal teaching and learning processes. We have had no previous experience to prepare us for such interlocking complexities. Industry, state, and education are being woven into a seamless garment. The school is no longer an isolated fortress. Education is everybody's responsibility, and the word for the future is *change*. It may be violent; it may be orderly; but it will surely be technological. It must consider the full gamut of cultural settings, social, political, economic, and psychological.

The concept of enclosing space where students might be instructed, whether the little red schoolhouse (of which 10,000 remain) or the multi-storied building designed a century ago (34,000 still exist), such concepts have to go! Even post World War II structures designed to accommodate a whole array of small group activities, individual and group projects, and greater flexibility in class scheduling are rapidly becoming obsolete. To-day's designs bear little resemblance to those of ten years ago, featuring new arrangements of space for future needs. Such arrangements reflect respect for persons, not the sterile institutional atmosphere of the past. A most important change is the development of a schoolhouse without interior walls, hence eliminating the ticky-tacky boxes tending to sort students into uniform sized groups according to age, grade, and other fixed criteria, a grouping assuming that students could learn at the same pace and way. Opening the classroom box offers the promise of effecting a style which acknowledges that each learner has no peer since learning is, after all, an individual matter. It recognizes individual differences in ability, readiness, and background, and the need for individualized approaches to both teaching and learning. It recognizes the need for an instructional program organized to encourage each pupil to make effective use of all his senses, to use his total environment. Such means go beyond simple reading, writing, and arithmetic to include field trips, work activities, and full use of electronic media.

The permissive architecture of the open school encourages diversity and individuality, inviting release from subjugation to so-called matched groups. In such an atmosphere, ability yields to compatibility. Whoever can work together profitably may do so, the young learning from the older, the slow from the quick, the brighter and more mature from their roles as tutors. Designed for the logistics of learning, the unrestrictive physical environment permits students and teachers to move throughout the schoolhouse in whatever way makes sense, alone or in clusters of 10, 30, or 100 for brief or long periods, with single or large arrays of material. All learners, both students and staff, can organize and reorganize in readily shifting combinations, depending upon requirements.

Probing the planning frontier even further, schools as we know them will evolve so radically that they may completely lose their schoolhouse identity, embodying entirely new concepts. As William D. Firmen, discussing the idea of "School on the Moon," sees it,

> The concept of a school on the moon can be a useful one for educators because it projects beyond the ruins of earlier civilizations, the weathered structures of earlier establishments, the jungles of overlapping jurisdiction, the swamps of tax and debt limitations, the morasses of bureaucracy and special privilege, the walls of unilateral planning and programming and action, the forest of control mechanisms, the mountains of prejudice, and ignorance and resistance to change. . . . It permits the educational planner to work side by side and in harmony with those who will plan to satisfy human needs for food, water, shelter, transportation, security, and human dignity. In short, it permits us to describe the school of the future in terms of first, the goals to be achieved, and second, the arrangements to be created. . . ."[2]

Educators, architects, urbanologists, and other specialists are being forced into hitherto undreamed of togetherness. They must eliminate from their mind's eyes both today's and yesterday's influences in order to perceive futuristic possibilities to develop for man's benefit. They cannot look at a single school building as divorced from a social context. Hence, the individual designer is rapidly giving way to teams of architects, sociologists, economists, transportation and educational specialists, and large-scale environmental planners. And this is only a beginning! By the year 2000 attitudes will be different than they are today. The right to learn will be added to our inalienable rights, learning as experience, as well as preparation. We will move from the dominant stress on the cognitive to greater appreciation for the affective. We will be spending less time acquiring skills and factual knowledge, more developing wisdom and concepts.

How much of this can be accomplished? Electronic equipment including educational television and correspondence courses by TV and radio will be commonplace in homes, stores, and shops. Libraries will be on microfilm and computer linked for rapid retrieval. Programmed learning will be more sophisticated and more readily available. Home developers are already planning houses to include instructional aids, a concept in keeping with a view that learning is a life-long process.

At the more formal level school designs must become part of a comprehensive community program. In keeping with this view, the Board of Education in Pontiac, Michigan, is developing a human resources center that will serve as a focal point for activities designed to improve the life changes for citizens of all ages. It is a wholistic approach, the professional designers considering demographic, economic, land use, and transportation structures through close collaboration with the Board of Education, Area Planning Council, city and country planning agencies, and a wide variety of citizens groups. This center will be more then a school. It will not only offer varied programs to the elementary students of all races in the immediate area, but it will also cater to the widest possible range of ability and interest of the entire community. This means developing auditorium and exhibition facilities, in-service training programs for Pontiac's educators, adult training and retraining programs, community services in health, welfare, and family counseling, preschool and day-care programs, and a variety of civic activities.

This is but one example of a total approach. Others would surely include the Parkway School in Philadelphia where there is no school building per se at al! Rather, there are places in museums, libraries, offices, and shops which are utilized as regular learning spaces. Curricular patterns are independently developed; clocks and calendars have faded into the background. The Pontiac and Philadelphia examples illustrate the need for facilities which coincide more closely with accepted principles of educational psychology than age-old principles of social organization. As Harold S. Gores, President of Educational Facilities Laboratories, suggests, a school is three things: people ideas, and a place—and, in *that* order.[3] The people, of course, are the pupils, the teachers, the parents, and the citizens. And each has his own special function. The learner must have the opportunity to grow. The others must facilitate that growth by the most humane processes possible. If this means that teachers, parents, and citizens must recognize the need for changing roles, for a flexibility hitherto unheard of, for the hardest thinking and planning they have ever known, then so be it. If they have to relearn their psychology, economics, and social dynamics, again, so be it—if they want to humanize the child and not destroy him. And how closely pedagogy, psychology and school design are related may be noted in the following series of if-then-hence statements:

IF . . . THEN . . . HENCE . . .

If a feeling of security and belongingness is crucial to the learning process, **then** school programming must be designed to improve social development through small but distinct units; **hence**, schools require a variety of small spaces for highly specialized activities such as photography, science, radio and television, and social clubs.

If individual differences are as paramount as the rhetoric of two generations suggests, **then** educators must be realistic in designing programs making it *possible* to attend to each student; **hence,** a school must offer a wide variety of learning experiences which may feature teaching machines, the whole spectrum of audio-visual equipment, charts, and models. Also, small workshops and offices are necessary for teachers to offer individual instruction.

If there is a relationship between attention span and learning competence, **then** the curriculum should be geared to this reality; **hence,** building spaces should permit teachers to shift easily from one type of activity to another. This might include easily movable partitions, strategically placed work benches, easily accessible equipment.

If the transfer of learning occurs most effectively when there are similarities between two activities, **then** learning situations should closely resemble real-life situations; **hence,** office practice rooms, shops, and laboratories should be designed to simulate the work-a-day world.

If readiness for learning dictates, as Robert G. Simpson suggests, that "...the child be prepared not only in the mental requisites...but also in the emotional and physical prerequisites,"[4] **then** every means should be used to determine individual readiness and bolster those deficiences where they occur; **hence,** buildings should be designed to accommodate nongraded classrooms in which students can "seek their own levels" or compatibilities.

If we have concern for the anomalous student, **then** develop teaching strategies to accommodate persons on both the gifted and retarded ends of the spectrum; **hence,** buildings must be designed to incorporate special exits, walks, thresholds, elevators and loading zones; also, places are needed for remedial instruction in speech, reading, and physical development.

If fatigue retards learning and we know that such fatigue results from the struggle to overcome psychical, psychological, and pedogogical obstacles, **then** we need to redesign curriculums to reduce boredom, monotony, and poor motivation; **hence,** we must design suitably controlled environments including visual, thermal and accoustical, as well as non-Procrustean furniture in which the chair fits the child rather than the child fitting the chair.

The Computer Challenge

No matter what happens in education, we can be sure that computer technology will make its impact, possibly creating a complete break from present programs. As Kenneth Boulding speculates,

The crucial problem here is whether the development of electronics, automation, cybernation, and the evolutionary process, the implications of which are as yet only barely apparent. The computer is an extension of the human mind in the way that a tool or even an automobile is an extension of the human body. The automobile left practically no human institution unchanged as a result of the increase in human mobility which it permitted. The impact of the computer is likely to be just as great. . . . It seems probable that all existing political and economic institutions will suffer some modifications as a result of this new technology. . . .[5]

In the same vein, William T. Knox of the Office of Science and Technology, Executive Office of the President, Washington, D.C., predicted:

. . .the invention of these new technologies has made it possible, for the first time since the invention of writing, for man to enjoy the best of two modes of communication—the written and the oral modes. He can now almost "talk" with substantial amount of recorded information, manipulate and organize it to serve his purposes, and leave the newly-organized information in the memory for others to use. The impact on United States society of this development will exceed the impact of the automobile.[6]

Other developments doubtlessly affecting the future of American life are the transition from the physical sciences and the extent to which the world will be nationally or globally oriented. In terms of the former, some observers believe that physics is fading as queen of the sciences. For instance, Robert Wood observes that we must realize that the physical sciences will yield the stage to the life sciences as problems evolve from advances in genetics, pharmacology, artificial organs, and medicine.

Other factors that will affect education and facilities include the population explosion, urbanism and metropolitanism, higher per capita income and gross national product, creative federalism, increased leisure time, the knowledge explosion, and housing.

Again, we might ask, "What will education be like in the year 2000 or 2500? Barring such unforeseen "systems" breaks as major wars, atomic catastrophes, and biological transformations, the innovative and experimental activities which enliven American education today should be setting the stage for an even more exciting and fruitful future. According to William Van Til, both the pursuit of knowledge and the pursuit of leisure will be important to students of all ages in 2000.[7] He predicts that homes will come with electronic learning and information centers which will include video communication for both telephone and television, rapid transmission and reception of facsimiles, including news, library materials, and instantaneous mail delivery. Hence, teachers will have to grow every year; no longer may they have one year of experience thirty times! Teachers will come in many roles, secretarial, lecturer, discussant, counselor, technician, evaluator, researcher. A coordinating teacher may be the master drawing upon all material and personnel resources for instructional purposes. Van Til suggests that a third of the coordinating teachers' six-hour workday may be spent supervising student learning of content in existent disciplines and interdisciplines, a third in staff planning, and a third practicing his speciality.

In view of technological pressure and new views of the learner, learning space in the future will be seen in more dynamic terms. As already suggested, it may not even be a school building as we know it. William Caudill suggests that it may be "...a point, the convergence of paths of communication—including telephonic paths, television paths, as well as people paths...a junction at which people and ideas gather and from which people and ideas go out in all directions."[8]

It is important, too, to note that both economic and educational factors lie behind schoolhouse dynamics. We have focused thus far on the needs of the individual. On the other hand, scarcity of land, rising real estate costs, rapidly increasing construction and operational costs, spreading population, all are making the single-purpose, part-time facility economically unfeasible. The Parkway School circumvents the problem even as it contributes to student self-direction; Philadelphia is both the campus and the curriculum. The Satellite School in Rochester, New York, a classroom established on the fourth floor of a department store, features the integration of elementary school learning, shoppers, and everyday living. Although set up as an experiment, it was planned carefully to incorporate all of the aesthetic, acoustic, thermal, and visual properties conductive to an excellent learning environment.

Other approaches are equally as exciting and productive. Davis and Shaver propose several solutions to educational needs, two of which are described here. In the first the objective would be to provide equal educational opportunities in an urban sprawl consisting of widely divergent socio-economic levels and a complete social and ethnic mix. The district would be divided into into subareas each with an area center. Subarea centers would include neighborhood learning nodes and home labs. The nodes would help reduce alienation by accenting the individual by (1) providing a "second family" to relate to; (2) cross culture; (3) cross ethnic; (4) cross race; (5) mixed age levels; (6) creative problem solving. A second level transportation linkage—utilizing busses, helicopters, and the monorail—between the centers would facilitate movement of students, faculty, and resource materials. A communication linkage of all educational facilities, the neighborhood learning nodes and the homes via television and radio would facilitate efficient transmittal of all audio and visual information. Home study units with audio visually equipped carrels would put learning into the neighborhoods to draw the entire community into the educational program.[9] Davis and Shaver also propose a briefing center, a supplemental educational facility linking the many resources of the total community to the school. The center would be a series of small auditorium-like spaces with audiovisual communications, gallery-like spaces for exhibits, and lounge-like space for discussion groups. Its operation would combine city agencies and groups and a professional staff from various disciplines and endeavors to prepare exhibits, organize briefings, and conduct tours. It would be served by a major terminal of the rapid transit system.[10]

The New York City Educational Construction Fund was created under special legislation to carry out a new program of urban development, the construction of elementary and secondary public schools in combined-occupancy buildings. The program is intended to provide new schools in several kinds of settings. In commercial areas, specialized high school programs, such as a co-op program offering experience training together with skills training, could develop the highly skilled graduates which the business community requires. In residential areas, schools and housing in the same structures should foster a more cohesive neighborhood. Other areas scheduled for redevelopment will lend themselves to combinations of facilities such as child care and preschool centers. It will make maximum use of scarce land and at the same time provide income from lease of air rights for construction and operation of the educational facility. Although unique among public school planning programs, private school trustees have several such projects underway.

Other schemes and proposals for meeting space requirements for learning opportunities are many and varied. With the widespread prevalence and use of the automobile, we may soon see educational "service stations" located on convenient drive-up corner lots in individual neighborhoods. The station would be equipped with educational television and other learning aids. Or we may see a series of "drive-in study units" located in neighborhoods or on convenient access roads to expressways similar in structure to drive-in bank facilities. They would be connected to a central education computer bank and include an adjustable remote-control console and video screen. Or imagine a mobile study carrel, controlled by computer and incorporated with a central system to form an important unit of public transportation. While in transit the carrels would run along electrical tracks and require no attention from the occupants once the destination was indicated. Thus, commuting time could be study time since the carrel would be equipped for individual study, data retrieval, thought, and rest. Such vehicles would be controlled by a transit system, forming a new revolutionary step in urban transportation.

In short, educational programs of the future will rely heavily upon technology. Telecommunications devices and systems will make possible an educational system that may preclude classrooms and lecture halls. Such systems can enrich every area of life, since education can take place in home, factory, neighborhood—in fact, *anywhere.*

VI

Futuristic Programs and Views

Introduction

One of the several themes which runs through this book might be summed up thus: the student is *not* product! Strange as it may seem to say this negatively, it does stress the frightfully dehumanizing attitudes and language evolving with American schools. Teachers, principals, superintendents, deans, and college presidents often use the language of industry in referring to persons involved in formal learning processes. Hence the need for more self-awareness of the educator's condition. As Jersild argues, teachers need to "face themselves." As Jourard contends, educators need to see the human enhancement which results from evolving a "transparent self." And the authors included here discuss both the assumptions for developing futuristic programs as well as some of those programs.

The late Abraham Maslow was certainly among the first order of humanistic psychologists. His seminal work in delineating man's "peak experience" is notable not only for its nonpathological characteristics but also because it constitutes a springboard for man's hope. Those impressed by Professor Maslow's insights relating artistic, educational, and peak experiences may wish to follow up his challenge to the positivist, behavioral, and objectivist psychologists, for are there not profound implications in various ways of discovering oneself? Or you may wish to ask yourself one of Professor Maslow's most fruitful questions, "What was the most ecstatic moment of *your* life?" and how do such moments relate to other moments, before or after, up or down, over, across, and beyond? Then, too, a question which may have both logical and existential answers: Could all living be peak experiencing? And do you agree with Maslow's view of classical music vis-à-vis rock? Could it be that he (literally!) never felt the vibrations? If, as Maslow suggests, the future is now, what does this do to the work ethic?

Robert Theobald has had much to say about that question. At a poverty symposium I once heard him respond to Leon Keyserling's demand for full employment with a suggestion that we needed full *unemployment*. He may have been joking, for the published version of the conference in question "clarified" his view, distinguishing between his discontent over full employment and his positive attitude toward work—so long as people work at tasks they deem worthwhile. He then went on to advocate the guaranteed income as a way of making such a condition possible.[1] In the essay which follows, he and his colleague, Noel McInnis, point out the crippling impact of education as preparation, the categorical necessity for perceiving and working for the impossible, the need for meandering dialogue and "goofing-off" time to permit creativity, the imperative need for treasuring uncertainty and ambiguity. But readers who remain skeptical may still wish to ask why it's so difficult to unlearn facts, why the curious kindergartener becomes the cynical college senior, why students wish to escape from freedom, and why the assumptions which Theobald and McInnis hold, seemingly so relevant in coming to grips with the issues of our times, are not more widely held—AND *acted upon!*

But it is pleasant to report that these assumptions are the foundation for the kind of learning setting which Judson Jerome discusses in his essay; his "ideal college" has become reality in Columbia, Maryland. These ideas are operative in some of the free universities which Ralph Keyes considers below.

And yet questions remain. Even when Jerome's "shoulds," "mights," and "coulds" are translated into action at Antioch-Columbia (Baltimore-Washington), one must ask how long it will be before such a program becomes more widely adopted. Is such a system replicable for the tens of thousands of students who enroll at the Universities of California, the Ohio States and the Wisconsins? Will alternative forms and modes of education, to be discovered in the small colleges (some hanging on by the skin of their financial teeth), in the cluster college concept at Santa Cruz or Buffalo (SUNY), in the University Without Walls associated with the Union for Experimenting Colleges and Universities, gain currency when funds are so short and commitment so low?[2] Will the "new breed of teacher," one who perceives himself as midwife-catalyst-facilitator-friend rather than fact-dispenser-authority-specialist (see Chapter 7), be "found" or educated in sufficient quantity to constitute the critical mass to turn American education around at every level? Are most Americans psychologically prepared to make the total commitment to dismantling educational institutions as easily as they take down the last generation's skyscrapers or industrial complexes when they are no longer functional? Are they prepared for the implementation of a view that learning may occur anywhere and be legitimized and credentialed when students are "without teachers,"[3] libraries, books, other generally accepted forms which normally spell "education"?

The critical nature of such questions is well illustrated by Ralph Keyes' piece on the free universities. When students and faculties setting up new institutions tend to adopt the same learning modes (classrooms, lectures, syllabuses, etc.) as those characterizing the institutions from which they revolt, is it to be expected that laymen will understand the subtle importance of evolving a curriculum, for instance, whose major thrust may be to evolve curricular processes? If the free university maintains the posture and self-image of being a counterculture, should those involved in running the new forms expect their ideas to be to be wholeheartedly adopted? Or does the free university constitute such a vital and viable example of an alternative that it will be disregarded only at the expense of further campus rioting, alienation, and contempt? Or is it merely a minor safety valve for those participating in it? Will they—*can they* overcome the criticisms of both their proponents and opponents, avoiding both hemophilia and hardening of the arteries! Are you as convinced as Keyes that learners in the free universities will drag the unfree institutions "kicking and screaming along with them"? And if not that, what?

18

ABRAHAM MASLOW

Education, Art, and Peak Experiences

Something big is happening. It's happening to everything that concerns human beings. Everything the human being generates is involved, and certainly education is involved. A new *Weltanschauung* is in the process of being developed, a new *Zeitgeist*, a new set of values and a new way of finding them—certainly a new image of man. There is a new kind of psychology, presently called the humanistic, existential, third-force psychology, which at this transitional moment is certainly different in many important ways from the Freudian and behavioristic psychologies, the two great comprehensive, dominating psychologies.

There are new conceptions of interpersonal relationships. There is a new image of society. There is a new conception of the goals of society, of all the social institutions, and of all the social sciences, which are a part of society. There is a new economics, a new conception of politics, revolutions in religion, in science, in work. There is a newer conception of education that I will mention because it forms the background for my ideas about music and creativity.

First, most psychologies of learning are beside the point—that is, beside the "humanistic" point. Most teachers and books present learning as the acquisition of associations, of skills and capacities that are *external*

This article appeared, in a slightly different form, as "Music Education and Peak Experience," in Music Educators' Journal, **54**, No. 6 (1968), 72–75, 163–71. *Copyright © Music Educators' Journal, February 1968. Reprinted with permission.*

and not *intrinsic* to the human character, to the human personality, to the person himself. Picking up coins or keys or possessions or something of the sort is like picking up reinforcements and conditioned reflexes that are, in a certain, very profound sense, expendable. It does not really matter if one has a conditioned reflex; if I salivate to the sound of a buzzer and then this extinguishes, nothing has happened to me; I have lost nothing of any consequence whatever. We might almost say that these extensive books on the psychology of learning are of no consequence, at least to the human center, to the human soul, to the human essence.

Generated by this new humanistic philosophy is also a new conception of learning, teaching, and education. Such a concept holds that the goal of education—the human goal, the humanistic goal—is ultimately the "self-actualization" of a person, the development of the fullest height that the human species or a particular individual can come to. In a less technical way, it is helping the person to become the best that he is able to become. Such a goal involves very serious shifts in learning strategies. Associative learning is certainly useful, for learning things that are of no real consequence, or for learning techniques which are interchangeable. And many of the things we must learn are like that. If one needs to memorize the vocabulary of another language, he would learn it by sheer rote memory. Here the laws of association can be a help. Or if one wants to learn automatic habits in driving, responding to a red signal light or something of the sort, then conditioning is of consequence. It is important and useful, especially in a technological society. But in terms of becoming a better person, of self-development, self-fulfillment, or "becoming fully human," the greatest learning experiences are very different.

In my life, such experiences have been far more important than listening, memorizing and organizing data for formal courses. More important for me have been such experiences as having a child. Our first baby changed me as a psychologist. It made the behaviorism I had been so enthusiastic about look so foolish that I could not stomach it any more. It was impossible. Having a second baby, and learning how profoundly different people are even before birth, made it impossible for me to think in terms of the kind of learning psychology in which one can teach anybody anything. Or the John B. Watson theory of, "Give me two babies and I will make one into this and one into the other." It is as if he never had any children. We know only too well that a parent cannot make his children into anything. Children make themselves into something. The best we can do and frequently the most effect we can have is by serving as something to react against if the child presses too hard.

Another profound learning experience that I value far more highly than any particular course or any degree was my personal psychoanalysis: discovering my own identity, my own self. Another basic experience—

far more important—was getting married, certainly more instructive than my Ph.D. If one thinks in terms of the developing of the kinds of wisdom, understanding, and life skills that we would want, then he must think of what I call *intrinsic* education—*intrinsic* learning; that is, learning to be a human being in general, and second, learning to be *this* particular human being. I am now very busily occupied in trying to catch up with all the epiphenomena of this notion. Our conventional education looks mighty sick. Once you start thinking in terms of becoming a good human being, and then ask about your high school courses—"How did trigonometry help me to become a better human being?"and echo answers, "By gosh, it didn't!" In a certain sense, trigonometry was for me a waste of time. My early music education was also unsuccessful because it taught a child who had a profound feeling for music and a great love for the piano *not* to learn it. My piano teacher taught me in effect that music is something to stay away from. And I had to relearn music as an adult, all by myself.

I am talking about ends. This is a revolutionary repudiation of nineteenth-century science and contemporary professional philosophy, which is essentially a technology and not a philosophy of ends. I reject thereby, as theories of human nature, positivism, behaviorism, and objectivism. I reject thereby the whole model of science and all its works derived from the historical accident that science began with the study of nonpersonal, nonhuman things, which in fact had no ends. The development of physics, astronomy, mechanics, and chemistry was in fact impossible until they had become value-free, value-neutral, so that pure descriptiveness was now possible. The great mistake that we are now learning about is that this model, developed from the study of objects and of things, has been illegitimately used for the study of human beings. It is a terrible technique. It has not worked.

Most of the psychology on this positivistic, objectivistic, associationistic, value-free, value-neutral model of science, as it piles up like a coral reef of small facts about this and that, is certainly not false, but merely trivial. But I do not want to sell my own science short; rather, we do know a great deal about things that *do* matter to the human being. But I would maintain that what has mattered most has been learned mainly by nonphysicalistic techniques, by the humanistic science of which we have become more conscious.

In speaking of the world situation at the opening ceremonies of a Lincoln Center Festival, Archibald MacLeish said in part:

> What is wrong is not the great discoveries of science—
> information is always better than ignorance, no matter what
> information or what ignorance. What is wrong is the belief
> behind the information, the belief that information will
> change the world. It won't. Information without human

understanding is like an answer without its question—meaningless And human understanding is only possible through the arts. It is the work of art that creates the human perspective in which information turns to truth.

In a certain sense I disagree with MacLeish, although I can understand why he said this. What he is talking about is information *short of this new revolution*, short of the humanistic psychologies, short of the conceptions of the sciences that not only repudiate the notion of being value-free and value-neutral, but actually assume as an obligation, as a duty, the necessity for discovery of values—the empirical discovery, demonstration, and verification of the values that are inherent in human nature itself. This work is now busily going on.

What Mr. MacLeish said was appropriate for the 1920s. It is appropriate today if one doesn't know about the new psychologies. "And human understanding is only possible through the arts." That *was* true. Fortunately, it is no longer true. It now is possible to gather *information* that can contribute to human understanding, that carries imbedded within it value hints, vectorial and directional information, information that goes someplace instead of just inertly lying there like flapjacks.

"It is the work of art that creates the human perspective in which information turns to truth." I deny that, and we had better argue about it. We must have some criteria for distinguishing good art from bad art. They do not yet exist in the realms of art criticism so far as I know. They are *beginning* to exist, and I would like to leave one hint, an empirical hint. A possibility is beginning to emerge that we would have some objective criteria for discriminating good art from bad art. At the moment we seem to be in complete and total confusion of values in the arts. In music, just try to prove something about the virtues of John Cage as against Beethoven. In painting and architecture similar confusion is present. We have no shared values anymore. I don't bother to read music criticism. It is useless to me. So is art criticism, which I have also given up reading. Book reviews I frequently find useless. Chaos and anarchy of standards reign. When Archibald MacLeish says that works of art lead to the truth, he is thinking about particular works of art that Archibald MacLeish picks out. But would his son agree? And then, MacLeish really has nothing much to say. This may be why I feel that we are at a turning point. We are moving around the corner. Something new is happening. There are discernible differences, and these are not differences in taste or arbitrary values. These are empirical discoveries. They are new things that are being found, and from these are generated all sorts of propositions about values and education.

One is the discovery that the human being *has higher needs*, that he has instinct-like needs which are a part of his biological equipment, the need to be dignified, to be respected, to be free for self-development. The discovery of higher needs carries with it all sorts of revolutionary implications.

Secondly, in the social sciences, many are discovering that the physicalistic, mechanistic model was a mistake, leading us—to where? To atom bombs. To a beautiful technology of killing, as in the concentration camps. To Eichmann. An Eichmann cannot be refuted with a positivistic philosophy or science. He just cannot; and he never got it until the moment he died. He didn't know what was wrong. As far as he was concerned, nothing was wrong; he had done a good job. He *did* do a good job, if you forget about ends and values. I point out that professional science and professional philosophy are dedicated to the proposition of forgetting about values, excluding them. This, therefore, must lead to Eichmanns, to atom bombs, and to who knows what! The tendency to separate good style or talent from content and ends can lead to this kind of danger.

We can now add to the great discoveries Freud made. His one big mistake, which we are correcting now, is that he thought of the unconscious merely as undesirable evil. But unconsciousness also carries in it the roots of creativeness, of joy, of happiness, of goodness, of its own ethics and values. There is a healthy unconscious as well as an unhealthy one. And the new psychologies are studying this at full tilt. The existential psychiatrists and psychotherapists are putting it into practice. New kinds of therapies are being practiced.

So we have a good conscious and a bad conscious, a good unconscious and a bad unconscious. Furthemore, the good is real, in a non-Freudian sense. Freud was committed by his own positivism, having come out of a physicalistic, chemicalistic science. He was a neurologist. And a sworn oath called for a project to develop a psychology that could be reduced to physical and chemical statements. This is what he dedicated himself to, though he himself disproved his point!

And about this higher nature that I claim we have discovered, the question is, how do we explain it? The Freudian explanation has been reductive. Explain it away. If I am a kind man, this is a reaction formation against my rage to kill. Somehow, here the killing is more basic than the kindness. And the kindness is a way of trying to cover up, repress, and defend myself against realizing the fact that I am truly a murderer. If I am generous, this is a reaction formation against stinginess. I am really stingy inside. This is a very peculiar thing. Somehow there is a begging of the question that is now so obvious. Why did he not say, for instance, that maybe killing people was a reaction formation against loving them? It is just as legitimate a conclusion and, as a matter of fact, more true for many people.

But to return to this exciting new development in science. I have a very strong sense of being in the middle of a historical wave. One hundred and fifty years from now, what will the historians say about this age? What was really important? What was going? What was finished? My belief is that much of what makes the headlines is finished, and the growing tip of mankind is what is now developing and will flourish in a hundred or two hundred years, if we manage to endure. Historians will be talking about this movement as the sweep of history; that here, as Whitehead pointed out, when you get a new model, a new paradigm, a new way of perceiving, new definitions of the old words, suddenly you have an illumination, an insight. You see things in a different way.

One consequence generated by what I have been talking about is a flat denial, an *empirical* denial (not pious, or arbitrary, or a priori, or wishful) of the Freudian contention of a necessary, intrinsic, built-in opposition between the needs of the individual and the needs of society and civilization. It just is not so. We now know something about how to set up the conditions in which the needs of the individual become synergetic with, not opposed to, the needs of society, and in which they both work to the same ends.

Another empirical statement is about peak experiences. We have made studies of peak experiences by asking groups of people and individuals such questions as, "What was the most ecstatic moment of your life?" Or, "Have you experienced transcendent ecstasy?" One might think that in a general population, such questions might get only blank stares, but there were many answers. Apparently, the transcendent ecstasies had been kept private because there are few if any ways of speaking about them in public. They are sort of embarrassing, shameful, not "scientific," which many believe is the ultimate sin. But we found many trippers to set them off. Almost everybody seems to have peak experiences, or ecstasies. The question might be asked in terms of the single, most joyous, happiest, most blissful moment of your whole life. You might ask questions of the kind I asked. How did you feel different about yourself at that time? How did the world look different? What did you feel like? What were your impulses? How did you change if you did? I want to report that the two easiest ways of getting peak experiences (in terms of simple statistics in empirical reports) are through music and through sex. I will push aside sex education, as such discussions are premature— although I am certain that one day we will not giggle over it, but will take it quite seriously and teach children that like music, like love, like insight, like a beautiful meadow, like a cute baby, or whatever, that there are many paths to heaven, and sex is one of them, and music is one of them. These happen to be the easiest ones, the most widespread, and the easiest to understand.

For our purposes in identifying and studying peak experiences, we can say it is justified to make a list of these kinds of triggers. The list gets so long that it becomes necessary to make generalizations. It looks as if any experience of real excellence, of real perfection, of any moving toward the perfect justice or toward perfect values tends to produce a peak experience. Not always. But this is the generalization I would make for the many kinds of things that we have concentrated on. Remember, I am talking here as a scientist. This doesn't sound like scientific talk, but this is a new kind of science. We know that from this humanistic science has come one of the real childbearing improvements since Adam and Eve, natural childbirth, a potent source of peak experiences. We know just how to encourage peak experiences, how women can have children in such a fashion as to have a great and mystical experience, a religious experience if you wish—an illumination, a revelation, an insight. That is what they call it in the interviews—simply to become a different kind of person because there ensues what I have called "the cognition of being."

We must make a new vocabulary for all these untilled, unworked problems. "Cognition of being" really means the cognition that Plato and Socrates were talking about; almost, you could say, a technology of happiness, of pure excellence, pure truth, pure goodness, and so on. Well, why *not* a technology of joy, of happiness? I must add that this is the only known technique for inducing peak experiences in fathers. It occurred to us in the first surveys of college students that, while women talked about peak experiences from having children, men didn't. Now we have a way to teach men also to have peak experiences from childbirth. This means being changed, seeing things differently, living in a different world, having different cognitions, moving toward living happily ever after.

Let's proceed to music in this relation. So far, peak experiences are reported only from what we might call "classical music." I have not found a peak experience from John Cage or from an Andy Warhol movie, from abstract expressionistic kind of painting, or the like. I just haven't. The peak experiences that were reported as the great joy, the ecstasy, the visions of another world or another level of living, have come from the great classics. This melts over, fuses into dancing or rhythm. So far as this realm of research is concerned, there really isn't much difference between them; they melt into each other. Music as a path to peak experiences includes dancing. For me they have already melted together. The rhythmic experience, even the very simple rhythmic experience—the good dancing of a rumba, or the kinds of things that the kids can do with drums: I don't know whether you want to call that music, dancing, rhythm, athletics, or something else. The love for, awareness of, and reverence of the body—these clearly good paths to peak experiences. They in turn are good paths (not guaranteed, but statistically likely) to the "cognition of being," to the perceiving of the Platonic essences, the intrinsic values, the ultimate values of being, which in turn is a therapeutic-like help toward both the curing-of-sicknesses kind of therapy and also the growth toward full humanness.

In other words, peak experiences often have consequences, very important consequences. Music and art can do the same; there is a certain overlap. They can do the same there as psychotherapy, if one keeps his goals right, knows just what he is about and is conscious of what he is going toward. We can certainly talk, on the one hand, of the breaking up of symptoms, like the breaking up of clichés, anxieties, and the like; or we can talk about the development of spontaneity, courage, Olympian or God-like humor, sensory awareness, body awareness, and the like.

Far from least, music and rhythm and dancing are excellent ways of moving toward the discovering of identity. Such triggers tend to do all kinds of things to our autonomic nervous systems, endocrine glands, feelings, and emotions. It just does. We do not know enough about physiology to understand why it does. But it does, and these are unmistakable experiences. It is a little like pain, which is also an unmistakable experience. In experientially empty people, including a tragically large proportion of the population, people who do not know what is going on inside themselves and who live by clocks, schedules, rules, laws, hints from the neighbors—other-directed people—this is a way of discovering what the self is like. There are signals from inside, there are voices that yell out, "By gosh this is good, don't ever doubt it!" This is a path we use to teach self-actualization and the discovery of self. The discovery of identity comes via the impulse voices, via the ability to listen to your own guts and what is going on inside of you. This is also an experimental kind of education that may eventually lead us into another parallel educational establishment, another *kind* of school.

Mathematics can be just as beautiful, just as peak producing as music; of course, there are mathematics teachers who have devoted themselves to preventing this. I had no glimpse of mathematics as a study in aesthetics until I was thirty years old, until I read some books about it. So can history or anthropology (in the sense of learning another culture), social anthropology, paleontology, or the study of science. Here again I want to talk data. If one works with great creators, great scientists, the creative scientists, *that* is the way they talk. The picture of the scientist must change—the image of the scientist as one who never smiles, who bleeds embalming fluid rather than blood. Such conceptions must yield to an understanding of the creative scientist, and the creative scientist lives by peak experiences. He lives for the moments of glory when a problem solves itself, when suddenly through a microscope he gets a new perception, a moment of revelation, of illumination, insight, understanding, ecstasy. These are vital for him. Scientists are very shy and embarrassed about this. They refuse to talk about it in public. It takes a delicate kind of midwifery to extract them, but I have gotten them out. They are there, and if one manages to convince a creative scientist that he is not going to be laughed at for these things, then he will blushingly admit the fact of having a high emotional experience from the moment in which the crucial correlation turns out right. They just don't talk about it. As for the usual textbook on how you do science, it is total nonsense.

My point is that if we are conscious enough of what we are doing and are philosophical enough in the insightful sense too, we may be able to use those experiences that most easily produce ecstasies, that most easily produce revelations, experiences, illumination, bliss and rapture. We may be able to use them as models by which to reevaluate history teaching or any other kind of teaching.

Finally, the impression that I want to try to work out—and I would certainly suggest that this is a problem for everyone involved in arts education—is that effective education in music, art, dancing and rhythm is intrinsically far closer than the usual "core curriculum" to intrinsic education of the kind I am talking about, of learning one's identity as an essential part of education. If education doesn't do that, it is useless. Education is learning to grow, learning what to grow toward, learning what is good and bad, learning what is desirable and undesirable, learning what to choose and what not to choose. In this realm of intrinsic learning, intrinsic teaching, and intrinsic education, I think that the arts are so close to our psychological and biological core, so close to this identity, this biological identity, that rather than think of these courses as a sort of whipped cream or luxury, they must become basic experiences in education. This kind of education can be a glimpse into the infinite, into ultimate values. This intrinsic education may very well have art education, music education, and dancing education as its core. It could very well serve as the model, the means by which we might rescue the rest of the school curriculum from the value-free, value-neutral, goal-less meaninglessness into which it has fallen.

19

ROBERT THEOBALD / NOEL McINNIS

A Certain Education
for an Uncertain Time

The world of the future will not be our world. It will be created by young people who know how to live in a new environment. I [Theobald] once talked about this with a young colleague, and he quite correctly saw that I have considerably more problems than he does in working within this world, although I think he would probably agree that I understand it better. But I understand it intellectually and he understands it emotionally. He understands it because he already lives in it! Thus, within this framework I challenge those of us who are older to be willing to work for something we may dislike, to accept things they cannot understand, and to start a process, the conclusion of which is uncertain and probably undesirable to many of us. This must be said because I believe that common humanity, love, honesty, responsibility, and humility are going to be very difficult for many of us to accept. We were not reared on such qualities!

The possible is irrelevant, so it is only worth trying for the impossible. This is why education is crucial! For it is the task of the educational system to make the impossible *appear* relevant. Thus the educational act and the political act are exactly the same.

The guaranteed income is a prime example of what I mean. Several years ago, I brought out a book, *Free Men and Free Markets*, in which

A reconstruction of the last two chapters of Robert Theobald, et al., An Alternative Future for America *(Chicago: Swallow Press, 1968). Reprinted by permission.*

I proposed the guaranteed income. Everyone agreed that it was a ridiculous idea, except for two or three people who said that it was very prescient—but unfortunately this would not be realized. In the intervening years, the guaranteed income has become a prime option open to this country. And not in the normal way; there have been no pressure groups, no people putting vast resources into pushing this idea—just a few people going round and round the country indigenizing the issue. It is only since the issue became "accepted" that pressure groups have formed around it.

A Major Problem . . . or Crisis

It is in the field of education that impossible actions are perhaps most difficult. Few educators have yet caught up with the fact that the patterns of the past, in which it was assumed that the old knew what the young must learn, is no longer valid. So long as the speed of change was relatively slow, this was a valid assumption. Entire societies were structured around a prestige structure, a knowledge structure, in which the old perpetuated knowledge through the young. But the enormous speed of change in our time, brought on by the cybernetic revolution, necessitates a total change in this structure. We can no longer assume that simply because somebody has been studying an issue all of his life, he knows it best. The fact that someone understands a discipline is not necessarily very helpful. This becomes particularly distressing when the systems are tightest as, for example, is a grading system which forces the regurgitation of existing factual knowledge.

We are presently doing several questionable things. We continue to perpetuate a most pernicious assumption; namely, that education is "preparation for life" when it becomes increasingly clear that education as life-preparation becomes, in fact, the postponement or in many instances the crippling of life. We continue to teach young people to respect authority at a time when authority is no longer possible, and when *we ought to be struggling together* to understand our world. We still say, *listen and learn* rather than *strive with us*. The dangerous pattern runs right through our educational system from kindergarten through graduate school, from trustee to faculty member.

We teach children to believe that questions are closed and soluble rather than teaching them to live with the uncertainty inherent in real life. If one cuts knowledge into sufficiently small strips, one can achieve certainty; this is the trick that economics brought off, for economics managed to reduce men to "economic men." We then discovered, not unexpectedly, that if men *were* economic men, the society would operate in a certain closed way. But men are not economic men. Therefore, the conclusions of existing economic theorizing are similar in relevance to the conclusions of chess—both are very interesting intellectual exercises but have no necessary relationships to the real world. Economics is dangerous when individuals apply the results presently achieved by the discipline to the real world. So long as it remains an intellectual game, its real problem is the intellectual waste it engenders. Whereas some believe that our society's greatest problem is that of wasting individuals on military exercises, I believe our greatest problem is the waste involved in irrelevant, intellectual exercises.

We also teach children individual facts and relationships rather than gestalts. And although we do not yet know how to teach gestalts, Marshall McLuhan makes it clear that we must learn quickly. The individual fact, the individual relationship cannot be valid at electronic speeds of communication.

In effect, we are "producing" people who are only capable of giving answers to already structured problems—inferior computers. It is at this point that the "black box" issue arises. To what extent can computers and teaching machines in general be used in the educational process? Computer technology, at the present time, is only capable of passing on facts and structured relationships. We should surely have learned by now that there is nothing more difficult to *unlearn* than facts. It is rather like a city: once you put the first road through the middle of it, if the road is in the wrong location it is very difficult to plan rationally. In much the same way, once you have begun to teach a child a set of patterns, he will retain them, or at least they will be extraordinarily difficult to *unlearn*.

This raises the issue of propaganda manipulation. How much propaganda manipulation does a child need and how much can he learn for himself? Although I have no adequate answers to this, I suggest that he needs much less at all ages that we are presently throwing at him. The child's capacity to learn for himself is infinitely greater than we are willing to admit—at all ages. Thus we face the problem that both the school and the university, which are built around the concept of passing on structured knowledge, are irrelevant and obsolete. In most schools, a teacher stands in front and students sit in neatly ordered rows. I would suggest to school principals and college presidents everywhere that they could improve their systems more by throwing out classroom desks and laying carpets on the floors than by any other single action open to them at low cost.

Consider the small child. He has a tremendous natural capacity to learn and is learning constantly as long as meaningful experience is available to him. But unfortunately our educational system often extinguishes this spontaneous joyful enthusiasm for learning. Formal education converts the learning process into a burden. Learning becomes toil, under an especially pernicious form of child labor. It is especially pernicious because in the education factories from which child labor laws do not protect our youth, injury and damage are not the result of having to process raw material. It is the result of their *being processed* as raw material. Now, assembly-line procedures are fine for converting inanimate raw materials into standardized products, but they succeed only because the initial raw material is itself standardized. We are no more prepared to accept differentiated raw material in the educational process than was Procrustes prepared to accept guests of different sizes at his inn in Ancient Greece. Some students come to us with knowledge which does not conform to our data, so we promptly cut them down to size. Others come with insufficient background to manipulate our data, so we shove it in all the harder. Most who pass through our classes are thus standardized to the specifications of *our* data. But I am convinced that the assembly-line model of education is inefficient, dehumanizing, dishonest, and just plain stupid. It is inefficient because most of the data are either never learned or shortly forgotten. It is dehumanizing because it reduces both teacher and students to a mechanical process of manipulating external signs and symbols which seldom are made relevant to the living experience of either party. It is dishonest because it encourages teachers to be deceptive about their objectives, lest too many students achieve them; also it similarly encourages students to be deceptive with one another, lest it be discovered that they either do or do not have the data most likely to be helpful at exam time. This became apparent to me [McInnis] during my first semester of teaching. When I sat down to make a final exam and found it necessary to consult both lectures and readings, I found myself asking, "If I can't remember enough data to *give* an exam, why should I expect my students to remember enough data to *take* one?"

Possibilities for Change

So the question remains: Is change possible? A great deal of evidence suggests a negative answer to this question. Having tried to change primary, secondary, and college education, I have a good deal of sympathy for those who claim that the educational establishment is virtually unyielding to fundamental change, in fact, more difficult to move than a cemetery!

Let me indicate why this is so. First, a professor sees the preservation of his discipline as his prime motivation. This is his intellectual capital, his way of earning a decent living until retirement; and unless he is very energetic, he is not about to let anyone destroy the disciplines as *the* relevant way of communicating knowledge. What about the student? The student really does not desire change either. He has been reared to adjust to a system of unfreedom. Having been taught to value protective structures, he is deeply suspicious of, and incapable of dealing with, the freedom essential to creative thinking. I [Theobald] have visited colleges and said to students, "I am now your president *pro tem* and am willing to offer you four years of studying what you want to study. No grades; no required courses. Of course, as a *quid pro quo*, the teachers do not have to teach any of you unless you can convince them that you want to learn. I will give you a week to decide whether you would like such a system. And I will guarantee that the degree you get when you leave this college will be worth as much as any other degree." Unfortunately, most students don't want that kind of freedom.

But suppose we attempt to change the system. What if we tried to produce an educational system designed to develop each individual's uniqueness? Let's look at some of the elements necessary for such a system—a system made possible because cybernation relieves us of inhuman toil. First, we must find ways to stop the fragmentation of knowledge, and find for both child and adult an environment in which they can discover reality from their own experience. We must recognize that lashing and bribing children into action are equally immoral. Both the carrot and the whip are immoral! Neither are motivators; they are simply different ways of ensuring that *my* motivation is put onto an "object"— the other person. We must help people find out what *they* want to do. Sidney Hartzburg points out that there is no difference between the bribe or the lash; they are both instrumental techniques for manipulating people. In the school setting a major answer to this problem, of course, is the abolition of grades and required courses.

We must also use the new technologies to contribute to the humanization of teaching and the elimination of regurgitative techniques. This is a much more important issue than some realize. The big industrial corporations which want to market large quantities of hardware and software are selling computer learning-systems—systems designed for structured, programmed education—and unless educators forcefully remind the corporations that such systems represent bad education, we will be unable to reverse this pattern.

A Fresh Start

What we need most urgently in this country is a top-level group of people to sit down today, tomorrow, and the next day, perpetually if necessary, to examine the true meaning of education in a cybernated era. What do we mean by the process of socialization for a world in which toil is unnecessary? This is totally different from the approach we normally follow. We normally ask: What can we do now? What we can do now is very small; and what we can do now without a clear-cut goal as to what we want is even less. We want very few educators on this top-level panel; and of these, fewer still who have national names. Such a group should abandon the assumption that the school and the university are necessarily valid structures and look at what can be done to give true, lifelong education to everyone. The group should not start by examining where we are now and then consider how much can be realistically achieved. Rather, it should first look for the ideal and then examine how we can bridge the gap between the present actuality and the ideal. I repeat, the possible is irrelevant, so it is only worth trying for the impossible.

It is obvious, of course, that even if we knew the ideal, we could not achieve it immediately. Let me, therefore, suggest certain policies and procedures which would contribute substantially toward starting us toward a better educational system. First, *all* colleges and universities could reduce the number of required academic hours or credits by some 40 percent and actually improve the learning climate. Already this is happening in some institutions, as a consequence of student pressure, because the students know that with five courses in an ordinary semester they can't do much thinking. Indeed, the points-credits-hours system could not be better designed to ensure that the students do not think. Obviously, with the 40 percent out, there would be a certain amount of "goofing off." I delight at the thought. I can't think of anything better. I do not mean this simply because we should give both students and graduates an opportunity to enjoy time off; we all need that. We must provide unstructured time because the only thing we really know about creativity is that it *happens* when you are "goofing off," when your brain is "playing" rather than working. While you may learn to be creative under pressure, I am quite convinced that it is not the first step. The first step is to allow your brain to start being creative, and that requires time off.

Next, we might introduce an intelligent first-year curriculum, one encouraging the student to benefit from his college education, recognizing that the high school does not presently do this. A freshman needs to know three things: he needs to know how to think, he needs to be able to art (i.e., create), and he needs to discover the nature of the world in which he lives (i.e., that which is worth thinking and creating about). Hence, his first course would be in logic and take the place of freshman English, because thinking comes before writing. Students do not know how to think because they have never been taught. American textbooks on logic would be unsuitable for such a course because they treat logic as a discipline and not as a practical way to help a person learn how to think. He needs to confront a body of data which needs analysis, structure, interpretation, and evluation in order that he experience those processes.

We might also introduce a course in social reality. This could be a three-week-cycle course introduced during the first week by a first-rate film and a first-rate person. The person introducing such a course would speak not in terms of how the discipline is structured, but about what problems are being posed by the development of the discipline. In biology, for example, one could ask: What does the statement, "The gene chain can be manipulated," mean? The students could then be placed under the leadership of upperclassmen for two weeks to talk about these issues on the basis of other data prepared specifically to sharpen awareness of social reality. With a shift in topic every three weeks and a focus on the way in which his own assumptions invent his reality and the reality of his fellows, he should have a better idea of what the world is like by the end of the first year. There is a fascinating balance here between the two suggested courses: Logic is a course that is "taught" by someone and in which one must really understand; the course in social reality is a course in which one learns to be creative in a rather nonstructured way. A third course might bring art, music, and humanities out of the museum, auditorium, and library into the live-a-day world; after all, the media revolution *is* relevant; TV, the paperback revolution, movies, and youth music have made their effect; youth have broken loose from their cultural smothering and are restoring contact with the realities of touch, smell, sight, and sound.

We must also move from competitive grading to cooperative grading. As stated earlier, I would like to abolish all grades, but we are not prepared to do this wholesale—yet. But if we adopted cooperative grading instead of stating, in effect, "It is good for you to kick other students in the teeth. Above all, do not help them because they may get above you on the curve," we should say, "We will grade the whole class at the same level. If you have a bad member of your class, a weak member, and you do not help him, you all will suffer." In this way we might create a system whereby the dynamic of the class is that of building itself into an alternative system wherein cooperation becomes a prime value.

We should recognize that the student at school and in the university is working just as relevantly as the person in the factory or the office. This is related to the guaranteed income, although it is not exactly the same issue. It speaks to the question of how we might more profitably use the billions we saved if we eliminated those armaments which, paradoxically enough, reduce rather than increase our security. In my opinion, students have a right to a substantial amount of it.

Finally, and most importantly, we need to challenge what Gregory Bateson calls "third levels of learning" or theories about how the world works. Do people react instrumentally? Is it a Pavlovian world? Is it a Skinnerian world? The strange thing, as Bateson points out, is that if an individual believes that it is any one of these, the world will "kindly" oblige and behave in the way he expects it to behave. Further, it is also true that individuals will react as you expect them to in terms of whether you expect them to be hateful or loving. In other words, if you believe that everyone in the world is hateful, you will act in such a way that individuals will oblige by hating you. If you behave, on the whole, as if individuals are loving and responsible, they will, in general, respond that way.

How can third-level propositions about the nature of the world be challenged? We need dialogue, true dialogue. Dialogue has become a fad of school, church, and government. But what they usually mean by dialogue is, only too often: "Let us talk together until we agree with the person in authority." This is not dialogue. This is debate and discussion under a new propaganda name. True dialogue is unstructured, open, and it leads nobody-knows-where. It is based on a study of problems rather than of disciplines, of gestalts rather than partial knowledge; on a recognition that authoritarian relationships cannot exist in real education; and that faculty, students, and citizens must cooperate in the development of new knowledge. The result of this is that adults have to become humble—a difficult thing—and students have to become responsible, which is equally difficult. Dialogue requires at least a minimum of love and trust. Without these elements, individuals talk only from their heads. I have tried to begin dialogue on campuses and found it a difficult experience. In general, people don't want to talk. We are willing to make statements *at* each other, but are not willing to enter into dialogue. For unless we are convinced that others will not use our remarks against us, we are unwilling to talk openly. Thus it is impossible to maintain an authoritarian structure and at the same time create dialogue; the two are mutually exclusive.

I am aware that dialogue is disruptive and dangerous. This is so because it leads from minimum love and trust to maximum love and trust, to the creation of a viable community. And when one creates a viable community, he may have the proverbial tiger by the tail. Such community proceeds ravenously through all administrative structures. It says that individuals are human beings, not numbers, and cannot be treated as numbers. If dialogue is started on campuses, campuses will change. Nice tidy administrative lines become irrelevant. We have to find a way to work a community through cooperation, through leadership that initiates and helps growth rather than through an administrator who uses authority. This is difficult and implies great risks.

Open-ended dialogue can lead to who-knows-where; the impossible and the uncertain become relevant. Educators and students accepting such initiative and responsibility for developing their own learning conditions will discover that *they* are *the reality*.[1]

20

RALPH KEYES

Freeing the University

The Phenomenon

The educational arm of the counterculture is, of course, the free university. Since Berkeley/64 and under a variety of headings, free university, antiuniversity, alternate university, experimental college, counterinstitutions have sprouted and folded like converts at a revival meeting.

A free university can have no general definition since each is unique. Most of them have been started by students at existing institutions of higher learning to join together students, faculty, resource people, and community members in the study of topics not normally available in the curriculum. Typically, such courses federate Marx, Mao, and Marcuse with Hesse, Alan Watts, and Bill Schutz, and sometimes a dash of Immanuel Velkovsky or Henry George. No accurate tabulation has been made of their number, a task probably impossible since they rise and fall so quickly, though educational reform monitors at the National Student Association estimate that between 300 and 500 free universities currently live. A poorly publicized free university conference held in Lawrenceville, Kansas, in the fall of 1968, drew 250 participants from about sixty counterinstitutions.

The original free universities grew out of civil rights "Freedom Schools" and Vietnam teach-ins. These early efforts, cropping up in New York, Berkeley, Chicago, Detroit, and Los Angeles in 1965, tended to be more militant than free. Observer-participant Harvey Wheeler of the

202

Center for the Study of Democratic Institutions expressed concern at the time about their "suffocating Marxist commitment."[1] SDS picked up the idea, and soon universities like Michigan, Texas, Colorado, Ohio State, Florida, and Wisconsin became nervous hosts to "counteruniversity" squatters.

But an interesting evolution began to occur in the academic fifth columns. If free university founders were often Left ideologues, many of the teachers and most of the students usually proved more interested in teaching and learning in a freer atmosphere. Typically, the radical founders of free universities set up their courses to study power elites, imperialism, cane-cutting, and whatever; then threw open the doors for all to come and be saved. Invariably, the radical courses were quickly overshadowed by others in astrology, yoga, card-playing, weaving, and the like. And more often than not, newly formed free universities attracted much greater numbers of students than they expected, most of whom chose the groovy over the correct.

The Meaning

What does it all mean? It is common for officials of conventional institutions to debunk their educational parasites as only a step above sandboxes, just as it is common for free university founders to announce the imminent demise of their hosts. Both are wrong.

In and of themselves, the hundreds of free universities our country has known in the past decade can hardly be termed a flaming success. Typically, after an initial burst of enthusiasm, their enrollment nosedives, courses are killed off, student organizers and administrators tire. For all the talk of finding new and better ways to teach and administrate, lectures and bureaucracy have proved embarrassingly common in these attempted laboratories.

Harold Taylor has called the free university "essentially conservative in its educational philosophy...and...as an offshoot of the regular university [it] stays with the tradition of the academy, meeting classes, holding lectures and discussions, and differing from conventional curricula only in its subject matter and choice of teachers."[2]

The charge is only partially valid. Anyone observing the encounter-yoga-I Ching-touchy-feely-dope-crazed-get-in-touch-with-your-feelings sessions which are common at free universities could hardly conclude that all of their pedagogy is conventional. But too much is, particularly at those with hard-revolution orientations. When Mark Rudd calls for "radicalized" education, he is less concerned with finding new ways of teaching-learning than that "the truth" be taught rigorously. New York's Alternate U began with courses on "Marxist Economics," "Black Power Housing," "The Mimeograph as a Revolutionary Tool," "Life in Hanoi,"

"The Assassinations of Kennedy and King," "The Stock Market," and "Art as a Revolutionary Tool."

But the attempt to blend political with cultural revolution is increasingly common to the free universities, particularly on the West Coast. There, says Jan McClain, 22-year-old founder of the Experimental College at the University of California in Davis, "In order to survive you must be political."[3] He and his colleagues worked hard at courting "the right people" within the university, sponsored a rent strike in town and unsuccessfully ran four students for city council. San Francisco State's Experimental College, the largest early effort which had a strong touchy-feely orientation at the outset, became much more politicized before and during the 1969 strike and went down after the conflict. Palo Alto's huge Midpeninsula Free University has since its inception taken an activist role within the community—publishing an underground paper, winning a federal court case against the city's use of public land, and working on rent strikes. At the same time, Midpeninsula remains a hotbed of arts and crafts, psychodrama, mysticism, and candle-making (literally).

In territory less responsive to such ways, the free university has been used as a tool for awakening consciousness. "We have tried to use the 'college' as a tool to acquaint these people with the issues of educational and university reform," says founder Bill Moody of the New Alabama Experimental College and its mostly "straight" enrollees. Moody, 23, and his wife had to drop out of the University of Alabama to handle the 500-plus students who overwhelmed their first offering in 1968. The courses offered ranged from the highly academic like "New Economics" and "Social Issues" to sensitivity workshops and one on motorcycling. Though Moody concedes that most registrants were mainly curious, he says that through the College "we now have many students who have made commitments to change the system here who still consider themselves 'good, southern boys and girls' and who still honor the past and continue to go to their fraternity and sorority parties."[4]

Today, the educational arm of counterculture, as with so much else, is dribbling down to the high school level. "Free schools" are now common in parts of Canada as well as California and Great Neck, Long Island. There a student-organized and administration-condoned Free School not only offers high school students the usual countercourses on film, street theatre, puppetry, Yiddish, and sensitivity, but also has set out to evaluate the regular faculty and offer draft counseling. The latter effort has run into stiff community-school resistance.

An Evaluation

What is the meaning of the free universities? As could be expected, the typical academic responds, "Not much." President John R.

Everett of yesterday's counterinstitution, the New School for Social Research, doubts that they have any serious academic purpose. Samuel B. Gould, formerly Chancellor of the State University of New York, while anticipating the influence of free universities on conventional curriculums, worried early in their inception that, "It's not enough to get together and discuss ideas and be stimulated. . . . There has to be some form of discipline in all education."[5]

Within the academic value system, this response is correct. Free universities hardly meet academic standards of rigor, discipline, pomposity, and bibliographies. Even sympathetic faculty, faculty who have risked their colleagues' ire to take or teach an alternate course, tend to feel uncomfortable with the bull session quality of it all. "The faculty couldn't really get into a free bag," says Moody of their experience. He also feels that their most successful courses have been taught by students because the faculty "have a hard time loosening up, getting away from the feeling that they have to get things done."[6]

Get things done.

And it's not just the stuffies who are skeptical. *Newsweek* Education Editor, Peter Janssen, has called the movement "too small to change institutions," and feels it has had "little more than minor impact on most established schools."[7]

Again, this position would be hard to contest within the usual educational perspective.

But is that the correct perspective?

It may be that the normal academic-bureaucratic standards are not the correct ones by which to judge the free universities. Such standards stress caution, deliberation, rigor, the "long-range view of things." But it is precisely these values that the counterculture is challenging. Whether the free universities survive for a decade and get a grant is not only not pertinent but also impertinent to the new style. More important is the question of whether it is a good trip for those aboard while it floats. How many people grow how much, not how many facts are assimilated.

Secondly, I think the hundreds of free universities that have lived and died in the past few years have had an intangible but enormous effect on the various revolutions at work in this country. Typically, the free university joins political radicals, cultural radicals, and straight students with faculty members and townies. Also, it often becomes a center of extra-educational activity. In places like Seattle, Palo Alto, Manhattan (Kansas), and most other locations, the local Free U is a clearing house for a great variety of countercultural activity.

Finally, I suspect that the impact free universities have had on teaching-learning styles in the unfree university can never be calculated. In some instances, however, a direct relationship is evident. The University of Pennsylvania started noncredit seminars on "relevant" topics soon after their Free University opened shop. Dartmouth started a faculty committee to develop more experimental opportunities in the curriculum which the Dean of Students called "directly related to the success of the [student-organized] experimental college."[8] Jan McClain and Bill Moody both say their universities have used them as a laboratory to test courses before incorporating them into the regular curriculum.

If nothing else, the free university is profoundly free market education, and not a bad gauge of consumer taste. No one enrolls in anything evcept by choice. Attendance cannot be enforced. The topic and teaching must attract and hold an audience. Deadwood is constantly being shaken out of the curriculum.

The reforms typical in higher education today—pass-fail, "relevant" course topics, more seminars, field work for credit, a broader pool of faculty—all of these things are typical of the free university style. It would be impossible to attribute the reform directly to their insurgence, but who would be so bold as to deny any correlation?

In the history of American higher education, the extracurricular has a proud history. The "side shows," wrote President Woodrow Wilson of Princeton over half a century ago, "have swallowed up the circus, and those who perform in the main tent must often whistle for their audience, discouraged and humiliated."[9]

While the sideshows normally were not too cerebral, this has not always been the case. In his book, *The Amerioan College and University*, Frederick Rudolph documents the degree to which mid-nineteenth-century student literary and debating societies became the intellectual hub of the sterile university of the time. "When the students were finished they had planted beside the curriculum an extracurriculum of such dimensions that in time there would develop generations of college students who would not see the curriculum for the extracurriculum. . . .[10]

And Rudolph argues that these early educational parasites revolutionized their host as well. "In a sense," he writes, "these nineteenth-century collegians, in taking charge of themselves, took charge of the American college and shaped it according to their wishes. . . and what is remarkably instructive about what they did is how much more effective they were than the would-be reformers in the ranks of the presidents and the professors."[11]

Perhaps it is the fate of American higher education to flow from periods of congruence with its students' needs to periods of incongruence, when the learners themselves protest with their feet, dragging the institution kicking and screaming along with them.

The consumer revolution need not be limited to supermarkets.

21

JUDSON JEROME

Toward an Ideal College

I

When the Rouse Corporation, developers of a planned city that is emerging at Columbia, Maryland, invited Antioch College to suggest a plan for a college, a number of us—Antioch faculty and students—began to dream. A loosely formed committee met; we aired our dissatisfactions with available educational institutions and our notions of how they might be changed. But this essay is by no means a committee report. It represents purely my own thoughts about what is presently wrong with colleges and how an educational facility at Columbia (I hesitate to call it a college—and certainly refrain from calling it "liberal arts") avoids them.

I will start with discontents, what I call the four diseases of American education today: compartmentalism, sequentialism, essentialism, and credentialism. This is a process of clearing the field, undermining many of the assumptions we bring to education as preparation for building anew.

(a) Compartmentalism—the notion that knowledge can be sorted and filed in areas, departments, disciplines, and courses: The model of education is that of the bottling works, filling each container, stamping on a cap. Scholars or scientists accumulate and verify data, sorting it into appropriate pigeonholes. They become experts regarding the contents

This article was originally published in The Humanist, **29,** *No. 2 (1969), 10–12, 19. Reprinted by permission.*

of their particular pigeonhole. Education is a kind of training or programming: A student is "exposed" to the contents of various pigeonholes. Each expert stresses the worth of his own field. Both the experts and the students become fragmented. Integration of knowledge and experience is left to the uncertain processes of the individual nervous system.

Today students are talking about "getting themselves together." We are recognizing, finally, that the integrative process requires conscious attention—and may, indeed, be the central educational need. That is, instead of thinking of education as systematic exposure to a variety of specialties, we should think of it as active integration of specialties. Instead of worrying about acquiring knowledge, we must think of using it—and acquiring more when there is a clear and definite need. I do not mean exclusively a "vocational" need—though I believe it is time we got over our snobbery about vocational education. Basically I mean the need of every man to have his own life make sense to him, to find some coherency in his human experience.

The hope of filling each citizen's head with at least a sampling of the important fields of knowledge is a vain one at best in this era of knowledge explosion. Before the invention of banks each man stored his own wealth—and carried much of it on his back. In Samuel Pepys's diary, at the time of the great London fire of 1666, the private burgher was much concerned about his "plate," literally silver plates and utensils that represented his savings and that had to be buried in the garden before he fled his burning house. In those days much of a man's wealth went into his garments—and he sometimes walked the streets wearing several layers of wool simply because that was the simplest and safest way of guarding his holdings. Today all a man needs is a pocket to carry his credit card; so fluid have our economic processes become that even the checkbook is out-of-date.

In education we still proceed as though the individual head were the best bank—and we carry our layers of resources around with us, even to bed. If we thought of education as learning to use knowledge rather than getting it, if we concerned ourselves with developing ready access to the world bank, if we measured people less by what they knew than by what they could do, we might free them, permit them to get themselves together—and we might begin to solve some of the problems that beset our culture.

Compartmentalism is passive; it receives without digesting. Even computers sometimes break down from a kind of psychosis called "information overload." We are systematically clogging minds with discrete bits of information and leaving it to the students to discover if and where these bits may be converted into active functions in their lives. We are like secretaries who believe problems disappear if one knows where to file them. Our cabinets bulge—and we founder in a polluted world, not knowing how to use what we know. This comes from our habit of emphasizing "content" in education, of regarding our job as educators as one of putting things into people rather than one of evoking what they know and are and what they are capable of becoming..

(b) *Sequentialism*—the notion that there is, if we could only find it, one right linear order in which things can best be learned or done: The myth is that in each compartment of knowledge there are "fundamentals," that step one must precede step two. Our language is shot through with notions of levels, progression, advancement, and often these terms reflect no reality other than our own conditioning.

I believe that sequentialism has something to do with habit, as well as our desire that others suffer what we have suffered, that they pay their dues. It is not unlike the indignation one used to hear from middle-class people who saw forests of television aerials over ghettos or Negroes driving Cadillacs. Men who once carried spears are now flying jets in Africa. Like it or not, we must accept the fact that there are short cuts to industrialization, that nations build atomic weapons without having taken all our required courses, just as we must accept the fact that young people emerge from their media-choked homes with more information and more life experience (albeit vicarious) than many of us have in middle age. There are thousands of routes to learning, and the young are swarming into the modern world like the throngs that stormed the Winter Palace. It is pathetic to think of some teacher telling students that they cannot go on until they have passed Algebra I.

We need—and are learning how to achieve—instant fluency in languages, instant industrialization, instant alteration of ancient cultural patterns. One of the most interesting developments is the proliferation of various kinds of encounter groups, achieving instant intimacy, instant honesty, perhaps instant friendship, instant courtship. Everywhere we are seeing more evidence of quantum leaps in our cluture that seem to belie the need we have always assumed of intervening steps, of continuity. And we hardly know how to live in the simultaneity that is appearing. Riots break out in China, New York, and Rome as though they had more to do with phases of the moon than what we have assumed to be social causes and effects. Perhaps the species is developing some more sophisticated kind of communication that bypasses words—such as that which enables a cloud of gnats to maintain flight formation over the evening water. Waves of information, gestalt perception, leaps, conversion, "vibes"—these terms are appearing everywhere as we struggle to comprehend our present experience and to liberate ourselves from the sequential modes in which we were trained.

(c) *Essentialism*—the notion that we can decide (as members of a community, as parents, as educators, as elders) what is "essential" that a person know: Compulsory education, required courses, general education—all these educational formulations are based on the essentialist premise that the tribe defines the initiation rites. All served some useful social function in the past, but it is becoming clear today that they are elitist, conformist, and unrealistic. One wonders whether literacy, which has long served as an index of civilization, can be defended as essential for citizenship in a world where such vast proportions of critical communication do not require reading and writing. When we add to literacy the strange variety of other skills and areas of knowledge that we have argued a person should master before being granted a diploma, the absurdity of our design becomes apparent. If we forgot about the number of units of world history, foreign language, mathematics, driver training, sex education, use of mass media, and computer programming, we might more nearly approximate the essential areas of education of the average citizen. If we add to that list urban affairs, race conflict, the military-industrial complex, the uses of atomic power, and a few other such subjects, we could perhaps prepare citizens to read *Look* magazine. But I am not suggesting that we bring essentialism up to date. Above all we should see the futility of the effort to define what is basic, the cultural bias that lies behind most of our concepts of essential education, and— with mass education—the deadening effect of standardization in textbooks, course structures, sequences—the classroom conformity and depersonalization in the name of objectivity and standards. Essentialism is a doctrine of programming, of conditioning citizens to the regulations of mass society. Once we thought of it in terms of the need for an educated electorate in a democracy. Now I think it is becoming evident that it produces not independent thinkers but zombies, the "good" student being the one who attends, performs on schedule, learns what is taught, and does not rock the boat with questions about what lies beyond the curriculum. .

(*d*) *Credentialism*—the notion that we can meaningfully certify things about people, about what they can do and what they know: This myth leads directly to the authority hangup—the disastrous confusion between authority as special knowledge and authority as power. Our system is now a complex of authorizations on the basis of credentials—and the credentials are, for the most part, either bogus or trivial.

What do we mean when we label someone? I am a poet. That sentence may mean that I have written and published poetry—something that can be verified—but to express that better I might say I *was* a poet. Whether I *am* a poet and will be one tomorrow remains to be seen each time I roll paper into the typewriter with the intention of writing a poem. "I am a Ph.D." is a much less meaningful statement. It gives you no assurance that there is anything in particular that I know or can do (except, probably, read and write English). Yet the statement is accepted as much more factual than "I am a poet," and it gives me tremendous influence over the lives of people. It gives me the authority to prescribe what they will do and to punish them, if I choose, for what they think.

Credentialism works into our minds and filters through our structures like cancer. Degree requirements are its most concrete manifestation. Compulsion and education are as contradictory as compulsion and love, yet most of our educational activity is conducted by means of the dynamics of compulsion. Credentials lure people into easing demands on themselves: If they have the document and have met the standards, they are largely relieved of the necessity of growing and doing, of proving themselves in each engagement, of questioning their own authenticity, of justifying their demands on others. And yet we stack our diplomas together like a house of cards that becomes magically transformed into a prison. Students are locked into their seats by our diplomas when there are no other chains. Why do they not rebel more furiously than they have? Because they want diplomas. It is a game invented for Parker Brothers by Franz Kafka. Compartmentalism, sequentialism, essentialism, and credentialism—these constitute the antilife in our system, the slow replacement, molecule by molecule, of organic tissue by solid rock.

II

If, then, one had a clean slate on which to diagram a new system, how would he begin? I believe that an educational institution primarily for young adults (old enough to be free from parental custody, young enough to be unencumbered with dependents) has a twin mission: to enable people to free themselves from their miseducation in the past and to enable them to develop ability for self-determination and survival in the only available world. On the horizon, like the glow of dawn, is the possibility that our institution might enable them to achieve more than that—what progressive educators are calling ecstasy. But it is probably much too soon to expect an institution in our society to stipulate ecstasy as an educational aim.

We need to create the opportunity for young adults to get, as one student put it, "un-hungup." Patterns of dependency, conformity, misdirected rebelliousness, and self-hatred have already been ingrained. And our problem is compounded by the fact that there is no sure way to "teach" people to be independent, self-directed, self-fulfilling. All we can do is provide the setting and support that may enable this transformation to take place.

I believe it would be a great mistake for a college to relinquish its parietal function, for we know that most education on campuses takes place in peer relationships and in the living situation as significantly opposed to the classroom. I would be tempted to say that living in college residences ought to be required, except that I believe nothing should be required. And the residences provided by the college should be almost the opposite of the dormitories traditionally provided: They should encourage interaction between the sexes and provide settings of privacy, informality, and great personal choice in life style. They should encourage some sense of community with others, be small enough so that the residents know one another well, large enough so that no one is trapped by too limited a set of relationships. Though it is important that young adults learn to relate successfully to their own age group, it is also important that there be some vertical range in the ages of people with whom they live: Children and older adults should be part of the community.

I am thinking of complexes of apartments housing no more than about a hundred individuals in each complex. Most apartments would be for two or three people, but some would be for one person, others for larger groups such as families. Housing should not be assigned but chosen—and available on the same basis to students and faculty. Each complex should have common rooms, a small auditorium, green space, and recreational facilities. Each apartment should be connected by closed circuit systems to the information and resources centers of the college.

Some faculty in each complex should have, as their primary educational responsibility, the charge of fostering the use of the living environment for learning. They should sponsor group activities, help people with similar interests get together, bring in resources (i.e., visitors, programs, exhibits, books) that are relevant to the learning needs of the residents. Their role is consciously therapeutic: They strive to create the conditions under which people can be liberated from their mental obstacles to learning. It should be understood that students will spend a great deal of time, as much time as needed, in the residential setting and the activities associated with it. This is no less a legitimate part of their education than time spent in the institutes, on jobs, or in other learning situations. In fact, because of society's tendency to think otherwise, some special emphasis upon the validity and necessity of residential or environmental education may be necessary. The residence is home, and home is, in large part, the center of our lives. "Leisure" is a pejorative word today, but in the future that may be the principal business of many of us. It is important that we be able to conduct ourselves well alone, in free time, and in intimate relationships with others.

But it is premature to gear ourselves for a society of leisure. Truly independent people are those who are freed not merely to do what they like but those who are in some sense self-supporting. "Self-supporting" means, of course, deriving support from others in some mutual relationship; the individual avails himself of the services of others by serving them. In that context of mutual dependency, freedom is possible only to the extent that the individual has as wide a range as possible of competencies, so that he may choose the ways in which he will serve and so that he can choose the services of others that will enable him to pursue his purposes. At the very least, a person who has been to this college should be able to cope—to perform real tasks in the world, to support himself not because he has a diploma but because he has developed marketable, effective skills. In this respect liberal-arts colleges are usually deficient because of basically elitist orientation that disdains application.

Therefore, as an alternative to departmental structure, the chief organizational units of the college should be problem-oriented institutes in such areas as race and poverty, communications, education, human development, urban studies, arts and society, and pollution. Though institutes suggest specialization and compartmentalism, each would, in fact, address a cross-section of human problems, and the institutes would be forced to rely on one another for information, ideas, and energy in attacking practical issues. As social problems change, the problems addressed by the institutes would continually change, requiring new personnel, new foci of interest.

Each institute would have three components: research, application, and education. Unlike departments, institutes can seek funds for their programs and broker their services for actual social needs. The programs they undertake in research and application should be designed in ways that permit the easy absorption of unskilled and unlearned students into their tasks. That is, "undergraduates" should be able to learn by participation even at the expense of some inefficiency in the operations.

In addition to the institutes, the college would make educational use of other functioning organizations in the community (i.e., factories, theaters, schools, publishing plants, churches), and it might, in fact, manage some such organizations, staffing them chiefly with students. That is, the college would conceive of itself primarily as an agency to get students into situations in which they can learn, to facilitate their learning there, and to provide the resources for study in greater depth than regular employees, scholars, or researchers are likely to discover. Because students would move fluidly from one institute or organization to another, have the stimulation of an enriched living and learning environment and free time to explore, think, and study, they would acquire not only the skills necessary to perform tasks but the perspective to see those tasks in relationship to the whole complex of social needs and their personal needs.

For most of the work students do in the institutes or on jobs in organizations, they should be paid—at a rate that would enable them to subsist in the college without outside support. Perhaps it would be possible—and desirable—to standardize the rate of pay throughout the system, so that a student "earns" as much working in a theater or reading philosophy as on a job in a biochemical laboratory or in business. Moreover, it might be advisable to handle this "salary" in such a way that no money changes hands, but the salary is applied to residential costs by a transfer on the books. It may be educationally advisable to insist that he *not* receive support directly from his parents or other outside sources. Rather, his parents might be encouraged to donate to the institution as a whole and therefore indirectly increase the rate of remuneration to all students.

One of the faculty in the student's residential complex would serve as his adviser, a guide to the array of educational possibilities in the college as a whole. He might study independently, work in one or more of the institutes, take a part-time job in one of the cooperating organizations, engage in projects or study ventures with other students or resident faculty—in short use the enriched environment in whatever way seems most relevant to his intellectual and personal growth. Movement of people among available learning slots in the institutes and on jobs would be coordinated by a computerized reservation system such as is used by motels and airlines. Dossiers of recommendations could be accumulated by the students or by a central office; letters collected there from supervisors would testify to the exact nature and quality of the student's performance in various areas of work or study, and these would be the student's chief demonstration to graduate schools or employers of the content of his education. Standardized examinations would be available, administered by the college at the student's request, if he chose to collect that kind of data about himself for the information of others.

Since at the present time the social demand for degrees is so great that a person is handicapped without one, and since there should be no penalty on a person who educates himself at this college rather than another, a process would be established for granting a degree, though no student is compelled to become a degree candidate. Such a degree program would have a residential stipulation (i.e., a minimum of three years of full-time participation in the college program). The student himself should define his objectives, the means by which he seeks to achieve them, and the evidence he wishes to submit of accomplishment. A staff or faculty committee would advise him in the formation of his plans, review his achievements, and write a descriptive paragraph to appear on the individual degree that indicates the student's aims, his accomplishments, and the committee's judgment as to their quality. Thus the degree would mean no more nor less than it said on its face—and one might hope that in time even this degree would wither away.

Thus the institution would consist of overlapping networks—of residences designed for educational purposes and of opportunities for direct engagements with real problems in the world. The units in the network (the residential complexes, the institutes) would be as autonomous as possible in governance, budgeting, formation and pursuit of goals. Since the networks would be compounded of modular units, they can be infinitely expanded, the size of the college being a reflection of what the traffic will bear. The central administration would be an agency, a device for enabling education to occur. It would operate central learning resources centers, recreational facilities, public relations, recruitment, and admissions and other such college-wide functions. It would initiate institutes and residential units, decide when these should be phased out or replaced, and help find appropriate staff.

To those who think of education as doing things to other people's minds these flexible networks will not sound like a college at all. "Why, that is just living," one person responded when I revealed my educational design. This is true—just living, in an environment in which there is a conscious effort to remove barriers to learning and growth, in which the machines have plastic housing to reveal their working parts, in which the individual is nurtured like a plant rather than conditioned to a maze (as a mouse might be by electric shocks). The aims of this college would be to develop originality, independence, competence in coping, to release human potential. That is a vision of excellence that sounds very strange in our present educational world.

VII

Personal
Humanism
in Action

Introduction

In a society as violent as ours, where so many human "contacts" are means to ends, mere transactions, where men, women, and children are often like the proverbial ships passing in the night, it is, indeed, radical to be human. Worst of all, being human creates credibility gaps. Surely, there is a tendency for people so used to be "taken," "conned," "screwed," "fucked over" (choose your own metaphor), and a tendency to inquire, "Is he for real?" if he comes across genuinely.

This is not to suggest that billions of human touches are not real. No doubt, they are. But their transmission and translation into the public realm almost by nature of the transmission distorts them. This is the existential dilemma. This is what so many encounter or T-group situations are designed to overcome. And this is why the ecstasy of the flower people cannot be discounted as a cultural aberration; it's a cultural reaction. This is why the hippy or youth countercultures, insofar as they remain nonviolent and sensitive, are evidences of radical humanism.

People who are open, sensitive, genuinely friendly, must face the flak if they begin to talk about what it is they're about, where their heads are. This may not produce less talk, but it may drive these types to haiku, the construction of Japanese gardens, other oriental practices such as Zen; after all, if the major result of self-revelation within conventional western contexts is to take abuse, then why *say* much about one's own radical humanism. Few see the use of taking such abuse.

How difficult it is to get public figures to "open up" is well illustrated by the difficulty *humanist* editors have experienced in getting well-known persons to write for a series, "How I Live." Human vulnerability is more palatable as fiction than reality.

Neither of the articles in this section are total "true confessions." At best they are mere shadows of reality on the cave walls. My own article is a most impressionistic approach to the tens of thousands of hours I have talked with students, not as a perambulating encyclopedia, not as a psychiatrist or professional counselor, not as much more than friend—although the student-teacher relationship was the basic one. I have tried to raise a host of questions which sensitive teachers must ask: What is the price of *not* listening with the third and fourth ear? To what extent and under what conditions does the teacher become a hypocrite? If a student flunks, who is the victim, the student or the teacher who may be a party to a grading process in which he has no confidence? When can a teacher "let go," not stand in the student's light? If his institution would kill the student, who is responsible? How much do we know about the learning processes from first-hand experiences? What kind of risks must both teacher and student take if they are to communicate on the same wavelength or within a similar gestalt? In short, some of the basic questions which Ben Thompson raises in the Epilogue.

Kaare Bolgen asks similar questions, but does it more beautifully. He demonstrates an incredible phenomenon. For rare is the adult who can see and hear like a child, feel like a child, think like a child. And rarer still the adult who will take the time, the energy, and insight to identify with children whom physicians, psychiatrists, teachers, and parents have given up. Such a person is Kaare Bolgen, educator, psychologist, poet, musician, concert violinist, and friend of children. Here he gives us a view of the inner relationships he has had with six of the many children with whom he has worked, not only discussing some of the fundamental assumptions serving as his working hypotheses, but more importantly revealing the application of his painstaking techniques for literally reconstructing human beings from would-be vegetables. Largely unsung for his efforts as a unique educator, he reflects a rare humanism in action.

Shortage of space precludes the richness of detail which I hope he will someday include in a full-length book—if for no other reason than to establish the fact that most "hopeless" children *can* be helped if adults determine that they *will* be. Having heard Kaare Bolgen discuss some of these individuals for hours at a time, I know how much he has sacrificed to telescope his insights and make them public (although fictitious names are used here to preserve the anonymity of the specific children).

22

KAARE BOLGEN

There Are No Hopeless Children

The Children

When the doorbell rang, Ralph and his mother were waiting, hand in hand. His mother told him to be a good boy and remember everything I told him. Ralph looked down at her, muttered something in a barely audible voice, and entered. Once inside, he stood blindly, silently. I asked him into my study. He followed obediently. I joked with him and outlined our work. Finally he whispered hesitantly, "Do I have to study Dick and Jane?"

Ralph was sixteen, six feet tall, handsome, and used a vocabulary of a six year old, but without the fluency of that age group. Every word seemed painful. His knowledge of the world was that of a first grader. He knew, for example, that there were cities, but had no concepts of states, nations, or society. His memory was nonfunctional. He could not remember a new word or sentence for one minute. Naturally he could neither read nor write. He was so timid that he dared not leave the house without his mother. He had lived for five years at a famous psychological clinic. Not sufficiently "disturbed" to require hospitalization, he was returned to his parents and a private psychiatrist. A hopeless case?

Donald had been a sickly child. Rheumatic fever kept him out of the

This article was originally published in The Humanist, **30**, *No. 4 (1970), 14–22. Reprinted by permission.*

first and second grades. At third grade age, he began school—in third grade. The next year, he was back in bed. Then he went to a parochial boarding school. Here he spent years in and out of classrooms, alternating work in the kitchen with hospital beds. At fifteen he was sent home, a hopeless case, a nonlearner in a hazy, unreal world consisting of a few people with whom he was in immediate contact and a vague landscape of two-dimensional nature flashing by him on his way to schools and hospitals, three-dimensional only when it expanded into the security of his own room. When I first saw him, he was back in bed, empty-eyed in an empty room, occasionally staring without comprehension at a couple of comic books.

Peter belonged to the group classified loosely as "brain-damaged" children. When I began to work with him, in his second year of school, he had gone through all the special help available, the entire gamut of testing and psychological measuring, and had come out of it fairly untouched, one way or the other. His small coordination was on an infantile level. He could not even grasp a pencil. His large movements were better, but his walk was jerky and uncontrolled. His eyes were largely unfocused, his speech clumsy and of elementary vocabulary. He could not read, write, draw, or partake in any natural activities of children his age. He could walk to school, that was about all. Hopeless?

Andy was classified as a moron. He could sit for hours staring straight ahead. In school he did exactly that. No matter what task his teacher pushed him into, soon she found him gazing into space. Like a toy, he could be wound up to go through some simple mechanical motions. But his spring was very weak. Soon he would run down and again stare at nothing. He was a second grader when I began working with him.

Roger almost died at birth and he had been on the verge of dying ever since. His early years had been a continuous succession of doctors and hospitals. An impressive string of leading specialists had examined him, treated him, and given him up. At five, his physical development was that of a child of three, and in one year he had not grown a fraction of an inch. His weight remained unchanged for almost a year. His voice, completely uncontrolled, had the deep texture of a boy entering adolescence. His skin had the yellow tint of a mongoloid. He had difficulties in eating, and his food intake was absurdly inadequate. In all the treatments, massive doses of vitamins, minerals, and protein supplements had never been given. He could walk, but otherwise his control and general coordination was on a poor three year old level. At five, he would soon be expected to begin kindergarten, and beyond loomed school. His mother was in a panic and hired me to work with him. Hopeless?

Nancy was sweet and pliable. Although she seemed intelligent, she did poorly in school. In the third grade, she still could not read, and at the mention of numbers, she would freeze and her mind go blank—visibly. Always cooperative, her cooperation invariably ended in failure. At our first interview, the locus of her problem was instantly clear—she looked out at the world with eyes filled with stark fear.

Some Problems

In working with such children I have tried to keep in mind the platitude that each has a unique personality and unique problems. But these six children loosely represent five types or groupings of children with problems that I have helped, or tried to help. They also represent types that are frequently met with, chiseled, hammered, and shoved into channels of development moving toward failure, failures as children and failures as adults. Educators are aware that these problems exist. Departments of special aids are growing like Topsy. The best institutions have experts in psychological guidance, classes for the "brain-damaged," the "retarded," and the "reading problems," in short accepting the educational responsibility for the less gifted and less fortunate. Yet, the problems of society, community, family, nation, and civilized world are also growing. As the facilities to aid "problem children" expand, the number of "problem children" increases at perhaps an even greater rate. It is a serious question whether the facilities will ever catch up with the need.

But no matter how closely problems follow certain patterns, the child himself is always unique. There simply is no way of putting Ralph, Donald, Peter, Andy, Roger, and Nancy into a class to work with them as a group. This does not mean, however, that it would be impossible to put $Ralph_1$, $Ralph_2$, $Ralph_3$, etc., into a room with a teacher and expect desirable and meaningful results. It means that there may be a number of Ralph-like children, a number of Rogers, etc.

Since such classifications are loose but perhaps helpful generalizations, Ralph could be said to represent the children who escaped, victims of the schizoid character of our time. Donald stands for the shockingly large percentage of children who as victims of illnesses receive a poor start in life. Peter is the representative of the "brain-damaged" ones, the results of careless, outdated medical practices, sometimes unavoidable accidents, natal or prenatal. Andy represents the group of children who are prematurely and often quite superficially and incorrectly assigned a low I.Q. Roger is a member of a rarer group, a combination of vaguely identified serious illnesses, growth problems, malnutrition, glandular imbalances and malfunctions, and a slow development of mental capacities which often lead to a childhood wasted as a retarded child. Nancy represents the group of children whose docility or aggressiveness hide fear and a chronic state of anxiety and insecurity.

The borderlines between these groups are, of course, loosely defined. They flow into each other, and there are numerous in-between stages. But with these reservations, they are representative of some of the problems that are much more common than many educators would be ready to admit. The "normal," "problem-free" child is a myth. There are only degrees.

These six children, then, represent the educational fringe, the "hopeless" ones, the problems, the unfortunates who cannot be reached through ordinary educational practices nor regular psychological counselling. But they have one thing in common: they require a continuous person-to-person relationship, deepening into friendship and complete trust, while a method of communication is established concurrently.

How is this accomplished? How is the first step taken? The beginning is always slow. It is not education, not psychology, but an art, depending partly on intuition, partly on experience, partly on love and affection, and partly on the ability to see every reaction of the child and grasp it instantly, with no hesitancy, and transform it into a steadily widening bridge. The person who asks "How do I establish contact with such children?" is asking the wrong question. If he has to ask, he can't.

There is no "method" in reaching the unreachable. It is an all-out effort, opportunistic, using the entire arsenal of human communication: touch, feel, song, sounds, drawing, music, psychology, games, words, objects, illustrations, allegories, fairy-tales, action, acting, projects, hobbies, sports, physical and mental exercises, jokes, humor, nature, animals, affection, love, hero-worship, father-figure, identification, suggestion, auto-suggestion, hypnosis, rewards, dreams, science, history, logic, semantics. Whatever works is the method.

Naturally communication must be established first. And this is often a major accomplishment, sometimes constituting the half-way mark in the child's progress although there may be no visible changes. But no matter how communication starts, eventually it must expand to include words. Verbal communication is both difficult and vital. It must be approached with caution as well as eagerness. We know that words to these children, far from being a means of communication, often represent the enemy, the danger, the meaningless, the threats, the emptiness, or even weapons of isolation. Few thinkers today accept words unreservedly as rational means of communication. Words communicate, yes, but hardly rationally and hardly as a method. In children words are largely emotionally colored, and an amazing number of childhood trauma are verbal in their nature. Therefore a new language often has to be created, i.e., each word already in the vocabulary of the child must be restored to its original meaning. Only gradually can one build a language that communicates.

It is also difficult to generalize a schedule, a method, or a step-by-step procedure by which these children can be reached and helped. With each child I spent an hour or two a week for two years or more, and two years can contain a large number of steps. Sometimes months of work occurred between each step; at other times they followed one another within the compass of a forenoon.

There were periods when each item of the following list was dominant: A period of building confidence and establishing contact. A period of establishing communication. Of building a structure of reality. Of creating out of the labyrinths of the unconscious a viable, dependable memory. Of the laying of ghosts. Of developing digital coordination. Of discovering the world. Of laying foundations of understanding on which to build technics. Of arranging experiences into structures of knowledge. Of learning to respond to everything that happens. Of stimulating imagination and creativity. Of rebuilding the senses so that the children can see, hear, smell, touch, feel, and reach freely.

Each period naturally contains many steps of development often spread over a long time. Always there is an overlapping and improvisational quality that make cataloging and brief descriptions unsatisfactory.

Any set technic or procedure must be fluid, readily adjusted to each individual child at each moment. Even to devise a scale of importance is meaningless. At each stage, one particular need may override the others, and it may never be the same one. Most children, however, have one crucial need that must be answered at the earliest moment: the development of a functional memory.

In varying degrees all children develop a habit of forgetting. There simply is too much to remember. Almost automatically, recall becomes selective. In children with problems, trauma and the all too common succession of clashes with the environment, the need to forget becomes vastly increased. Soon the past ceases to exist. The child lives in a flux of the present, made bearable by the skills and blessings of instant forgetting. As new experiences become increasingly meaningless, they become increasingly easy to forget. Basically, new experiences and newly introduced skills fail to make a meaningful impression from the very start and float into the range of consciousness without the means of being hooked onto an existing structure where they are needed. Thus they may float out as easily as they floated in.

Observation, attention, mnemonic confidence, determination to remember, need to remember, habitual recall, absence of blocks, all of these elements of memory are commonly lacking in our children with problems and to some extent in all children.

The technics of free association have little relevance in dealing with children. Here the explorations into the memories of the past must be much more direct and probed with more calculated care. The discovery that the forgotten can be uncovered and remembered again is of incomparable importance to the child. More than anything, it builds a confidence in the previously elusive memory that forms an excellent foundation for further memory work. Ralph, for example, whose memory of the past was close to a blank—except for the vague nightmare of Dick and Jane—soon could recall with startling accuracy whole sequences of his life at the clinic, quoting the doctors verbatim with excellent mimicry. Day after day was uncovered, and it was a revelation to him to discover the power of his memory. It contributed significantly to his self-confidence and became scaffolding for building his memory.

How does the memory work? What really is it? Such questions usually would lead us into the physiology and psychology of memory that added valuable elements to our understanding. The child could now stand aside and observe his own and others' memories at work. The nature of the memory, the forces inimical to its development, the grasp of its complexities and acceptance of its vagaries, all added to the construction.

In the beginning, the "actual memory work" is carried on through games. Such games range from the simplest observation of objects to complex ones involving abstract patterns. While the whole thing appears spontaneous to the child, a funny game out of the blue, it is, of course, part of a logical developmental structure.

In the beginning, the teacher's mind must run on several parallel tracks, one permanent track being the memory work. It must permeate every working hour. The child's reactions must be constantly watched and evaluated. The slightest change in ease of recall must be seized upon, welcomed, praised, and further built upon.

These few remarks about the building of the memory must suffice. It is of primary importance to all future progress and must be a continuous process for at least the entire first year. Without such a foundation, the results that I shall briefly outline would not have been possible.

Ralph (16–18)

As expected, Ralph's progress began slowly. He was extremely fearful of himself, his abilities, his possibilities. He was convinced he would fail at anything he might try. The origin of his anxieties, his inability to function, his entire "retardation syndrome" had to be largely ignored for several reasons: (1) they were obviously rooted in an environment that could not be changed; (2) to lead him to a precise understanding of himself would probably have required years of analysis and psychological treatment; furthermore, it had been tried without success; (3) he was incapable of basic verbal communication.

So instead of groping for origins, we concentrated on developing a new personality. Soon we spoke of the old Ralph as some strange person that had been nice to have known, but for whom we really didn't have much time. The great breakthrough came when we discovered that the old Ralph had a good memory which we could use. (Speaking of "old" and "new" Ralph, I must mention that Ralph quickly grasped the fact that one and the same personality could have several facets, and he reacted to this with wit and maturity.) We found at times a mnemonic ability approaching total recall.

When in the space of a few months his vocabulary made the leap from kindergarten to high school, we decided to skip all the years in between! So we started high school subjects, first orally; then as his reading improved gradually, we studied written documents, at first edited and prepared by me, later directly from regular textbooks. Thus we by-passed Dick and Jane entirely. We never used second, third, fourth, or eighth grade printed materials. Working phonetically on vocabulary building, we made our own sentences, then related them to the subjects studied as soon as words began to take shape.

In all directions we had tremendous discoveries waiting for us, the entire modern world, its present and past, the entire universe whose existence he had not even suspected. At times it was overwhelming. Here was a five-year-old suddenly becoming sixteen, darting across through a short-cut in the chronos. Astronomy, the structure of the universe, was the tearing aside of a curtain of darkness, but so was the study of economics, the structure of the promises we live by. The ecological chain of nature gave endless fascination, but so did the ecology of the community. The fact that both individuals and nations had personal histories opened other horizons. In fact, every week was a drama, with ever-expanding horizons.

As Ralph approached his seventeenth birthday, he also began to question. Again and again he was struck by the illogic, the blunders and stupidities of mankind. His sense of justice was becoming very strong; and his growing sense of logic was constantly offended by the many inconsistencies and gargantuan mistakes of the human society.

Simultaneously other things began to happen. He started working in his father's factory, with a momentous added feature—he walked to the station, took the train to New York and the subway to the factory, *all alone!* This was an achievement comparable to any heroic journey into the darkest of continents.

Probably one of the most daring adventures of all time was our decision for him to learn to drive and obtain a driver's license. When he announced our decision to his parents, he was greeted with incredulity. His successes had gone to my head. This was both ridiculous and impossible, irresponsible and dangerous. Fortunately, Ralph was by now quite independent of old environmental influences as well as in the possession of a certain amount of stubbornness. If I said he could learn to drive and obtain his license, he was certain it could be done.

The next few months we added driving and preparing for his tests to our program. After some practice, he enrolled in a driving school for practical instruction. When he went for his oral and written test, his nervousness got the better of him. He flunked. We laughed it off and continued working. A month later, he took another test and easily passed. He passed the road test quickly, obtaining his New York State driver's license right on schedule. With money he had saved, he bought a car. Later, with the help of his father, he got still another car, a new, modern mechanical marvel, almost worthy of his accomplishment.

That summer he spent his vacation on a bicycle tour of Europe with a youth group.

At about his eighteenth birthday, he also acquired a girl friend, a charming, intelligent and good looking girl of seventeen. He now began preparing for the New York State Regents' examinations to give him a high school equivalency certificate. For a boy who only recently had been afraid of Dick and Jane, this was a gratifying development.

Throughout his growth, Ralph's sense of logic, common sense, justice and fair play had also flowered. Approaching draft age, he naturally became interested in the Vietnam war and increasingly critical of it. Socially, politically, and economically, he became increasingly liberal without any particular urging from me. This led to disagreements with his aggressively conservative father and anxiety and fears on the part of his timidly conservative mother. One morning I received a telephone call from his mother telling me that they were discontinuing his lessons. . . .

Donald (15–17)

The first time I saw Donald, I was mostly aware of his pleasant, cheerful, and innocent smile. He was in bed, where he had spend approximately half of his lifetime, with a crumbling socket in his hip-bone. Before that, it had been with rheumatic fever, a poor heart, and a succession of related minor illnesses. When serious, his face had a vacuous expression, matching well his vacuous mind. But when he smiled, his face lit up. Obviously, this was not the smile of a feeble-minded nonlearner or a child in the stage of retardation that his record indicated.

Nevertheless, his mind was as total a blank as the mind of a fifteen-year-old boy can be and still be alive. I knew his history well, and in the first interview it became clear how this blank had come into being. It was the old story, a combination of events and conditions conspiring against the child. The accidental nature of the problem was unmistakable. One of the tragic aspects of working with so-called "hopeless" children is the frequency of accidental origins: if there had not been a mistake here, an accident there, an omission here, and an unfortunate coincidence there, it might not have arisen.

So there was Donald, smiling up at me from his bed, a healthy mind in an unhealthy body. After a few sessions, it was clear that Donald would have no basic difficulties. The only reason for proceeding with caution was the temptation to pour it on too quickly. In other words, the teacher needed the self-discipline, not the student. Starting from scratch, he learned to read very rapidly and his handwriting was better than Ralph's.

His life became a succession of adventures and discoveries. Not possessed with a great potential brilliance, but with a more limited range, Donald learned with amazing speed. "Drinking it in" and "Lapping it up" were expressions that often came to mind. Although not as serious-minded and intense as Ralph, he learned of pollution, wars, crimes, and men's stupidities without feelings of bitterness. When he began to understand the enormity of his misfortunes, the illnesses with their complements of educational failures, he could view these, too, with equanimity. He was a sleeper awakening and not about to moan over time lost in his sleep. The fact that he might have slept his whole life away did bother him a little. But then he smiled, because—after all—I was there.

The two years I worked with Donald were entirely pleasant, a time of zest and joy. At times the road was difficult, often a result of vacant spaces and missing parts in a personality (and education) growing too quickly, a time when an observer might have marvelled at my patience. But the question of patience never comes up when working with "problem children" although an outsider might perceive it as "superhuman patience." Actually, what appears as patience is merely a chain of necessities, tied to inevitable and often exciting logic: a certain effect is necessary, or a certain muscular movement, or skill or understanding. At this point, you, the teacher, can no longer stand outside and watch. You must become the child. You must know and feel exactly why the desired results are difficult. You must—on the child's level, with the child's mind—solve *his* problems. Then you must transmit this entire experience to the child, who now must feel that you are acting and thinking together. Soon you don't quite know who is the student and who is the teacher. You are becoming one, and at the student's level. The only difference is that you can see the glimmering of a solution while he can't. During such concentration, in such a desperate situation, it is an absurd *non sequitur* to speak about patience. Often a long time spent on one tiny, insignificant thing seems to require "patience." Nothing could be more meaningless than the time element in such situations. Time ceases to exist. As for "insignificant" things, such do not exist when working with children with problems.

In two years, Donald covered all subjects to a considerable distance into the high school curriculum. While not outstandingly brilliant, he did well and was getting ready for his high school diploma.

When I terminated my work with him, it was not because two years was a magic limit; rather, I no longer could find time to commute to the little town where he lived. Donald continued studying and developing. Shortly after I left, he met a girl, married, opened a successful business, and soon became the head of a happy family.

Peter (8–10)

Peter presented a number of unusual problems. Much of the beginning work was physical, such as training muscles, coordinating both large and small movements, developing a sense of rhythm in all muscle actions, posture, walking, sitting, and standing. Finger control was particularly undeveloped. His control of eye muscles required a year of special attention before his technic of seeing began to match the acuity of his vision.

Working with Peter offered many opportunities to demonstrate what is commonly classified as "patience." The work on his handwriting is illustrative. At the outset, we spent hours learning to hold a pencil. Then we proceeded to draw small circles and lines in varying patterns. Through all this, I would often have to guide his hand and identify each muscle used, dictating every movement as our hands moved slowly over the paper. When we finally arrived at the incredible complexities of writing letters and numbers, our powers of concentration were tested to the utmost. Nothing but the ultimate intensity of effort could have conquered such difficulties. Hour after hour we searched for the feelings of rhythm without which all movements remain clumsy. Hour after hour we left our tracks on growing heaps of paper. When the letters began to assume recognizable forms, we started to associate the sounds with the letters. Immersed in Peter's mind, I found every moment filled with obstacles that often seemed insurmountable. It was a personal triumph when a muscle responded properly or when a letter took on a shape to indicate that the unconscious was beginning to cooperate. There were times when it seemed as if I knew no other world than this reluctant, slow-motion, obstinate world of physical weakness. We had to learn to breathe, walk, lift our arms, and execute other complex actions that other children take for granted.

Working with Peter was especially demanding because nothing could be left to itself. There were no departments of learning, skills, or understandings where we could draw a sigh of relief and say, "Well, here at least is something you can do on your own."

We were always too busy to stop and think whether our hours of concentration were wasted and the whole thing futile. We were in a world where the slightest improvement loomed like a landmark of gigantic proportions. Time and again, we felt like a candidate being awarded the Nobel Prize, and all for microscopic improvements where an outsider would have seen nothing.

An added aid was Peter's steadily growing sense of humor. He made jokes at our expense, sharp and amusing insights into the world around him. His observations and evaluations of other people became both penetrating and witty. He could see the humor of both situations and individuals. He could at times be sarcastic, both of himself and others, but it was sarcasm steeped in kindness and thoughtfulness. Such humor helped us preserve perspective, also serving as an excellent antidote against developing attitudes of martyrdom or unjust disadvantages. It would be difficult to suspect that our work was not the common, ordinary occupation of all common, ordinary children of our age.

While Ralph and Donald never attended school except for a year or so in early childhood, Peter, through the devoted stubbornness of his mother and the excellent cooperation of the public school, attended classes throughout my work with him. In the early years, school attendance was largely a matter of form, but it did accomplish one important thing: it kept him in contact with other children so that he grew up with friends and normal social standards. We saw to it that he understood exactly why he was different and that this was only a temporary state of affairs.

During the three years that we worked together, Peter's greatest triumph, easily comparable to Ralph's triumph of earning a driver's license, was learning to ride a bicycle. With his feeble sense of balance, he would undoubtedly swerve crazily into the path of a speeding car or crash into an immovable object, not to mention the constant possibility of his falling victim to the treacherous force of gravity, with which he was not even on comfortable, friendly terms when walking or standing!

In working with children with problems, it is imperative to set goals that may appear ridiculously impossible. The work is, in truth, a continuous succession of doing the impossible. Without a little of this irresponsible daring, nothing would be accomplished beyond routine compromises. Here no compromise is acceptable. We don't want to do "pretty good" considering our disadvantages. We want to be normal children.

So we started Peter's bicycle adventure with totally irresponsible optimism. Every sign pointed to failure, if not disaster. But no disaster skulked in our lanes or streets. Irresponsibility triumphed. We may have set a new record for a boy of eight since we accomplished the undertaking without a single fall.

In the beginning, I was always there behind him, holding on, guiding his thinking, feeling, and action. As we speeded up, I would still be there, running behind with a firm grasp on the bicycle, following each shift in the center of gravity and each appearance of centrifugal forces in turns with directions of how to respond, balance, follow and counteract. We made a fine team, and one fine day I just let go of my hold. He was soloing! For a while, he soloed without knowing it, while I was preparing the psychological background for his complete take-over of all responsibilities. Finally I showed him by suddenly running up beside him and in front of him that he was, indeed, on his own. It was a field day for irresponsible optimism.

Peter learned how to read. During the third year, we began typing. He gradually acquired most of the skills and knowledge of his peers and continued being promoted in school until he was actually able to work on his class level.

As with all these children, it would have been preferable to have continued a few years more, but we decided that since my working schedule was becoming very full, Peter should try working on his own; there were now many children who needed help much more than he did. He is now a fine, successful boy in high school.

Andy (8–16)

The work with Andy was complicated by his temper tantrums and by an inflexible stolidity difficult to penetrate. His case was one of the few in which I used suggestion and autohypnotism extensively. I would have preferred to have used outright hypnotism; it would have been a tremendous timesaver in penetrating his layers of resistance, obstinacy, and animosity to learning, but children of his mentality and age can rarely be hypnotized. A form of suggestion under hypnotic conditions proved, on the other hand, to be quite successful. Where reason, admonitions, bribery, rewards, and encouragement had been fruitless, this intense program of suggestions against a background of hypnotic techniques had obvious results in stirring him to the beginnings of cooperation and desire to grow and learn.

His mother was extremely intelligent and talented and understood to the fullest what was required to work with him successfully. She had the patience to accept the necessary slowness in building a center from which his education could radiate. With Andy it was, indeed, a radiation. All directions had to be tried, since it seemed so true that we were up against an incurable mental deficiency.

I spent more than seven years with Andy, seven years so filled with failures and creeping progress that it often seemed foolish to go on. With ordinary parents, the work would undoubtedly have stopped; after all, why throw away money on such a hopeless case? Fortunately, Andy's mother would not give up.

So we crept along at our snail's pace. We battled our way to expand a memory that was almost incapable of grasping abstractions. Slowly some foundations were laid, and we began to hunt for ways of escaping his prisons. Physically he was awkward, and his stumbling improvement only served to accentuate his awkwardness. He was years behind his peers in running, jumping, and other physical skills. He was slow to acquire reading skills. His writing begain to take shape, but without sudden leaps. Plodding was the word for Andy.

But of course, any progress was a victory and usually would have been regarded as such. In Andy's case, I felt strongly that this was not enough. I could see no promise of surprises ahead, sudden dawnings of brilliant sun. It was obvious that abstract thinking would always remain difficult. The intricate symbols and signs of written language and logical discourse, except on a fairly elementary level, would probably always be beyond his range.

As mentioned before, there is a first maxim in working with such children: we cannot accept the permanence of any problem. The end result may not always be "normal" children, but we want them to be persons capable of full, rich lives. If one thing does not work, we must try something else.

In Andy's case, the something else did not seem very promising. Since abstraction presented such obstacles, we had to try the concrete. But here his clumsiness, his lack of both large and small coordination, seemed to make it a poor alternative. Nevertheless, we had to try.

Since he lived in a house in the country, with a farm next door, we began to build an interest in animals and farming. The using of tools, leading in the beginning to near disasters, was constantly encouraged. He began to do work on the farm. I brought things for him to take apart. Then I brought things to dismantle and reassemble. The next step: give him things in need of repair. I presented him with my alarm clock, my watch, an automatic timer, a bicycle, a radio, a toaster; suddenly all my mechanical possessions seemed to break down, a veritable mechanical epidemic! I developed into a sort of Typhoid Mary; wherever I went, technology collapsed, and I took it to Andy to be fixed. Gradually he began to repair everything.

Naturally, all the steps in this amazing metamorphosis must be omitted from this brief account; but the startling fact is that Andy developed into a mechanical genius. Farmers from all around began to take things to Andy that has been given up by professional mechanics. Soon he was fixing tractors, cars, machine tools, anything mechanical. If it was devised to run, he would make it run.

One of our early projects, after he fixed a decrepit bike, was to learn to ride a bicycle. Next followed driving a tractor, then a car, in each after having rebuilt them from old wrecks. This led to preparation for the driver's license, although he was still too young for it. Now our work with abstractions became of tangible importance. It gave new impetus to his efforts. He quickly learned all road signs and mastered all required knowledge for a driver's license, including the ability to read and answer the printed questions.

My work with Andy was stopped, as with Donald, because I could no longer commute the long distance to his home. Suffice it to say that today Andy, barely out of his teens, is married and the master mechanic in a large garage, the youngest member of the staff. It gives me a great pleasure, and a certain of sardonic humor, that his annual income is considerably higher than mine.

Roger (4–11)

Roger's case was more complicated than any other of this representative group. First, he was a medical problem of international proportions, having been examined and given up by specialists at home and abroad.

With due respect to experts in medical science, certain of their failures were unacceptable. At no time was Roger prescribed an all-out nutritional program, an anomaly in a case where a child is obviously starving to death. This is important, for nutritional deficiencies are very common in children with problems. Exceptions are few, and I commonly find both vitamin and mineral deficiencies. And yet I cannot recall a single case where a medical advisor had prescribed vitamin therapy. As for a comprehensive program of natural vitamins, natural supplements, and the fullest possible development of a dietary, physical, and emotional regime, this is tragically beyond the capacity or interest of most medical practitioners.

Roger's medical history would have been radically altered for the better if his mother during pregnancy had been given a fully supplemented diet, if he had been treated from his first medical examination with vitamins and minerals in assimilable natural organic (in case of minerals, colloid) forms, if he had been breast-fed implemented by natural supplements, and upon weaning placed on the extraordinary diet he obviously required. Instead, he was a serious medical problem. Unfortunately his parents did not agree on the nature of his problems. His father believed nothing was possible. His mother was ready to try anything. As a result, I never got the full cooperation so necessary in such extreme cases. Thus my efforts to build his appetite were regularly sabotaged by his father who brought home candy, ice cream, cakes, soda pop, exactly the things most detrimental to my efforts and which I had specifically proscribed with all urgency possible. This was a critical time, since there was still hope to undo much damage through massive doses of vitamins, minerals, concentrated protein, and a sensible diet of natural nutrients.

Lack of understanding on the part of well-meaning, kind parents has often destroyed children, figuratively. Roger was being destroyed, literally. For a long time, it looked as if the doctors who gave him up were right. He was fading rapidly. However, his mother managed to carry out at least part of the vitamin program, and he survived.

At this stage Roger showed no will to live, and we had to build that, too. The will to live, so closely related to interests, affections, and love, can be brought out exactly through those channels, and we gave them all attention possible. In long talks with his mother, I showed her how she could intensify and bring to Roger this triumvirate of life: interests, attentions, and love. At this time, a number of other problems needed attention. His coordination was almost nonexistent. He could neither dress nor feed himself. His voice, of a deep, uncontrolled adolescent quality, seemed beyond repair, his speech poorly developed.

To illustrate the kind of battle in which we were engaged, let me mention an early victory that may have been the turning point; and that came only after preparation, prolonged practice, and a concentration that is inconceivable to the normal person: Roger learned to tie his shoelaces. The moon-landing may be a corresponding feat in the adult world—although it is improbable that the moon-landing will be followed by as much progress as the shoelace tying.

From then on, Roger's progress was punctuated by stupendous landmarks. He learned the numbers, how to count, how to write the alphabet, how to read and recognize the alphabet, the phonetic foundation of the language, the beginning of reading—all before he entered kindergarten.

He began to control his voice. His speech improved. He learned how to run. He mastered a number of physical exercises that were distinct and advanced skills. By the time he finished kindergarten, he excelled in running, a distinction he retained through the early grades. This was an amazing accomplishment for a boy about half the normal weight and several years younger in general physical development.

By the time he entered first grade, he could read. His mathematics was outstanding. He begain to make friends. His personality became more positive, straightforward, and pleasant. His grasp of abstractions became exceptional.

A triumph, as tremendous as that of tying his shoelaces, was his learning to bicycle. As in the case of Peter, when we started this project, it seemed like an impossible pipe dream. And yet, Roger's learning period was shorter than Peter's. Soon he was an expert cyclist, where along with his running, he was on equal terms with his peers, no matter the size, an equal among equals.

Roger's progress was highly satisfactory. Here was a really successful case, a dream case, so to speak. He was alive, thriving, developing into a brilliant boy, going from success to success, scholastically at the head of his class.

But troubles began casting their shadows. I was not satisfied with his progress for a simple reason: his rate of physical growth was still far below the normal. My program of vitamins and special diet had been virtually given up by his mother because the rest of the family opposed it. I was prepared to battle any future emotional complications when Roger reached adolescence. I would gladly have taken on his problems, the problems of a very short person, bordering on the semimidget physique, but I could not do it without parental cooperation. After six years, I stopped working with him.

Nancy (8–9)

Nancy's fears were centered on the break-up of her parents' marriage. About this nothing could be done. The break-up was too far gone for healing, and neither of the parents were interested in rebuilding a marriage that alone could give the girl security.

In such cases, we can only hope to patch things up as well as possible and hope for the best. The patching consists of preparing the child for a world where certain elements are missing, making the best of an imperfect world. Philosophically, a pretty convincing case can be made. All in all, this is a beautiful world, and its imperfections are illusions, created by selfish individuals, which do not really have the power to destroy the world. The eternal truths are not touched. The beauty is there. The sunsets and sunrises are not wiped out. Psychologically, a wound is a wound and leaves traces that cannot be covered up without the almost certainty of paying for it later.

Strong interests, a capacity for love, an understanding of the nature of the human being, his institutions, conventions, and weaknesses, are all of help. Although the past has done its damage to a child, it is possible to prepare her for the future. You cannot undo the past, but through the building of a rich, flexible personality you can prevent debilitating reactions of insecurity in the future.

The purely technical side of working with a child like Nancy is extremely simple. The memory responds quickly to training. The steps to reading are without complications. I worked with Nancy only one year, at the end of which her difficulties in mathematics had evaporated. She could read with ease and pleasure.

Many of her fears had been allayed. She had found a person—and a man at that—who in working with her had shown her own worth, one concerned and interested. She had seen that all of us have fears; and that in facing a fear, its cause will not disappear but its power will.

All in all, it had been a successful year. It was, however, with sadness that I said goodbye to Nancy. So much more could have been done.

Through a recent follow-up, I know that she appears to be happy and successful. But I cannot help feeling that her parents failed her, and so did I, by not insisting more forcefully on solving the problems of the entire situation. Usually such speculations have no place when working with problems. There are always things that one should have done that he doesn't do. But I know that Nancy possesses vast possibilities that we shall never see.

Usually, we don't speculate thus. We generally go ahead and help where we can, hoping for the best. As teachers we must realize that our major goal is to put ourselves out of work. . . .

23

ROY P. FAIRFIELD

A Teacher as
Radical Humanist

A Teacher

...feels the "urge to kill" a student.
...feels the urge to hug one of her fifth graders.
...receives an invitation to speak on a controversial topic at the local Rotary Club.
...knows that a colleague is plagarizing a friend's textbook.
...refuses to turn in grade reports because they are being used in ranking students for Selective Service.
...joins the American Federation of Teachers and organizes a strike.
...finds his files rifled the night before a final exam.
...tries to teach a seventh grade class of 42 in a ghetto school.
...is approached by a football coach who makes "discreet" inquiries about his star quarterback.

A Student

...tells her teacher that she had become pregnant, had an abortion at Dr. X's office.
...is always late with his projects or term papers.
...reports to his DAR mother that his civics class is studying Karl Marx and the United Nations.
...asks for a two-hour conference to discuss "personal matters."
...says "Shi!" or "Mother fucker" during a class discussion.
...tells his teacher that he's leaving school because he can't afford books and clothes.
...changes his financial aid statement when he learns that money is available
...runs a stop light to "show off" before his teacher.
...asks his teacher to come to dinner

This article originally appeared in The Humanist, **37**, *No. 3 (1967), 92–96, under the title "Critical Conflicts in Education." Reprinted by permission.*

A Teacher   *(cont.)*   *A Student*   *(cont.)*

. . . hears a college president: advise his students "If you drink, don't get caught."

. . . stays in bed and "takes sick leave" when he can't face a Monday class.

at his fraternity to discuss Vietnam and the C.I.A. influence on American students.

. . . breaks a "speaker ban" rule to protest his school's showing files to federal authorities.

. . . protests a grade upon return of an exam.

I picked up the Sunday paper a few years ago to learn that one of my social science students in a course called "Citizenship in the Modern World" had been apprehended by FBI for putting pipes on a railroad track. I spent much of that day wondering what was really happening in that class of sixty students. It was an embarrassing Monday when I faced the fellow sitting in the front row!

There is probably not a teacher in America living at the knife-edge of the learning process who has not had a similar experience, nor one who could not talk for several hours about the micro- or capsule-situations above. Sensitive teachers who value each moment of learning time, both in and beyond the classroom, confront an incalculable number of such situations during a career. Some days find a teacher confronted by a dizzying number of crucial junctures of relationship, with his students, colleagues and senior officers. Many delineate the broad frontier between *seems* and *is*. Others are much more brutal, demanding decisions within split seconds. Still others are so subtle that one's antennae of awareness may not pick up the wave lengths for days or even years.

Ethics on the teaching frontier are not radically different from others which involve human relationships. However, situations are often dramatic because the teacher is keenly aware that he is in a position "to play God." The magnitude of his potential influence is enormous. Knowledge is now perceived as a precious commodity in an urbanized-industrialized civilization, and the home is no longer capable of fulfilling specialized need. Therefore, the teacher's burden becomes heavier. The stakes are considerably higher than they were when learning was not so clearly related to making a living. Today, the teacher assumes a large number of roles—parent-surrogate, authority figure, counselor, friend. Teachers themselves do not always understand their conflicting roles or the implications when students do not understand roles which seem to conflict.

More brutally: can a teacher perform a number of roles which, from the student's point of view, conflict? How can a sensitive teacher, however aware of the filament-like communication between himself and the student, prepare for situations which become ever more intricate in an increasingly complex and demanding society?

It would not be too difficult to outline systematically a set of ethical propositions for each of several competing ethics, then indicate how any teacher might follow his code in responding to some of the micro-situations listed here. For instance, a teacher taking an absolute position regarding obedience to law would immediately report the name of the doctor performing an abortion and call the police about the smart aleck student running a red light. Nor would the absolutist tolerate tardiness when establishing rules for turning in projects or term papers. In fact, he would find comfort in a rather rigid set of rules. At the other end of the continuum, the complete relativist or situationalist would sense no real conflict: anything might go, including him, if his principal had alternative principles!

The humanist teacher might have problems attempting to find a referent between these extremes, because the humanist teacher must locate value in the total human welfare of the students involved. He must also ask: What happens to me and my values in the total process of human interaction? How does one discover the locus of importance in the student's life? Can one really know what his perspectives are? What difference does it make to the student when a particular course of action is taken?

> A flunking college senior asked me to review his notes with him before the final. I agreed and spent an hour with him going over them page by page. It was soon obvious that he was using his fiancee's notes from the previous year. I suggested this subtly by pointing out that "This year we are not reading this, and that." He did not acknowledge the fact, left my office with a "Thanks"! He passed the course, but did he ever recognize the ethical problem comprised in his action? And what kind of a high school history teacher is he today?

Implicit in this micro-situation as well as that pertaining to the abortion is the prerequisite of knowing about the student's out-of-classroom life. There are also some critical right-of-privacy questions embodied in such teacher-student relationships. Teachers becoming a party to information from the mouths and hearts of their students will in all probability be those teachers in whom the students believe they can confide. Such confidence imposes special obligations. Such confidence requires lengthy discussion, much pondering and weighing of alternatives. It is surely no place for assemblyline, forty-hour-a-week education or routinized counseling.

The teacher may serve more as a sounding board than a prescription writer in many micro-situations. Above all, the humanist needs to be a good listener. He must also be an expert in searching for alternative methods of solving problems. He needs to know the law, needs skills in analyzing conflict, needs to recognize when he is out of his depth in handling serious psychological disturbances.

A micro-situation involving a protested grade may be more profound than meets the eye. Eliminating one implication: few students protest because their grades are too high. Most protests come from the other direction. Whether or not protesting is a valuable process depends upon several variables: the climate which the teacher establishes in the course; the student's perception of teacher flexibility and/or personality; and what the grapevine says about a teacher's willingness to change a grade.

Over the years I have enjoyed needling dormitory, sorority and fraternity groups about "Coursemanship—Tactics and Strategy of Passing Courses Without Necessarily Giving a Damn." One quasi-humorous way of handling the most obnoxious and persistent protestors (those who care more for the external implications of a grade than the value of knowledge) is to say innocently and simply, "You know, the first 10,000 papers I graded were the most difficult." The twenty-four hour cooling-off period is also effective. After a giraffe-like basketball center, standing a foot over my head, threatened me, I insisted that there would be no discussion of grades for twenty-four hours after the papers were returned. This reduces chronic and picayune complaints, but it may miss a basic point, one illustrated by a concrete case:

> A young woman once remained after a three o'clock class to review a C+ exam. Within twenty minutes we had analyzed the paper and agreed that it could have been half a grade higher or lower without much stretch of the imagination. Finally, I asked why she was so worried since the semester was young and C+ wasn't "so terribly bad." She replied that it was a "psychological flunk" that she was "on scholarship and couldn't afford to get anything less than a B." Pressing further, I discovered that worry over the C+ was symptomatic of other worries. During the next four hours I learned that she feared her mother had cancer and was angry because her mother wouldn't go to a doctor; a sister needed an expensive operation; another sister was experiencing marital difficulties; her brother was in prison.

No wonder this girl did "poorly" on the exam! No wonder students have difficulty studying when homesickness, girl trouble, social pressures, conflicting family tensions, the draft, ambiguity of purpose, and dozens of other common garden-variety of daily crises press for solution. No wonder teachers sometimes feel obsolete and helpless when they observe such personal tensions but have so few means for getting to the root of such problems.

However, once a teacher is involved in helping a student, whether kindergarten or a graduate, he may wish that he had never started with such personal interest. Such situations often require hours and hours, days and days of attention; time which the teacher may be unable to afford while trying to become acquainted with his particular field, serve as parent to his children, attend PTA and committee meetings, balance his budget, and meet the thousand other "slings and arrows" to which flesh is heir.

Fortunately, the C+ situation came early in my teaching experience. It sensitized me to the importance of probing gently-gently when surface evidence doesn't add up to the impending catastrophe perceived by a student. This case was the first of many leading to hundreds of hours of discussion on such pointed questions as:

> Have you ever felt the urge to murder your mother? Will you help me fall out of love with Professor X? What happens if I become a conscientious objector? Maybe I shouldn't have had sexual intercourse with him? Where can I find money to continue school? Why won't my father stop trying to run my life? Do you think that Professor Z should have been fired?

Such questions raise more questions about the human comedy than they can settle. Do you *tell* a student even if you have felt the urge to kill? How *does* one help a person "fall out of love" with anybody? Where is the line to be drawn between advocating that a student serve as a conscientious objector and inciting him to become one? Can one properly discuss sexual intercourse between others objectively? How many teachers are in a position to know people who are willing to assist students who need money to continue in school? How can it be given without imposing indignity upon the recepient? Who can control a father who insists upon telling his teenager or college senior what to do?

> Among the tensest situations I have experienced was a face-to-face encounter with the parents of a student. They could not manage their own lives, let alone the young woman's and reenacted their mutual hatreds and hostilities in my living room. What more to do, after they had asked my opinion, than to suggest that they seek the assistance of marriage counselor and psychiatrist?
>
> The girl graduated and now has a family of her own. The mother and father send me a Christmas card each year.

The student's search for information about a colleague raises complex issues about disclosure of information. If an issue becomes public as it once did in Berkeley, California, when a teacher admittedly aroused controversy by discussing his LSD trips with his high school students, then a colleague may well express an opinion. But in certain instances, expressing an opinion may disclose information violating a colleague's right of privacy. A teacher has responsibility to all parties in a given case. A student's innocent question may not be so innocent.

> I have seen my classes grow in average from thirty to sixty to ninety. I have been told by a college president, "Roy, you know that you can teach a hundred as easily as you can teach fifty, and two hundred as easily as a hundred." I have heard colleagues say in despair, "I've stopped learning my students' names"..."I've stopped assigning term papers and including essays on my examination"..."I want no students phoning my home."

While teachers watch the rising flood of students and cry, "Impossible, we can't keep up!"—while teachers adopt the so-called objective, true-and-false, and multiple-guess approach to the examination process, our students cry, "Alienation! Alienation!" And "law and order" is the counter productive scream.

T. S. Eliot caught the spirit of life's fragmentations when Prufrock remarked, "I have measured out my life with coffee spoons." The sensitive teacher is all too aware of this quality of the human dilemma. Teachers do not have time nor facilities to record the dimensions of teaching micro-situations in order to reflect carefully upon them. A teacher has to operate by rule of thumb, by common sense, or by the thinnest scratch of chalk. Tape recorders and video recorders might be of help but in using such aids, one runs into the obvious problem of, perhaps, upsetting the evidence by the means of recording it. Furthermore, one can never be certain when he begins to talk with a student just how far and where it will go. One thing is clear: the teacher's task does not stop at the classroom door.

That ancient humanist, Socrates, knew this when he used all of Athens for his discussions. Millions of teachers have followed in his steps, adding the dimension of caring enough to walk the tenth mile, play ball on the playgrounds and accompany students through field, forest and suburb.

Today the teacher has a major handicap: the student all too frequently sees the teacher (literally) in the classroom context only. The net result is more impersonality, deepened alienation. The student, confined to a bus schedule, does not find time to meet teachers after school, even when teachers are willing. A teacher, hooked by routine, does not make extra time to help the bewildered student. A routinized society generates routinized situations, and vice versa, squeezing human relations into non-human patterns.

The cries of "Alienation" have been justified in Berkeley, New York, and Madison. The experimental colleges rising from the ashes of impersonality and the rekindled fires of anger have been justified at San Francisco State, at Berkeley, at Wayne State. One should not jump to the conclusion, however, that smaller classes necessarily promote humanistic rapport between partners in the learning process. I have seen graduate seminars of twelve, high school and elementary classes of twenty-five and even individual conferences which generated alienation. Students perceived teachers as authority figures and teachers behaved more like stuffed shirts than persons who would bleed if scratched! All teachers might well ask, while applying lipstick or shaving in the morning, "Am I a phoney?"

> When meeting students on the campus I often cannot tie a face to a name. My classroom seating chart is gone! So, while I'm biding for time, I say, "Hi there!" (Cheerily, of course.) Need one do more to make the world safe for hypocrisy?

The humanist, searching for the locus of human value, impact and meaning, may well remember that it is criminal to regard any educational micro-situation as routine, normal, something-to-be-lived through. Nothing could be farther from the truth. Any classroom is a vivid kaleidoscope of multiple perceptions, multiple apperceptions, multiple cognitive potentialities, multiple emotional preparations, multiple objectives, multiple urges. The teacher who believes that he or she "has the truth" and *will* dispense it may obtain uniform responses, in laughter, in grade curve patterns, in agreements over classroom procedures. That teacher, however, may have to face the bar of conscience for having committed manslaughter if his action has stunted growth rather than promoted it. Isn't the stoppage of human growth a kind of killing since time's passage is an irreversible process?

> He was a G.I. and he sat in the second row. He insisted that the course I was teaching would "never buy him a cup of coffee" and that such courses existed only to give people like me a job. I laughed. The class laughed when he expressed such views bluntly. But what might I have done to promote his growth, rather than resist his views?

We have heard a great deal of nonsense for half a century about meeting the needs of individual children. Few will deny that individuals have different perceptions. But taxpayers, school officials and other laymen of self-proclaimed expertise on school affairs have not won any international prizes for maximizing conditions which permit teachers to study individual human learning units to optimize the learning process. We are all familiar with reasons why this can't be done—high costs, inefficiency, lazy teachers, pressure-group activity, etc. Far too much of the educational process is hypocritical by humanistic standards. We don't meet the needs of the growing individual in this changing, value-shifting, potentially explodable, and relativistic world.

The teacher who is serious about a student's growing edge of confrontation with the world (seen through any subject, from block-building to atom-smashing) has the task of serving as midwife between the known and the unknown, between the felt and the unfelt, between the perceived and the perceivable. He must know one hell of a lot, not only about his own subject-matter field, but about the student's growing awareness and the socio-economico-psychological climate which claims the student.

The humanist teacher must be familiar with the alternative techniques or tools for best serving as midwife. Today's tools include more than spoken and written words. Marshall McLuhan suggests when advocating radical changes in education, "You must be literate in umpteen media to be really 'literate' nowadays." He further points out that education should abandon its commitment to print and cultivate the "total sensorium."[1] This is not to advocate what is often a sterile audiovisual technology, but to suggest that the teacher cannot risk illiteracy at any point, substantively or pedagogically. Even if one introduces the quasi-cynical notion that no teacher should take himself too seriously or believe that his influence is more than marginal, a teacher would be a genuine charlatan if he did not have some confidence that his effort had some relevance to his students' lives.

> I have discovered that evidence of "making a difference" is sometimes difficult to find. Grades can be deceiving. Spoken expressions often carry a wary overtone. And, caring is hard to indicate through conventional words like "love," "I care" and "thank you." But I am grateful for hundreds of letters, cards and phone calls—as evidence.

Assuming the teacher's humanistic attitude and willingness to work the proverbial twenty-five hour day, assuming his giving of self to his students in every context possible: can he pursue the learning process with his students if he teaches in a power vacuum? He cannot. Like any citizen in the public eye, the teacher is likely to be whipsawed between quanta of power toward which he may have a whole range of attitudes and/or awareness.

The humanistic teacher, willing to devote his life inexorably to assisting students in the growth process, is almost inevitably "in for trouble." He may want too much money to do too many things for the average community. His sense of devotion may not be appreciated by colleagues willing to follow the asphalt paths. His determination to become immersed in the learning process and to make decisions for educational reasons will often be thwarted by those making decisions for political, public relations, financial and other non-educational reasons—and non-reasons.

Administrators, usually caught between the pro and con factions, are not renowned for their courage. They are more often authoritarian than humanistic. Rules are to be obeyed.

> My department chairman once refused to let me arrange the meeting time for a seminar although there were only eight students in it, because he had received one complaint from a student, the previous semester, that some of my seminar meetings lasted until 12, 1 and 2 a.m.

Far too many teachers at every level of teaching are exceedingly naive when confronting the relationship between their classroom functioning and the power framework in which they exist. Many teachers believe they are free to practice their profession until they encounter a specific situation which reveals the restraint of their academic straightjackets. Men and women of every ethical persuasion have some profound thinking to do in relating teaching and power processes. They must ask: Do I and should I participate significantly in setting policy governing my classroom and/or my involvement in the total learning process in my school? If I have no power, what am I willing to do in order to obtain it? If it is unobtainable in any realistic sense, how far am I willing to move, geographically, professionally, financially, and with what probability of correcting dissatisfactions or contradictory conditions?

> An academic supervisor once said to me, "If you don't like it here, why don't you move?" I held my tongue, but I thought, "I like it here fine, it's *you* I don't like." Making the world safe for hypocrisy?

Authoritarian teachers have less difficulty than non-authoritarian in answering some of these questions. Since policymaking in almost every branch of American education tends to move from the top down, the authoritarian can hardly complain. However, careful study of professional journals at every level of teacher concern, observation of the growth of teacher unions, and recognition of strikes, boycotts and private griping suggests a growing resentment about the dichotomies and trichotomies of teacher involvement in the educational power structure. Teachers surely cannot dodge the responsibility of coming to grips with such divisiveness any more than they can evade issues which upset their students, napalming Vietnam peaseants, CIA subversion of student groups, and methods of countering the double standards of the selective service system. A teacher's ethics will be formed on the basis of his knowledge of and commitment to confronting such problems.

It is difficult for a teacher to maintain understanding and empathy with student perception and to keep his perspective when he grows older every year, but his students remain the same age. How can teacher and student maintain a dialogue so that old and new can be discussed with appreciation, openness and communication?

> "What is a spade?" I asked. He looked at me with surprise,
> but answered, "Negro." "What is a drug rhythm?" Again
> he tried to explain, patiently, to one approaching fifty.

The popular media may help teachers over thirty. Early 1967 issues of *Look* and *Time* devoted space to the problem, the latter even making youth their "Man of the Year." But the popular media are not enough. The teacher must read what youth are reading, read what they are writing, write what they are reading, hear what they say about what he is writing, listen to music and criticism which they are hearing. And, if the teacher has the courage to bridge the generational gap, but is fearful of getting too close to his own students, let him take a sabbatical or visit a neighboring city or state. Let him stand on a corner listening, smelling, seeing, tasting life as youth perceives it. If he has children, the generational and emotional gaps may preclude impartial observation. He must face the implications of that awareness, however, and still seek to discover what "turns on" his students, even if it is pot or smoking bananas. If his ethical perspectives include every angle of vision on all planes of reality, he will not be hung up with prejudgments about digging jive, LSD trips and other phenomena which he may not have experienced and may not wish to experience. His teaching acts and attitudes will affect students, however, despite his intentions, and he cannot afford to be unselfconscious about his knowledge of self and the implications of his contact with students.

How difficult it is to cross the generational gap is illustrated by the experience of a former neighbor, a life-long fighter for the American Civil Liberties Union, the League of Women Voters, the Anti-Defamation League, etc. One day her 17-year-old son returned from school complaining bitterly about "the Establishment." After she had challenged him to support his statements with evidence, the boy exclaimed in exasperation, "Oh, mother! You don't know what it is to fight the Establishment!"

> Upon occasion I have kept a log of hourly and daily
> experiences. It has helped sharpen my ears. But there aren't
> enough hours in the day.

We are in need of teachers' daily logs which reflect the decision making process as it is related to ethical commitment; all kinds of ethical commitment, not merely humanistic. We will then need publishers fearless enough to publish them. As Abraham Maslow suggests, life on the knife-edge of peak experience can be exhilarating—but it can also be dizzyfying. High sensitivity on those peaks, communicated in some way across the generations, could improve the learning process. We need men and women willing to risk exploration in such rugged ethical terrain.

VIII

Campus
Power

Introduction

The most visible of all problems facing higher education in America during the past decade has been the struggle for campus power. That struggle has commanded the most television tape, the most newspaper print, and probably the largest number of outcries from both petty and important officials. That struggle has ostensibly been the greatest threat to public order although the competition for campus power, as at San Francisco State, really was a symptom of more contagious dis-ease and diseases—the disease of our involvement in Vietnam, of racism and poverty, and general malaise over the American dream's having become a nightmare.

For all the repressive events growing out of the conflict between students and administration, students and faculty, students and police, students and politicians, some results were sanguine, too. Much as they disliked it, many midstream Americans were forced to examine their consciences over the crucial issues of war, racism and affluence. Members of academic institutions, including those in the public schools, were suddenly required to develop listening techniques or face a bulldozing into oblivion. And laymen, perhaps for the first time in American history, had to learn more than they may have wished about academic freedom, curriculum processes and governance, topics formerly kept fairly comfortably inside the ivy walls. Laymen were stunned by the incidents which began as Berkeley and continued at Kent and Jackson State. It was so out of character to convert campuses into National Guard bivouacs. But students, faculty, administrators, and trustees seemed equally bewildered as is evidenced by the tide of periodical literature and books on campus dissent which has swept into bookstores and newstands during the past decade. Wrangling over governance has become standard fare, both curricular and extracurricular. The positions represented here reflect almost every position except that which might advocate blowing up the buildings simply to watch the cornices fly. On the one hand we have Professor Sidney Hook, a tower of liberal strength for several decades, advocating measured reason unless we wish to destroy democratic processes. Milton Konvitz, a renowned scholar of civil rights and liberties, holds a similar position, remarking that students should go to college to study; if they want to remake the world, they should go "someplace else." On the other hand, Linda Roberson, a graduate student, advocates any means short of violence to achieve a "redistribution of power." Charles Frankel and Edward Brooke sound pretty much like "business as usual" while John Seeley recommends that universities need "not only radical restructuring" but must also *become quite other sorts of institutions.*" James Dixon, President of Antioch College, sees our institutions of higher learning as "hopelessly obsolete." For him, the revolution is "real," but the opportunities for developing new patterns for learning and living leave him optimistic—unless violence prevails. Short of that, Dixon would have faculty join students to eliminate the "colossal obsolescence" of our institutions; Hook and Frankel on the other hand believe students and faculties should keep their traditional distance.

There's ample room for a symposium about this symposium of ten views, for many questions remain both unanswered and unasked: One may, for instance, question Hook's belief that all campus storms are "synthetically contrived"; or Dixon's view that patronage is a "very special kind of violence"; or Konvitz' belief that students "want the rights of adults and the exemptions of young children"; or Linda Roberson's statement that "the university caters exclusively to...capitalistic demands" of the military-industrial complex! But what, if any, *are* the conditions under which faculties should be more activist, as Louis Kampf advocates earlier in this volume? Hasn't the university long since outgrown its corner on the truth-seeking market? Does it not reflect both the ugliness and the beauties of the greater society of which it is a part? And can it be exempted from the revolutionary hurricanes howling through so many other parts of our society? Wherein is it more a part of the problems of racism and violence than the solution to those problems? Can institutional spokesmen insist that students and faculty search for "moral relevance" if they take an amoral position regarding the crucial issues of our times? Can we as a so-called democratic sociey afford to tolerate intolerance, physical or intellectual, when the intolerant, if gaining control, would no doubt suffer little difference of opinion or stirring to action? But how can we as a people exercise controls without *seeming* intolerant?

It is doubtful if any of these problems are going to go away. Although the level of the conflict may differ on each campus, administrators and faculty who boast that they've had no "disturbance" at their college are living in a fool's paradise. If they've frightened their students with threats of coersion, they'd best take the pious language about academic freedom from their catalogues. If the students are content, maybe they aren't reading the papers or watching television to "hear it like it is." In any case, if the students aren't asking difficult or embarrassing questions, the college can't be doing its job! Far from being involved in the "politics of absurdity," as Professor Hook contends, I would argue that never before in American history have we had such a bright opportunity to rebuild institutions or erect counterstructures which can deal with *total* men and women, *persons,* not just those who cerebrate. It's the challenge of risk-taking rather than the conservation of the obtained. And to cite Theobald and McInnis again, "The possible is irrelevant, so it is only worth trying for the impossible." This is the bias of hope, not the certainty of despair. Few generations have the expectation that acting on such hope will give meaning to life.

24

SIDNEY HOOK

Prospects for
the Academic Future

I began my college career in the fall of 1919, hence my academic lifetime spans a dozen revolutions in American education. But I am not going to reminisce. I want to stay young, at least in spirit, and I learned from my teacher, John Dewey, whom I observed closely for the last twenty-five years of his life, what the secret of staying young is and that is *not* to reminisce about the past. Actually, I never heard John Dewey reminisce until he was in his nineties, and that was as a reluctant response to my deliberate prodding in order to extract biographical data from him.

However, there is a way of talking about the past which is not merely reminiscence or idle reverie. It occurs when we make comparisons of the past and present for the sake of a present purpose or for the sake of finding a new way out of present difficulties.

Fifty years ago, it would be no exaggeration to say that the belief in academic freedom was regarded as faintly subversive even in many academic circles. The AAUP, organized by two philosophers, Arthur Lovejoy and John Dewey, was in its infancy and without influence or authority. Today, except in some of the cultural and political backwaters of the United States, academic freedom, although not free from threats, is firmly established. In some regions it has the support of law.

This article originally appeared, in slightly different form and under the title "The Prospects of Academe," in Encounter, **31**, No. 2 (1968), 60–66. *Reprinted by permission of* Encounter *and the author.*

Fifty years ago, the power of the chief university administrator was almost as unlimited as that of an absolute monarch. Today the administrator is a much harried man with much less power and authority among both faculty and students than his forebears. Today there may be temperamentally happy administrators, but their present life is an unhappy one. There seems to be an open season on them and to such a degree that for the first time in history there is an acute shortage of candidates for the hundreds of vacant administrative posts in institutions of higher learning. When I did my graduate work at Columbia, Nicholas Murray Butler was both the reigning and ruling monarch. I don't believe that in his wildest dreams he could have conceived of the Columbia scene today. The strongest argument I know against the resurrection of the body is that if it were within the realm of possibility, Nicholas Murray Butler would have risen from his grave and would now be storming Morningside Heights.

Having been an administrator in a small way myself, I have learned what an ungrateful job it is and at the same time how necessary. Without administrative leadership, every institution, especially universities, whose faculties are notoriously reluctant to introduce curricular changes, runs downhill. The greatness of a university consists predominantly in the greatness of its faculty. But faculties, because of reasons too complex to enter into here, do not themselves build great faculties. To build great faculties, administrative leadership is essential. In the affairs of the mind and in the realm of scholarship, the principles of simple majority rule or of "one man, one vote" do not apply. The most "democratically" run institutions of learning are usually the most mediocre. It takes a big man to live comfortably with a still bigger man under him, no less to invite him to cast his obscuring shadow over the less gifted.

The paradox today is that, as administrative power decreases and becomes more limited, the greater the dissatisfaction with it seems to grow. The memory of favors or requests denied remains much stronger than the memory of requests granted. Faculties are fickle in their allegiance. Overnight, the most beloved of administrators can become the target of abuse, a figure of obloquy in the eyes of the very faculty, or a large section of it, which he himself has helped to build. In the very year that Clark Kerr received the Meikeljohn Medal for academic freedom, the faculty at the University of California campus at Berkeley panicked in consequence of the events resulting from the *fourth* student sit-in. In effect it repudiated him by adopting a set of resolutions that made him the scapegoat for the student lawlessness which it conspicuously refused to condemn. The faculty even voted down a motion that would have given the students complete freedom of speech except to urge the commission of *immediate acts* of force and violence. Another example: Vice President Truman of Columbia University was vigorously applauded at

Columbia's commencement in June 1967 for, among other things, opening new avenues of communication with students. In the spring of 1968 he was roundly booed by a section of the Columbia faculty.

Why any scholar (and administrators are largely recruited from the ranks of scholars) should want to become a full-time administrator has always puzzled me. The duties, sacrifices, and risks seem altogether disproportionate to the rewards. In speaking of administrators, one is tempted to characterize them with the words Lecky used in his great history of European morals about the fallen women of Europe, "the eternal priestesses of humanity blasted for the sins of their people." Well, university administrators are no longer priests, but whenever a crisis arises, they are sure to be damned if they do and damned if they don't.

One thing seems clear. In the crisis situations shaping up throughout the country, administrators are not going to enjoy a peaceful life. Their prospects of weathering the storms that will be synthetically contrived for them depends upon their ability and willingness to win the faculty for whatever plans and proposals they advance in the name of the university. For if they permit students or any other group to drive a wedge between them and the faculty, they will discover the sad fact of academic life that in such rifts the faculty will either play a neutral role or even assume a hostile one.

Not only on good educational grounds, therefore, but on prudential ones as well, the administration must draw the faculty into the formulation of institutional educational policy. I say this with reluctance because it means the proliferation of committee meetings, the dilution of scholarly interest, and even less time for students. But this is a small price to pay for academic freedom and peace.

In talking about academic freedom, nothing signifies the distance we have come in the space of my lifetime so much as the fact that we now are concerned with the academic freedom of *students*. For historical reasons I cannot explore here, academic freedom in the United States meant *Lehrfreiheit*, freedom to teach. *Lernfreiheit*, freedom to learn, has only recently been stressed. It does not mean the same as it meant under the German university system which presupposed the all-prescribed curriculum of studies of the *Gymnasium*. If academic freedom for students means freedom to learn, then two things should be obvious. There is no academic freedom to learn without *Lehrfreiheit* or academic freedom to teach. Where teachers have no freedom to teach, students have obviously no freedom to learn, although the converse is not true. Second, students' freedom to learn was never so widely recognized, was never so pervasive in the United States as it is today—whether it be construed as the freedom to attend college or not, the freedom to select the *kind* of college the student wishes to attend, or his freedom of curricular choice *within* the kind of college he selects. Above all, if academic freedom for students means the freedom to doubt, challenge, contest, and debate within the context of inquiry, American students are the freest in the world and far freer than they were when I attended college. The incident Ernest Nagel recalled when we were students together in the same government class at CCNY is authentic. The teacher conducted the class by letting the students give reports on the themes of the course. All he contributed was to say "next" as each student concluded. But when, in reporting on the Calhoun-Webster debates, I declared that it seemed to me that Calhoun had the better of the argument, that his *logic* was better than Webster's although his *cause* was worse, the instructor exploded and stopped me. After emotionally recounting his father's services in the Civil War, he turned wrathfully on me and shouted, "Young man! When you're not preaching sedition, you are preaching secession!" Whereupon he drove me from the class. (The "sedition" was a reference to an earlier report on Beard's economic interpretation of the Constitution which he had heard with grim disapproval.) And this was at CCNY in 1920! The incident wasn't typical, but that it could happen at all marks the profundity of the changes in attitudes toward students since then. John Dewey's influence has made itself felt even in the colleges today.

Of course, there is still a large group of potential college students who are deprived of freedom to learn because of poverty, prejudice, or the absence of adequate educational facilities. And, as citizens of a democratic society whose moral premise is that each individual has a right to that education which will permit him to achieve his maximum growth as a person, our duty is to work for, or support, whatever measures of reconstruction we deem necessary to remove the social obstacles to freedom of learning. It is perfectly legitimate to expect the university to study these problems and propose solutions to them. All universities worthy of the name already do. This is one thing. But to conclude, therefore, that these problems must become items, not only on the agenda of study, but for an agenda of action, is quite another. For it therewith transforms the university into a political action organization and diverts it from its essential task of discovery, teaching, dialogue, and criticism. Since there are profound differences about the social means necessary to achieve a society in which there will be a maximum freedom to learn, the university would become as partisan and biased as other political action groups urging their programs on the community. Its primary educational purpose or mission would be lost. It would be compelled to silence or misrepresent the position of those of its faculty who disagreed with its proposals and campaigns of action. Class and group conflicts would rend the fabric of the community of scholars in an unceasing struggle for power completely unrelated to the quest for truth.

If the university is conceived as an agency of action to transform society in behalf of a cause, no matter how exalted, it loses its relative autonomy, imperils both its independence and objectivity, and subjects itself to retaliatory curbs and controls on the part of society on whose support and largesse it ultimately depends.

This is precisely the conception of a university which is basic to the whole strategy and tactics of the so-called Students for a Democratic Society. I say "so-called" because their actions show that they are no more believers in democracy than the leaders of the so-called Student Non-Violent Co-ordinating Committee are believers in nonviolence. And, indeed, the leaders of the SDS make no bones about that fact. In manifesto after manifesto they have declared that they want to use the university as an instrument of revolution. To do so, they must destroy the university as it exists today.

With more space I would list some of the clever stratagems they have devised to polarize their opposition. On every campus there are always some grievances. Instead of seeking peacefully to resolve them through existing channels of consultation and deliberation, the SDS seeks to inflame them. Where grievances don't exist, they can be created. One group of chapter members was urged to sign up for certain courses in large numbers, then denounce the university for its large classes!

Freedom of dissent, speech, protest is never the real issue. This is, of course, always legitimate. But the tactic of the SDS is to give dissent the immediate form of violent action. The measures necessarily adopted to counteract this lawless action then become the main issue, as if the original provocation hadn't occurred. Mario Savio admitted after the Berkeley affair that the issue of "free speech" was a "pretext"—the word was his—to arouse the students against the existing role of the university in society. One of the leaders of the SDS at Columbia is reported to have said: "As much as we would like to, we are not strong enough as yet to destroy the United States. But we are strong enough to destroy Columbia!" He is wrong about this, too—the only action that would destroy Columbia would be faculty support of the students—but his intent is clear.

Actually, the only thing these groups, loosely associated with the New Left, are clear about is what they want to destroy, not what they would put in its stead. In a debate with Gore Vidal, Tom Hayden, one of the New Left leaders, was pointedly asked what his revolutionary program was. He replied: "We haven't any. First we will make the revolution and *then* we will find out what for." This is truly the politics of absurdity.

The usual response that present-day academic rebels make to this criticism is that the university today is nothing but an instrument to preserve the *status quo* and therefore faithless to the ideals of a community of scholars. Even if this charge were true, even if the universities today were bulwarks of the *status quo,* this would warrant criticism and protest, not violent and lawless action in behalf of a contrary role, just as foreign to their true function. But it is decidedly not true! There is no institution in the country in which dissent and criticism of official views, of tradition, of the conventional wisdom in all fields, is freer and more prevalent than in the university. The very freedom of dissent that students today enjoy in our universities is in large measure a consequence of the spirit of experiment, openness to new ideas, absence of conformity, and readiness to undertake new initiatives found among them.

The first casualty of the strategy of the campus rebels is academic freedom. It is manifest in their bold and arrogant demand that the university drop its research in whatever fields these students deem unfit for academic inquiry and investigation. This note was already sounded in Berkeley. It was focal at Columbia. It is a shameless attempt to usurp powers of decision which the faculty alone should have. After all, it is preposterous for callow and immature adolescents, who presumably have come to the university to get an education, to set themselves up as authorities on what research by their teachers is educationally permissible.

Unless checked, it will not be long before these students will be presuming to dictate the conclusions their teachers should reach, especially on controversial subjects. This is standard procedure in totalitarian countries in which official student organizations are the political arm of the ruling party. Already there are disquieting signs of this. At Cornell, even *before* the martyrdom of Reverend King and before the gun-carrying incident of 1969, a group of Black Nationalist students invaded the offices of the chairman of the economics department and held him captive in order to get an apology from a teacher whose views on African affairs they disagreed with. It seems only yesterday that another group at Northwestern demanded that courses in "black literature" and "black art" be taught by teachers approved by the Negro students. And there are spineless administrators and cowardly members of the faculty who are prepared to yield to this blackmail even as they did at San Francisco State prior to the presidency of S. I. Hayakawa. Under the slogans of "student rights" and "participatory democracy" the most militant groups of students are moving to weaken and ultimately destroy the academic freedom of those who disagree with them.

Let us not delude ourselves. Even when these militant students fail to achieve their ultimate purpose, they succeed in demoralizing the university by deliberately forcing a confrontation upon the academic community which it is not prepared to face and which is fearful of accepting its costs. In forcing the hand of the academic community to meet force ultimately with force, the citadel of reason becomes a battlefield. The students glory in it, but the faint of heart among their teachers turn on their own administrative leaders. These militants succeed in sowing distrust among students who do not see through their strategy. They also succeed in dividing the faculties. There is always a small group—a strange mixture of purists and opportunists desirous of ingratiating themselves with students—who will *never* condemn the violence of students, but only the violence required to stop it. These students succeed, even when they fail, in embittering relations between the administration and some sections of the faculty. They succeed, even when they fail, in antagonizing the larger community of which the university is a part, and in arousing a vigilante spirit that demands wholesale measures of repression and punishment that educators cannot properly accept.

How is it possible, one asks, for events of this character to happen? There have always been extremist and paranoid tendencies in academic life, but they have been peripheral—individuals and small groups moving in eccentric intellectual orbits. But not until the last decade has the norm of social protest taken the form of direct action, have positions been expressed in such ultimatistic and instransigent terms, have extremist elements been strong enough to shut down great universities even for a limited time.

There are many and complex causes for this. But as I see it, the situation in the university is part of a larger phenomenon; namely, the climate of intellectual life in the country. I do not recall any other period in the last fifty years when intellectuals themselves have been so intolerant of each other, when differences over complex issues have been the occasion for denunciation rather than debate and analysis, when the use of violence—in the right cause, of course!—is taken for granted, when dissent is not distinguished from civil disobedience, and civil disobedience makes common cause with resistance and readiness for insurrection. A few short years ago, anti-intellectualism was an epithet of derogation. Today it is an expression of revolutionary virility.

In the fifties I wrote an essay entitled "The Ethics of Controversy," trying to suggest guidelines for controversy among principled democrats no matter how widely they differed on substantive issues. Today I would be talking into the wind for all the attention it would get. Fanaticism seems to be in the saddle. That it is a fanaticism of conscience, of self-proclaimed virtue, doesn't make it less dangerous. During the past few years we have seen the spectacle of militant minorities in our colleges, from one end of the country to another, preventing or trying to prevent representatives of positions they disapprove of from speaking to their fellow-students wishing to listen to them. The spectacle shows that we have failed to make our students understand the very rudiments of democracy, that to tolerate active intolerance is to compound it. If we judge commitment by action, the simple truth is that the great body of our students is not firmly committed to democracy or to the liberal spirit without which democracy may become the rule of the mob.

I do not know any sure way or even a new way of combating the dominant mood of irrationalism, especially among students and even among younger members of the faculty whose political naiveté is often cynically exploited by their younger, yet politically more sophisticated, allies. What is of the first importance is to preserve, of course, the absolute intellectual integrity of our classrooms and laboratories, of our teaching and research against any attempt to curb it. We must defend it not only against the traditional enemies, who still exist even when they are dormant, but also against those who think they have the infallible remedies for the world's complex problems and that all they need is sincerity as patent of authority. Fanatics don't lack sincerity. It is their long suit. They drip with sincerity—and when they have power, with blood—other people's blood.

We need more, however, than a defensive strategy, safeguarding the intellectual integrity of our vocation against those who threaten it. We need—and I know this sounds paradoxical—to counterpose to the revolt of the emotionally committed the revolt of the rationally committed. I do not want to identify this with the revolt of the moderates. There are some things one should not be moderate about. In the long run, the preservation of democracy depends upon a passion for freedom, for the logic and ethics of free discussion and inquiry, upon refusal to countenance the measures of violence that cut short the processes of intelligence upon which the possibility of shared values depends.

These are old truths, but they bear repeating whenever they are denied. Even tautologies become important when counterposed to absurdities.

We, as teachers, must make our students more keenly aware of the centrality of the democratic process to a free society and of the centrality of intelligence to the democratic process. Democracy has our allegiance because of its cumulative fruits, but at any particular time the process is more important than any specific programs or product. He who destroys the process because it does not guarantee some particular outcome is as foolish as someone who discards scientific method in medicine or engineering or any other discipline because of its failure to solve altogether or immediately a stubborn problem.

There is one thing which we cannot deny to the intransigent and fanatical enemies of democracy. That is courage. Intelligence is necessary to overcome foolishness. But it is not sufficient to tame fanaticism. Only courage can do that. A handful of men who are prepared to fight, to bleed, to suffer and, if need be, to die, will always triumph in a community where those whose freedom they threaten are afraid to use their *intelligence* to resist and to fight and ultimately to take the same risks in action as those determined to destroy them. Yes, there is always the danger that courage *alone* may lead us to actions that will make us similar to those who threaten us. But that is what we have intelligence for —to prevent that from happening! It is this union of courage and intelligence upon which the hope of democratic survival depends.

25

JAMES P. DIXON

Permanent Campus Revolution?

I once had an experience in a little town in New Hampshire. I was driving along about 60 miles an hour, rounded a corner, and landed right in the lap of a radar speed trap. Very angry, I was thinking what a stupid business this was, as the state policeman came up to the window. Before he even asked for my driver's license, he said, "You know, a couple of days ago there were some people killed on this corner and one of the responsibilities of police is to show concern. I'm terribly sorry that it happened to be you." In one simple sentence he had converted my affect from that of a miserable, angry sinner to a social reformer.

Knowing that when talking about the problems of our continuing campus revolution, one must always talk about it with some bias, I intend not to make a reasoned explanation—although I hope it is reasonable—but rather to provide a commentary from a happy warrior. I want to hypothesize that we indeed have a continuing revolution, and to say a little bit about how it came about as a way of defending it as a genuine revolution.

Keeping in mind Adlai Stevenson's famous adage that no suggestions for social reform are moral unless they are accompanied by some reasonable alternative solutions, I will lapse (as it is very easy for college presidents to do) into the role of prophet.

Somebody has observed that we ought not to worry too much about

Reprinted by permission of the author and the Commission on Higher Education of the City of Philadelphia.

the fact that we are having trouble, because in all times in which we lack a national consensus, we are bound to go through trouble before we locate a new national consensus.

How is it that we have lost our consensus—our consensus concerning the role of young people, and some over thirty—in our society? I suggest that we have lost it and we have lost it forever in its old terms.

How did it happen? It certainly started to happen around the episodes of World War II, when the parochial ideologies of American youth were blasted and the world was discovered by a whole generation of American young people. It was blasted by Sputnik. It has been affected by the phenomenon of instantaneous communication which smashes human isolation. There is no place to go; there is no place to hide.

Another factor in this situation is obviously affluence, for affluence is modifying the mores of the middle class establishment and, I think, drastically modifying also the mores of other parts of our social class structure.

Finally, a single significant act has taken us over the watershed. This single act contains potential for great change and possibilities of considerable disaster along the way. After a century of talking about the meaning of liberal education, we succeeded by official action to make education beyond the high school virtually compulsory in this country.

By that single act we merged the pluralistic ideologies of our diverse educational establishment with the national ideology. We put our individual institutional moralities at the risk of the national morality and the national morality at the risk of the individual institutional moralities. It is too early to say what is going to be the theology of this new "church."

As if this weren't enough, we finally have come to an understanding that man is not really a simple Pavlovian animal. He is not just the arithmetic sum of simple muscle twitches but a very complicated set of human reactions. It is now possible to distinguish between political man, cognitive man, affective and emotional man, vocational man, and a social-transactional man.

The political man is the man who understands the meaning and use of authority—where it is located and how to use it. He is the man who has made his career through the use of a very special form of violence known as patronage—a humane substitute for physical violence, as Loren Eisely is apt to remind us.

The social-transactional man is different from political man because he has the skills to create a group loyalty, not held together by anything as ephemeral as patronage, but held together by common commitment to a common cause that makes the activities of the members of the group somewhat predictable—or sufficiently predictable so as not to be threatening.

We can no longer, then, deal with the simple definitions of man. We now understand why the computer, with its binary logic, can't replace him because it takes a much higher order of logic to deal with the variables of man than the computer can presently handle.

Then we have the phenomenon of alienation. Older people talk about the alienation of youth and I hear youth saying that those of us who are over thirty are alienated too. We see a reduction in trust, a reduction in confidence, and an increasing mischievousness in the use of manipulative tactics throughout all of the organizations of human life. We see mischievousness in the collection and selective use of information, in the highly sophisticated way in which information can be selectively used so that only the information logically relevant to a given solution enters into the making of the solution.

Goodness, in terms of the old ideology around which we built our old consensus, has for Western man been specified in terms of behavior. Each specific piece of man has a characteristic kind of behavior. The political man exercises his franchise; the cognitive man is the custodian of the concept of excellence; the affective man is the custodian of, shall we say, compassion, love, sensitivity. The vocational man is the custodian of craftsmanship. The social-transactional man is the custodian of the process of human involvement. If we define man in these terms and define education as being required to nurture these characteristics, then it is small wonder that we are having trouble. All of these behaviors can in some way or other be modified by the learning process.

Now that we have mandated education, and mandated it so severely that it is a cause for deferment from military obligation at least at the undergraduate level, we are busy packing our young people—their political, their cognitive, their affective, all of the forms of their life—into our institutions of higher learning. We are escalating the institution, traditionally the custodian of the habits of the mind and intellect, to be the custodian of the whole person. And we are placing this demand on the institutions as a matter of public policy.

Now this wouldn't be so bad if it were not for the fact that the institutions into which we are packing them are hopelessly obsolete. They are not only obsolete in terms of the new consensus, but they were already obsolete in terms of the older order.

In the first place, they are obsolete in their policy-making structures. They are among the least democratic in society—much less democratic than our churches. There are few, indeed, of our educational institutions that have a congregational concept. They are oligarchic custodians of the problems of scholarship. They operate with something called a curriculum, which is nothing but a collective-bargaining agreement between the faculty and the students—with all of the moral, political, and intellectual validity of such an agreement.

It's small wonder that students are concerned about the curriculum. When they move out of secondary school they hope there's going to be something different—some higher degree of openness in their under-graduate experience and some recognition that an emerging adult is capable of taking charge of his own processes of knowing.

Our educational institutions are, if not paranoid, then schizophrenic, because at one and the same time they can support academic freedom and the CIA. They are Victorian, or at least if they have any moral out-look in a conventional sense they could be called Victorian. They are, in their statements about priorities of moral values, completely out of touch with the realities of moral affairs of individuals and themselves.

It could be argued that all this sets up a situation of creative conflict.

Institutions are still in an era in which it was ordained that they should be democratic and present individuals with equal opportunity. At the same time, institutions are essentially elitist. They preselect, they have scores, and there are even those that have implicit racist policies.

What I am saying is that the revolution is real, that these are some of the reasons why it is real, and that there is no particular reason to believe that we can go back. The old forms will simply not meet the new needs.

Now, what are the evidences that this is indeed a revolution? Or is it merely a fantasy of a frustrated old-fashioned liberal? (I recognize that one has to defend himself on this score as he passes the midcentury mark.) Let me try to defend myself with some objective evidences that suggest that this is indeed a real revolution.

The most important evidence I have is that for the first time in this century the role of both faculty and students is problematical. The faculty are rushing to protect themselves by instruments of collective bargaining. This is not an act of great intellectual courage—not an act supported by great faith in one's ability to manage the teaching and learning process. Particularly and peculiarly it is not this in a setting which prides itself on being able to manage the problems of consent and dissent and learning and mind-changing.

The students are pushing toward the free university movement. It isn't always called a free university, but if you look you will see every curriculum opening up, or you see a change in the definition of inde-pendent study or in the definitions of student-initiated courses.

There's something going on in the articulation of the roles of student and faculty. This may mean that we must begin to understand teaching and learning as a phenomenon and then understand that one can play the role of both teacher and learner simultaneously, But at the moment we are not accepting that to be true. We're digging in our heels and hop-ing somewhat that the wall will hold when we finally push back there.

Another evidence of the revolutionary impact of the turn toward public support, and all that means with respect to the role of the edu-cational institution as the historic custodian of ideologies, comes through clearly when you consider that the private academic establishment is about to collapse financially. It is being either pushed out of existence or pushed into the public sector. I don't think I even need cite examples to point out that this is a major trend. Paradoxically, at the same time there are new private institutions coming on the line, but it is nonetheless true that the private establishment which prided itself on its custody of ideologies is being collapsed into the public establishment and we're moving toward a wholly different structure.

One hardly need cite as evidence of revolution political action on the campuses—power and the use of power—but that is an important component of revolution. When you reach a situation, as we did in the southwestern corner of Ohio, where you have to call the National Guard to get a single student off the campus in a Negro institution, for my money you have revolution.[1]

I don't know where you go from there. As a matter of fact, I do know. You stop. You close up. At that moment you have had it.

It would be a gross misstatement, however, to say that the problems of revolution, whether associated with violence or not, are necessarily racially connected. If you talk to white middle-class students on campuses across the country—on private college campuses, large universities, state teacher colleges—you will hear them say, "We are suffering too."

It is popular to associate that kind of suffering with analogies to the problems of the development of less socially advantaged people. And I think that kind of suffering grows from the same roots, in part. The roots are in the sense of loss of consensus and ability to participate in consensus that seems to have a relationship to race and geography of origin. It is an oversimplification to say that this is a revolution of any group. It is a revolt against the entire process.

One of the things that characterizes the revolution on all fronts is the quest for moral relevance. You see this in the actions of civil disobedience. You see it in the tremendously earnest claims that students are making upon their institutions of higher education to take moral stands. It is a very strange thing that institutions of higher education, which essentially grew out of moral traditions in our country (very diverse moral traditions, distributed among various kinds of theologies or nontheologies), now find it impossible as institutions to take moral stands on human issues because, it is said, this violates the ethic of academic freedom.

We have an inescapable dilemma here which we must solve. If we fail to be supportive of moral ideology, then as institutions for education we are going to be left with a little corner of the cognitive blanket. Some other social institution, some new church, some new form of government is going to have to take over the problems of the development, isolation, and the identification of moral values.

So much for the evidence that it is a revolution, that it is a common revolution, and that young people are the most involved in it. Young people are the most concerned and the most threatened in terms of their roles and the future. And they are much freer than those of us who have so much wisdom and knowledge to say, through explicit behavior, what it is that concerns them.

What does all this mean? What does it say about the emergence of public policy? You can take a pessimistic view, of course, a view that has been taken sometimes by ethologists who simply say, "Well, that notion of free will was really a fantasy. You know it was an environmental accident of man's affluence. It never really did exist and when one has difficulties in his environmental accommodations, he reverts to what he really is." This is the pessimistic, reactionary view. If you take this view, you don't do anything. You build bomb shelters, as a matter of fact. You sit it out if you can.

I would rather take a view, however, that is more optimistic because I don't really want to build a bomb shelter and because I don't want to give assent to the possibility that I might need it. I want to suggest that what is really going on could be put together by a synthesis, of all things, between a point of view of Eric Hoffer's and a point of view of Nehru's. Those who remember the Sevareid-Hoffer interview on television a few years back may recall, among his magnificent collection of *non sequiturs*, that Hoffer said that one of the things that gave him encouragement for the development of the American dream was what he called the American genius for development without supervision. He's the best exponent of independent study I've heard in a long, long time—an American genius who developed without supervision.

Of revolutions Nehru observed that revolutions integrate ethical will and the search for justice, probably an Eastern viewpoint. If you can believe what Hoffer had to say, and if you can believe what Nehru had to say, then you have perhaps a position around which to understand, in an optimistic fashion, the revolution that is going on, and relate to it at least pragmatically with some sense of carrying on.

My predictions, then, would be in terms of this optimism.

Under the present situation, I see no possibility that we won't have political activity on our campuses and probably this political activity will for a time seem to erode the old *laissez faire* freedoms. It will erode faculty freedoms and be pushed into the packaging of collective bargaining units. It will erode freedoms for students because force and dismissal will be used. (For the moment, you can use force and dismissal because the objective of having a space for everyone hasn't yet been realized. The time will come when the use of threat to the student's tenure as a way of making regular the affairs of campus will no longer, I think, have any power and force.)

Administrators, particularly with the press toward public institutions, are going to be plagued with problems of public accountability and probably plagued with problems of public standardization. They will probably try to counterfeit their public statements as much as possible in order that they, too, by selective control of information, can get enough of a hold on the situation to have confidence that they are playing their role. We will learn to be ambiguous. We will appear to be open but we will be lying better than we ever did because this will be the only way out for us.

There will be a reduction, as far as I can see, of the characteristic role of undergraduate education as the carrier of ideologies. I think this has to go. I've worn it, I was weaned on it, but it's going to go.

It's not going to go because it is antithetical to academic freedom. It's going to go because the institutions of higher learning no longer have the moral authority to make the case.

The computer is going to come of age and that's going to mean that there's going to be a lot more spare time for activism. Once we get that geared in we'll either have to cram the four undergraduate years with a lot more stuff or one will go through them in very much of a breeze. If other kinds of education are any evidence, we won't shorten the period, we'll lengthen it, and we'll lengthen it in the name of excellence. My own profession of medicine has now lengthened its period of study so that you are often under treatment for arthritis before you can treat somebody else for it. So the custodial period is likely to go on and on and on.

On the brighter side of things I think we will shift our curriculum subtly and with all kinds of perverse reasons toward a problem-solving basis. Our small college, for instance, is associated with a group of some twelve colleges now involved in what one would hope would be creative relationships with urban school systems.[2]

We are going to have a sharp period of experimentation with decentralized education. We are going to have to deal somehow with this problem of a new democracy. The old democracy which worked for political purposes at its most elementary level—the participatory level— and then later at the consensual level, and then even later at the representative level, is not adequate to deal with problems that have a high content of information and knowledge. We are probably going to be forced in some of our educational institutions to experiment internally with models of the new democracy.

General education will change. There probably will be education in the crafts. That will come back into the hallowed temples of learning because we turn out into an affluent society more and more people to perform service roles and many are going to have to find their expressions of excellence and satisfactions of excellence through some kind of craftsmanship. It is not by accident that there are a million and a half painters in the country. It is not by accident that there are heaven knows how many million do-it-yourself, weekend hobbyists who cut off their thumbs occasionally. We are going to develop a social criticism for craftsmanship which in a sense will replace the social criticism of vocationalism that undergirded our experiences of an earlier era.

We are going to be forced to attend to the magnificent problems— the magnificent problems of war and peace; the magnificent problems of the politician who has to design and manage a state that will work; the problems of the scientist who has to be free to pursue the truth without worrying about its application.

Let me make a final comment which ties what I have been saying back to the very special concerns of unrest and upset and violence which characterize our educational scene at the moment. If this revolution proceeds by violence, then for the period in which the violence occurs, much may be lost in the quality of human life even though the violence may be thoughtfully and intelligently directed by those who believe that violence is the only means by which the centers of power in the establishment can be repopulated. To the extent that we can avoid violence, the baccalaureate of the future—the post-Renaissance man who plays in the string quartet in the evenings, works on the assembly line in the daytime, and betweentimes is a member of his city council—may emerge more promptly. For this to happen, in the face of the colossal obsolescence of our institution of higher education, faculty and administrators must join students in the campus revolution. To be able to do this without being purged, defeated, or demoralized requires either that society protect these radical roles or that the radical roles go underground.

The question then becomes not whether we have a permanent revolution, but whether our institutions of higher education will be able to change in the open or in secret. This is the question that the revolutionaries are asking the establishment. For an affirmative answer they will, indeed, perfect the use of much violence. This is the crucial question of public policy. If there is a hallmark of civilized society for which the educational establishment feels in some way responsible, it is that civilized persons can substitute the violence of patronage for the violence of physical assault and the difficulties of anxiety for the difficulties of raw fear. Higher education, then, if it is to demonstrate its utility in this time of revolution, must have the protection of public policy to permit the whole institution to dissent.

26

Student Power:
A Symposium

Editors of The Humanist *wrote to many people concerned with education, asking them to participate in a symposium on student power. The questions below were provided as guidelines:*

1. Do you agree with the advocates of student power who claim that universities and colleges need radical restructuring? If so, what should have the highest priorities in restructuring?

2. What position of power do you think students should have in universities and colleges? Should they share all decisions equally with the faculty and/or administration? Should they have the predominant voice?

3. Should illegal and/or violent acts on campuses be condoned? How do you think universities should deal with violence? Should universities ever call police to maintain order? Should student militants who use violence be suspended or expelled?

The responses were many and varied. The Humanist *is pleased to present a sampling of views on this critical subject:*

Charles Frankel

I believe that colleges and universities do require fundamental reforms. The practice of liberal education is disappearing; even the theory of liberal education has become vague and uncertain.

This article originally appeared in The Humanist, **29,** *No. 3 (1969), 11–16. Reprinted by permission.*

However, the largest change needed is an *educational* change, a change that has to begin in the way in which college and university teachers themselves are educated and in their orientation towards their work. If I understand the complaints of the most serious and responsible students, they want more "philosophy" in the generic sense in their education—more analysis of premises, more examination of alternatives, more effort to connect facts with ideas, and more interest in showing the connection of the subject to other subjects, to the surrounding society, and to the larger themes of moral and intellectual life.

Given the premise that the primary purpose of any "restructuring" is educational, I think there would be advantages in arrangements that encourage the faculties to look at their common educational business together, and that challenge the narrow control of the curriculum by separate departments. Arrangements providing for the regular cooperative review by students and faculty of the educational performance of their institution would also be useful for students and professors and would restore spirit to the higher educational enterprise.

For this same reason, I think it worthwhile to hoist a warning signal against excessive preoccupation with the external forms of governance of colleges and universities. This can divert students and teachers from the more important business of educational reform. It is useful to review the governing structures of educational institutions and to reform them where desirable; the main purpose of such an exercise is to improve the educational performance of such institutions, and not to try to copy in some mechanistic way constitutional arrangements derived from other kinds of social organization, such as government.

The phrase "student power" has certain unfortunate connotations, because it suggests an approach to the politics of a university inappropriate to the kind of institution a university is. However, in so far as the phrase stands for a general effort to make students more active participants in the designing of their educational experience, I am sympathetic with it.

More specifically, the question of student participation in university decision-making depends upon the kind of issue involved. Students should have formal grievance procedures available to them where questions of discipline or dormitory conditions are involved; they should be consulted about curriculum; depending on local conditions it may well be desirable to have them represented in small numbers on a board of trustees, and it will, almost always, be desirable to provide them with the channels of formal communication with the trustees. On the other hand, students should not participate formally in the selection of faculty. This would be incompatible with a professional relationship between teacher and student, and with the academic freedom of teachers.

In general, a university is a hierarchical organization, which can do its work only on the premise that some people know more than other people. To make a wholesale case for "student power" by appealing to democratic principles is to say that democracy should make no distinctions between the abilities of individuals, even when there are clear standards available, and even when the making of such distinctions is essential to the accomplishment of important social purposes. This is to parody the idea of democracy.

To my mind, the basic political problem in today's colleges and universities is a problem of communication, not a problem of the distribution of power. If "student power" means better and steadier communication with students, it makes sense.

I do not see how illegal or violent acts on campuses can be condoned. Violence on the university scene is incompatible with the fundamental obligation of the university to be a place of free, unintimidated inquiry and discussion. As for illegality, the university can maintain its autonomy only if its members recognize an obligation not to use their right to self-government to create protected enclaves of illegality.

Since a university administration has a fundamental responsibility to protect free speech and free inquiry for all members of the university, it cannot permit the use of force to abridge these rights. I can see no objection, in principle, therefore, to the use of police to defend a free and pluralistic community, if that becomes necessary. Obviously, because the use of police leads to consequences that greatly damage the cohesiveness of the university community, such a course of action is always regrettable, and I sympathize with those who try to avoid it. But it is not "repression" to prevent people from repressing other people's rights, and the consequences are even worse if a university, through vacillation, tolerates intolerance. Student militants who use violence should certainly be disciplined. Such discipline should be administered in a spirit appropriate to an educational institution, but the institution, if it must defend itself, should certainly not regard suspension or expulsion as inappropriate.

In the end, all these questions come down to the old issue of the relation of means and ends. I can well understand why there are people who think that the ends invoked to justify current student activism are so important as to throw out concern about the limits of the tactics employed. But I think there is an elementary test that any political program should be asked to meet: It is whether that program, if put into practice, will help or hurt the cause of honest study and free education. This is not the only test of a political program, but it is a significant one, and, to my mind, it renders all disruptive actions on a university campus illegitimate.

Milton R. Konvitz

The turmoil on American campuses has not been brought about by students advocating a restructuring of the universities but by the means used in thrusting demands on them. I know from my many years at Cornell that student proposals for significant and even radical changes are nothing new; and many such changes were made in an orderly way and without sensationalism. But now on many campuses students shout so loudly that one cannot hear what they say. It is not the nature of the demands that is unsettling but the way they are made.

There are some 2,500 colleges and universities, each with its own history, traditions, policies, and procedures. Each has its merits, I suppose, though some have probably outlived their reason for existence. The least one can say is that each of them can stand improvements. But I see no sense in a blanket judgment that "universities and colleges need radical restructuring," a claim often made by young people who barely know their way around their own institutions. Each case calls for painstaking study, hard work, long hours of talk—as any member of an important faculty committee knows. The bull-in-the-china-shop approach can only lead to destruction. And when one sees the temper and means of student demonstrations, one may rightly ask if their purpose is to reform or to destroy the institution. Means and ends have relevance to one another.

I am old-fashioned enough to think that students should come to a university to study—to read, to learn, to think, to acquire information, knowledge, and wisdom, and certain skills and a degree of competence. If this is not their main purpose, they should not be on the campus. The place to remake the world is someplace else.

Assuming that their purpose is to study, they should then have an interest in what the university does to foster and advance this purpose, what it does to improve the environment that may maximize the qualities of the institution as a place of study. To this end students should feel themselves involved in the work of the faculty, administration, and trustees, and the machinery of the institution should be ordered in a way that will stimulate, reflect, and utilize this legitimate student concern.

At Cornell for many years faculty-student committees have dealt with this problem in its many phases, and ways have been found to share duties and interests from which everyone has benefited.

But there should be no concern to share "power." A university board of trustees or a faculty or a student group that thinks in terms of "power" instead of functions and duties has gotten off the right track and is on the way to struggle and disaster.

Students, as any other citizens, must be held responsible for their actions. They are not a privileged group that is above or ouside the law. It is no favor to our young people to treat them in such a way as to instill in them the notion that "anything is all right as long as you can get away with it." If they want to be treated as adults, then they must be held accountable as such. The fact is, though, that they seem to want the rights of adults and the exemptions of young children—children subject to outbursts of rage and ill-temper, as if they were mentally incompetent.

When students choose threats, turmoil, and violence in the place of rational and orderly discussion, it is morally and educationally unjustified to tolerate such actions—toleration which, to many people, seems to imply acquiescence to conduct that is violent and criminal.

This does not necessarily mean that the administration must at once call the police and place hundreds of students under arrest. But if they persist in their unlawful and violent ways and thumb their noses at authority, then it would be an abdication of moral judgment and of intelligence to let mob rule take over the institution. A militant minority that is led to think that it is immune to the dictates of morality and the processes of law can easily subvert an institution, and their example, when learned by others, can undermine any democratic society.

I may be oversimplifying, but, I think, the basic principle can be briefly stated: Students who by their actions show contempt for the rights of others have no place on the campus. They should be asked to take their venom and destructiveness elsewhere.

John R. Seeley

The will is good—at least, I take it that it is—that asks the questions: "Do you agree with the advocates of student power who claim that universities and colleges need radical restructuring," and "What position of power do you think students should have . . .?" But the very mode of asking the question, free of the present decisive historic and political context, makes the questions impossible of other than arbitrary-appearing answers. There are questions that are no longer susceptible of cool, intellectual discussion—or at least not with the *de facto* commander of the "tactical force" called to break the heads of my friends if they will not voluntarily renounce their constitutional, human, and moral rights, and with the ideologists who confect the pseudorationale for such actions.

What *is* a university today? A typical university like San Francisco State or Berkeley? It is the indispensable arm of the emerging garrison state, masked still with the grin of freedom, and mantled yet in the rhetoric of liberty. It could soon aptly substitute for the conventional "Let truth flourish" the total lie over the gates of the German labor camps: *Arbeit macht frei!* At least, as fraud, it is a near-equal. And if it is still a battleground, it is only because some of the prisoners—a fair number of students, a handful of faculty—have not been subdued by conditioning ("education") from within or batons, mace, fines, and jail from without.

The object of the university is to train manpower and to pursue enquiries of technological utility. The manpower is to man the positions in the table of organization that is the military-industrial-academic complex: The UCA, the United Corporations of America. The technologies to be served by the manpower are two—both highly rationalized functionally and both equally empty of substantive rationality. The two technologies look to the ancient control of man over nature, now driven beyond need or sense, while the new technology is to give man control over man. The second technology is doubly necessary if "law and order" are to be preserved; for as the increasingly Kafkaesque world produced by the first emerges into full and horrible visibility, either men must again be driven to their tasks under whip and gun, or a subtler technology of man-management must supervene. The first technology is to be served by the natural sciences; the second, by the so-called social ones. The humanities and theology and such, where they are not self-liquidated into pseudo-sciences, are to gild the gingerbread and provide an air of decorum like Wagner festivals at Bayreuth. There is one more job the university must do and does: prepare the teacher who in the public schools unman the men and unwoman the women, so that when these "pupils" reach the university they may create as little trouble as possible for their final processors.

Within that context, to your questions! The universities and colleges need not only radical restructuring—if that only means getting rid of their robber-baron regents and head-warden administrators—but need to become *quite other sorts of institutions:* self-governing communities of free, just men and women learning, while acting upon it, to bring into being a free, just—and, finally, loving—world. The "highest priority in restructuring" is to throw out, clear and clean, all boards and administrators. The next task is to hold a constitutional convention—to turn the whole university into such a convention—until a form of government appropriate to the proper task of the university and the only parties who make up the university (students, young and old) is worked out and instituted. There would be no "administration." Those should have the "predominant voice" who in any given matter make the most sense. As for "illegal and/or violent acts on campuses," the question is loaded. Legality is a trivial consideration in the face of oppression and injustice; it is only to be hesitated before if the law is itself a properly promulgated rule of reason directed to the common good. University law fails all three tests. As for violence, the question is again (apart from strategic and tactical considerations), in effect, a trick. Arbitrary and unreasonable and unjust government *is itself violence* in latency. When it persists and becomes merely brazen in the face of petition, *it* declares war, not the petitioners. It is well to love gentleness—but not to the point where you plead while police beat your brother into impotence as standing university policy.

Senator Edward W. Brooke

Whatever the causes of today's student unrest, I am more interested in what the results of that unrest will be. In the universities, as in the rest of society, we need to ask: Are we witnessing the start of a downward spiral of social dissension that will end in self-destruction? Or can we direct the energies now being mobilized on campus into channels that transform our universities and our nation into better and more viable institutions?

Some of the more outrageous student uprisings of recent years seem to me to have gone well beyond the bounds of sensible political action. I do not presume to tell student protesters what they should or should not do. I ask only that they consider the larger political context in which they act and judge for themselves whether their determined efforts to achieve local goals are important enough to jeopardize the other values at stake. Briefly stated but deeply felt, my own views are that the right to protest is the right to persuade, not the right to paralyze; that the authoritarianism of protest is no better than the authoritarianism of repression; and that the disruption of great universities is a disservice to a free society.

In my judgment the political result of these kinds of demonstrations has been to create the danger of a backlash that could do grave harm to the universities and to the country. They can only feed the latent anti-intellectualism that Richard Hofstadter and others have found to be a continuing element in American life and politics. Where the choice for society becomes one between freedom and order, it is freedom that will perish. This fact has been confirmed in the history of too many other nations for America to dismiss it lightly.

To the extent that the disruption on college campuses becomes a part of wider disruption in our national life, the requirements of social order may come to dominate public debate and attention in this country. And, to put it candidly, I don't believe we can afford to be distracted in this manner from the greater and more urgent human tasks that lie ahead. Order is the first responsibility of government, but it is not the only responsibility; and I think it would be tragic if, at a moment when the interests and capacities of this nation have begun to focus on the lingering social inequities that plague us, we should be drawn into an expensive preoccupation with the problem of public order.

When protest as a political technique is abused, it only provides fresh fodder for those who wish an excuse for inaction. They can and do harp on the theme that to respond affirmatively to the demands of disruptive protestors is to reward intimidation, even if they admit that the demands have merit. Few things are better designed to make it difficult for any-one in authority to respond to protests in a conciliatory way than to expose them to charges that doing so is an act of cowardice. Neither college administrators nor public officials are going to relish having their manhood and courage impugned.

Apart from the influence of campus protests on the general political climate of the land, I sense other implications that bear quite directly on the relationships between universities and government. Connections be-tween universities and government have become closely intertwined in the years since the Second World War. By and large the rising financial assistance by government to the academic community and the increased involvement of academics in matters of public policy have been fortunate and fruitful developments. The federal government, both through its research support and through its direct-assistance programs, has become a principal source of necessary funds to colleges and universities. Virtually no center of learning in America could continue to operate effectively if federal support were abruptly withdrawn.

Lately, however, research and development appropriations have leveled off or declined somewhat, and trouble spots have appeared in what was previously a smooth relationship. Considerable resentment has appeared in Congress and elsewhere toward those members of the academic community who have benefited from public support and who now are so vocal in attacking public policies and public institutions.

I wish that students could hear for themselves the way riots, campus disturbances, the crime problem, and other issues mingle in the conversa-tion of many of my colleagues. We are observing what could become a damaging reaction to disorderly behavior in many fields, including academic life, and the opportunities for political retaliation are numerous.

I am not at all suggesting that events will move inexorably in this direction. We are not in immediate danger of an exorbitant reduction in federal funds for higher education. I am only anxious to underline the way in which complex issues interact to affect public policy in this field. Campus protests are not about to cause a severance of these relation-ships. But indirectly and subtly, they contribute to an environment in which Congress is likely to be less rather than more generous in nourish-ing the institutions of learning in this country.

Linda Roberson

Anyone involved in the processes of higher education knows that a radical restructuring of the educational system is necessary. If I were asked to come up with one word which would indicate the type and direction of needed change, my choice would be "humanization." This process, as I see it, demands a fundamental reorientation concerning the university's position and purpose in our society. The university is a public-service institution; as such, it must serve the interests of all members of society. As it exists today, it is not fulfilling this function. Controlled through financial and political manipulation by corporate interests —the interrelationship between big business, big industry, and the military machine—the university caters exclusively to their capitalistic demands; thus, it not only ignores its obligation to less powerful segments of society but also aids in their exploitation and repression by providing the personnel and knowledge necessary to the perpetuation of the power structure and by denying them to those who are considered to be a threat to that power structure. In other words, the university is one more arm in the complex of societal institutions which serve to protect and preserve the interests and position of a moneyed elite and to repress its opponents. It provides the backbone of militaristic exploitation through defense contracts, ROTC, and recruiting for the armed forces. Its tools of knowledge and intelligence are directed toward destroying life rather than enhancing it. It churns out graduates, nothing more than human machines, who can efficiently occupy predetermined roles in a prestructured, rigid society. Compassion, human dignity, love for one's brothers have no place in this structure; they aren't profit-making. If the university is to serve the interests of the people, it must be controlled by the people. Power over the university must be taken away from the corporate body and given instead to those who are concerned not with money and the status quo but with the educational process itself: the providers of educational services and those who receive—or ought to receive—these services. Only when the university is controlled by all segments of society can it begin to deal with society's demands. Only when it belongs to the people can it meet the needs of the people and thus fulfill its function.

Positions of power within the university should be held by the people who are directly involved in its functioning and who operate in direct relationship to the institution. This is to say that the university ought to be governed by a coalition of faculty and students; the administration's function is to administer rather than to prescribe regulations and policy. In areas of student life, such as housing and social rules, students should have sole jurisdiction, since these matters concern them and no one else. In other areas of university life where interests are shared, the power must also be shared; the distribution of power areas should be proportional to the interests and involvement of both faculty and students.

As a person whose orientations are basically pacifistic, I cannot condone the use of violence on the campus; on the other hand as a realist, neither can I condemn it. The repression and exploitation so deeply ingrained in the structure of the university have forced the movement for human rights to become a revolution. When coercive tactics are employed to suppress the voice of the people, such tactics are also necessary to insure that the people be heard. In order to explain and justify the campus revolution, I would like to quote a man far wiser and more articulate than I. Thomas Jefferson, in the Declaration of Independence, said: "...that to secure these rights, governments are instituted among men, deriving their just powers from the consent of the governed, that whenever any form of government becomes destructive of these ends, it is the right of the people to alter or abolish it, and to institute new government...when a long train of abuses and usurpations, pursuing invariably the same object, evinces a design to reduce them under absolute despotism, it is their right, it is their duty, to throw off such government and to provide new guards for their future security." The structure of the university, which is necessary to serve the interests of the corporate society, is diametrically opposed to the guarantee of human rights for which campus militants are fighting. In order to maintain this structure, the university is directed to suppress, by repressive or violent measures, any form of serious, threatening dissent.

I deplore the actions of any person, be he student, police, or college president, who deliberately inflicts bodily injury upon another person. With regard to other questions of tactics (i.e., disruption by students and expulsion by the institution), value judgments of ought or ought not, right or wrong, are inapplicable. The situation is one of political fact: Campus militants strive to effect meaningful change, and the university reacts by suppressing these efforts in order to protect its vested interests. The basis of this struggle is the redistribution of power; while those who control the university will utilize any means to maintain control, their opponents believe the power base to be illegitimate, and thus consider their actions unacceptable. The crucial question, then, is not one of the appropriateness of actions initiated by either group, but rather of the legitimacy of the authority of the institution.

Marvin Zimmerman

The function and goals of the university are not confined solely to the needs and interests of students. The faculty, administration, and, indeed, society in general also have interests in the university that are no less important. But even if students were the exclusive concern of the campus, this would not sustain the view that they are "qualified" to cope with all the questions concerning the running of a university. One can make as good a case that patients in a hospital are the raison d'être for hospitals as one can that students are the raison d'être for universities. Should patients operate in hospitals because they constitute the main purpose of hospitals? Perhaps the analogy is not strict, but there are enough similarities to make us pause before capitulating to all of the demands of those who argue for student power.

Undoubtedly students have interests, needs, knowledge, and information relevant to the function of schools, just as patients have interests and needs relevant to the function of doctors and hospitals; these should be sought and provided for. But how to satisfy the needs and interests, how to utilize the knowledge and information, is a matter of competence; there is as little reason to believe that students are capable of fulfilling these functions as there is that patients are.

If varying competence of the academic and nonacademic world differentiates their roles in higher education, the same holds for different members of the academic community. Some suggest that students have proficiency comparable to faculty that distinguishes them (students) from the nonacademic sector. Some students may be more capable than some people off campus, but how they compare with faculty or anyone else obviously depends on the individual and the specific area of knowledge. There are varieties of background among faculty that qualify them for different kinds of decisions. Normally, no one expects the physics teacher to determine the sociology curriculum; indeed, the student majoring in sociology is ostensibly better equipped, though the sociology teacher would probably be the most proficient.

The question of curriculum control encompasses a variety of problems requiring different kinds of knowledge and experience: determining the courses required to fulfill a major field; deciding the programs necessary to satisfy degree requirements; planning budgets that affect the size, quality, and variety of classes, and so on. Many faculty members lack the knowledge and experience essential for coping with certain curricular problems, particularly budget matters. Students are precluded from determining curriculum not only because they lack proficiency but because of a conflict of interest between meeting educational requirements and setting those requirements.

No doubt there are teachers who are unsympathetic, boring, arbitrary, cruel, incompetent, oppressive, and deserving of dismissal. There should be machinery available to deal with this. But granting students authority to hire, fire, and promote faculty who in turn will pass judgment on students, may have unpleasant consequences; students not only lack competence but suffer from a conflict of interest with faculty that could lead to collusion, intimidation, and blackmail.

Granted that the university should be guided by the principles of academic freedom and competence, it is ultimately responsible to the citizens in a democratic society. As citizens, members of the academic community have the right to employ whatever legal means are permitted to seek changes in education. Thus students have a right to request curricula reforms and more voice in the university even if mistaken on judgment. Competence does not guarantee infallibility and benevolence and thus does not deserve exemption from suggestions and criticism. Though calls for student power sometimes stem from misunderstanding of democracy or revolutionary tactics, agitation is frequently founded on legitimate grievances, such as: poor teaching; overcrowded classrooms, eating facilities, and dorms; and excessive controls over student activities. The university is obligated to provide means for the expression of genuine complaints, and to investigate and respond to them, otherwise it makes for poorer education and unnecessary confrontations.

But it is also duty bound to uphold norms of competence, learning, and academic freedom, and not sacrifice them in response to intimidation, threats, illegal acts, or violence. Not every complaint is justified; not every request deserves to be met; and even where legitimate they cannot be acceded to in an atmosphere of atmosphere of harassment or lawlessness. Even if appeasement could purchase temporary tranquility on the campus, it might be over the corpse of higher learning.

David Evans

As the idealism of the first sit-ins in the South provided a source of moral energy for the northern peace movement, and the rhetoric of black power an excuse for similar demands by students, so an essay by a black psychiatrist in the mid-years of the rights movement provides the keenest insight into the causes of student unrest.

"The White African Queen Complex," by Dr. Alvin Poussaint, received little attention in the national media though scores of copies of the UPI story summarizing Poussaint's thesis were sent through the mails as a warning from distraught mothers in midwestern towns to their long-haired and disheveled daughters at Seven Sister schools. Poussaint's title is descriptive and his argument easily summarized. Those fair young lasses who traveled south in '63 and '64 carried with them the racism of the society in which they had been reared. They came not to serve but to lead the impoverished black masses, just a few generations from slavery and how many from the trees. To their very real horror they found that their missionary zeal had placed them at the center of a maelstrom of frustration, anguish, and hurt. The protection of southern womanhood, the flower of that misbegotten culture, from the swollen member of the black man was, of course, the justification for slavery. Those fine-boned, delicately featured lowerclassmen from Smith and Radcliffe became the objects of desire (midnight integration) for their black male co-workers and of hate for the black woman. As often as not their presence was the cause of dissolution for an otherwise promising community project. Many could not last a summer. None stayed more than a year.

The relevance of this analysis should be clear. The mother-fuckers up against the wall at Columbia, at Oshkosh, at San Francisco State are, of course, the fathers or their surrogates (*en loco parentis*) of those middle- and upper-middle-class revolutionaries screaming for liberation. Today's student has seen the neurotic and frustrated women who bore him thrust into the convenienced kitchens of Riverdale, Beverly Hills, or where you will. As the justification and excuse for their collective father's failure to recognize the dehumanizing conditions of his labor, today's student is out to recapture what is left in the now technetronic society of the pos- sibilities for achieving manhood. And their partners in this struggle are the daughters of those same spiteful women who have felt their synapses rot as they pop pep pills (who are the real speed freaks—at least the heads know what they're taking) and push the buttons of automatic ap- pliances, and understand the concept of womanhood only through the words of muted irresponsibility uttered by Molly Bloom. To the extent that universities serve as an acculturating force for a society without moral direction, without men and without women to sustain them, those universities will be fought; and if necessary destroyed.

The moral of which is that behind every good radical is a witch—or at least a member of the Women's International Terrorist Conspiracy from Hell.

Gerald Pinsky

The present so-called "advocates of student power" appear to consist mainly of New Left fascists who are contemptuous of democratic student power but who are utilizing demands for student power as a means of attaining their initial goals, personal power and publicity for themselves, and the establishment of totalitarian beachheads within the democratic society for their movements. Left-fascist disregard for student power is evidenced by putshist actions carried out without the consent of student majorities (and often against their expressed wishes). True advocates of student power would rely upon student elections and re- ferendums, which could be followed by a vote to decide whether or not to strike should it prove impossible to reach satisfactory agreements with administration and faculty.

Supporters of democracy should welcome a more active role of stu- dent majorities and their representatives in most areas of decision-making in universities and colleges. These institutions have often been run in dictatorial and arbitrary fashion by old-guard administrators (and some- times faculty) who have arrogantly disregarded student rights. Now, faced by violent student fanatics, often led covertly by extremist faculty, many of these erstwhile tyrants display the cowardice of the bully. They allow those extremists to impose a new arbitrary and dictatorial rule on the university community, and rush to surrender the rights and sacrifice the careers of their faculty and administrative colleagues, to say nothing of the rights of the disorganized nonextremist student majority.

Campuses have come to be the breeding-ground of what the social critic Martin L. Gross calls the "New Religion"—a mixture of Trotskyism, Leninism, and highly distorted versions of the ideas of Freud and John Dewey. Because of their special awareness of the dangers of religious irrationality when it passes through a particularly fanatic phase, humanists should take the lead in protecting democracy against New Left bigotry and extremism. What is required of democrats now is activism and unity against both the escalating threat on the left and the inevitable counterthreat on the right. Conservatives, moderates, liberals, and socialists devoted to freedom must recognize that their shared values greatly exceed what divides them from one another. This basic operational principle requires that the democratic left unite with the democratic center and right to oppose the fascistic left—both for its own good and for democratic and even human survival. The same duty is incumbent, *mutatis mutandis,* upon democratic conservatives.

The precise details of the way in which these principles (and others) can best be applied to the university scene will necessarily differ greatly from campus to campus. Faculties, students, and administrators should firmly resist any attempts to stampede them into yielding to violence, other direct action, or threats—whether from the reactionary New Left, from inflamed racial or other minorities, or from right-wing extremists or hysterical politicians. However, any proposal presented should be examined carefully, on its merits, regardless of source. Due process should be accorded to ideas as well as persons in the bodies established to carry out this function.

Faculty members must be willing to take strong independent action against the spineless administrations that are willing to sacrifice academic freedom and institutional integrity to appease extremists. On the other hand, they must be willing to concede to students the right to take certain actions to back up their unsatisfied demands when these actions are voted by a majority of students. Among these rights should be the right to engage in nonviolent strikes.

The consequences of the *de facto* removal of the campus from the laws of the democratic state is today seen not only in the harassment, physical action, and threats against nonextremists but in continual arson, bombings, and even murders on campuses. One effective way of bringing the campus back within the framework of democratic law would be to remove the discretion of college presidents in this matter and explicitly provide that any member of the academic community whose rights are violated may summon the civil authorities. The elimination of extralegal private threat systems is supposedly a basic principle of democratic communities and they should not be tolerated, particularly on campuses, which are supposed to be centers of rationality.

I would like to add two points, which I consider of vital importance to the current campus disorders. The first is that actions that are tolerated from one group and measures that are adopted respecting them should not be different from those accepted for any other group. If one tolerates or condones direct action from the extreme left, one must do likewise for the extreme right. If one sets up a separate, biased course of study and proportionate quotas for blacks, one should be willing to do the same for militant "Aryans."

The second point is that current college violence is a symptom of the fact that the atmosphere in many academic institutions has become poisonous and destructive of the political sanity of many vulnerable young persons. The greatest crimes of history have been *political* crimes and the most dangerous form of insanity has been *political* insanity. To help clear this atmosphere, faculty members must redefine their moral and professional responsibilities to include making the university a place in which arguments for democracy are at least as intensively disseminated as is the cleverly disguised antidemocratic propaganda. Without such an effort, it is difficult to see how free universities can survive.

IX

International Education

Introduction

Barbara Ward and Buckminster Fuller have "blown our minds" with talk about our "global village" and "spaceship earth." And most of us *know* that we are but split seconds from instant communications with men on the moon or those in an Asian typhoon via satellites and other electronic communications. Yet we often seem to be living proof of the concept of territoriality, we so closely guard the grass in our backyards, declare loyalty to local village, state, or nation with such uncritical fealty. We often act as though it were impossible to be loyal to more than one territory or one community at a time! And, of course, maybe it *is* impossible if the values of one are in direct conflict with those of another. More often, it's difficult to sort out the true from the false, the evil from the ugly. But one thing is clear: there is no clear One Thing! Whether one travels widely in person or vicariously via books, magazines, and television, the variety of food, clothing, and custom, the incredible variety of language and creed, and the pluralism of the world's people are most manifest. Hence it is demoralizing to hear an Adolph Hitler and his latter-day disciples ranting that "...history is the science which demonstrates that one's people is always right..."[1] It is destructive to watch Jews and Arabs shooting it out in the Middle East, threatening to blow up the entire world, because each is certain that the other is wrong. It staggers the imagination to realize what the hundreds of billions of dollars going into the Vietnam War might have bought for Southeast Asians in the way of food, clothing, and peace! Nor is it comforting to know that our schools continue to brainwash American students year after year with patriotic virtue and ardor while the knowledge and feeling which we generate for other peoples and lands is miniscule in comparison.

Again, we know better, but we don't do better! Witness the passage of an international education bill and the failure of our Congress to appropriate funds to implement it! Witness the constant rearguard battle that the Daughters of the American Revolution have carried on "to get the United States out of the United Nations and the United Nations out of the United States." And this is only symptomatic of the viewpoint of other righteous rightists who would rather be dead than red or even well-read. They are part of the not-so-silent majority who support the insanity of antiballistic missiles.

And this is the kind of matrix into which a Francis Shoemaker would attempt to bring reason and appreciation for other cultures. Of course, Professor Shoemaker is correct when he says that "we find many of our definable concepts of self rudely challenged, both abroad in modern pluralistic planetary culture and on home ground in ghetto, campus, and complacement suburb." He is also mind-streching when he reminds us of the vast literatures of Islam, of Hindu-Buddhistic-Taoist cultures, of the Japanese and Africa. And we would agree that "It is obvious that we have a lot of exciting study ahead of us as we add a wholly new aesthetic to our understanding. . . ." But I am compelled to add quickly to the last comment, *if there's time*. Too, what is the probability that the number of persons reading widely about other cultures will form a critical mass to make a difference in the affairs of state? If we get involved in a nuclear holocaust, it may make no difference. But if we continue to plunge into brushfire wars, will the informed student of our global village muster enough pressure to restrict the publicity mill from grinding out stereotypes such as "Hun" during World War I or "Jap" during World War II? And we're back to the problem which Jack Nelson outlined in his review of nationalism in education (Chapter 14). When jingoism is in, sensibility is out!

Yet Professor Shoemaker and Harold Taylor provide an optimistic balance to such gloomy questions. The world could well be the teachers' training grounds—if we but willed it and funded it. And one hopes that Harold Taylor is right when he declares that there *is* "beneath the surface of the visible world society an inner community of persons—peasants, teachers, doctors, scientists, poets, lawyers, architects, men of religion, writers, readers, students, lovers, composers—linked together intuitively by common concerns and interests, and reaching out to each other across the divisions of the world and its governments." In such a *reaching* there is hope.

There is little doubt that Dr. Taylor's vision, for teachers and for mankind, is one of the impossible practicalities on which we have focused throughout this book. If the billions of dollars spent on war could be converted into ship and plane tickets, to increase appreciation for other cultures and peoples, to develop international social service and teacher corps, perhaps the world's peoples would be too busy to fight wars! Spaceship though we may be, it is doubtful if we'd lose gravitational equilibrium if all three billion of us became mobile at once!

Harold Taylor's is a clarion call to action. Groan as we may about our government's irresponsibilty, loathe nationalistic education as we may, condemn as we should obsolescent educational structures, each of us can do what he can to cultivate that greatest of the liberalizing arts, the skill to communicate via the written and spoken word as well as the medium of listening. Since nobody to my knowledge has come up with the perfect scheme for training teachers, Taylor's imaginative suggestions may provide an overall design for developing more detailed blueprints. Here is a field for the fertile imagination. Here is a field for inventions which may not enrich the inventor but may benefit mankind for generations to come. Here is a field ready for the ploughing.

If, as Harold Taylor says, we are "a nation of volunteers," a minority of one can take action.

27

FRANCIS SHOEMAKER

New Dimensions
for World Cultures

We are currently engaged in a second revival of the Humanities in American education. Many of us participated in the first one during the fifteen-year period before War II, when within the remarkable growth of broadfield Humanities, Social Science and Natural Science courses in General Education programs in colleges and universities, the Humanities brought together previously scattered offerings in literature and other arts, and frequently history, philosophy and religion, predominantly of Western Civilization.[1] Today's revival constitutes a comparably dramatic growth in American high schools of courses variously titled Humanities, Culture Area Studies, World Affairs and the like. Central to many is concern for literature and other arts, but almost universally within the total cultural context of other cultures than the so-called Western. Where Western culture is included, a prominent concern is to place it in perspective among other world cultures.

The revivals resemble one another in their search for both breadth and focus in times of cultural crisis. The world-wide Depression and World War II challenged us in the unprecedented measure to testify to the value of the individual in society. We sought the testament in the individually formulated values embodied in the arts of Western Culture. In some colleges—Stephens and Antioch, for example—we used basic aesthetic principles as the focusing factor for the tremendous breadth of

This article originally appeared in the Teachers College Record, **69**, *No. 7 (1968), 685–97. Reprinted by permission.*

material. In other colleges—Columbia and Chicago, to name two—we found focus in selected Great Books as representative of great ideas. By 1940, drawing on the social sciences of history, anthropology, psychology and human ecology—as in Stanford, Colorado State College of Education and Teachers College, Columbia University—we had begun to point up successive cultural epochs in Western civilization, each embodying a new and enlarged conception of self in Western man.[2] With each new organizational framework we increased the scope in our material and sharpened the aesthetic focus in philosophy and method.

Today we find many of our definable concepts of self rudely challenged, both abroad in modern pluralistic planetary culture and on home ground in ghetto, campus and complacent suburb. Just as insistently we find ourselves studying to redefine values and redesign course content and patterns of inquiry. Thousands of us are returning from assignment overseas as exchange teachers, Fulbright lecturers and tutors, USIS and USAID technicians and Peace Corps Volunteers. What designs and emphases are we likely to find significant, when everyone on our communities knows that manned satellites sweep over the European peninsula before we can call the names of such epoch embodiers as Sophocles, Dante, Shakespeare, Goethe, Melville, Tolstoy and Steinbeck—and that the United Nations now includes more than 130 members, half of which are less than twenty years old? Will Eastern Humanities and Western Humanities suffice? Or White-skinned Humanities and Dark-skinned Humanities? Or Greco-Roman-Judeo-Christian Humanities? Or Islamic Humanities? Or Buddhist Humanities? Or African Autochthonous Humanities? Or Humanities based on universal Aesthetic Principles, culturally defined? Or on concepts of imaginative individuals speaking for or against prevailing and intuited ideas and values of their societies?

My guess is that many of us lean toward the last of these, but that we also want a serviceable design within which to observe and compare these ideas and values. With this in mind, I would like to explore one such design which, after thirty some years of teaching Humanities in the United States, has begun to take shape through my day-to-day involvement in international education in Latin America, Africa and Asia. The process that Matthew Arnold calls "artistic simplification" leads me to think of the nations of the world as constituting four major world cultures. The nations comprising each world culture share common and differentiated values. They participate in the contemporary world through common and differentiated patterns of symbolization. It is their fundamental values and symbol systems that both provide and denote their integrity. While the nations in each world group share some geographic proximity, it seems important to designate them by terms that suggest their centers of loyalty and devotion rather than their geographic location.

In consequence, I find it helpful to think of our own world cultures as Classico-Judeo-Christian, and simultaneously of two other world cultures as Islamic, and Hindu-Buddhistic-Taoist, and the fourth as African Autochthonous—to suggest a world culture in the marking.

Redefining "Western"

In using the grographical term "Western" to designate our world culture, we have for the most part limited ourselves to Europe and the United States; we have ignored the linguistic, political, religious, literary, educational and familial ties of Latin America with Mediterranean and Biblical cultures. And the continent of Australia, with its rich new literature, we have yet to relate to its Anglo-Saxon origins. In the Classico-Judeo-Christian culture design, then, I would suggest that we include Europe, the Americas, Australia and the Philippines. And there can be little doubt that the great books of "Western culture" notwithstanding, the most pervasive formulation of values for this world culture exists in the Bible in its many versions and derivative myths and symbols in art, literature, music and architecture.

It is momentarily staggering to think of adding to an already over-ambitious content any concern for Incan art or Caribbean music, Mexican painting, recent Latin American novels in English translation, the architectural promise of Brasilia, or Randolph Stow's prize novel of Australian life, *A Haunted Land,*[3] or Leonard Casper's *New Writing from the Philippines.*[4] But I take courage from the publication in April of William H. McNeill's *A World History*[5]—not because it is a tremendous *tour de force,* but because it exemplifies the principle of simultaneity. Application of this principle, plus judicious use of touchstones in selected art mediums will permit us, I believe, to help students intensify the quality of their experience and heighten their feeling for the reality of their study.

Knowing the Middle East

As we move on to consider the second world culture within this planetary design we realize that a number of schools have introduced new courses with titles resembling "The Middle East." If we follow the lead of such a geographic designation to its farthest dimensions, we immediately list twenty nations, speaking several major languages but all sharing in the inspiriting precepts of the *Holy Koran.*

Islamic world culture today stretches over 160 degrees of longitude, from the Islamic Republic of Mauretania on the Atlantic coast of Africa, across Morocco, Algeria and Tunisia, skirting the northern provinces of

Mali, Niger and Chad into the whole of the Sudan and then throughout Egypt, Arabia, Jordan, Lebanon, Turkey, Iraq, Iran, Afghanistan, Pakistan and the Republic of Indonesia—with an additional 50,000,000 Muslims in India. The history and geography of this vast area shows pervasive problems of land and water management that are directly related to food supply and national and regional self-sufficiency. The frequency of reference in the *Holy Koran* to "gardens underneath which rivers flow" helps us to read this great book with something of the seventh-century Arab's ear for metaphor and survival.

With no prior study each of us can read the A. J. Arberry[6] translation of the *Holy Koran* or *Aspects of Islamic Civilization* and find himself caught up in the seventh century return to monotheism, the security of a new legal structure, and a strengthened code of ethics. He can virtually feel himself cleansed of tradition-bound depravity when he reads

> There is no fault in those who believe and do deeds of righteousness...God loves the good-doers.

A thoughtful reading of this key literary document of Islam can bring our students to understand, with Bernard Lewis in *The Arabs in History,* that "Islam...was not only a system of belief and cult. It was also a system of state, society, law, thought and art—a civilization with religion as its unifying, eventually dominating, factor."[7]

Architecture provides another symbol of culture for Islam. It introduces us to the sequence of the culture epochs of national leadership—Arabian, Egyptian, Persian, Turkish, Moghul, with Egypt bidding again today for primacy. From the Alhambra Palace in Spain to the Taj Mahal in India magnificent structures reveal superb engineering, artistry, and affluence. Palaces and citadels reveal the brilliance of princely society, and congregational mosques and their decorative themes (of course devoid of painting and sculpture) speak of "a religion of triumph in success, of salvation through victory and achievement and power."[8] And today, alongside the ubiquitous Hilton Hotel, each country is making its adaptation of international architecture.

Islamic Perspectives

The educational system provides a third perspective on the unity of Islam. This will be particularly true for those who can assume the point of view of the Islamic student in his own country, not that of the American scholar gathering data in comparative education. From grade one every child throughout Islamic culture memorizes sections of the *Koran.* He later reads parts of it in his national language; but he also studies

Arabic in which to recite the *Koran;* he studies his nation's history and geography in the context of Islamic history; he studies calligraphy as an art form, and other arts and crafts. Knowing the fairly uniform curriculum, we can ask ourselves what Islamic humanities contributes to the young person's development and national pride. What are his feelings of wonder at Islam's replacing the Roman Empire in North Africa and Spain within a hundred years of Mohammed's death in Arabia?—and at the founding of the oldest university in the world in Cairo (enrollment now 50,000) and of other university centers at Aleppo, Baghdad, Teheran and Balkh in Northern Afghanistan while Europe groped through the darkest years of the Dark Ages? What are his feelings when he learns that Greek culture and science reached Europe through Arabic-to-Latin translation?

When he reads George Sarton's *History of Science,* how does he respond to the tribute that "...from the point of view of the development of mankind as a whole, the Arabic-Islamic culture was of supreme importance, because it constituted the main link between the Near East and the West, as well as between the Near East and Buddhist Asia"?[9] What kind of perspective does he gain on himself when he compares the descriptions of Arab character by fifteenth-century historian, Ibn Khaldun, and those of twentieth-century social scientists, Edward T. Hall and Daniel Lerner? How does he regard the tragedy of the leveling of the great cities of Afghanistan, Iran, Iraq by Ghengis Khan between 1220 and 1260? And the elimination of 1,000,000 Muslims in Spain at the end of the sixteenth century? Does he recall that 900 years elapsed from the sack of Rome to *The Divine Comedy*—and that today his culture may be on the threshold of a new age after only 700 years of recuperation from holocaust in Asia and 350 years in Spain?

This kind of historical perspective is valued in Islamic culture. Islam's greatest modern poet Mohammad Iqbal writes,

> What is history, O stranger to thyself?
> A tale, a story or a fable?
> No! It makes thee conscious of self
> Capable in action and efficient in quest!
> Sharpens thee like a dagger on the whetstone
> And then strikes thee on the face of thy world?[10]

Historical information is readily available to students in the paperback editions of such books as Bernard Lewis's *The Arabs in History* and Wilfred Cantwell Smith's *Islam in Modern History.* Direct approaches to other humanities are available in T. Cuyler Young's *Near Eastern Culture and Society,* and James Kritzeck's *Anthology of Islamic Literature.*[11]

Again it is instructive to read six more lines of Iqbal to let him reinforce the thought that education may open the key window on Islamic culture.

> What is the school-master?
> An architect of the souls of men!
> How attractively has the philosopher, Qaani,
> Remarked for his guidance:
> "If you will have your courtyard flooded with light,
> Do not interpose a wall in the path of the Sun . . ."[12]

The Hindu-Buddhistic-Taoist

Hindu-Buddhistic-Taoist world culture is the third in this brief exploration. It involves twelve countries: Ceylon, India, Nepal, Tibet, Thailand, Burma, Laos, Cambodia, Vietnam, China, Korea and Japan— in all of which, according to F.S.C. Northrop in his monumental *The Meeting of East and West*, Buddhist culture is a major and persistent component.[13]

Buddha had completed fifty years of teaching a thousand years before Mohammed was born. As happened in the later recording of the teachings of Christ and Mohammed, groups of Buddha's one-time Hindu followers assembled after his death and set down from memory the canon of the *Tripitoka*. This is now the basic document of Hinayana Buddhism in Ceylon, Thailand and Burma; its literary, artistic and philosophic continuity in India is evident in the much repeated *Jataka Tales* of the rebirths of Buddha, the symbolic representations of his life and work in the temples of Sarnath and Sanchi, and the codes of law and humane conduct inscribed on the pillars of Asoka and abbreviated in the *chakra*, or the Great Wheel of the flag of modern India.

At a later date other philosophically inclined disciples of Buddha set down in the form of discourses with Buddha the *Surangama Sutra*. This is the major document for Mahayana Buddhism in Tibet, China, Korea and Japan. With its sustained discussions of mind and perception we may find that it leads us in the direction of what Northrop calls the undifferentiated aesthetic continuum of Chinese Buddhist and Taoist painting, and the Sumiye and Haiku of Japanese Zen. What new aesthetic will emerge from Chinese Communism we may sense presently.

But the close reading to arrive at these discriminations can be very dull reading for high school students. It seems more important that they take Hindu-Buddhistic-Taoist relationships as a given, and then briefly, in impressive visual maps and graphs, grasp the simultaneity of parallel culture epochs in the three major secular components of the Hindu-Buddhistic-Taoist world culture, India, China, Japan, and in turn, their relation to contemporaneous culture epochs in other world cultures. This could bring students quickly to the modern context of three world cultures.

The striking fact about contemporary India, China and Japan, of course, is that they entered the present epoch at almost the same time: Hiroshima (1945) for Japan, Independence (1947) for India, Communist dominance (1949) for China.[14, 15] It seems essential that we continue to deal with them simultaneously in their modern phase. Their own interrelations multiply, with India and China disputing territorial boundaries, Japan according to Hajime Nakamura, diligently researching the roots of its own Buddhism in India, and India using Japan as a national model for its developing education and industrialization.[16] As we come to know more about Buddhist humanities and their Indian, Chinese and Japanese components, we may well develop a touchstone approach to the diverse factors in this world culture. Let me sample here one or two aspects of such an approach, using Indian material primarily and touching lightly on possible leads into Chinese and Japanese culture patterns.

Indian Emergence

Pre-Independence Indian education was largely set by an English Government document known as the Macaulay Minute. This called for the education of persons, "Indian in blood and color, but English in taste, in opinion, in morals and in intellect." There was little room in this system for Indian geography and ecology, Indian archaeology and history, Indian mother-tongues, or indigenous art.

But in the twenty years since Independence, India has moved dramatically on all these cultural fronts. As in our efforts to achieve empathic identification with Islamic culture through the eyes of Islam's youth, so may we with Indian culture. To further what India calls "national integration," each of her sixteen states teaches the physical and economic geography of each other state. Each State Education Ministry maintains a science institute, which helps youngsters to observe indigenous flowers, trees and birds rather than memorize the characteristics of English daffodils, oaks, and robins. The Indian Archaeological Survey has become the largest national archeological endeavor in the world—virtually lifting an inspiring national history from the prehistoric sites of Harappa and Mohenjo-daro, from Buddhist stupas in Sarnath and Sanchi and the temple caves of Ellora and Ajanta, from such Muslim tombs as the Taj Mahal, and fortress cities like Fatephur Sikri, and even from the consciously preserved monuments to British governors and kings. Dance groups—Bharatanayam, Kathakali, Manipuri, Kuchipudi, Odissi—travel among the states, reembodying traditional values in regional classic forms. Comparably in literature, Indian youngsters recite the *Koran,* read and retell the *Jataka Tales* of the rebirths of Buddha, the animal stories of the *Panchantantra*, tales from Kalidasa, the epic of the *Ramayana*, and the historico-philosophic drama of the *Mahabharata* with its religious center in the *Bhagavad Gita*. The classic Indian humanities become part of a living present from which India is consciously constituting her modern synthesis.

One of Nehru's great interests was the founding of the Children's Book Trust to develop a children's literature for India. Little has yet come from the Book Trust that provides modern role models for modern children. But last year the Sahitya Akademi published a book, *Contemporary Indian Short Stories*,[17] one from each state, that sets a good example. And since 1964, following the work of Professor Constance McCullough as a member of the Teachers College, Columbia University advisory team, young authors are learning to look at their village communities and to write stories about today for school primers. Also, I venture a guess that increasing American interest in the Indian Tolstoy, Premchand, will lead to the reprinting of many of his short stories and novels, both in English and in Indian languages.

Modern Indian Art Forms

Film, it seems to me, may play a unique role in Indian humanities. In the hands of Satyajit Ray, of course, it provides a realistic mirror for Indian youngsters—quite different from the four-hour productions of the Bombay and Madras studios. But those of us who have taught Humanities in its western form look at all Indian film from a special perspective. We know that the high degree of consciousness of self in Classico-Judeo-Christian culture dates from Gutenberg and subsequent preoccupation with the printed word. Millions of Indian people are illiterate in print but fully literate in film. They are coming into their literary heritage through sound-color film. There are implications in this for the development of Indian national personality. It may, indeed, develop along lines of much greater social conscience than characterizes the privatism of our culture. Both G. Morris Carstairs' *The Twice Born*[18] and Nirad C. Chaudhuri's *The Continent of Circle*[19] provide us with psychological insights for reading Indian literature.

Humayun Kabir writes in *The Indian Heritage*. "The modern world is instinct with the urge for a new and impatient life. To the old tradition of unity of life has been added the new demand of equality and justice. . ."[20] There are intimations of this in much of contemporary Indian literature, certainly in the many biographies and writings of Gandhi and Tagore, which seem to be "musts" in any program we develop. But there are also novels such as Khwaja Ahmad Abbas' *Inquilab*,[21] which deals with the freedom movement; Raj Anandi's *Coolie*,[22] which cuts deeply into values of aspiration, injustice and denial; Khushwant Singh's *Train to Pakistan*[23] and *Mano Majra*,[24] which treat the inanities of partition; and Thakazhi Pillai's *Chemmeen*,[25] which examines young love thwarted by custom. And R. K. Narayan's new book, *The Vendor of Sweets*,[26] asks us to look again at the conflict of the generations with an overlay of the conflict of world cultures.[27]

Our responsibility to our students, it seems to me, is to help them with the criterial questions with which they can continue to read the increasing amount of Indian literature available. What, for instance, are the tension points in the behavior of characters? Do they arise because characters are using ancient epic heroes as role models? Or because literary characters may have had no modern role models from which to learn the consequences of varied behavior patterns? And—perhaps most important— what new role models are contemporary Indian literatures of print and film creating for Indian youth?

There is some likelihood that painting will become the major expressive form for Indian youngsters. For the past thirteen years the Shankar on-the-spot painting contests and the Shankar International Children's Art Festival have enlisted hundreds of thousands of perceptive interpretations. Indian children seem to come closer to self understanding through painting than through literature.

In architecture, India has tried her hand at two all-new state capitol cities, Chandigarh in the Punjab and Bhubaneschwar in Orissa—answering affirmatively Le Corbusier's and Lewis Mumford's insistence that our old cities are not redeemable. With public school providing extensive experiences in virtual space in painting, we may expect a new generation of city planners to come into university programs in engineering and architecture, bringing a new respect for Indian traditions in tropical shelter and their relation to human survival.

Simultaneous with our study of touchstones in Indian culture it should be possible to observe comparable touchstones in Japan and in China. Unless we press ourselves to perfect this kind of method we will continue the vast culture lag that characterizes much of contemporary education.

Japanese Touchstones

Turning to Japan we can, as in India, look at education as a key to national culture. The address of Japan's Education Minister, Abe Yoshishige, to the U.S. Education Mission, March 8, 1946, eight months after Hiroshima, provides a starting point, but one quite unlike the English Macaulay Minute.

> After this miserable defeat...Our people have suddenly turned their eyes on education and become keenly aware ...that the present condition of our country is due to errors

and defects in education, and also to [our] low cultural standard. . . as individuals. . . [28]
. . . the characteristics of a tradition that is still alive among the people should be respected. Thus I would like to ask America not to deal with us simply from an American point of view. . . America as a victorious country, is in a position to do any thing it pleases with Japan. I hope I am not making too bold in expressing the wish that America may not avail herself of this position to impose upon us simply what is characteristic of America or of Europe. . . if this is . . . the case. . . I fear that we shall never be able to have a true Japanese education. . . firmly rooted in our soil and which can work on the inmost soul of the. . . people.[29]

Leads for understanding of the "inmost soul" of Japan, prewar and contemporary, are opened to us in *Approaches to Asian Civilizations*,[30] edited by Theodore de Bary and Ainslee Embree. But we come much closer in Ruth Benedict's wartime analysis of Japanese culture patterns, *The Chrysanthemum and the Sword*,[31] and UNESCO's postwar *Without the Chrysanthemum and the Sword*,[32] a study of personality structures and values of young people. Focus on personality orientation sharpens in L. Takeo Doi's essay, "Amae: A Key Concept for Understanding Japanese Personality Structure."[33] The social science perspectives of these and other studies[34] inform our reading of seventeenth-century dramas of Chikamatsu and twentieth-century novels of Tanizaki. They prepare us for cross-cultural insight into Japanese popular culture as reported by Hidetoshi Kato,[35] and as reflected in the UNESCO anthology of *Modern Japanese Stories*,[36] and Donald Keene's *Modern Japanese Literature*.[37]

Chinese Touchstones

To this simultaneous approach to Indian and Japanese humanities we need to add comparable concern for Chinese humanities, starting with the now available *Red Book* of Mao Tse Tung and moving to the excellent new book of Liu Wu-Chi, *An Introduction to Chinese Literature*.[38] It will be no surprise that Chairman Mao, as early as 1942, was demanding "a unity of politics and art, a unity of content and form, and a unity of revolutionary political content and an artistic form of as high a standard as possible."[39]

Matching theory with talent, Lao She provides insight into a new Chinese national personality in the conclusion to *Rickshaw Boy* (1938) with this paragraph:

The face-saving, emulative, dreamy, self-seeking, individualistic, robust, and great Hsiang-tzu. No one knew how many funeral processions he had attended for others, nor was it known when and where he would bury himself, this degenerate, selfish, luckless product of the sickly womb of society, the wayworn ghost of individualism.[40]

African Autochthonous Humanities

In sub-Sahara Africa, new nations date their independence within the last ten years; remaining ones expect theirs within the next ten years. Political newness is matched with the newness of visible and transmittable formulations of African values. Vigorous and prolific literature is either newly created by a new generation of writers or newly transcribed directly from the story tellers. In consequence, as W. E. Abraham says in *The Mind of Africa*, "Our interest in our own cultures is not historical and archeological but directed towards the future..."[41]

Dr. Abraham's personal cultural roots are in Ghana, but he speaks for the fifty nations of Africa which are trying to heal what he calls the "multiple wounds" of diverse European exploitations and to find the "Agreement which would draw the skin together and give Africa a continental outlook."[42]

Here again it seems to me that entry into African culture through African education is particularly appropriate. One of the key books studied by Nigerian youth for the Nigerian Secondary School Certification Examination is Chinua Achebe's *Things Fall Apart*.[43] The beginnings of modern African humanities for Africans and for us must include this classic effort of an author to get life into form for his people, who have witnessed personal deteriorations and tribal disintegrations from the incursion of commercial, political and missionary interests. *Things Fall Apart* renders into highly charged form Abraham's factual account in "Paradigm of African Society" of tribal social-religious-aesthetic values.

As in other world cultures, education is being looked to to provide the personality resources to fuse the finer qualities of tradition with the most promising aspects of modernity. At this juncture the center for this synthesis seems to be the concept of *the African personality*, "...that complex of ideas and attitudes which is both identical and significant in otherwise different African cultures..."[44] Philosophically, "the African personality" seems to share something with our own conception of transactional participation in environment. The African thinks much about the world but not, indeed, as the world inside which he finds himself, but as the world of which he forms a part.[45]

Aesthetics and Culture

Nothing is more central to the realization of the African personality than comprehension by us and our African friends of the culture-based characteristic of any aesthetic. In the well-intentioned vandalism of missionaries, countless thousands of objects of art were destroyed. A little anthropological understanding would have shown that for peoples without writing, normal expression of values is through art—through, as Abraham writes, "...the timeless, immemorial, silent, and elemental power so characteristic of African traditional art. Indeed this is the main reason why it is not lifelike in a representational sense. Forms had to be distorted." He continues, "In art there was a moral-philosophical preoccupation which led it to portray forces of the world, and to portray a force it is essential that it should not be treated like something assimilated, and consequently like something overcome, as the rendering of it in lifelike figures would have been."[46]

It is obvious that we have a lot of exciting study ahead of us as we add a wholly new aesthetic to our understanding, or following Susanne Langer's lead in her latest book, *Mind: An Essay on Human Feeling*,[47] search out the biological bases of art forms in world cultures, including the African Autochthonous.

Scholarly organizations will be increasingly helpful to us. The University of Leeds publishes *The Journal of Commonwealth Literature*.[48] The Association for African Literature, based in Fourah Bay College in Freetown, Sierra Leone, publishes its *Bulletin*[49] replete with perceptive reviews of current literature of all types. The Department of English at the University of Ibadan is behind *New Approaches to African Literature*,[50] a comprehensive bibliography and commentary.

These organizations are essentially extensions of the modern aesthetic of African authors. Onuora Nzekwu's *Wand of Noble Wood*[51] reflects the self-conscious effort to use literature to make Ibo society understandable to English-speaking audiences. And Chinua Achebe goes the distance in making his art an integral part of African cultural evolution. In an essay entitled "The Novelist as Teacher" he writes:

> Perhaps what I write is applied art as distinct from pure. But who cares? Art is important but so is education of the kind I have in mind. And I don't see that the two need be mutually exclusive. In a recent anthology a Hausa folktale having recounted the usual fabulous incidents ends with these words: "They all came and lived happily together. He had several sons and daughters who grew up and helped in raising the standard of education of the country." As I said elsewhere, if you consider this ending a naive anti-climax then you cannot know very much about Africa.[52]

It is not only the self-conscious author who has access to emerging ideas of social conscience though. In contemporary African literature, read in the spirit of inquiry, we can put down a number of test cores to assay the quality of values being nurtured in the culture. William Conton's *The African* affords one example. After years of provocation by an unreconstructed bigot, the narrator of this story has a perfect opportunity for vengeance. He writes:

> He lay very still as I stood over him, and as the first drums began to send their throbbing message out across the night it was pity I found in my heart for him, not hate. I stooped quickly, lifted him gently, and bore him through the easing rain to the safety of his home.[53]

There can be no summary to this exploration of a potential organizational framework for the study of world cultures. There can only be projection into the methods it implies. It implies the need to deal with parts only in the context of wholes. It implies the need to find new ways to deal in lifelike simultaneity with wide spectrums of materials and values. It implies the need for staff and students to work together at their respective levels of inquiry. It constitutes a new opportunity to demonstrate the scholarly method is an integral part of teaching method.

28

HAROLD TAYLOR

The Teacher in the World

The education of teachers lies at the heart of everything that matters in the life of the world's people. We who are teachers have a chance we have never had before to teach and learn on a world scale, and to join forces with a world community of those who have the good of humanity at heart. For the principal fact of the modern world is not its massive unrest, although that is its most visible characteristic, but its growing and necessary unity—the interpenetration of all lives by every other, the coming-together of peoples, cultures, and societies to accomplish common purposes. We are groping toward something named by Adlai Stevenson just before his death, "impartial protection for the whole wide society of man."

A transformation is under way, partly through blind and unavoidable impulses in contemporary history, partly through conscious changes in the thinking of those with political, social, and intellectual power. The international social and political systems are now affecting each other in fundamental ways. So are the educational systems. Secular and religious beliefs are finding new accommodations; the great religions are in the process of discovering, through a world-wide ecumenical movement, a set of shared truths which have to do, not with theological dogma, but with what Pope John in *Pacem in Terris* called, "the common good of the entire human family."

This article originally appeared in The Humanist, **28**, *No. 1 (1968),* 16–19. *Reprinted by permission.*

It is with this common good that I am concerned; this is the heart of the matter. There exists beneath the surface of the visible world society an inner community of persons—peasants, teachers, doctors, scientists, poets, lawyers, architects, men of religion, linked together intuitively by common concerns and interests, and reaching out to each other across the divisions of the world and its governments. That community has within it a kind of power, a growing sense of unity, a common culture coalescing into new forms which add the flavor of regional differences to a newly developing heritage of man.

The teacher and the student are at the center of this new community. They share, in whatever country they live, a common interest in the advancement of learning for human benefit. In the United States, a new generation of students has created a national community among themselves, with national and international interests, of which the problems of peace and war, human rights, the politics of change and the reform of education are central. The solutions they propose and act upon, their unifying beliefs, are based on the idea that the older generation and the established order in any society cannot assume the right of authority and control over the younger generation. The young have equal rights as citizens; they have their own ideas about how to run a society and its educational system. Since they are the ones education is done to, they have special qualifications for knowing what it is.

Elsewhere around the world there is a comparable constituency—the young Indonesians who were united against Sukarno, the Korean youth who opposed the dictatorship of Rhee, the Spanish students who reject educational control by Franco, the Soviet young who question, through poetry, the politics of their elders. In international and world education, here is where we must start—with the living reality of the world community of students and teachers. We must bring that community together, put it in touch with itself. The education of the teacher and the student (the two are inseparable) must now draw upon the cultural and intellectual resources of the entire world, no matter to which part of it the teacher's habitat confines him. For the American teacher and his students, the cultural and intellectual resources of the world are at his feet, and if he does not find them there, he can go to the places where they are.

At this point in history, we in America *are* the world's most powerful economic, social, military and political force. We are also the ones who have mastered the technique of mass communication, the ones with the most technology, the most educational institutions, museums, art galleries, science laboratories, television stations, cultural centers, educational programs. Whether we like it or not, we are the forerunners of what mass societies will some day be. Despite our Western geography, we live in the middle of the world. The world has come to us, we travel into it by the millions every year, we serve as a point of linkage between the thousands of elements which make up the cultural and social fabric of world society. What is at stake now is the question of how we use the power at this center, with what degree of imagination and good will we can enter the lives of the rest of the world's people.

We have not yet come to terms with the fact that we have a latent cultural power of fantastic proportions, and that we could very well fritter it away. A large part of this power lies in the sheer amount of interest the rest of the world has in us. We are watched and listened to, criticized and condemned, opposed and supported. Our daily lives are scrutinized from abroad and at home by a stream of foreign experts, and the whole world seems to feel free to take part in our politics, liking or disliking our Presidents, our habits, our customs, our arts, and ourselves.

If we have not fully realized what a radical change our world position means to our educational thinking and in the use of our own resources, this is perfectly understandable. The years of rapid change in America's position were years in which educators at home were inundated with the practical problems of expanding radically an inadequate educational system while at the same time reforming its content. The educators were building a system of mass education without having thought first about how they were doing it. So concentrated has been the attention given to the practical problems of enrollment, buildings, and rising budgets, that questions about the world and where it is going have very seldom been raised among working educators. They have tended to do what they have been asked to do, having discovered during the fifties that reforming the science and mathematics curriculum was safe, good and rewarded, while meddling with international issues could turn out to be nasty, brutish, and short. Reforms in the curriculum of world affairs were based on a philosophy of strengthening and rationalizing our side of an ideological conflict with Communism. In the case of foreign visitors and programs to bring them here, the aim was to win friends and allies to our side.

That philosophy has been outdated by events, if it could be said to have had validity in the first place. Our purpose in American education is not to induct our visitors into an American curriculum so that they will appreciate and support America and the West, but to enrich our curriculum and their education with the points of view and knowledge of those from elsewhere around the earth. We should now ask them to join us in teaching ourselves.

First, let us declare that teaching is a form of national and international service. Let us then call the country's youth to that service as volunteers for a national Student Corps. Let us say what is true, that to prepare oneself to teach is to give to liberal education its true meaning—to use knowledge for the improvement of human life—and that the normal expectation for the college graduate is that he should give at least two years of his life to the service of his country by teaching to others what he has learned in college.

We have already begun this in part, by calling upon volunteers for the National Teacher Corps, Head Start, the Domestic Service Corps, the Peace Corps, and the Poverty program, but we have stopped short of making the call for service into a philosophy of education for a democratic society. Let us give our youth a chance to serve.

We should then provide the volunteers with subsistence and tuition, just as we did in an earlier time through the G.I. Bill, when a whole new generation of youth was brought into the main stream of American society. Let us give 50,000 student-teachers a year abroad in practice teaching, foreign languages, and service in communities. Let us assume that foreign service is a natural part of the education of teachers, both for those already teaching and those being prepared. For those at home, let us send 50,000 student volunteers into the Spanish-American, Indian, Puerto Rican, Negro, poor white, and other communities for a "year abroad" in the United States. Let us follow out the implications of the Peace Corps, and think of it as a teacher education program of world dimension by making it mutually international, with 15,000 foreign students brought to America yearly to teach in our schools, help us with our foreign languages, our studies of Asia, Africa, Eastern Europe, South America, to teach us about their countries and join us in our effort to make a world community and a world curriculum.

Let us make of America a meeting-ground for the teachers and peoples of the world, a place where we can pool the world's resources for the benefit of all. Let them bring their instruments and play their music, act their plays, read their poems, dance, sing, compose, paint, and write with us in an all-year, every-year world festival of the arts. Let everyone teach everyone whatever it is he knows. Abroad, we can take the initiative to create, not merely East-West Centers for client countries and potential allies, but World Centers on the seven continents, world centers on our own campuses, where students, teachers, and scholars from everywhere can work together on common tasks.

We would then find ourselves closer to the place we ought to be. Having been handed the leadership of the world as a gift from history, a gift seldom given and quickly taken away, we would have shown that we had chosen to use that gift and our power to secure the peaceable welfare and education of all mankind.

Before these proposals are dismissed as visionary, let me say that they are simply attempts to put into operation the declared intention of the President of the United States and the United States Congress. The proposals deal simultaneously with the problems of producing the Great

Society and creating a peaceful world order. Beginning with President Johnson's Smithsonian Institution address of 1965, moving on to his subsequent message on international education to Congress, and the passage of the International Education Act in 1967, a straight line of argument has developed about the American intention.

For the first time in the history of the United States, a President of this country has called for a conception of American education which makes it part of a world system. The United States has formally accepted an obligation to share her cultural resources with the world and to advance the cause of education everywhere, in cooperation with "all nations, friend and foe alike," with a wish to "receive as much as we give, to learn as well as to teach." The United States has declared explicitly that we are one among many cultures, willing to do our part in uniting them all. These new developments, and the extraordinary opportunities they provide, bring a whole new set of energies, ideas and talents into the work of educating teachers. There is enormous power in the individual acts and singular persons who, in the communities, colleges and schools of America have simply taken it upon themselves to do something and have set about doing it. We are lucky enough to be a nation of volunteers.

The parents of a school child who started the Ogontz plan for foreign students teaching in the schools, the Colorado student who formed an exchange with Brazilian students for community action and education, the faculty at Michigan State who proposed and established an international curriculum at Justin Morrill College, with four hundred students, the dozens of international projects in the colleges of the Midwest, the pilot projects of the member institutions of the Association of Colleges for Teacher Education, the major programs and projects of Stanford, Indiana University, the University of Wisconsin, and the new plans and achievements of Universities in California and New York State—all of these were originally started by the initiative of either a single or just a few persons. The issue of reform in education is not as important as the simple task of taking on the right projects and doing them. After a while, if enough good projects are done, you find that education has been reformed. I call upon all educational institutions to set in motion at least one new project, to appoint at least one faculty member, to make at least one new program in the education of teachers which will help to extend education into the world and the world into education.

I am deeply devoted to the idea of teachers colleges, to the idea that learning to teach is the ultimate liberal art, and that the best way to learn something is to try to teach it. Against the current of contemporary opinion, I deplore the mass movement of educators away from the idea of teachers colleges and toward the multi-purpose university, or toward that alarming and inelegant hybrid, the multiversity. I think I know why the educators have moved that way. They have been dislodged from their belief in the primacy of teaching and learning by those with the power and prestige of the knowledge industry behind them. There can be no genuine multi-purpose university no matter what diversity of clients it claims to serve. In the true university there is a single purpose, the advancement of learning. Learning depends on the capacity and commitment of students to learn, and this, in large part, depends on the talent of scholars to teach.

The powerful social and intellectual force which exists within the new generation of students has been greatly underestimated by educators and the public, who have tended to think of student activists and those concerned with civil rights and world affairs as a general nuisance, a motley group of radical dissidents, draft-dodgers, or young rebels who will soon get over it. On the countrary, what we have is a new and significant national asset. The core of the student protest movement is composed of a serious and informed body of young people who act out of a sense of personal commitment to each other and a sense of compassion for those who have been blocked from a place in society. They care very much for the quality of their own lives and are sensitive to the effects of their acts on the lives of others. They are responsible critics of the society and its educational system, and the best of them have a political sophistication and social energy which is in advance of many of those appointed to educate them. In short, by their acts of engagement and their intellectual commitments, they have shown that they are already teachers. They have trained themselves.

But, as I have talked among them, I have found a curious paradox. The motivations and interests which have brought them into a direct confrontation with the problems of world society and its educational system are exactly those which turn them away from entering the teaching profession. Within their ideas, their persons and their social idealism lies a formidable force for educational change of exactly the kind the country has been calling for. Two hundred and fifty thousand of them are volunteer tutors in the urban and rural slums. Thousands more are at work on educational reform, tens of thousands have volunteered for service in social welfare programs. Yet most of these do not intend to be teachers.

When asked for the reasons, they say two things: they refuse to spend what they think to be wasteful time in taking education courses which they contend are without serious intellectual content or relevance to their own experience as teachers and tutors. They want to work out their own methods and curricula directly with the children and teachers in the school, with such help as they can get from educators who welcome their questions. They then say that once properly certified and installed in a teaching post, they would not be able to teach about the world with any real sense of integrity because the system—the school board, the superintendent, the principal, the other teachers and the community—has a set pattern of political, social and educational attitudes in which they would, by conforming, lose their personal identity. To which I have replied, then how do you hope to reform either the society or its educational system if you refuse to get into the game? I usually win the argument while losing the candidate.

The way to win them is to take them seriously. Until we create programs in the undergraduate and graduate colleges of education which can speak to their concerns and yield to them the satisfaction of learning to act in the world and of using their lives in an ideal cause, we will not engage the most promising among them in our profession. We have been going about it backwards. When we should have been creating an education which could enlist their energies, we have been organizing a system which instructs them in how to behave.

A college or university which took seriously the education of teachers would take the world as its campus and move the world into its curriculum and into its student body and faculty as a perfectly natural thing to do. It would be an example of how liberal education can best be conducted. It would be an institution for the education of students, whether or not they were to become teachers. I use the words, teacher and student, not to describe the people you see in the halls or read about as parts of schools and colleges. By teachers I mean those who have learned, or who know intuitively, how to set the minds of others into motion and who place their own knowledge, whatever it may be, at the disposal of those who are learning.

The college for these teachers and students would be a staging ground for expeditions into the world, a central place where the student could prepare himself, through the study of the arts and sciences, to understand what he would find beyond the campus. As a regular part of his education he would both live in his society and study at the college, bringing to his seminars and courses the information, ideas and insights which he had gathered at first hand. He would become an intern in society, here and abroad, learning from the experience it has to give him. He would be proving to himself that what he learned from his academic colleagues, their books and their imparted knowledge, squared with the facts as he saw them in his experience. The time of the student on the campus would be a time for doing the things which can best be done there, in some cases can *only* be done there, in the science laboratory, the library, the art studio, the theater, the classroom, the seminar.

Some, or most, of the students in a college of this kind would become teachers after graduation, the others would have had the crucial experience of learning through teaching and learning how to create their own education out of the materials at hand. The graduate student would become a partner of the undergraduate in a community where each would help the other. They would all be practice teachers and practice learners at the same time. The faculty, as is so often said, would become colleagues with the students in the enterprise of learning.

There are already models among the experimental colleges for institutions of this kind, as well as colleges and universities where these conceptions are taken with the seriousness which they deserve. Among other examples, I can mention the fascinating developments at San Francisco State College, where both the students and the College of Education have invented new educational forms which take full advantage of the natural capacities for learning and teaching which lie within the student body. There the faculty is evolving a World Urban Teaching Center to which educators and education students from a sweep of foreign countries come together to work on the crucial educational problems of the cities of the world, using the inner city of San Francisco as a laboratory. There the students have formed their own internal Experimental College of more than six hundred students enrolled in courses taught by other students.

There is of course Antioch College, where at a given point in time, half of the 2000 students are studying and working away from the campus, many of them in foreign countries. But what appeals to me most in this idea of a college is the fact that it is central to the tradition of American public education. More than that, it *is* the tradition of the State Colleges whose philosophy is that of the land-grant university, whose origins are in the teacher college movement, the majority of whose students intend to become teachers, where one out of every five American college students is enrolled, and where a very large part of the expanding enrollment in higher education is going to take place.

As the universities, from Berkeley to Harvard, move farther and farther away from the undergraduate education of teachers to concentration on producing what Harvard has called the Missing Elite, the field is left open for a whole new movement of innovation and experiment in the reform of undergraduate education at large and teacher education in particular. It is clear to me, after surveying the field, that the most interesting and imaginative reforms in mass education are now likely to take place in the State Colleges and the urban universities. Pressures for change and reform are coming from a new generation of students with new needs, without cultural antecedents or social inhibitions. Because of their constituency and often because of their location, institutions like these are confronted, directly and daily, with the problems of poverty, cultural deprivation and radical social change.

It is therefore possible to develop a theory of education within such institutions which links them directly to the social and educational innovations represented by the Domestic Service Corps, Head Start, the National Teachers' Corps and in its world dimension, the Peace Corps. If we were to internationalize the National Teachers Corps by including foreign students and a new curriculum, and were to think of the Peace Corps as a program of teacher education in world affairs, we would have the model we are seeking for a major solution to the problems of the education of teachers in world affairs.

In the present situation I believe that the colleges of education are going to have to take their own initiatives, make their own alliances, invent their own programs, recruit their own scholars, artists, foreign teachers, scientists interested in curriculum, sociologists interested in education, and prepare to teach a much more varied student body of social activists, young poets, composers, internationalists, and others. Only when they do take such initiatives will the students wish to come to them with a sense of commitment to act upon the world by first learning how to act in it.

Epilogue

BENJAMIN F. THOMPSON

Education:
The Most Dangerous Game

A friend asked me why I felt education was the most dangerous game. My reply, in the style of intuition and reason, was to say: "because we take it seriously," or in the "spirit of seriousness" as Jean-Paul Sartre would have it. The "Spirit of seriousness" views man as an object and subordinated to the world. It thinks of values as "having an absolute existence independent of human reality."[1] More about that later. There was another image that suggested the title, an image that comes from the short story, *The Most Dangerous Game*, by Richard Connell. The story, in brief, tells about Ship-Trap Island, a mysterious land, visible from the yacht upon which a big-game hunter named Rainsford is arguing with a companion about whether a jaguar has feelings. Rainsford thinks not; his companion argues that the jaguar understands one thing—fear—the fear of pain and death. Rainsford argues that the world is made up of two classes, the hunters and the hunted. He falls off the yacht in the dead of night, swims toward the sound of shots heard earlier, and reaches a shore where he is greeted by a General Zaroff. Rainsford soon learns the secret of Ship-Trap Island. You see, General Zaroff was a hunter also. He had hunted his entire life, all over the world. Tired of his easy prey, he had searched for the ideal game, an animal with courage, cunning, and reason. Yes, Ship-Trap Island was the hunting ground for men. Rainsford protested that this was not hunting but murder, and soon he became the hunted. He learned about fear, and in the end the hunted killed the hunter.

Suffice it to say that today in education and other spheres we have seen the hunted become the hunter. You may protest that the imagery is too strong, but I can only reply that I think not.

My first thesis: I believe the major responsibility of education is to test whether freedom will work. Contained in this assumption is my estimate that generally education has not enabled men to change—and it seems to me this is the greatest freedom. If we are willing to start with this assumption, perhaps we will be able to stand the internal strife upon which growth can be begun.[2]

My second thesis: that the "how" of education is more important for a free and open society than the "what." If the "how" is correct, then the individual can go beyond teachers, textbooks, and schools into the area of personal choice where he must begin to accept his aloneness and responsibility. This, to me, is the juncture of effort and cognition or mind and body—which leads me to my last thesis.

Education correctly conceived is play. Some may be inclined to observe, "Now he has done it—talking like a progressive 'educationist.'" Far from it! As Schiller remarks in *Letters on the Aesthetic Education of Man,* "Man only plays when in the full meaning of the word he is man, and he is only completely a man when he plays."[3] Also, Sartre observes, "As soon as man apprehends himself as free and wishes to use his freedom ...then his activity is play."[4] Or the theology of Jacob Boehme, "In 'play' life expresses itself in its fullness; therefore, play as an end means that life itself has intrinsic value."[5] For now, let us ask: if play as an end means life, what does school mean?

My request of the reader is for reflection on free play with some ideas, dropping any defenses as in play and not needing to reject or accept. My questions begin with "how" rather than "why" to assist the free play.

1. How is it that we expect one person can choose what another should learn; furthermore, that he will learn it?
2. How is it that we believe failure can build success?
3. How is it that we believe some should be at the "top" and some at the "bottom"?
4. How is it that we believe that thirty students should and can be learning the same thing at the same time?
5. How is it that students are assembled in classrooms most of their school lives?
6. How is it that we do not accept the view that to think is to doubt and to make mistakes?
7. How is it that we fail to recognize that each person needs acceptance?
8. How is it that in their early years children are imaginative and original in speech, play, and thought, only to have these qualities disappear or go underground as they "mature"?

9. How is it that rarely does one see students using the property of an institution except under specific rules and surveillance?

10. How is it that we hold to the idea that thinking and learning are conscious?[6]

11. How is it that when we sense efficient learning is effortless, we continue to talk about learning as work?

12. How is it that it is the very rare curriculum offering that takes as its subject matter self-knowledge?

13. How is it that we believe values exist independent of man rather than that values are what men wish?

14. How is it that we do not use fantasy and imagination directly in the classroom?

15. How is it that student-teacher planning has never taken hold in education—is it still teacher planning?

16. How is it that the school years force a person to concentrate on himself—all the while we are urging him to think of others?

17. How is it that we do not see the schoolroom as a place where we face surrogate parents and siblings?

18. How is it that we believe man is evil and must be controlled?

19. How is it that rather than stressing tolerance and amelioration of weakness we acquire intolerance and punishment of weakness?

20. How is it that we do not see that "drill and drill" only hardens the processes of repetition in the human—and in this sense practice makes imperfect?

21. How is it with all the talk of innovation—individualized instruction, team teaching, independent study, mixed media presentations, sensitivity training, etc.—when we look around there is little evidence of any of these functioning in the schools?

22. How long will it be before education pays attention to unconscious forces?

23. How is it that we have not been able to transmit to new generations what has been learned in the past?

24. How is it that we believe learning matures man rather than vice versa, that maturity makes it possible to learn?

25. How is it that thinking about such questions soon becomes work? that we do not allow ourselves to play?

Now, perhaps, the notion "Education: The Most Dangerous Game" makes more sense. And who of us has the knowledge and will to live dangerously?

References

Preface

1. Paul Kurtz, ed., *Moral Problems in Contemporary Society: Essays in Humanistic Ethics* (Englewood Cliffs, N.J.: Prentice-Hall, Inc., 1969), pp. 1–14.
2. J. P. van Praag, "The Humanistic Outlook," *International Humanism,* III, No. 1 (1969): 14–15.
3. Cf. below, Chap. 19.
4. Seen at Saco-Lowell Shops, Biddeford, Maine, 1943–45.
5. van Praag, p. 15.
6. See Theodore Roszak, *The Making of a Counter Culture* (Garden City: Doubleday & Company, Inc., 1969).
7. Harold Kaplan, "In Defense of Anti-Communism," *Bennington Review,* I, No. 3 (Summer 1967): 14–15.
8. By Jonathon Kozol and Nat Hentoff.

I. General Diagnoses

Introduction

1. Roy P. Fairfield, "Release from Fearful Bondage," *Miami Interaction,* I, No. 5 (1969): 4.

1. Brameld

1. Jack Star, "Our Angry Teachers," *Look,* XXXII, No. 18 (September 3, 1968): 64.
2. *Ibid.*
3. Alaine Touraine, "Western Europe: The New Industrial State on Trial," *Saturday Review,* LI, No. 33 (August 17, 1968): 42.
4. John Dewey, *Interest and Effort in Education* (Boston: Houghton Mifflin Company, 1913).

5. W. Warren Wagar, *The City of Man* (Baltimore: Penguin Books, Inc., 1967), p. 10.

2. Fantini

1. Freedom School Students, *The Modern Strivers* (Washington, D.C., n.d.).
2. Montgomery County Student Alliance, "Wanted: A Humane Education. An Urgent Call for Reconciliation Between Rhetoric and Reality," *A Study Report on the Montgomery County Public School System* (Montgomery County, Maryland, February 11, 1969).
3. Jerry Farber, *The Student as Nigger.*
4. Mario Fantini and Gerald Weinstein, *Making Urban Schools Work: Social Realities and the Urban School* (New York: Holt, Rinehart & Winston, Inc., 1968), pp. 24–25.
5. R. F. Mackenzie, *Escape From the Classroom* (London: Collins, 1965), p. 173.

3. Friedenberg

1. For a vivid descriptive analysis of this process at work, see Arthur D. Vidich and Joseph Bensman, *Small Town in Mass Society* (Princeton, N. J.: Princeton University Press, 1958).
2. Indianapolis: The Bobbs-Merrill Co., Inc., 1963.
3. Frank Zappa, "Plastic People," Mothers of Invention Album, *Absolutely Free* (V6-5013). Used by permission of Frank Zappa Music, Inc. "We hope it helps."
4. *Ibid.*

II. Some Specific Problems

4. Rapoport

1. *University of Michigan Record* (October 26, 1967), p. 2.

5. Kampf

1. André Gorz, *Strategy for Labor* (Boston: Beacon Press, 1967), pp. 12–13.

7. Fairfield

1. Marjorie Barrett, " '19th Century' Piano Teaching Hit," *Rocky Mountain News* (Denver, Colorado), July 6, 1970.

8. Shaw

1. For a summary of Catholic school statistics, 1960–61 to 1968–69, see *Catholic Education 1969: An Overview* (Washington, D.C.: The National Catholic Educational Association, 1969). For more detailed statistics through the 1965–66 school year, see the annual *Summary of Catholic Education* (Washington, D.C.: The Department of Education, United States Catholic Conference).
2. For a detailed discussion of Catholic School finances, see Ernest Bartell, "Efficiency, Equity and the Economics of Catholic Schools,"

in Michael P. Sheridan, S. J., and Russell Shaw, eds., *Catholic Education Today and Tomorrow* (Washington, D.C.: The National Catholic Educational Association, 1968).

3. See, for example, James F. Schuster, "School Consolidation: A Rationale and a Method," *NCEA Bulletin*, LXV, No. 3 (February 1969): 13–25.

4. For a report on one recent survey of Catholic attitudes toward Catholic schools, see George Elford, "The Community Speaks," *NCEA Bulletin*, LXV, No. 3 (February 1969): 3–12.

5. Seymour Warkov and Andrew M. Greeley, "Parochial School Origins and Educational Achievement," *American Sociological Review*, XXXI (June 1966): 406–14; Andrew M. Greeley, *Religion and Career* (New York: Sheed & Ward, 1963), pp. 82–83.

6. For a detailed survey of research on the outcomes of Catholic schooling, see Michael O'Neill, *How Good Are Catholic Schools?* (Dayton: The National Catholic Educational Association, 1968).

7. For a detailed discussion of this point, see Neil G. McCluskey, *Catholic Education Faces Its Future* (Garden City: Doubleday & Company, Inc., 1969), pp. 185ff.

8. For an examination of several philosophies of Catholic education, with preference given to the concept of "integration," see James Michael Lee, *The Purpose of Catholic Schooling* (Dayton: The National Catholic Educational Association, 1968).

9. "Minds at Work," from an address given at St. Peter's College, Jersey City; quoted in *Catholic Mind*, LXII (September 1964): 32.

10. See Andrew M. Greeley and Peter H. Rossi, *The Education of Catholic Americans* (Chicago: Aldine Publishing Company, 1966), pp. 53–76.

11. "A New Opportunity for Catholic Education," *NCEA Bulletin*, XLV, No. 1 (August 1968): 22–27.

9. Blanshard

1. Board of Education of Central School District No. 1, etc., et al., Appellants, *vs.* James E. Allen, as Commissioner of Education of New York, et al., *Supreme Court Reporter*, V. 88a, pp. 1923–1941: 392 U.S. 236.

2. Florence Flast, et al., Appellants, *vs.* Wilbur J. Cohen, Secretary of Health, Education and Welfare, et al., *Supreme Court Reporter*, V. 88a, pp. 1942–1970: 392 U.S. 83.

10. Darcy

1. These values include, for example, the quality of life, income distribution, and environmental quality. See *Resources*, XXXIII (Washington, D.C.: Resources for the Future, Inc., January 1970), 16.

2. "Why Is Economics Not an Evolutionary Science," in *The Portable Veblen*, Max Lerner, ed. (New York: Viking Press, 1958), pp. 215–240.

3. The leading contemporary American economist who has contributed to the study of value, in the generalized sense considered here, is Prof. C. E. Ayres of the University of Texas, past president of the Association for Evolutionary Economics and author of numerous articles and books including *Toward a Reasonable Society* (Austin: University of Texas Press, 1961). Another distinguished economist,

Professor Kenneth E. Boulding of the University of Colorado, delivered his presidential address to the American Economic Association in 1968 on the topic, "Economics as a Moral Science," *American Economic Review*, LIX, No. 1 (March 1969): 1–12. Also see C. West Churchman, *Prediction and Optimal Decision: Philosophical Issues of a Science of Values* (Englewood Cliffs, N.J.: Prentice-Hall, Inc., 1961).

4. *Economic Opportunity Act of 1964*, Section 2, as Amended (Washington, D.C.: U.S. Government Printing Office, 1968) (0–291–704).

5. To do so in a manner that preserves work incentives and affords equity to income earners would increase the total cost to about 2–3% of GNP.

6. For a discussion of the relationship between knowing what *is* and what *should be*, see J. Bronowski, *Science and Human Values* (New York: Harper & Row, Publishers, 1965).

7. Alan B. Batchelder, *The Economics of Poverty* (New York: John Wiley & Sons, Inc., 1966), pp. 73ff.

8. See John Maynard Keynes, *The General Theory of Employment, Interest, and Money* (New York: Harcourt Brace Jovanovich, Inc., 1936) pp. 324ff.

9. George Bernard Shaw, *The Intelligent Woman's Guide to Socialism and Capitalism* (New York: Bretano's, Publishers, 1928), pp. 42–43.

10. Edward F. Denison, *The Sources of Economic Growth in the United States and the Alternatives Before Us,* Supplementary Paper No. 13 (New York: Committee for Economic Development, 1962), p. 269.

11. *Manpower Report of the President* (Washington, D.C.: U.S. Government Printing Office, 1968), p. 47.

12. Washington, D.C.: U.S. Government Printing Office, 1969 (0-332-383, Paperbound), p. 101.

13. See R. L. Darcy and P. E. Powell, *Manpower and Economic Education* (New York: Joint Council on Economic Education, 1968), pp. 57ff. and 309–311.

14. Remarks made by Ian McHarg in an address at Colorado State University, Fort Collins, Colorado, on January 22, 1970.

15. Reed Whittemore, "A Prejudiced View of the Social Sciences," a review of National Academy of Science and Social Science Research Council, *The Behavioral and Social Sciences–Outlook and Needs* (Englewood Cliffs, N.J.: Prentice-Hall, Inc., 1970) in *The New Republic*, CLXI, Nos. 25–26, (December 20 and 27, 1969): 21ff.

16. Indeed, Kenneth Boulding goes so far as to suggest that "Economic education...may well be one of the most important keys for man's survival in the coming centuries or even decades. In a complex world, unfortunately, ignorance is not likely to be bliss, and a society in which important decisions are based on fantasy and folk tales may well be doomed to extinction." In "Economic Education: The Stepchild Too is Father of the Man," *The Journal of Economic Education*, I, No. 1 (Fall 1969): 11.

17. Norman Cousins, "Hail Automation, Hail Peace," *Saturday Review*, XLVII, No. 3 (January 18, 1964): 20.

III. Look Back to the Future

Introduction
1. *New York Times,* May 2, 1952.
2. Otto Krash to Roy Fairfield, February 7, 1970.

11. Krash

1. *The Humanist*, XXVIII, No. 3 (1968): 1.
2. *Ibid.*, 16.
3. *Ibid.*
4. *Ibid.*, 18.
5. *The Humanist*, XXIX, No. 1 (1969): 23.
6. *The Humanist*, XXVIII, No. 6 (1968): 24.
7. From Dewey's definition of "Philosophy," Volume XII, reprinted in Seligman and Johnson, eds., *Selections from the Encyclopedia of the Social Sciences* (New York: The Macmillan Company, 1944), pp. 18–19.
8. John Dewey, *Logic: The Theory of Inquiry* (New York: Holt, Reinhart & Winston, Inc., 1938), p. 107.
9. Paul A. Schilpp, ed., *The Philosophy of John Dewey* [New York: Tudor Publishing Co., 1939 (now published by The Open Court Publishing Co., La Salle, Ill.)], p. 597.
10. Ernest Nagel, *Sovereign Reason* (New York: The Free Press, 1954), pp. 132–33.
11. John Dewey and Arthur Bentley, *Knowing and the Known* (Boston: Beacon Press, 1949), p. 317.
12. See *ibid.*; also Dewey, *Logic*; and "Theory of Valuation," *International Encylopedia of Unified Science*, XI, No. 4 (Chicago: University of Chicago Press, 1939, 1947).
13. "The Applicability of Logic to Existence," *The Journal of Philosophy*, XXVII, No. 7 (1930): 176.
14. *Ibid.*

IV. Relevance Like It Is

14. Nelson

1. See especially Mark Krug, "The Teaching of History at the Center of the Cold War—History Textbooks in East and West Germany," *School Review* (1961); Grace Conant, "German Textbooks and the Nazi Past," *Saturday Review* (July 20, 1963); William Medlin, "Analysis of Soviet History Textbooks Used in the Ten Year School," in *Teaching in the Social Sciences and the Humanities in the U.S.S.R.* (U.S. Office of Education, Division of International Education, December, 1959); Cyrus Peake, *Nationalism and Education in Modern China* (Columbia University Press, 1932); Theodore Hsi-en Chen, "Education and Indoctrination in Red China," in *Current History* (September 1961); Dixon Miyauchi, "Textbooks and the Search for a New National Ethic in Japan," *Social Education* (March 1964); J. Merton England, "The Democratic Faith in American Schoolbooks, 1783–1860," *American Quarterly* (Summer 1963).
2. Ray Allen Billington, *The Historian's Contribution to Anglo-American Misunderstanding: Report of a Committee on National Bias in Anglo-American History Textbooks* (New York: Hobbs, Dorman and Company, 1966).
3. *Ibid.*, p. 38.
4. Jack L. Nelson, *Nationalism and Education*, Buffalo Studies No. 1 (Buffalo: University of Buffalo, April, 1968).
5. Florida Statutes, Section 230.23(4) (1) (as of 1967).

6. California, State Board of Education, "Teaching About Democracy and Communism," *California Schools* (November 1962).

7. New Hampshire, "An Educational Platform for the Public Schools," Concord, Department of Education, 1952.

8. Nelson, "Nationalism and Education."

9. Bessie Pierce, *Citizens' Organizations and the Civic Training of Youth* (New York: Charles Scribner's Sons, 1933); Howard Beale, *Are American Teachers Free?* (New York: Charles Scribner's Sons, 1936); and *A History of Freedom of Teaching in American Schools* (New York: Charles Scribner's Sons, 1941); William Gellerman, *The American Legion as Educator* (New York: Teachers College Press, Columbia University, 1938); Donald Robinson, "The Teachers Take a Birching," *Phi Delta Kappan,* February, 1962; Everett Moore, "Intellectual Freedom", *ALA Bulletin,* March, 1963.

10. V. O. Key, Jr., *Public Opinion and American Democracy* (New York: Alfred A. Knopf, Inc., 1961), p. 316.

11. See footnote 1 above.

12. N. B. Shurtleff, ed., *Records of the Governor and Company of the Massachusetts Bay in New England* (Boston, 1853): II, 6, 203.

13. Bessie Pierce, *Public Opinion and the Teaching of History in the United States,* (New York: Alfred A. Knopf, Inc., 1926). See especially footnotes in Chap. 1.

14. Statutes of Massachusetts, 1780–1807, Section 4, Vol. I, pp. 470–71, as found in Bessie Pierce, *Public Opinion.*

15. U.S., Department of the Interior, Bureau of Education, *Bulletin Number 30, 1920, Laws Enacted in 1918 and 1919* (Washington, D.C.: U.S. Government Printing Office, 1921).

16. *Laws* of North Dakota, 1897, par. 742; *Laws* of Idaho, 1897, Sec. 17.

17. *Laws* of Kentucky, 1862, ch. 636.

18. *Laws* of Nevada, 1907, ch. CLXXXII, Sec. 30, p. 386; as found in Bessie Pierce, *Public Opinion.*

19. David Spitz, "Politics, Patriotism and the Teacher," *The National Elementary Principal,* XLIII, No. 3 (January 1964): 19–20. [Copyright 1964, Department of Elementary School Principals, National Education Association. All rights reserved.]

20. Daniel Sisson, "Toward a New Patriotism," in *The Center Magazine* (May 1969).

15. Bay

1. *The Social Contract.* Book III, Chap. IV, last lines.

2. *Politics.* Book I, Chap. 2.

3. This approach to the definition of freedom is developed at greater length in Bay, *The Structure of Freedom* (New York: Atheneum Publishers, 1965), especially in Chap. 3. What is here called "autonomy" is there called "potential freedom."

4. Edward P. Gottlieb to Roy P. Fairfield, February 16, 1970; by permission.

V. Technology and Education

Introduction

1. Friedrich Georg Juenger, *The Failure of Technology: Perfection Without Purpose* (Hinsdale, Illinois: Henry Regnery Company, 1949).

2. This is Lewis Mumford's thesis in his most provocative and insightful study, *Technics and Civilization* (New York: Harcourt Brace Jovanavich, Inc., 1934), pp. 12–18.

17. Chase

1. Basil Castaldi, *Creative Planning of Educational Facilities* (Chicago: Rand McNally & Co., 1969), p. 173.
2. William D. Firman "The Challenge of Change in School Finance" (Paper presented at the 10th National Conference on Education Finance of the National Education Association, April, 1967).
3. Harold Gores, "Facilities for the Future," *Liberal Education*, XLIX, No. 1 (March 1963).
4. Robert G. Simpson, *Educational Psychology* (Philadelphia: J.B. Lippincott, 1949), p. 153.
5. Kenneth E. Boulding, "Expecting the Unexpected: The Uncertain Future of Knowledge and Technology," in *Prospective Changes in Society by 1980*, Edgar L. Morphet and Charles O. Ryan, eds. (Denver, *Designing Education for the Future,* 1966), p. 209.
6. William T. Knox, "The New Look in Information System," in Morphet and Ryan, *Designing,* p. 223.
7. William Van Til, *The Year 2000: Teacher Education* (Terre Haute: Indiana State University, 1968), p. 27.
8. William W. Caudill, *In Education the Most Important Number Is One* (Houston: Caudill Rowlett Scott, Publishers, 1967).
9. Donald L. Davis and John A. Shaver, "New Ideas in Urban Education," *Nations Schools,* LXXXIII, No. 3 (March 1969): 67–82.

VI. Futuristic Programs and Views

Introduction

1. Robert Theobald, "Programs: Present and Future," in Don Benson, ed., *Dialogue on Poverty* (Indianapolis: The Bobbs-Merrill Co., Inc., 1967), p. 107. (A Symposium on Poverty, St. Francis College, Biddeford, Maine, May 5–7, 1966.)
2. Harold Taylor, *Students Without Teachers* (New York: McGraw-Hill Book Company, 1969).
3. Those interested in both relevance and futuristic programs may wish to contact the Union for Experimenting Colleges and Universities, Antioch College, Yellow Springs, Ohio, 45387, to learn of both undergraduate and graduate programs. Also the Antioch-Putney Graduate School of Education, Yellow Springs, Ohio, has had one of the most innovative Master of Arts in Teaching programs since the mid-sixties.

18. Maslow

1. Archibald MacLeish, "Thoughts on an Age That Gave Us Hiroshima," *New York Times,* July 9, 1967, Section 2, p. 1 .

19. Theobald and McInnis

1. Since completing this piece, Robert Theobald has written a participation fiction/science-fiction/nonfiction book entitled *Teg's 1994.* This volume explores the educational system to be expected in 1994 and the society in which it will be embedded, for education will no longer be a separate function. This book is being circulated privately.

20. Keyes

1. *New York Times,* December 12, 1965.
2. Harold Taylor, *Students Without Teachers,* pp. 233–34.
3. Jan McClain, interview, August, 1969.
4. Bill Moody, interview, August, 1969.
5. Quoted in "Profiles," *The New Yorker,* XLIII, No. 39 (November 18, 1967): 116.
6. Moody, interview.
7. Peter Jannsen, "Free U. and Old U.," *Change,* I, No. 6 (November-December 1969): 13.
8. Thaddens Seymour, interview, Spring 1967.
9. Woodrow Wilson, "What is College For?" *Scribners,* XLVI, No. 5 (1909): 576.
10. Frederick Rudolph, *The American College and University* (New York: Alfred A. Knopf, Inc. 1962), p. 137.
11. Frederick Rudolph, "Neglect of Students as a Historical Tradition," in L. E. Dennis and J. F. Kauffman, eds., *The College and the Student* (American Council on Education, 1966); reprinted in *Issues in Higher Education,* Rita Dershowitz, ed. (Student Press Association mimeo., February, 1966), pp. 11–12.

VII. Personal Humanism in Action

23. Fairfield

1. Richard Kostelanetz, "Understanding McLuhan (In Part)," *New York Times Magazine* (January 29, 1967): 18ff.

VIII. Campus Power

25. Dixon

1. At Central State University, Wilberforce, Ohio, November 1967.
2. Antioch is a member of the Great Lakes College Association, a consortium of twelve colleges with an urban school project in Philadelphia.

IX. International Education

Introduction

1. From *Mein Kampf,* quoted in Peter Viereck, *Conservatism Revisited* (London: John Lehmann, 1950), p. 79.

27. Shoemaker

1. Patricia Beesley, *The Revival of the Humanities in American Education* (New York: Columbia University Press, 1940).
2. Francis Shoemaker, *Aesthetic Experience and the Humanities* (New York: Columbia University Press, 1943).
3. See *The Journal of Commonwealth Literature,* No. 1 (September 1965).
4. Leonard Casper, *New Writing from the Philippines: A Critique and Anthology* (Syracuse: Syracuse University Press, 1966).
5. William H. McNeill, *A World History* (New York: Oxford University Press, 1967).

6. A. J. Arberry, trans., *The Koran Interpreted* (New York: The Macmillan Company, 1956).
7. Bernard Lewis, *The Arabs in History* (New York: Harper and Row, 1960), p. 133.
8. William Cantwell Smith, *Islam in Modern History* (New York: New American Library, 1957), p. 39.
9. T. Cuyler Young, ed., *Near Eastern Culture and Society* (Princeton: Princeton University Press, 1966), p. 90.
10. K. G. Saiyidain, *Iqbal's Educational Philosophy* (Lahore: Muhammad Ashraf, 6th ed., 1965), p. 63.
11. James Kritzeck, *Anthology of Islamic Literature from the Rise of Islam to Modern Times* (New York: New American Library, 1964). For further reading: *Islamic Literature,* An Introductory History with Selections by Najib Ullah (New York: Washington Square Press, 1963).
12. Saiyidain, *Iqbal's,* p. 39 .
13. F.S.C. Northrop, *The Meeting of East and West: An Inquiry Concerning World Understanding* (New York: The Macmillan Company, 1960), Chaps. 10 and 11.
14. Lin Yutang, ed., *The Wisdom of China and India* (New York: Random House, Inc., 1942).
15. Hajime Nakamura, *The Ways of Thinking of Eastern Peoples* (Japanese National Commission for UNESCO, 1960).
16. Hajime Nakamura, *Japan and Indian Asia, Their Cultural Relations in the Past and Present* (Calcutta: Firma K.L. Mukhapodhyay, 1961).
17. *Contemporary Indian Short Stories* (New Delhi: Sahitya Akademi).
18. G. Morris Carstairs, *The Twice Born, A Study of a Community of High-Caste Hindus* (London: Hogarth Press, 1961).
19. Nirad C. Chaudhuri, *The Continent of Circe, An Essay on the Peoples of India* (London: Chatto and Windus, 1965).
20. Humayun Kabir, *The Indian Heritage* (Bombay: Asia, 1960), p. 20.
21. Khwaja Ahmad Abbas, *Inquilab* (Bombay: Jaico, 1955).
22. Mulk Raj Anandi, *Coollie* (London: May Fair Books, 1962).
23. Khushwant Singh, *Train to Pakistan* (London: Four Square Books, 1961).
24. Khushwant Singh, *Mano Majra* (New York: Grove Press, Inc., 1956).
25. Thakazhi S. Pillai, *Chemmeen* (London: Victor Gollancz, 1962).
26. R. K. Narayan, *The Vendor of Sweets* (New York: The Viking Press, Inc., 1967).
27. Milton Singer, ed., *Traditional India: Structure and Change* (Philadelphia: American Folklore Society, 1959).
28. Herbert Passin, *Society and Education in Japan* (New York: Teachers College, Columbia University, and The East Asian Institute, 1965), p. 274.
29. *Ibid.,* p. 277.
30. Theodore de Bary and Ainslee Embree, *Approaches to Asian Civilizations* (New York: Columbia University Press, 1964).
31. Ruth Benedict, *The Chrysanthemum and the Sword* (New York: Houghton Mifflin Company, 1946).
32. Jean Stoetzel, *Without the Chrysanthemum and the Sword, A Study of the Attitudes of Youth of Post-War Japan* (New York: Columbia University Press, 1955).
33. L. Takeo Doi, "Amae: A Key Concept for Understanding Japanese

Personality Structure," in Robert J. Smith and Richard K. Beardsley, eds., *Japanese Culture, Its Development and Characteristics* (Chicago: Aldine Publishing Company, 1962), pp. 132–40.

34. John W. Hall and Richard K. Beardsley, *Twelve Doors to Japan* (New York: McGraw-Hill Book Company, 1965).

35. Hidetoshi Kato, ed., *Japanese Popular Culture* (Rutland, Vt.: Charles E. Tuttle, 1959).

36. Ivan Morris, *Modern Japanese Stories, Anthology* (Rutland, Vt.: Charles E. Tuttle, 1961).

37. Donald Keene, ed., *Modern Japanese Literature* (New York: Grove Press, Inc., 1960).

38. Liu Wu-chi, *An Introduction to Chinese Literature* (Bloomington: University of Indiana Press, 1966).

39. *Quotations from Chairman Mao Tse-Tung* (New York: Bantam Books), p. 173.

40. Liu Wu-chi, *Introduction*, p. 275.

41. W. E. Abraham, *The Mind of Africa* (Chicago: © Copyright 1962, The University of Chicago Press), pp. 41–42.

42. *Ibid.*, p. 115.

43. Chinua Achebe, *Things Fall Apart* (New York: McDowell, 1959).

44. W. E. Abraham, *The Mind*, p. 39. For further reading, cf. Alex Quaison-Sackey, *Africa Unbound, Reflections of an African Statesman* (New York: Praeger Publishers, Inc., 1963).

45. *Ibid.*, p. 46.

46. *Ibid.*, p. 111. For further reading cf. Janheinz Jahn, *Muntu, The New African Culture* (New York: Grove Press, Inc., 1961).

47. Susanne Langer, *Mind: An Essay on Human Feeling* (Baltimore: Johns Hopkins Press, 1967).

48. Arthur Ravenscroft, ed., *The Journal of Commonwealth Literature* (Leeds, England: Heinemann Educational Books, annually.).

49. *Bulletin of the Association for African Literature in English* (Freetown, Sierra Leone: Fourah Bay College, Department of English, annually.).

50. J. A. Ramasaran, *New Approaches to African Literature, A Guide to Negro-African Writing and Related Studies* (Ibadan, Nigeria: Ibadan University Press, 1965).

51. Onuora Nzekwu, *Wand of Noble Wood* (New York: New American Library, 1961).

52. John Press, ed., *Commonwealth Literature, Unity and Diversity in a Common Culture* (London: Heinemann Educational Books, 1965), p. 205.

53. William Conton, *The African* (New York: New American Library, 1960), p. 192.

Epilogue: Thompson

1. Jean-Paul Sartre, *Being and Nothingness: An Essay on Phenomenological Ontology* (New York: Philosophical Library, Inc., 1965), p. 552.

2. For a longer discussion, see Van Cleve Morris, *Existentialism and Education* (New York: Harper & Row, Publishers, 1966).

3. J. C. Schiller, "Letters on the Aesthetic Education of Man," in *Essays Aesthetical and Philisophical* (London: G. Bell, 1884) quoted in

Norman O Brown, *Life Against Death* (New York: Random House, Inc., 1959), p. 33.

4. Jean-Paul Sartre, *Being and Nothingness*, pp. 580–81.
5. H. H. Brinton, *The Mystic Will* (New York: The Macmillan Company, 1930), pp. 217–18.
6. For further discussion see the writings of Lawrence Kubie.

Contributors

CHRISTIAN BAY: Professor of Political Science, University of Alberta. Native of Norway, he has served on the Faculty of Law at the University of Oslo as well as on the faculties of Michigan State and Stanford University and the University of California, Berkeley. An associate editor of the *Journal of Conflict Resolution*, he is author of *The Structure of Freedom* as well as many professional articles and chapters of books published here and abroad.

PAUL BLANSHARD: Member of the New York bar, author of many works on church and state, and for several years the representative of the American Humanist Association in Washington, D.C.

KAARE BOLGEN: A native of Norway (and husband of a superb elementary school teacher, Dorothy, who often assists in his important work), he is author of *Science and Violin Playing* and many records, "ABC's, Beginning Reading," "Numbers, How to Tell Them," and a series on ear training for use in the schools. Former editor of *Music Teachers' Review, Music Teachers Quarterly*, and *The Juvenile Musician*, he has written widely on musical, psychological, and related subjects. He makes his home in Great Neck, New York.

THEODORE BRAMELD: Professor of Educational Philosophy, Emeritus, Boston University. Member of several faculties, Long Island University, Adelphi University, University of Minnesota, and New York University. Dr. Brameld is author of a dozen books and scores of professional articles.

He is regarded as a leading proponent of the hopeful reconstructionist theory of education, encouraging schools to take an activist position regarding social and political ills.

ALSTON BROWER: Black student, Antioch College.

EDWARD W. BROOKE: Senator from Massachusetts. A native of Washington, D.C., he graduated from Howard University on the eve of World War II, served in combat duty in Italy, took LL.B. and LL.M. degrees at Boston University following the war. After two terms as Attorney General of Massachusetts, he won election to the U.S. Senate; he served as a member of the National Advisory Committee on Civil Disorders; chairman of the Ad Hoc Congressional Committee on the Poor People's Campaign; trustee of Boston University; and Chairman of the Board of Directors of the Opera Company of Boston.

WILLIAM W. CHASE: Deputy Director, Division of Facilities Development, and Chief of the Design and Materials Branch, Office of Construction Service, U.S. Office of Education. Holding a doctorate from Indiana University and formerly consultant in facilities planning at Ohio University, he also served as Director of the Division of Schoolhouse Planning for the State of Indiana. He is responsible for providing leadership in the planning and development of educational facilities, both at home and abroad, working closely with educational planners at local, state, and national levels.

ROBERT L. DARCY: Professor of Economics at Colorado State University, Fort Collins. From 1961 to 1968 he taught economics and served as Director of the Center for Economic Education at Ohio University. A native of Illinois, Dr. Darcy earned economics degrees from Knox College, Indiana University, and the University of Colorado. His special fields are manpower and human resources, poverty, and economic education. His recent publications include a research monograph, *Manpower Education in a Growing Economy* and a textbook for secondary schools, *Manpower & Economic Education.*

JAMES P. DIXON: President, Antioch College, since 1959. Between his graduation from Antioch and his presidency, he earned an M.D. from Harvard, M.S. from Columbia, and served as Health Commissioner of Denver and Philadelphia. Among his wide-ranging public and private services, he is a trustee of Goddard College, of the College of the Virgin Islands, and of the Institute for Policy Studies; he is co-chairman, with Dick Gregory, of the "New Party"; he is a member of the national committee of the American Civil Liberties Union and of the Harvard visiting committee for medical and dental schools. He has also served on many national committees, such as the Food and Drug Councils and the Peace Corps, and has traveled widely in Europe and Africa as an American specialist in education. He has masterly skills as a student and practitioner of institutional processes. He contributed to *Goals for Americans,* prepared by President Eisenhower's Commission on National Goals.

DAVID EVANS: Graduate of Amherst, he served for a year and a half as a Leader in Training with the American Ethical Union. While in college he worked in Mississippi and was active in Students for a Democratic Society. He is an editorial associate of the *Humanist*, and resides in Washington where he works on his writing.

ROY P. FAIRFIELD: Professor of Social Science, Antioch College; Coordinator of Graduate School, Union of Experimenting Colleges and Universities. Formerly a teacher at Bates, Hofstra, and Athens Colleges as well as Ohio University, he has long worked closely with students as faculty advisor, football trainer, trail companion. His writing includes a book, *Sands, Spindles and Steeples*, a history of his home town, Saco, Maine, as well as the editorship of the Anchor edition of the *Federalist Papers* and many magazine articles. Although he has taught widely in the fields of history, education, and the social sciences, he perceives his field as "Man" and responds to the nomenclature, "Maineac."

MARIO FANTINI: Program Officer, Ford Foundation. A native of Philadelphia, he did graduate work at Temple University and received his doctorate from Harvard. In addition to teaching at all levels of education, he has taught mentally retarded and emotionally disturbed children; he served as Senior Research Associate at Syracuse University while developing more effective ways of dealing with disadvantaged youth. He is author of *Designing Education for Tomorrow's Cities* and co-author (with Gerald Weinstein) of several books on community control, decentralization, and other aspects of urban education. He has also lectured widely in the United States.

CHARLES FRANKEL: Old Dominion Professor of Philosophy and Public Affairs, Columbia University. Between 1965 and 1967 he was Assistant Secretary of State for Educational and Cultural Affairs of the United States. Presently an editor-at-large of *Saturday Review* and a member of the New York State Commission on the Quality, Cost, and Financing of Elementary and Secondary Education, Dr. Frankel has authored many widely read books including *The Case for Modern Man, Education and the Barricades,* and *High on Foggy Bottom.*

EDGAR Z. FRIEDENBERG: Professor, State University of New York at Buffalo. Sociologist and educational theorist, he earned his doctorate at the University of Chicago after which he served on the Brooklyn College and University of California (Davis) faculties. Frequent contributor to *Ramparts, The New York Review of Books,* the *New York Times Magazine, The Nation,* and other periodicals, he is author of *The Vanishing Adolescent, Coming of Age in America,* and other widely read books.

SIDNEY HOOK: Professor of Philosophy, Emeritus, New York University. He is a founder of the Congress for Cultural Freedom and former President of the American Philosophical Association. Through a long and fruitful life of lecturing widely throughout America, he has written widely for both the periodical and the book press. Among the books he has authored are *The Paradoxes of Freedom*, *Heresy, Yes! Conspiracy, No!*, *Religion in a Free Society*, *Education for Modern Man*, and *Reason*, *Social Myths and Democracy*.

JUDSON JEROME: Professor of Literature, Antioch College, since 1953 except for a year as holder of the Amy Lowell Traveling Poetry Scholarship and two years' Chairman of Humanities Division at the College of the Virgin Islands. Extremely versatile, he is the author of two collections of poetry, *Light in the West* and *Ocean's Warning to the Skin Diver and Other Love Poems*, a novel, *The Fall of Dark*, a collection of essays, *The Poet and the Poem*, and a textbook. His work has appeared in *Harpers*, *The Atlantic Monthly* and other important journals throughout the land; he is an educational pioneer with Antioch–Columbia, Maryland.

LOUIS KAMPF: Professor in the Department of Humanities, Massachusetts Institute of Technology. Founder of the New University Conference; steering committee of Resist; teacher of literature and social inquiry; officer of the Modern Language Association; author of *On Modernism*, chapters for several other books, and articles for many periodicals.

RALPH KEYES: Member of the staff of *Newsday*, Garden City, New York, he graduated from Antioch College in 1967 where he was involved in movements for educational reform and served as community manager. He did graduate work in international history at the London School of Economics and Political Science; his work has appeared in *The Nation*, *Change*, and several newspapers.

MILTON R. KONVITZ: Professor of Industrial and Labor Relations and Professor of Law at Cornell University. Author of *Expanding Liberties* (1966), *Religious Liberty and Conscience* (1968), *Bill of Rights Reader* (4th ed., 1968), and many other books. Member of Institute for Advanced Study (Princeton), Fellow of Center for Advanced Study in Behavioral Sciences (Stanford), Guggenheim Fellow, Ford Foundation Fellow, Fund for the Republic Fellow, Visiting Professor at Truman Center for Advancement of Peace (Hebrew University, Jerusalem).

OTTO KRASH: Professor of Philosophy of Education, City University of New York. After teaching in the public schools of Wisconsin, he taught at Wayne State University, the University of Tennessee, New York University, Hofstra and Yeshiva. Frequent contributor to periodicals such as *Saturday Review and School and Society*; persistent contributor of letters to editors of newspapers, including *New York Times*, and the *New York Post*; claims that his "education was subsidized from kindergarten through the doctorate," hence is "attempting to repay that debt to the American public by working with teachers and extending the conditions of free inquiry in the public schools."

PAUL KURTZ: Professor of Philosophy at the State University of New York at Buffalo. He is editor of *The Humanist* and co-editor of the

International Directory of Philosophy and Philosophers and on the editorial board of the *Revue Universitaire de Science Morale*. He is author of *Decision and the Condition of Man*, co-author of *A Current Appraisal of the Behavioral Sciences*, and editor of *Sidney Hook and the Contemporary World* and *Moral Problems in Contemporary Society*. He has spoken widely throughout Europe and the United States and participated in the East-West Marxist-Humanist conferences.

ABBA P. LERNER: Professor of Economics at Berkeley. Born in Russia; grew up in London; taught at London School of Economics, Universities of Kansas City, Chicago, and Virginia, Amherst, the New School, Roosevelt, Columbia and Michigan State Universities. He has written widely in many areas of economic theory; his major works include *The Economics of Control*, *The Economics of Employment*, *Essays in Economic Analysis* and *Everybody's Business*. Formerly an advisor to the government of Israel and Distinguished Fellow of the American Economic Association, he is also revered as a teacher with great skill and patience and the courage of his convictions.

ABRAHAM MASLOW: Late Resident Fellow, W. P. Laughlin Charitable Foundation and Professor of Psychology at Brandeis University; past President of the American Psychological Association; recipient of the "Humanist of the Year" award; formerly taught at Brooklyn College; Andrew Kay Visiting Fellow at Western Behavioral Sciences Institute; author of *Religions, Values and Peak Experiences*, *Toward a Psychology of Being*, and more than 150 other books and articles.

NOEL F. McINNIS: Coordinator of the Center for Curriculum Design, Kendall College, Evanston, Illinois. As "Vice President in Charge of Heresy" at Kendall, he has initiated numerous innovative developments. Formally trained in journalism and American History at Northwestern University, he is primarily concerned with the development of a freshman integrative studies curriculum, "Comprehensive Thinking," one of several facets of a broader program entitled "Spaceship Earth Curriculum Project." He supervised the work of nine students who edited *An Alternative Future for America*, from which Chapter 19 in this book is adapted.

JACK L. NELSON: Professor in Graduate School of Education, Rutgers University. Has taught on faculties of SUNY at Buffalo, Los Angeles State, and Citrus Junior Colleges. Editor of *Social Science Record* and Book Editor of *Social Education*, his publications include articles in the *Journal of Teacher Education*, *School and Society*, *Social Studies* and similar journals as well as a book, *Teenagers and Sex*. He has co-authored or co-edited two other books, *Sociological Perspectives in Education: Models for Analysis* and *Patterns of Power: Social Foundations of Education*.

GERALD A. PINSKY: Director of Research and Controller of University Centers for Rational Alternatives, a nationwide organization whose members support academic freedom, rational deliberation, and the democratic process against extremist violence, intimidation, and administrative and semantic deception. Previously, Mr. Pinsky served as a researcher in the Department of State, instructor at Dartmouth, New York University, and Borough of Manhattan Community College; also he has been a free lance journalist and was co-founder of the student wing of Americans for Democratic Action and Coordinating Center for Democratic Opinion.

ANATOL RAPOPORT: Professor, Institute for Mathematical Statistics and Operations Research, Technical University of Denmark. Formerly at the University of Michigan, he has been guest professor at many other universities in the United States, England, Austria, and Scandinavia. Editor of *General Systems* and associate editor of three other journals, he is author of seven books, including *Strategy and Conscience* as well as *N-Person Game Theory*, and more than 300 articles published in American and foreign journals. His major research is in mathematical biology and mathematical psychology.

LINDA ROBERSON: Graduate of Oberlin College. She is a graduate student in education at the University of Wisconsin; secretary of the youth division and member of the Board of the American Humanist Association.

ESTHER SCHULZ: Marriage and Family Counselor. Formerly member of Bates College, Indiana and Columbia University faculties, Dr. Schulz, R.N., has researched and practiced widely in the fields of nursing and education. As a member of the SIECUS staff she traveled widely at home and abroad as consultant and speaker on sex education. She is co-author of *Family Life and Sex Education.*

JOHN R. SEELEY: Professor, California Institute of the Arts. Whether businessman in the thirties, student in the forties, teacher-philosopher-consultant in the fifties and sixties, Mr. Seeley's accomplishments as a student of mankind are widely known at home and abroad. Long a professor in Toronto and at Brandeis, he recently spent five years as Fellow and Dean at the Center for the Study of Democratic Institutions. He has held or now holds many editorships and consultantships, and has authored several books and 400 articles.

RUSSELL SHAW: Director, Division of Information, United States Catholic Conference. Formerly public information officer of the National Catholic Education Association and reporter for the National Catholic News Service, Mr. Shaw was educated at Georgetown University, is author of *The Dark Disciple* (a novel) and *Abortion on Trial,* co-author of *S.O.S. for Catholic Schools,* editor of two books on Catholic education and a frequent contributor to numerous periodicals.

FRANCIS SHOEMAKER: Professor of English, Teachers College, Columbia University, and Director of the Office of International Programs and Services. Consultant on English language teaching and textbook production to the Ministry of Education of India, also coordinator of Teachers College overseas projects in Afghanistan, India, Peru, and Egypt during the sixties, he is currently concentrating on the development of programs of world affairs study of American teachers. He is co-author of a series of science books for elementary schools; author or editor of three other books and numerous articles and chapters in journals and yearbooks here and abroad.

HAROLD TAYLOR: Former President of Sarah Lawrence College, he is internationally known for his leadership in the peace movement and progressive educational change. Distinguished author, his most recent books include *Students Without Teachers: the Crisis in the University, The World as Teacher, Art and the Future, How to Change Colleges*. Among other experiments in education he has conducted a pilot project in a world college and helped to establish the first Peace Research Institute in the United States.

ROBERT THEOBALD: British socioeconomist, born and reared in India. Educated at Cambridge and Harvard Universities, he has lectured widely on American college campuses, participated in numerous television discussion shows and authored both magazine articles and books. His best-known works include *The Rich and the Poor, The Challenge of Abundance* and *Free Men and Free Markets*. He has edited several other volumes and is general editor of a seris of *Dialogue* books on contemporary social issues. A more recent work, *Teg's 1994*, is a fascinating experiment to develop participation in the evolution of an idea.

BENJAMIN F. THOMPSON: Associate Professor of Education, Antioch College. Native of Indiana, educated at Ball State and Michigan State Universities, later taught at the latter. High school teacher, principal, and criminologist in the Youth Division of the Department of Correction in Michigan before teaching at Antioch and in the Antioch-Putney Graduate School where his course in "The Learner" is a *must*. Work includes two radio series for the National Association of Education Broadcasters, co-authorship of *Juvenile Delinquency: Culture and the Individual*, and articles and book reviews for the *Humanist*, *Journal of Correction*, and similar publications.

MARVIN ZIMMERMAN: Associate Professor of Philosophy, SUNY at Buffalo. Formerly President of the New York City chapter of the American Humanist Association, Dr. Zimmerman received his doctorate from New York University, and also taught there. He is author of *Contemporary Political Democracy*.